Essays for David Wiggins

B

Edited by
Sabina Lovibond
and
S. G. Williams

Essays for David Wiggins

Identity, Truth and Value

Aristotelian Society Series

Volume 16

BLACKWELL
Publishers

Copyright © Blackwell Publishers Ltd, 1996

First published 1996

2 4 6 8 10 9 7 5 3 1

Blackwell Publishers Ltd
108 Cowley Road
Oxford OX4 1JF
UK

Blackwell Publishers Inc
238 Main Street
Cambridge, Massachusetts 02142,
USA

British Library Cataloging in Publication Data

A CIP catalogue record for this book is available from the British Library.

Library of Congress Cataloging-in-Publication Data

Essays for David Wiggins: identity, truth, and value/edited by Sabina Lovibond and S. G. Williams.

p.   cm. – (Aristotelian Society series; v. 16)

Includes bibliographical references and index.

ISBN 0–631–19134–8 (alk. paper)

1. Philosophy.   2. Wiggins, David.   I. Wiggins, David.
II. Lovibond, Sabina.   III. Williams, S. G. (Stephen G.)   IV. Series.
B1674.W494E87   1996
100–dc20   95–42647
                                                         CIP

Typeset in 10 on 12 pt Plantin
by Pure Tech India Ltd, Pondicherry, India
Printed in Great Britain by T. J. Press Ltd, Padstow, Cornwall

This book is printed on acid-free paper

Contents

Notes on Contributors

ROGER CRISP is a Fellow of St. Anne's College, Oxford.

WILFRID HODGES is Professor of Mathematics at Queen Mary and Westfield College, London.

EDWARD HUSSEY is a Fellow of All Souls College, Oxford.

JULIE JACK is an Emeritus Fellow of Somerville College, Oxford and a former Fellow of King's College, Cambridge.

SABINA LOVIBOND is a Fellow of Worcester College, Oxford.

JOHN MCDOWELL is Professor of Philosophy at the University of Pittsburgh.

CHERYL MISAK is Associate Professor of Philosophy at the University of Toronto.

A. W. MOORE is a Fellow of St. Hugh's College, Oxford.

HAROLD NOONAN is Reader in Philosophical Logic at the University of Birmingham.

ANTHONY SAVILE is Professor of Philosophy at King's College, London.

P. F. SNOWDON is a Fellow of Exeter College, Oxford.

S. G. WILLIAMS is a Fellow of Worcester College, Oxford.

TIMOTHY WILLIAMSON is Professor of Philosophy at the University of Edinburgh.

Preface

David Wiggins is an unusual philosopher – unusual in his impact on the subject, in his style of thought and expression, and in his power to command the attention and affection of people who work with him. His pupils in particular have always appreciated the arresting and engaging quality of his instruction, as well as his unstinting regard for their welfare; many of them, partly as a result, are still at large in the subject. This collection of essays is presented to him (now a little belatedly) to mark his 60th birthday and to celebrate his accession to the Wykeham Chair of Logic at Oxford. With one exception[1], all the essays are published here for the first time.

Wiggins was born in London in 1933, and was educated at St Paul's School and Brasenose College, Oxford, where he read Literae Humaniores. He was appointed lecturer in Philosophy at New College, Oxford in 1959 and elected a tutorial fellow there in 1960. In 1967 he took up the post of Professor of Philosophy at Bedford College, London; he returned to Oxford in 1981 as Fellow and Praelector in Philosophy at University College. In 1989 he was appointed Professor of Philosophy at Birkbeck College, London, where he remained until he returned to New College as Wykeham Professor in 1993. He was elected Fellow of the British Academy in 1978 and a Foreign Honorary Member of the American Academy of Arts and Sciences in 1992.

These bare facts are filled out in our final chapter, in which Wiggins's detailed responses to the essays emerge out of a fascinating personal-cum-academic memoir – a glimpse of the early experience that was to inform his choice of specialization within philosophy. 'Specialization', however, may not be quite the right word here. What can one think of as the *special* preoccupation of a philosopher whose work has broached questions as seemingly remote from one another as the interpretation of Aristotle on

practical reason, the role of need in moral and political philosophy, the
treatment of adverbs in truth-conditional semantics, and the elucidation
of metaphysical concepts such as truth, substance, identity and necessity?

Even so, anyone who takes a reasonably large sample of Wiggins's work
is likely to sense an essentially unified system of concerns beneath the
surface, and despite his initial pessimism, his own account lends support
to these intimations. Philosophy, he writes, has never been for him an
exercise in rebutting scepticism or in securing the foundations of knowledge, religious or otherwise: his thought has been from the outset
thoroughly secular, both in the familiar sense and in the sense of content-
ing itself with an immanent exploration of the human point of view. One
recurring theme is the attempt to reconcile the 'anthropocentrist' ideas
suggested by this approach with a variety of objectivist positions –
whether in ethics, in the theory of individuation, or in the philosophy of
language – which they may at first sight appear to threaten. Another is the
need to construct (or reconstruct) an undogmatic rationalism that would
enable moral and political theory to stand their ground against positivis-
tic models of 'rational choice' derived from disciplines such as economics
or behavioural psychology. The outcome is a philosophy that is sensitive
both to the dangers of would-be scientific reductionism and to the
location of human life within the natural world.

As well as thanking our contributors for their forbearance in waiting for
the appearance of a book which has been some time in the making, we
must express our gratitude to those who have helped the editors and
dedicatee with bibliographical and word-processing tasks, especially Anne
Borg, Christoph Hoerl and Rachel Margolis. We have also benefited
from the advice of Tom Baldwin (as editor of the Aristotelian Society
Monograph series) and of Stephan Chambers and Steve Smith of Blackwell's. We hope the finished product is worthy of its *raison d'être* – that is,
to continue some of the debates that Wiggins has engaged in and to
record the pleasure, provocation and insight his work has brought to so
many philosophers, not least ourselves, over the years.

Sabina Lovibond
S. G. Williams

NOTE

1 The exception is Anthony Savile's essay, which first appeared in a slightly different
   form as Chapter 4 of his *Kantian Aesthetics Pursued* (Edinburgh University Press:
   1993) and is included here by kind permission of the publishers of that book.

1

The Necessity and Determinacy of Distinctness

Timothy Williamson

Any metaphysical caprice can be indulged in some more or less deviant formal system. The work of David Wiggins is a reminder of the depth to be gained in metaphysics from the constraints of orthodoxy in logic. His writing on the metaphysics of identity is a salient case in point.

Consider four claims:

(NI) If things are identical, they are necessarily identical.
(ND) If things are distinct, they are necessarily distinct.
(DI) If things are identical, they are determinately identical.
(DD) If things are distinct, they are determinately distinct.

NI and DI proclaim the necessity and determinacy of identity, ND and DD the necessity and determinacy of distinctness.[1] NI is provable with a modicum of fairly orthodox logic. A formally parallel proof can be given of DI. Similar proofs of ND and DD can be given only in an extended logic. Wiggins has endorsed NI and DI but not ND or DD, and considered sympathetically a view combining DI with the denial of DD. A parallel view would combine NI with the denial of ND. This paper assembles some considerations relevant to the assessment of such views. An alternative proof will be given of ND that is almost as compelling as the proof of NI. This result is quite consistent with Wiggins's position in *Sameness and Substance* and elsewhere; his defence of NI against supposed counterexamples can be extended to ND. On a common view of determinacy, the alternative proof of ND can be adapted as an alternative proof of DD, contrary to the view that accepts DI and rejects DD. This result would be consistent with the main lines of Wiggins's position; his

I thank Lloyd Humberstone and Stephen Williams for helpful comments on this material.

defence of DI against supposed counterexamples can be extended to DD.

If these considerations point in the right direction, identity is a metaphysically rigid relation. Either it necessarily and determinately relates a given pair of individuals, or it necessarily and determinately fails to relate them. In that sense, the facts about it form part of the necessary and determinate structure of reality. Any alternative to them is epistemic, not metaphysical. In what follows, the question of necessity will be discussed first; ideas from that discussion will then be applied to the question of determinacy.

NI and ND can be expressed in a simple formal language. They are universal generalizations, so individual variables 'x', 'y', . . . are needed, but there are no other singular terms (if NI and ND were sentence schemata, closed singular terms, such as names or definite descriptions, would be needed to provide them with instances). The only primitive predicate is identity (=). The primitive sentential connectives are negation, the material conditional and a necessity operator ($\sim, \rightarrow, \Box$). For simplicity, there are no quantifiers; instead, theorems are read like equations in mathematics, implicitly prefixed with universal quantifiers. The formation rules are standard. Thus NI is formalized as $x = y \rightarrow \Box x = y$ and ND as $\sim x = y \rightarrow \Box \sim x = y$.

It might seem natural to assess the validity of NI and ND by constructing a possible worlds model theory for the formal language.[2] A model would include a set of worlds, a relation of accessibility between them, and a domain of objects. The truth of a formula A at a world w relative to an assignment a of objects in the domain to variables would be defined recursively with respect to a model. Relative to a, $\sim A$ is true at w if and only if A is not true at w; $A \rightarrow B$ is true at w if and only if either A is not true at w or B is true at w; $\Box A$ is true at w if and only if A is true at every world w' accessible from (possible relative to) w. A is valid in a model if and only if it is true at every world relative to every assignment. When is an atomic formula true? The simplest idea is to make assignments independent of worlds, and have $x = y$ true, relative to a, at w if and only if a assigns the same object to 'x' and 'y'. NI and ND would then automatically be valid in every model, for $x = y$ is true at every world or at none relative to a fixed assignment. This may be the best policy in the end. However, it is not a good way of assuring oneself that NI and ND are correct principles.

NI and ND came out valid simply because the truth of $x = y$ at any world was assessed in terms of the identity of the assigned objects in the world in which the assessment was being made. Their validity was not made to depend on the modal behaviour of identity, or any feature distinguishing identity from other relations. If one introduced a new primitive predicate R to mean *richer than*, and defined xRy to be true at w relative to a if and only if the object assigned to 'x' is richer than the object assigned to 'y', the formulae $xRy \to \Box xRy$ and $\sim xRy \to \Box\sim xRy$ would be valid in every model, but this does not show that the rich man in his castle and the poor man at his gate could not have had each other's estate. Nor is the use of non-modal conditions in the world in which the assessment is being made to assess truth at an arbitrary world an incidental feature of the model theory. It is the source of its power, for it enables us to decide what modal principles are valid in all models by non-modal reasoning, and therefore without appeal to the principles whose validity is in question. If we rewrote the model theory in modal terms, we could make the truth of $\Box x = y$ depend on whether the objects assigned to 'x' and 'y' could have been distinct, but then we should be in no position to decide whether NI is valid in all models without already having decided whether it is correct on its intended interpretation.

We could construct a model theory in non-modal terms on which NI and ND would be uncontentiously invalid. The simplest way of doing this would be to make assignments of objects to variables relative to worlds. However, the effect of this model theory is just as independent of the modal behaviour of identity as before. The theory is also open to the charge of subverting the point of individual variables – to trace what befalls a single individual – by assigning them different objects in different worlds. As usual in modal logic, we cannot decide the correctness of contentious principles by appeal to model theory, for the latter comes in too many varieties. We can require any decision to harmonize with some variety or other, but it is not much of a constraint.

We need some proof theory. For inferences not turning on identity, we can adapt the basic modal logic K, replacing the propositional variables that are its atomic formulae with equations. K is the strongest logic all of whose theorems are valid in all possible worlds models like those above, without constraints on the accessibility relation. For truth-functional inferences, all tautologies are axioms and modus ponens (MP) a rule of inference. In practice, inferences derivable on that basis will often be abbreviated into a single step (PC). There is one modal axiom schema, named with harmless ambiguity:

K $\quad \Box(A \to B) \to (\Box A \to \Box B)$

There is also the rule of necessitation:

RN If A is a theorem, so is $\Box A$.

Together, K and RN require just that provable consequences of what is necessary are themselves necessary. As usual, the rules for identity are reflexivity and substitutivity. If Ay/x results from substituting 'y' for some occurrences of 'x' in A, the following are axioms:

$$= I \quad x = x$$
$$= E \quad x = y \rightarrow (A \rightarrow Ay/x)$$

Any variables in place of 'x' and 'y' give instances of $= I$ and $= E$. The system as a whole will be named $K =$.

Doubts might be raised about $= I$ in case x could have failed to exist. Doubts might also be raised about $= E$. These should not be doubts about Leibniz's Law, the principle that if things are identical they have the same properties. As Wiggins has emphasized, Leibniz's Law is fundamental to the logic of identity. The question is whether $= E$ is a consequence of Leibniz's Law. Is there a property such that A is true if and only if x has it and Ay/x is true if and only if y has it? Both kinds of doubt are relevant to the proof of NI.

A proof of NI was first published by Ruth Barcan (Marcus) in 1947. It may be adapted to $K =$ as follows:

(1)	$x = y \rightarrow (\Box x = x \rightarrow \Box x = y)$	$= E$
(2)	$x = x$	$= I$
(3)	$\Box x = x$	2, RN
(4)	$x = y \rightarrow \Box x = y$	1, 3, PC

Line (3) treats it as necessary that x is self-identical; could x have been self-identical without existing? Line (1) is in trouble unless there is a property a thing has if and only if it is necessary that x is that thing. Wiggins has tried to meet such doubts with a modification of the proof in which the sentential connective $\Box$ is replaced by a predicate modifier NEC applied to the identity predicate (as in the surface grammar of NI).[3] The free variables would fall outside the scope of NEC, a property would be visibly specified, and necessary existence not entailed. These modifications may well yield an increase in suasive force. It does not follow that the original argument was invalid, for philosophers often doubt valid principles of inference. (1)–(4) is a formally valid argument in $K =$, and the principles of $K =$ will henceforth be assumed to be correct on their intended interpretation.[4] The aim of this paper is not to answer objections to the proof of NI but to ask what attitude someone who regards those objections as answered should take to ND. Although the objections are assumed to be answerable without a retreat from $\Box$ to NEC, the arguments of the paper could be adapted to a predicate modifier approach. It is also worth repeating that the language of K= does not contain closed singular terms. If such terms '*a*' and '*b*' were added to the language, the sentence $a = b \rightarrow \Box a = b$ would not automatically be a theorem; it would depend on the treatment of '*a*' and '*b*'.

K = is a very weak modal logic. Neither of the following schemata can be derived in it:[5]

D $\Box{\sim}A \rightarrow {\sim}\Box A$
T $\Box A \rightarrow A$

D says that the necessary is possible; it is valid in a model if from every world some world is accessible. T says that the necessary is the case; it is valid if every world is accessible from itself. T (which entails D in K =) is compelling for both metaphysical and natural necessity. Even if K = is extended by T to the system KT =, the following schemata cannot be derived:[6]

B ${\sim}A \rightarrow \Box{\sim}\Box A$
4   $\Box A \rightarrow \Box\Box A$

B is valid in a model if accessibility is symmetric, 4 if it is transitive. If B is added to KT =, the result is the 'Brouwersche' system KTB =; if 4 is added, it is the S4 system KT4 =; if both, the S5 system KTB4 =.

ND cannot be derived in K =; indeed, it cannot be derived in KT4 =.[7] However, Prior showed that it can be derived from NI in S5.[8] As Kripke later pointed out, only the B schema is really needed.[9] The proof of NI can be extended to a proof of ND in KB = as follows:

(4)	$x = y \rightarrow \Box x = y$	Theorem
(5)	${\sim}\Box x = y \rightarrow {\sim}x = y$	4, PC
(6)	$\Box({\sim}\Box x = y \rightarrow {\sim}x = y)$	5, RN
(7)	$\Box({\sim}\Box x = y \rightarrow {\sim}x = y) \rightarrow (\Box{\sim}\Box x = y \rightarrow \Box{\sim}x = y)$	K
(8)	$\Box{\sim}\Box x = y \rightarrow \Box{\sim}x = y$	6, 7, MP
(9)	${\sim}x = y \rightarrow \Box{\sim}\Box x = y$	B
(10)	${\sim}x = y \rightarrow \Box{\sim}x = y$	8, 9, PC

The converses of NI and ND are not provable in KB =. However, they are provable in KTB =, which extends KB = by the uncontentious principle that what is necessarily the case is the case. More generally, all instances of $A \leftrightarrow \Box A$ are theorems of KTB = and even of KDB =. The result extends a fortiori to the strong S5 system KTB4 =. $\Box$ is a redundant operator in these systems; any formula is provably equivalent to the result of deleting all its occurrences of $\square$.[10] Facts about the identity of individuals are completely invariant across possible worlds; they are part of the necessary structure of reality. Of course, the redundancy of $\square$ depends on the restricted vocabulary of the language; if it were enabled to express facts of other kinds by the addition of new predicates, or quantifiers, the application of $\square$ to formulae involving them would not be redundant.

That the full strength of S5 is not needed for the proof of ND from NI might be seen as a point of little consequence. For S5 might be seen as the evidently correct logic for metaphysical necessity. S5 expresses the view that necessity and possibility are not themselves contingent matters. A proposition is either necessarily necessary or necessarily not necessary, and either necessarily possible or necessarily not possible; the iteration of modal operators is redundant. If one dispenses with the accessibility relation between worlds, treating metaphysical necessity as simply truth in all worlds whatsoever, one will adopt S5. This is an attractively simple and unrestricted view of metaphysical possibility. However, it is worth noting that objections have been made to it that do not extend to the weaker 'Brouwersche' system in which ND can be derived from NI as above.

Hugh Chandler and Nathan Salmon have argued that 4, the S4 schema $\square A \rightarrow \square\square A$, is subject to counter-examples. Their idea is that a particular artifact could have originated from slightly different matter, but could not have originated from completely different matter. For example, if a ship s is built from 1000 planks, it is metaphysically possible for s to have been built from 999 of its actual planks and one other plank, but not for s to have been built from planks none of which actually belongs to it (that would have been another ship). Let w_0 be the actual world, and w_1 a possible world in which s is built from 999 of its planks in w_0 and a new plank. Now apply the same principle again: if w_1 had obtained, a world w_2 would have been possible in which s is built from 999 of its planks in w_1 and a new plank, so that only 998 of its planks in w_0 are used. The argument can be repeated. The result is a sequence of worlds $w_0, \ldots,$ w_{1000}, where w_{i+1} would have been possible had w_i obtained, but in w_{1000} s is built from 1000 planks none of which is used in w_0, so w_{1000} is not possible in the actual world w_0. Thus the accessibility relation is not transitive. Schema 4 fails, for in the context of K it entails $\square A \rightarrow \square^{1000} A$, whereas although it is necessary that if s is built at least some of its actual planks are used, the necessity operator cannot be iterated a thousand times. The argument is flexible. Some regard the design of an artifact as more relevant than its matter; if they hold that an artifact could have had a slightly different design but could not have had a completely different design, the argument can play on that.

Arguments of the Chandler–Salmon kind pose no threat to the T and B principles. The arguments encourage the view that a world w' is accessible from a world w just in case w' is similar enough to w in certain respects. Such a similarity relation is presumably reflexive, symmetric and non-transitive. These constraints yield the modal system KTB. Thus one could accept the Chandler–Salmon argument and still derive ND from NI. Since □ is redundant in KTB =, facts about the identity of individuals would be part not just of the necessary structure of reality, but of its necessarily necessarily . . . necessary structure. The question whether one should accept the Chandler–Salmon argument will be left open here.[11]

Salmon allows that all instances of the B schema may be true, even necessarily true. However, he denies that they are *logically* true. B is contrasted with T. According to Salmon, anyone who knows how to reason correctly about metaphysical necessity is willing to accept as valid the inference from □A to A. Such a person need not be willing to accept as valid the inference from ~A to □~□A, even if intermediate steps are supplied (what would they be?). The logic of metaphysical necessity is KT, not KTB. Salmon's claims are hard to assess without a clearer conception of logical truth. T is certainly more obvious than B, but not all obvious truths are logical truths, nor is it clear that all truths of logic can be derived from obvious truths (obviousness is not a very helpful criterion if one is trying to decide which sentences of a second-order predicate calculus are logical truths). From a formal point of view, K gives a cleaner picture than KT of the logic of metaphysical necessity, for it corresponds to the idea that the logical truths are just those guaranteed by the form of the possible worlds model theory, with all constraints on the accessibility relation supplied by metaphysics rather than logic. In any case, the claim that the logic of metaphysical necessity is weaker than KTB but at least as strong as K suggests the intriguing thought that, while NI is a truth of logic, ND is at best a truth of metaphysics. Against this thought, a new derivation of ND will be offered, based on principles whose claim to logical truth is better than that of B.

The new derivation requires the addition to the language of a new operator @, to be read as 'actually'. In the model theory, a world w_0 is singled out as the actual world, and @A is true at a world w if and only if A is true at w_0. Validity in a model is defined as truth at the actual world of that model relative to all assignments of objects to variables. All instances of the following schemata are valid in all models, whatever the accessibility relation and the treatment of atomic formulae:

@K $@(A \to B) \to (@A \to @B)$
@D $@{\sim}A \to {\sim}@A$
@D$_C$ ${\sim}@A \to @{\sim}A$
@□ $@A \to □@A$
@T$_C$ $A \to @A$

Similarly, the following rule preserves validity in all models:

@RN If A is a theorem, so is $@A$.

If validity in a model had been defined as truth in all worlds (not just the actual one) relative to all assignments, only one of these principles would need to be dropped, @T$_C$. In the presence of @T$_C$, the rule of necessitation must be restricted, for if RN were applied to @T$_C$ the result would be $□(A \to @A)$, which is false even at the actual world if A is false but possible there. The restricted version of RN allows $□A$ to be derived if A can be derived without appeal to @T$_C$. Let K@ (K@ =, KT@, etc.) be the result of adding @K, @D, @D$_C$, @□, @T$_C$ and @RN to K (K =, KT, etc.) and restricting RN as above.[12] Even if the possible worlds model theory is regarded as merely an algebraic device, the principles about @ are logically compelling on their intended interpretation.[13]

ND is derivable in K@ = as follows:

(1) $x = y \to (@x = x \to @x = y)$ = E
(2) $x = x$ = I
(3) $@x = x$ 2, @RN
(4) $x = y \to @x = y$ 1, 3, PC
(5) $@{\sim}x = y \to {\sim}@x = y$ @D
(6) $@{\sim}x = y \to {\sim}x = y$ 4, 5, PC
(7) $□(@{\sim}x = y \to {\sim}x = y)$ 6, RN
(8) $□(@{\sim}x = y \to {\sim}x = y) \to (□@{\sim}x = y \to □{\sim}x = y)$ K
(9) $□@{\sim}x = y \to □{\sim}x = y$ 7, 8, MP
(10) $@{\sim}x = y \to □@{\sim}x = y$ @□
(11) $@{\sim}x = y \to □{\sim}x = y$ 9, 10, PC
(12) ${\sim}x = y \to @{\sim}x = y$ @T$_C$
(13) ${\sim}x = y \to □{\sim}x = y$ 11, 12, PC

The first four lines of the proof mimic the proof of NI, with @ in place of □. The only use of = E is at line (1); there is no rationale for allowing substitution within the scope of □ but forbidding it within the scope of @.[14] Line (4) could have been justified by direct appeal to @T$_C$, but then RN could not have been used at line (7). Since @T$_C$ is used at line (12),

RN cannot be applied to the conclusion. Fortunately, ND is not in danger of being a contingent truth about the actual world, for the effect of necessitation can be secured indirectly. $\Box^i\,(\sim x = y \rightarrow \Box^j\sim x = y)$ is a theorem of K@ = for any natural numbers i and j, where $\Box^i$ is a sequence of i $\Box$s.[15]

As before, if K@ = is extended by the D principle that necessity implies possibility, $\Box$ becomes a redundant operator. @ also becomes redundant. Any formula is provably equivalent to the result of deleting all its occurrences of $\Box$ and @.[16] Thus all instances of $A \leftrightarrow \Box A$, $\Box(A \leftrightarrow \Box A)$ and $\Box(A \leftrightarrow @A)$ are theorems. In KD@ =, facts about the identity of individuals are completely invariant across possible worlds; they are part of the necessary structure of reality. Of course, the redundancy of $\Box$ and @ depends on the restricted vocabulary of the language; if new predicates, or quantifiers, were added, the application of $\Box$ and @ to formulae involving them would not be redundant.

The provability of ND in some modal systems and not in others looks at first like a random phenomenon. However, an explanation can be given. ND says in effect that if $x = y$ is possible, it is the case. In trying to verify ND, we start at a world w_0, move to an accessible world w_1 at which the same formulae are true of x and y, and then have to show that the truth of $x = y$ at w_0 follows. In order to do this, we need a formula whose truth-value at w_1 is sensitive to the truth-value of $x = y$ at w_0. We need an operator that allows us to get back to our starting-point. If accessibility is symmetric, $\Box$ itself has this effect. Less would suffice. If one can get back from w_1 to w_0 by a series of k steps of accessibility, the truth of $x = y$ will be transmitted along the chain and finally reach w_0. This point is expressed in modal logic by the derivability of ND when the B schema is weakened to $\sim A \rightarrow \Box\sim\Box^k A$.[17] But if no number of accessible steps gets us back from w_1 to w_0, an 'actually' operator does it automatically. It does not matter that w_0 is not accessible from w_1, for accessibility plays no role in the semantics of 'actually'. If such a notion is needed, it is because not all worlds are possible worlds; although the notion of a world may be needed in the semantics of 'actually', the restrictive notion of possibility is irrelevant. Since the role of accessibility is only to record what would be possible in various circumstances, it should not figure in the semantics of 'actually'.

What all this suggests is that the underivability of ND in systems such as K =, KT = and KT4 = merely reflects their expressive limitations. Because they lack backwards-looking operators, the substitution schema = E does not have enough instances to ensure that = behaves as identity.[18] But given the intended interpretation of $\Box$, it would always be legitimate to introduce an operator such as @, and ND would then be provable.

Moreover, the principles about @ used in the proof seem to be purely logical ones, whose validity does not depend on any special constraints of a metaphysical kind. If so, ND is as much a truth of logic as NI. When one is working in a restricted language without @, and one's principles about the iteration of modal operators do not allow one to derive ND, one should simply add it as an axiom.[19]

Do the foregoing considerations about the necessity of identity and distinctness extend to their determinacy? Gareth Evans was impressed by an analogy between the operators 'necessarily' and 'determinately'. On one reading, his 1978 note 'Can there be vague objects?' transposes a version of the Barcan proof of NI into a proof of DI, and describes an extension of it to DD in an analogue of S5, corresponding to the Prior proof of ND.[20] If □ is reinterpreted as 'determinately', the proof of NI in K= becomes a proof of DI and the proof of ND in KB= becomes a proof of DD.

Several doubts have been raised about the soundness of such proofs.[21] The matter is still more fraught than in the modal case, for now the soundness even of classical propositional logic is in question. Indeterminate propositions cannot be assumed to be either true or false, so truth-functional tautologies formed out of them cannot be assumed to be true without special justification. An example is the PC inference from $x = y \rightarrow \Box x = y$ to $\sim\Box x = y \rightarrow \sim x = y$ in the KB= proof of DD. On some treatments, the premise is true and the conclusion indeterminate when $x = y$ is indeterminate.[22]

Unfortunately, most of the objections to DI and DD rely on many-valued (usually three-valued) semantics. The underlying assumption generalizes truth-functionality. The semantic value of a conditional, conjunction, disjunction or negation is assumed to be a function of the semantic values of its component sentences, but truth and falsity are no longer the only values. In the simplest case, indeterminacy is the third value. Yet in almost every attempted application of many-valued semantics, generalized truth-functionality is a quite implausible assumption.[23] For example, John is an adult male human whose intended wedding ceremony was beset by irregularities. It is so indeterminate whether he remains unmarried that 'John is a bachelor' and 'John is not a bachelor' receive the same semantic value. A many-valued semantics for the conditional will assign the same semantic value to 'If John is unmarried then John is a bachelor' as to 'If John is unmarried then John is not a bachelor', for their antecedents match in semantic value, as do their consequents. Yet the former seems true and the latter at best indeterminate. Such apparent counter-examples to generalized truth-functionality – which are quite independent of issues about identity – have been known for many years. No convincing redescription of them has been given. While this state of affairs remains, objections to the proofs of DI and DD from many-valued semantics carry little weight.[24]

A non-classical semantics of 'determinately' should be non-classical enough not to satisfy generalized truth-functionality. The obvious candidate is the method of *supervaluations*. This method is usually associated with the view of indeterminacy as semantic under-specification. Our linguistic practice is supposed to determine an incomplete specification of references for the expressions of our language. This incomplete specification may include constraints on the interconnections between the references of different words, for instance that if a man is counted as 'married' he must not also be counted as a 'bachelor'. A specification is *admissible* if it extends our incomplete specification to a complete specification of references for our expressions, including truth-values for our sentences. An admissible specification is two-valued. A sentence is assessed as true if it is true on every admissible specification, as false if it is false on every admissible specification, and as neither true nor false otherwise. In the example above, 'John is married' is true on some admissible specifications and false on others. 'John is a bachelor' is false on the former and true on the latter. Thus both sentences are assessed as neither true nor false. The material conditional 'If John is married then John is a bachelor' is assessed as neither true nor false, for it is false on those admissible specifications on which its antecedent is true but true on those on which its antecedent is false. But 'If John is married then John is not a bachelor' is assessed as true, for on any admissible specification on which its antecedent is true, so is its consequent. Thus generalized truth-functionality fails.[25]

The method of supervaluations may seem inappropriate when DI and DD are in question. For if it is indeterminate whether $x = y$, how could that be a matter of semantic under-specification? The reference of 'x' and 'y' is not under-specified, for they are simply variables; as Wiggins emphasizes, the question in which we are interested cannot be posed using singular terms whose referential determinacy is not assumed. As for =, it is not a good candidate for semantic under-specification.[26] However, someone who thinks that indeterminacy might not be confined to our language or conceptual scheme can still use the method of supervaluations: although it is hard to make sense of the idea of indeterminacy in the world, it is not much easier without supervaluations than with them. An admissible specification assigns truth-values to our sentences, and so may be regarded as specifying a way for the world to be. It may then be held to be indeterminate whether the world is that way. Why should the apparatus of supervaluations not be used to discuss this supposed indeterminacy?

Formally, a supervaluationist semantics for 'determinately' is very like a possible worlds semantics for 'necessarily', with admissible specifications playing the role of possible worlds. All classical tautologies are true on all specifications and MP preserves truth on all specifications. Since determinacy is truth on all admissible specifications, the schema K and the rule RN may be retained on the new reading of □. All instances of = I and = E will also be assumed to be true. Thus the proof of DI in K = is valid. How do the proofs of DD in KB = and K@ = fare?

An S5 system for 'determinately' admits first-order indeterminacy but leaves no room for higher-order indeterminacy. Although it may be indeterminate whether this rock is part of Ben Nevis, it is either determinate that it is determinate that this rock is part of Ben Nevis or determinate that it is not determinate that this rock is part of Ben Nevis. This is not a plausible view; the boundary of what is determinately part of Ben Nevis is no easier to locate than the boundary of what is part of Ben Nevis. The supervaluationist should not treat the set of admissible specifications as determinate. An accessibility relation between specifications must be introduced. Part of what a specification specifies is what specifications are admissible, just as a world determines what worlds are possible. Suppose, for example, that on specification s, both x and y are part of Ben Nevis; on s', x but not y is part of Ben Nevis; on s'', neither x nor y is part of Ben Nevis; s may also specify that s and s' are admissible, but that no specification such as s'' on which x is not part of Ben Nevis is admissible. Thus on s, x but not y is determinately part of Ben Nevis. The view just sketched confirms Wiggins's suspicions of the use of S5 in a proof of DD.

It is natural to assume that one specification assesses the admissibility of another by comparing it with itself. Those that are too unlike will be ruled inadmissible. For example, s does not admit s'', for s'' makes Ben Nevis smaller than s does by too much. But perhaps s' does admit s'', for s'' differs from s' by little enough. Thus s admits s' and s' admits s'' but s does not admit s''. Transitivity breaks down, and with it the S4 principle; it is determinate that x is part of Ben Nevis, but not determinate that it is determinate. However, as in the modal case, this is no threat to symmetry and the B schema. If admitting is a similarity relation, one might expect it to be reflexive, symmetric and non-transitive. That would make KTB = the logic of 'determinately'. Since DD is provable in KB =, it is provable in KTB =. Now admitting may not be strictly symmetric, for different specifications may assign different weights to similarity in a given respect; thus the similarity of s' to s according to s may be greater than the similarity of s' to s according to s', so that s admits s' but s' does not admit s. This threatens the B schema.[27] However, it might still be possible to find a sequence of k specifications leading from s' back to s, each member counted as similar enough to be admissible by its predecesor. Thus if s' counted x and y as distinct, s would do so too. Even if the B axiom $\sim x = y \rightarrow \square \sim \square x = y$ is false, the weaker $\sim x = y \rightarrow \square \sim \square^k x = y$ may still be true for some k, in which case $\sim x = y \rightarrow \square \sim x = y$ is true. DD remains plausible.

In the modal case, there was no need to rely on the proof of ND in KB =, for there was the proof in K@ = to fall back on. Is there any analogous proof of DD? At first sight it seems not. Within supervaluationist semantics, no operator stands to 'determinately' as 'actually' stands to 'necessarily'. The actual world matters to us as no other possible world does, but no specification is privileged for us above all other admissible specifications (if it were, no room would be left for indeterminacy). However, the only principle in K@ = to assign a privileged role to actuality is $@T_C$, which says in effect that true propositions are true in the actual world. All the other principles about @ are valid simply because the truth of $@A$ at an arbitrary world is equivalent to the truth of A at a fixed world. For any world w, these other principles would be valid if @ were read as 'in w'. When $@T_C$ is dropped from K@ =, one can still prove $@\sim x = y \rightarrow \square \sim x = y$ (line (11) above). Similarly, for any specification s, if @ is read as 'on s' there is a sound argument for $@\sim x = y \rightarrow \square \sim x = y$. Thus it is true on s. Moreover, this reading of @ makes $\sim x = y \rightarrow @\sim x = y$ true on s. Hence $\sim x = y \rightarrow \square \sim x = y$ is true on s. Since s was arbitrary, DD is true on all specifications, and so true. By earlier arguments, one can show that either $\square^k x = y$ is true for all k or $\square^k \sim x = y$ is true for all k. For the supervaluationist, facts about the identity of individuals are part of the determinate structure of reality.

Wiggins suggests that if we accept DI and refuse to accept DD,

> we can see how it is that singling out is such [so great] a task: because nothing then remains to prevent individual thinkers and the societies that breathe life into the individuative practices of individual thinkers from delimiting definitely what they single out, and counting as quite clear what they have singled out, *without* making absolutely everything definite about the frontier between that thing and that which is not that thing.[28]

Supervaluationists will have to find some other way to see how it is that singling out is such a task. Whether some other conception of vagueness – for example, an epistemic one – grounds a plausible asymmetry between identity and distinctness is a question for another occasion.[29]

NOTES

1 Necessity is understood as metaphysical necessity, although the arguments of the paper would extend to weaker kinds, such as natural necessity.

2 Various options are described in Hughes and Cresswell (1968), pp. 189–202.

3 See Wiggins (1975), (1976b), (1976e), (1980a) and (1980d).

4 One answer to the doubt about necessary existence is defended in Williamson (1990b). As for the use of = E, it is illicit only if the application of □ to an open formula is either unintelligible or intelligible but creates a context in which relative to an assignment co-referring variables are not intersubstituable *salva veritate*. Neither option is attractive. See also Cartwright (1979). Similar remarks apply to the other readings of □ considered below.

5 Proof: Consider the following model. There is just one world w; w is not accessible from w; every atomic formula is true at w. One can check that all theorems of K = are true at w (for = E, use induction on the complexity of A), but $\Box \sim x = x \rightarrow \sim \Box x = x$ and $\Box \sim x = x \rightarrow \sim x = x$ are not. Note that such independence results do not follow automatically from the independence of the corresponding systems of propositional modal logic; see n. 10.

6 Proof: Consider the following model. There are just three worlds, w, w' and w''; the worlds accessible from w are w and w'; those accessible from w' are w' and w''; only w'' is accessible from w''; at w and w', an atomic formula is true just in case it is of the form $v = v$; all atomic formulae are true at w''. All theorems of KT = are true at all worlds, but $\Box \sim x = y \rightarrow \Box\Box \sim x = y$ is not true at w and $\sim x = y \rightarrow \Box \sim \Box x = y$ is not true at w'.

7 Any reflexive symmetric relation is extensionally equivalent to $\sim \Box \sim x = y$ at some world in some model of KT4 = (Williamson (1990a), pp. 38–9), so the extension of $\Box \sim x = y$ can be empty when the domain contains more than one thing. Thus ND is not derivable in KT4 =.

8 Prior (1955), pp. 206–7, with sensible remarks about NI and ND.

9 Kripke (1972) and (1980), note 56 (see Wiggins (1980a), p. 217). Kripke there gives an alternative argument for ND: if two objects x and y are each identical with some object z in another possible world, $x = z$ and $y = z$, so $x = y$, presumably by the symmetry and transitivity of identity. However, those who deny ND will say that x and y are not identical with any such z, but could have been. The argument treats identity as though from a perspective outside any particular possible world; they may deny the existence of such a perspective.

10 The proof is a simpler variant of one given in note 15. It follows that independence results do not always transfer from propositional modal logic. If T! is the schema $\Box A \leftrightarrow A$, $p \rightarrow \Box p$ is a theorem of KT! but not of KDB, whereas KT! = and KDB = have the same theorems.

11 The denial of the S4 principle may lack the generality requisite of a solution to the difficulty, for it does not help with similar modal and temporal paradoxes of artifact identity; see Williamson (1990a), p. 142. Wiggins sug-

gests that our linguistic practices here are not always coherent; we may 'fall from the heights where we take conceptual risks in our management of artifact identity' (1980a), p. 97; the problem is not confined to artifacts; it also arises for such things as icebergs).

12 See Crossley and Humberstone (1977) and Hodes (1984) for more on the logic of 'actually'. In systems where $\Box A$ is interpreted as truth in all worlds, axiom schemata such as $\Box A \to @A$ and $\Diamond(\Diamond @A \to A)$ are valid (@RN is then redundant in the presence of RN). They are not derivable in K@. $\Box p \to @p$ can be false at the actual world if the latter is not self-accessible. The schema would be derivable in KT@, but $\Box(\Box p \to @p)$ would not be; it can be false at the actual world if it is not accessible from every world accessible from it (so accessibility is not symmetric). $\Diamond(\Diamond @p \to p)$ can be false at the actual world if it is not accessible from any world accessible from it.

13 @$\Box$ is the principle most likely to meet resistance. A full defence cannot be given here, but four points may be mentioned. (a) @$\Box$ has a sensible analogue in tense logic; if it is raining now, it will always have been raining now. (b) @$\Box$ also has an analogue in first-order predicate logic: the theorem $Fa \to \forall x\, Fa$, where 'a' is a closed term. (c) There is a notion easily confused with 'necessarily', in Humberstone's terms 'fixedly actually', for which the analogue of @$\Box$ does fail. (d) Consider the apparently valid argument 'It could have happened that everyone who actually went to the party stayed at home; John actually went to the party; therefore it could have happened that John stayed at home'. The premises are naturally formalized as $\Diamond \forall x\, (@Fx \to Gx)$ and $@Fj$ and the conclusion as $\Diamond Gj$. It can easily be shown to be valid on the basis of @$\Box$ and standard logical principles (there is an irrelevant complication about John's existence; purists should take as major premise 'It could have happened that John existed and everyone who actually went to the party stayed at home'). Without @$\Box$, how is the argument to be analysed?

14 Some may find substitution more plausible within the scope of @ than within that of $\Box$. The proof of ND in K@ = can be extended to a proof of NI in KB@ = involving no substitution within the scope of $\Box$, by reasoning parallel to that in the extension of the proof of NI in K = to a proof of ND in KB =

15 Proof: Let $*$ be $\Box^i (\sim x = y \to \Box^j \sim x = y)$. By application of RN and K to NI, $\vdash x = y \to \Box^i x = y$; by PC, $\vdash\quad x = y \to (\sim x = y \to \Box^j \sim x = y)$, so $\vdash \Box^i x = y \to *$, so $\vdash x = y \to *$. Since $@T_C$ was not used in the proof of line (11), $\vdash \Box^{i+j-i} @ \sim x = y \to \Box^{i+j} \sim x = y$ by RN and K; by @$\Box$ and K, $\vdash @ \sim x = y \to \Box^{i+j} \sim x = y$. By PC, $\vdash \Box^j \sim x = y \to (\sim x = y \to \Box^j \sim x = y)$, so $\vdash \Box^{i+j} \sim x = y \to *$ by RN and K. Thus $\vdash \dot{} @ \sim x = y \to *$, so by $@T_C \vdash \sim x = y \to *$. PC completes the proof.

16 Proof: Let dA be the result of deleting every occurrence of $\Box$ and @ in A. By induction on the complexity of A, for every sequence # of $\Box$s and @s $\vdash dA \to \#A$ and $\vdash \sim dA \to \# \sim A$ in KD@ =. Basis: Use the previous footnote, @$\Box$ and $@T_C$. Induction step: Suppose the hypothesis holds for every formula less complex than A. (i) A is $B \to C$. By hypothesis and PC,

⊢ $d(B \to C) \to (\sim\#\sim B \to \#C)$ and ⊢ $\sim d(B \to C) \to \sim(\#B \to \sim\#\sim C)$. By RN, K, @RN and @K, ⊢ $(\sim\#\sim B \to \#C) \to \#(B \to C)$ and ⊢ $\sim(\#B \to \sim\#\sim C) \to \#\sim(B \to C)$. Thus the hypothesis holds for $B \to C$. (ii) A is $\sim B$. Similar. (iii) A is $\Box B$. By hypothesis, ⊢ $dB \to \#\Box B$ and ⊢ $\sim dB \to \#\Box\sim B$. By RN, K, @RN and @K applied to D, ⊢ $\#\Box\sim B \to \#\sim\Box B$, so ⊢ $\sim dB \to \#\sim\Box B$. Since $d\Box B$ is dB, the hypothesis holds for $\Box B$. (iv) A is @B. Similar. Since # can be the null sequence, ⊢ $dA \leftrightarrow A$.

17 Chellas and Segerberg (1994) discuss conditions under which the theorem-hood of $A \to \Box A$ in a modal logic implies the theoremhood of $\Diamond A \to A$ (they give another example: if the necessary existence of God can be deduced from the existence of God, does it follow that the existence of God can be deduced from the possible existence of God?).

18 Humberstone (1983) makes closely related points. His backwards-looking operators stand to $\Box$ and $\Diamond$ as 'x is accessible from y' stands to 'y is accessible from x'; they permit a derivation of ND from NI even when accessibility is non-symmetric. He and Karmo (1983) also discuss analogous issues in tense logic (does 'If identical, always identical' entail 'If distinct, always distinct?'), where past tense operators are backwards-looking with respect to future-tense operators and *vice versa*.

19 If ND is not added as an axiom, one has the unsatisfactory situation that K@ = (KT@ =, etc.) is a non-conservative extension of K = (KT =, etc.): ND is a formula in the original @-less language but provable only in the extended system.

20 Evans's intentions are not wholly clear; see Lewis (1988) and Burgess (1989). What he gave is not strictly a proof of NI but a reductio ad absurdum of the supposition that it is indeterminate whether $a = b$, where 'a' and 'b' are to be replaced by singular terms of an unspecified kind; it therefore pays explicit attention to the relative scope of these terms and of 'determinately'. This issue is less urgent when, as now, the singular terms are variables. A proof more like the present one was given in Salmon (1982), pp. 243–6.

21 Doubts as to whether the existence of vague objects is incompatible with DI and DD are irrelevant in this context.

22 For example, if A is indeterminate, let $\sim A$ be indeterminate and $\Box A$ false; let a conditional have the same status as its consequent if its antecedent is true and be true otherwise.

23 See Urquhart (1986) and Williamson (1994). It is not denied that many-valued semantics may occasionally be a convenient technical device.

24 Could an objection to the proofs of DI and DD come from some other deviant logic? Wiggins (1986a), p. 176 emphasizes the mildness of the logical principles used in his proof of DI by pointing out that they are intuitionistically valid; in contrast, his proof of DD uses double negation elimination. However, both the proof of DI in K = and the proof of DD in KB = are intuitionistically valid if the B axiom is treated as an assumption.

25 Fine (1975) expounds a supervaluational theory of indeterminacy in detail. It is discussed critically in Williamson (1994).

26 See Williamson (1987/8), p. 114.

27 Parallel issues arises about the similarity of possible worlds; see Lewis (1973), p. 51 and Williamson (1988), pp. 459–60.
28 Wiggins (1986a), p. 179. The formula he envisages us refusing to accept is (in present notation) $\sim\Box x = y \to \Box \sim x = y$ rather than $\sim x = y \to \Box \sim x = y$, but since we are envisaged as accepting the equivalence of $\sim x = y$ and $\sim\Box x = y$, the difference is immaterial.
29 Williamson (1990a), pp. 103–8; (1994).

2

Absolute and Relative Identity

Harold Noonan

1. In *Identity and Spatio-Temporal Continuity* (1967) and its successor *Sameness and Substance* (1980a) David Wiggins defends an absolute, or Leibnizian, concept of identity against relative identity theorists.

The books contain much more, of course. In particular, there is Wiggins's examination of the concept of personal identity which (in its version in (1980a)) contains the radical suggestion that the debate over personal identity is misconceived so long as we do not appreciate that the concept of a *person* is parasitic on that of a *man* and cannot involve a distinct, non-coinciding, criterion of identity.

But it remains true that the attack on relative identity is at the heart of Wiggins's position. In what follows I attempt an assessment of the debate.

2. In both (1967) and (1980a) Wiggins begins by asking 'Can *a* be the same f as *b* but not the same g as *b*? Can this happen even when *a* or *b* is itself a g?' Here 'f' and 'g' range over sortal concepts and hence to give an affirmative answer to the question is to endorse Geach's famous thesis of the sortal relativity of identity (see for example Geach (1973)), which Wiggins refers to as 'thesis R'. Wiggins rejects thesis R and presents a case for its rejection comprising both general arguments and detailed examinations of particular cases which, at first sight, seem to support it. It is in the course of his discussion of these cases that Wiggins introduces his famous 'is' of constitution, which has since become a standard weapon employed by defenders of absolute identity against their relativist opponents.

I begin my discussion of thesis R, in the next section, with an analysis of what is going on in these cases. (I do not have space to discuss Wiggins's general arguments against thesis R, but I should say, to make my position clear, that I do not find them convincing) With respect to putative *diachronic* case of relative identity I argue that their *logical form* disqualifies them from illustrating thesis R – and hence that no appeal to the 'is' of constitution is needed by an opponent of relative identity to deal with them. With respect to putative *synchronic* cases of relative identity, the most well-known of which is the example of the cat on the mat, I argue that whilst their logical form is not inappropriate, an opponent of thesis R can nevertheless still reject them as illustrations of that thesis without appeal to the 'is' of constitution. Appeal to the 'is' of constitution is required, it emerges, only if not only Geach's relative identity thesis, but also his thesis of the irreducibility of restricted (sortal) qualification to unrestricted quantification is rejected. But I suggest that the linguistic facts in such a case as that of the cat on the mat do not enable a decision to be made either for or against the irreducibility thesis.

However, the fundamental point at issue between absolutists and relativists, I believe, is not to be found here. Rather, the crucial notion to be examined is that of *a criterion of identity* (this is implicit, of course, in the fact that thesis R is a thesis about identity under a sortal concept, for sortal concepts are precisely those with which a criterion of identity is associated[1]). Absolute identity theorists like Wiggins maintain that absolute equivalence relations (i.e. equivalence relations which ensure the indiscernibility of their terms) can constitute criteria of identity but that relative equivalence relations (i.e. ones which do not ensure indiscernibility) cannot; relative identity theorists, like Geach, maintain that relative equivalence relations can constitute criteria of identity. I argue, in the last two sections of the paper, that when the expression 'a criterion of identity' is used in one sense that can be given to it, the absolutist is right; when it is used in another sense that can be given to it the relativist is right, but when it is used in the sense which is its most common in the philosophical literature, neither is right. I suggest, however, that the sense which can be given to the expression by the absolutist is of doubtful legitimacy and hence that only relativists have anything useful to offer.

3. I begin, then, with the putative examples of relative identity discussed by Wiggins and Geach.

An example of relative identity would be a situation correctly describable by a statement of the form:

(1) aRb & not-aSb & for some z, $(aSz \lor bSz)$

– where both 'R' and 'S' stand for relations of sortal relative identity and hence, minimally, for equivalence relations. (1) entails:

(2) $(aRa \& bRb) \& (aSa \lor bSb)$

by the reflexivity of R and S.

Now the crucial point to make about all the *diachronic* cases of relative identity discussed by Wiggins in (1967) and (1980a) is that they fail to satisfy schema (2). Hence no appeal to the 'is' of constitution is necessary to show that these cases are not examples of R.

To illustrate, consider Wiggins's case (β) ((1980a), p. 27ff.; (1967), p. 8ff.). A jug is shattered and the pieces cemented together to make a coffee-pot. The coffee-pot is the same collection of bits as the jug but not the same utensil. Wiggins appeals to the 'is' of constitution to argue that this is not an illustration of thesis R, but such an appeal is unnecessary. Since the two have non-overlapping life-histories, the coffee-pot is the same collection of bits as the jug only in the sense that it *is*, at the later time, the same collection of bits as the jug *was* before the accident. But this being so it is false that the jug *is* at the later time the same collection of bits as the jug *was* before the accident. Similarly, it is false that the coffee-pot *is* at the later time the same collection of bits as the coffee-pot *was* before the accident. Hence we do not have the conjunction required by the first half of schema (2) and so, however the 'is' of 'is the same collection of bits' is interpreted, case (β) does not illustrate thesis R.[2]

Again, consider Wiggins's case (δ) ((1980a), p. 28ff.; (1967), p. 9ff.). The river on which my vessel is now moored is the same river as the river on which I moored it yesterday, but it is not the same water, despite the fact that rivers are water. But, however we interpret the 'is' of 'is the same water as', this is a correct description of the case only in the sense that the river on which my vessel is now moored is not *now* the same water as the river on which I moored it yesterday *was yesterday*. It is not true that the river on which my vessel is now moored is *now* the same water as the river on which my vessel is now moored *was yesterday*, nor is it true that the river on which my vessel was moored yesterday is *now* the same water as the river on which my vessel was moored yesterday *was yesterday*. Hence we do not have the disjunction required by the second half of schema (2), and so case (δ) does not illustrate thesis R.

The same point holds for all putative diachronic cases of relative identity; appeal to the 'is' of constitution is never needed to show that they are not illustrations of R, since in every case schema (2) is bound to be unsatisfied however the relevant occurrences of 'is' are interpreted.

Matters stand differently with the putative *synchronic* examples of R presented by Geach. For in these cases there is no problem about schema (2) being satisfied. But in these cases, too, the opponent of relative identity need make no appeal to the 'is' of constitution.

To see this point it will suffice to look at the well-known case of the cat on the mat.

Geach presents this case as follows. Tibbles is sitting on the mat, and is the only cat sitting on the mat. But Tibbles has at least one thousand hairs. Geach continues:

> Now let c be the largest continuous mass of feline tissue on the mat. Then for any of our 1,000 cat-hairs, say h_n, there is a proper part c_n of c which contains precisely all of c except the hair h_n; and every such part c_n differs in a describable way both from any other such part, say c_m and from c as a whole. Moreover, fuzzy as the concept *cat* may be, it is clear that not only is c a cat, but also any part c_n is a cat: c_n would clearly be a cat were the hair h_n plucked out, and we cannot reasonably suppose that plucking out a hair *generates* a cat, so c_n must already have been a cat. (Geach (1980), p. 215.)

The conclusion, of course, is that *same cat* must be a merely relative identity relation, for there is only one cat on the mat and hence all the *distinct* entities present on the mat must be the same cat.

It is clear that this argument will not convince an opponent such as Wiggins, who will simply deny that any of the entities distinct from Tibbles on the mat *is* a cat – pointing out in support of his denial that there are modal and historical properties possessed by Tibbles not possessed by the other entities (e.g. being capable of losing all her hair, having chased a mouse two years ago last Wednesday).

On the other hand, a defender of Geach will want to know with what right it is assumed that possession of any of *these* properties is regarded as essential to being a cat.

But, in fact, it is clear that there are *three* possible lines of solution to the puzzle of the cat on the mat (and that these solutions are applicable *mutatis mutandis* to any of the other examples Geach employs):

(1) As noted, one can just say that Geach is wrong and that the correct definition of 'cat' applies to *none* of the entities present except for Tibbles herself. If one takes this line one needs to explain why, despite this, it is correct to *say*, e.g. of each of the continuous lumps of feline tissue $c_1, c_2, c_3 \ldots$, that it 'is' a cat. At this point one may appeal to Wiggins's 'is' of constitution.

(2) Or one can say, to elaborate the Geachian position outlined briefly above, that what the puzzle shows is that it is a mistake to suppose that in everyday life counting is always by identity, i.e. that x and y are to be counted as one just in case x = y. In fact, in counting cats we count, as the puzzle shows, by a weaker equivalence relation R. This equivalence relation obtains between each of c_1, c_2, c_3 and the next, and between each

of these and Tibbles. Consequently we are speaking correctly when we describe the situation as one in which there is just one cat even though the situation contains 1,000 distinct objects each of which qualifies as a cat. But, of course, in counting cats, the relation we count by can be none other than the one we express by 'is the same cat as'. This, then, must be the relevant relation R. Thus 'is the same cat as' is an expression for a relative equivalence relation.

(3) Finally, one can reject *both* of these suggestions and say that the solution to the puzzle lies in recognising that in counting cats not everything that qualifies as a cat counts. 'There is just one cat on the mat' means 'some cat is on the mat and every cat on the mat is identical with that one'. Thus the only entities present to be counted when counting cats are those which fall within the range of the natural language quantifying expressions 'some cat' and 'every cat'. But it is only if 'some cat is F' is equivalent to 'something is a cat and is F' and 'every cat is F' is equivalent to 'everything, if it is a cat, is F' that these quantifying expressions must be taken to range over everything which qualifies as a cat. A solution to the puzzle can thus be found in denying these equivalences and maintaining that, of the 1,000 items in the situation which qualify as cats, only one – Tibbles herself – falls within the range of 'some cat' and 'every cat' (which, in fact, is a central component of Geach's position anyway, required in order to assign the intuitively correct truth-conditions to statements such as 'some cat is on the mat now and was also on the mat yesterday').

It seems clear that the linguistic facts are consistent with each of these solutions and hence that to continue to dispute about such putative synchronic cases of relative identity is idle. But the availability of the third type of solution also makes it clear that, anyway, opposition to the concept of relative identity, by itself, provides *no* motive for insisting on the type (1) solution or for endorsing the 'is' of constitution. What is required for providing such a motive is an argument for rejecting the thesis of the irreducibility of restricted (sortal) quantification to unrestricted quantification, but it is hard to see what form such an argument might take. The crucial point at issue between the proponents of the type (1) solution and the type (3) solution is whether *'is a cat', understood as a syntactically simple predicate in which the 'is' is merely the 'is' of predication – a mere fragment of a predicate which expresses no property or relation by itself, applies univocally both to Tibbles and to (at least one of) the entities present in the situation described which are distinct from Tibbles.* If so, the type (3) solution can be accepted; if not the type (1) solution must be accepted. But how this issue might be decided, and even whether there is any fact of the matter to *be* decided is, I suggest, wholly unclear.

Of course, the linguistic facts might have been otherwise. It might have been that it was the untutored reaction of any competent speaker of English, when presented with the case of the cat on the mat, that it was simply *incorrect* to describe any of c, c_1, c_2 etc., as 'cats'. If so this would be conclusive evidence that (1) was the only possible line to take about the case – and no appeal to the 'is' of constitution would be either required or possible. The case would then be no puzzle at all. But the linguistic facts are not like this, and even if they were this would not settle the matter in general. For the debate between opponents and proponents of thesis R concerns the *conceptual possibility* of examples of R, not their *actuality*. However, as I have indicated, it is hard to see how any case, actual or hypothetical, in which the linguistic facts were such as to provide *prima facie* evidence of a synchronic illustration of thesis R, could ever provide an unambiguous proof of that thesis because of the availability, not only of the type (1) and type (2) solutions, but also of the type (3) solution.

4.   If we had to leave matters in this state, I submit, the debate between relativists and absolutists would not be worth considering. But there is a notion which is central to the debate which has, so far, been left unexamined, namely, the notion of a criterion of identity. The relativist view is that a relation equivalence relation can serve as a criterion of identity; the opposing absolutist view is that only absolute equivalence relations can serve as criteria of identity. But what is a criterion of identity?

There are three elements constitutive of the notion of a criterion of identity as it is usually understood by philosophers:

(E1)   A specification of a criterion of identity is a specification of a relation.

(E2)   The specification of the criterion of identity for f's (where 'f' is a sortal term) is the specification of a relation which holds between f's.

(E3)   The specification of the criterion of identity for f's is an essential part of a full account of the sortal concept f.

I shall argue (a) that a relative equivalence relation *can* serve as a criterion of identity in the sense of a relation satisfying (E1) and (E3), but not as a criterion of identity in the sense of a relation satisfying all of (E1), (E2) and (E3), and (b) that an absolute equivalence relation *can* serve as a criterion of identity in the sense of a relation satisfying (E1) and (E2), but, again, not as a criterion of identity in the sense of a relation satisfying all of (E1), (E2) and (E3).

Let us first consider the relativist position.

The basic argument the relativist can put forward goes as follows. Consider any relative equivalence relation R, say Geach's famous (or notorious) relation *same surman* – the relation which holds between two men if they have the same surname. Then it is easy to see how a stock of proper names can be introduced into the language in association with that relation as the criterion of identity associated with them. Suppose we wish to introduce 'Chones' as the name of the one and only surman all the Joneses are. Then we can explain the contribution of 'Chones' to the truth-conditions of sentences in which it occurs in two ways. We can stipulate that where 'G' is a simple predicate applicable to men, 'Chones is G' is to be true if and only if *every* man surnamed 'Jones' is G. Alternatively, we can stipulate that 'Chones is G' is to be true if and only if *some* man surnamed 'Jones' is true. Thus, on both accounts, 'Chones is a man' will be true, as will 'Chones is a surman'. But on the first account neither 'Chones is alive' nor 'Chones is dead' will be true, whereas on the second account both will be true. When we consider complex predicates either account will, therefore, yield oddities: on the first account 'Chones is alive or dead' will not be true, although 'Chones is a man' will be true and every man is alive or dead; on the other hand, on the second account 'Chones is both alive and dead' will be true, although 'Chones is a man' will also be true and no man is both alive and dead. But when we analyse these complex predications into truth-functions of simple predications we see that the claims they make are perfectly straightforward; it is just that the way these claims are expressed (consequent upon the decision to introduce as simple predicates of surman predicates equiform with simple predicates of men) is unusual.

We can proceed in the same way to introduce a name for the surman all men surnamed 'Brown' are, another for the one all men surnamed 'Smith' are, and so on; and at the same time introduce simple relational predicates applicable to surmen. Then we can go on to introduce restricted quantifiers 'some surman' and 'every surman' explained in such a way that 'some surman is G' is true if and only if '*a* is G' is true where '*a*' is a name *for* a surman, i.e. is a name introduced or introducible by the means just sketched.

The possibility of thus proceeding to introduce a miniature 'language game' in which surmen are spoken of is familiar from the writings of Geach and Dummett (see Dummett (1981b), ch. 11; Dummett (1991b); Geach (1973)), and it is clear that the proposal involves no incoherence. Hence, the relativist might say, his case is proven: since no special feature of the relation *same surman*, not possessed by *all* equivalence relations, was appealed to in the description of the proposed manner of introduction of names *for* surmen, *any* relative equivalence relation can serve as a criterion of identity, and, at least, which is all, strictly speaking that he seeks to claim, *some* relative equivalence relations can serve as criteria of identity.

However, this overlooks a crucial point. The equivalence relation *same surman* is indeed a relation in which every surman stands to itself, and so every surman is in its domain, but it is not a relative equivalence relation *in that domain*, in fact it is an absolute equivalence relation in that domain. For, if '*a*' and '*b*' are two names *for* surmen, then if '*a* is the same surman as *b*' is true, *a* and *b* will be indistinguishable.[3] *Same surman* is, indeed, a relative equivalence relation as it holds between men, and men are, indeed, surmen, but it is not a relative equivalence relation as it holds between surmen. Hence we do not have in this case, and could never have, a case in which a relative eqivalence relation is serving as a criterion of identity in the sense of 'a criterion of identity' specified by all three of conditions (E1)–(E3) above. The only sense in which a relative equivalence relation can serve as a criterion of identity – and *same surman* does thus function in relation to names *for* surmen – is as a relation satisfying the two conditions (E1) and (E3).

The absolutist might now conclude that his case has been made. This, however, is also untrue.

The notion of a criterion of identity is tied to the notion of a sortal concept: sortal concepts are precisely those a full explanation of which requires explanation of the associated criterion of identity. This is why element (E3) is a component of the sense of the expression 'a criterion of identity' as philosophers are accustomed to use it. Thus, the thought is, where 'f' is a term for a sortal concept, as well as the question 'What is it to *be* an f?', that is, 'What are the necessary and sufficient conditions for being a member of the sort f?', there is also the question 'What are the identity conditions of the sort f?', that is, 'What is it for an f identified at one time or by one description to be the same f as an f identified at another time or by another description?' – and a full account of the concept of an f requires an answer to the second question as well as an answer to the first.

However, this thought cannot be correct if the criterion of identity associated with a sortal concept is to be given by the specification of an absolute equivalence relation. For if it is, the *conditions of f-hood*, which can be specified without explicit use either of the concept of identity *simpliciter* or of the concept of f-identity (in an 'identity-free' way, as I shall say), fix uniquely the conditions of f-identity.[4]

If the criterion of identity associated with the sortal concept f is given by the absolute equivalence relation R then a specification of a necessary condition of f-identity would presumably have to take the form:

(i)   for any x, for any y, if x is an f and y is an f then x is the same f as y
      only if xRy,
      but if *same f* is an absolute equivalence relation this is equivalent to:
(ii) for any x, for any y, if x is an f and y is an f then x = y only if xRy,
      which is in turn equivalent to:
(iii) for any x, if x is an f then xRx.

But (iii), of course, says nothing about f-*identity*, rather it simply specifies
a necessary condition of f-hood, so its equivalent (i), despite appearances, does the same. Once the necessary conditions of f-hood have been
specified, then, there is no need for further specification of necessary
conditions of f-identity along the lines of (i).

What of sufficient conditions of f-identity?

A specification of a sufficient condition of f-identity would presumably
have to take the form:

(iv) for any x, for any y, if x is an f and y is an f then x is the same f as y
      only if xRy.

But if *same f* is an absolute equivalence relation this is equivalent to:

(v)   for any x, for any y, if x is an f and y is an f then x = y if xRy, which
      is equivalent to:
(vi) for any x and y, if xRy and it is not the case that x = y then (x is not
      an f or y is not an f).

(vi), which denies the existence of distinct R-related f's, cannot be
represented as specifying a necessary or a sufficient condition of f-hood,
since it is not equivalent to anything of the form:

for any x, x is an f only if Cx,

or of the form:

for any x, x is an f if Cx.

But what (vi) does do is to specify a necessary condition of a concept's
being the concept of an f, i.e. a constraint on the *concept* of an f. In this
respect, it is like the proposition 'there is at most one divine being', i.e.
'for any x and y, if x exists and y exists and it is not the case that x = y then
(x is not a divine being or y is not a divine being)', which denies the
existence of distinct divine beings. This proposition does not specify any
necessary or sufficient condition of being a divine being (a 'mark' of the
concept in Frege's sense), since it is not equivalent to anything of the
form:

for any x, x is a divine being only if Cx,

or of the form:

for any x, x is a divine being if Cx.

but what it does do is to specify a second-order constraint that any concept has to satisfy to *be* that of a divine being.

However, once we have specified the necessary and sufficient conditions of being a divine being (which can be done in an identity-free way), this specification, together with the facts, will determine the truth-value of 'there is at most one divine being'. Thus, if true, this will be a derivative truth, which does not need separate mention.

The same is true with respect to the concept of an f and assertions of form (vi). Once an identity-free formulation of the necessary and sufficient conditions of f-hood has been given this, together with the facts, will determine which, if any, assertions of the form (vi) are true, and those which are true will be merely derivative truths which do not need separate mention.

But if *same f* is an absolute equivalence relation, assertions of the form (vi) are the equivalent of assertions of the form (iv), and so the same must be true of the latter. In other words, specifying in an identity-free way the necessary and sufficient conditions of f-hood fixes the sufficient conditions of f-identity just as it fixes the necessary conditions of f-identity.

Thus, unless it is denied that if a relation R gives the criterion of identity for f's a full specification of the meaning of the sortal term 'f' must specify, in terms of R, the necessary and sufficient conditions of f-identity it follows that *no* absolute equivalence relation can be regarded as giving the criterion of identity associated with a sortal concept.

In other words, an absolute equivalence relation can serve as a criterion of identity only in the sense of a relation satisfying elements (E1) and (E2) of the notion of a criterion of identity given above. Like a relative equivalence relation it cannot serve as a criterion of identity in the sense of a relation satisfying all of (E1)–(E3).

5.   Hence, neither the absolutist nor the relativist position is wholly correct. But to get clearer about the situation we need to distinguish two sorts of case. In the first sort of case our understanding of a sortal concept f is dependent on a grasp of a relative equivalence relation holding between entities distinct from f's. In the second sort of case no such relation of dependence holds.

The paradigmatic examples of sortal concepts of the first kind are those under which abstract objects fall.

Consider the abstract sortal term 'shape'. It seems clear that the correct account of its semantics is along the lines sketched out by Frege in the *Grundlagen* using the concept of a direction as his model.

According to this account the sortal term 'shape' may be thought of as introduced into the language as follows: we begin by introducing an expression 'has the same shape as' for a relative equivalence relation between material objects; we then introduce the functional expression 'the shape of' explained in such a way as to yield the equivalence of 'the shape of x is the same as the shape of a y' and 'x has the same shape as y', and finally we explain 'x is a shape' to mean 'for some y, x is the shape of y'. Simple predicates of shapes may now be introduced in terms of predicates (simple or complex) of material objects with respect to which identity of shape is a congruence relation, and complex predications of shapes will be determined as true or false in accordance with their composition from simple predicates.

What makes this account compelling is that it reflects the necessary order of language acquisition. There *could not* be a language in which it was possible to make reference to shapes but did not contain any functional expression with the sense of 'the shape of'. This is because shapes, unlike, say, colours, are not possible objects of ostension: even against the background of an appropriate criterion of identity one cannot pick out a shape by pointing and saying 'this'. The only way to refer to a shape is as the shape of some already identified object or region (or as the shape satisfying a certain description in terms of predicates of shapes introduced by means of the account sketched above). Thus, a language could not contain the predicate 'is a shape' unless it also contained the functional expression 'the shape of' and the Fregean account is in accord with this fact.

We can now see that Geach's account of how the sortal term 'surman' and predications of surmen may be introduced into the language is merely a variant of the Fregean account. What makes it seem different, and what explains its oddities, is merely that it involves introducing as simple predicates of surmen predicates equiform with simple predicates of men. This is why it is possible on the Geachian account to say that surmen *are* men. But once this point is recognised there is no difficulty in appreciating that in the case of surmen, as in the case of shapes, the relation grasp of which is essential to understanding the concept is, indeed, a relative equivalence relation, but one holding not between surmen but between objects of a distinct ontological category – men.

However, it is not just in the case of abstract nouns that it is plausible to suppose that understanding the concept expressed requires a grasp of a relative equivalence relation holding between objects distinct from those falling under the concept. The same is true of mass nouns.

Consider the mass noun 'gold'. Like shapes, parcels of gold are not possible objects of ostension. Pointing and saying 'this gold' will not determine which is the object to which I am referring. This is because any proper part of a parcel of gold is itself a parcel of gold, but a distinct parcel from that of which it is a proper part. Thus, just as in order to identify shapes we must relate them to some other already identified objects or regions – as the shapes *of* those objects or regions – so, in order to identify a parcel of gold, one must relate it to some already identified object as the gold *of* that object: just as one may identify a shape as the *shape* of so-and-so's wedding ring, so one may identify a parcel of gold as the *gold* of her wedding ring, and as the possibility of reference to shapes depends upon the existence of such means of identification the same holds of the possibility of reference to parcels of gold. And so a language *could not* contain the means of making reference to parcels of gold – and hence could not contain the predicates 'is gold' and 'is the same gold as' (understood as applicable to parcels of gold) – unless it contained a functional expression with the sense of 'the gold of', as it occurs in 'the gold of her wedding ring'.

But in the light of this, the Fregean pattern of explanation seems to have as much plausibility for 'gold' as it has for 'shape'. The basic relation one must grasp, in order to be able to talk of parcels of gold, is that which holds between material objects x and y when they are constituted of the same gold. This relative equivalence relation serves as the criterion of identity for parcel of gold in just the sense in which the relative equivalence relation *having the same shape as* serves as the criterion of identity for shapes.

If these suggestions are correct, abstract sortal terms and mass terms *may* be thought of as associated with criteria of identity given by relative equivalence relations, just as the relativist claims, but the relative equivalence relations in question cannot be thought of as holding between the items falling under the concepts expressed by those terms.

But, in addition to abstract sortals and mass terms there must also be what we can call 'basic count nouns', like 'man'. However, in the use of such basic count nouns it cannot be that comprehension of the concept expressed requires grasp of a relative equivalence relation holding between entities distinct from those falling under the concept. Hence, it may seem that in this type of case, if we wish to speak of an associated criterion of identity at all, we *must* regard such a criterion as being specifiable by a specification of an absolute equivalence relation holding between the entities falling under the concept.

However, as we have seen, an absolute equivalence relation cannot serve as a criterion of identity in the sense of a relation *whose specification as such is an indispensable part of a full specification of the concept*. But that there is *something* which plays this role in relation to basic count nouns, just as there is something which plays it in relation to abstract sortals and mass terms, seems evident. How can this be understood?

I believe that the solution to this puzzle has been given by Dummett (1981b), ch. 11). In the case of basic count nouns the crucial point to recognise is that the associated criterion of identity is not an equivalence *relation* at all – where a relation is thought of as something holding between *objects*.

We cannot give a correct representation of that level of our language at which we quantify over and refer to objects, Dummett argues, unless we recognise a lower level at which no reference to objects exists. At the lower level, what takes the place of the use, at the higher level, of proper names and other singular terms to refer to objects, is the use of demonstrative pronouns in what Dummett calls 'crude predications'. The distinctive feature of this use of demonstratives is that no criterion of identity has to be invoked to make their utterances understood; no answer to the question 'this *what*? need be available. In such crude predications the predicate cannot, therefore, be one applicable to an *object*, but must be one expressing what Strawson has called a 'feature-placing concept'. Examples of such predications are 'This is sticky', 'This is red', 'This is smooth'.

The transition to the higher level, Dummett suggests, is mediated by what he calls 'statements of identification', that is statements of the form 'this is the same X as that', where 'X' is a basic count noun. A child does not actually acquire the word 'cat' in the first place by learning to point simultaneously to, say, the head and tail of a cat, and say, 'that is the same cat as that'. Nevertheless, this correctly represents what is involved in the move from the lower level of language to the higher, namely the acquisition of a criterion of identity by which we can determine where one cat leaves off and another begins.

But a statement of identification, like a crude predication, does not *itself* involve any reference to objects, since, in itself, it is merely a crude relational statement, like 'This is darker than that'. Hence, the criterion of identity associated with a basic count noun is not an equivalence relation between objects – either objects of the sort to which the count noun applies, or objects of another sort; for though '. . . . is the same X as . . .', as used in statements of identification, is *like* an expression for an equivalence relation, it does not *stand for* such a relation.

Let us now take stock. We began this section by listing three elements constitutive of the notion of a criterion of identity most commonly employed by philosophers. We then saw that no relation could serve as a criterion of identity in the sense of a relation satisfying all three of these conditions, but that a relative equivalence relation could serve as a criterion of identity in the sense of a relation satisfying the first and the third, and an absolute equivalence relation could serve as a criterion of identity in the sense of a relation satisfying the first and second. What we have now seen is that we *do* have a use for the first of these notions of a criterion of identity – in the case of abstract sortals and mass terms, but that this is not so with regard to the second notion of a criterion of identity. For in the case of the remaining category of terms which can be regarded as associated with criteria of identity, namely basic count nouns, the appropriate notion of a criterion of identity is best thought of as not given by a relation at all. Indeed, it is, I think, appropriate to say that the second suggested sense for 'a criterion of identity', that is, the sense in which an absolute equivalence relation *can* serve as a criterion of identity, is not actually a legitimate sense for this expression at all. For the essential element in the idea is the third one: that the criterion of identity for f's should be something a grasp of which is essential to a full understanding of the concept f, and this is precisely the condition no absolute equivalence relation will satisfy.

Thus, I suggest, though neither the position of the relativist nor that of the absolutist is wholly correct, the relativist position is nearer to being so. The main emphasis of Geach's work on identity has always been on the uselesness of the notion of absolute identity, and on its inability to provide any usable criterion of identity. If the arguments given in this paper are correct, this point is vindicated.

NOTES

1 In a well-known passage, referred to by Wiggins, Strawson draws the distinction between sortal and non-sortal concepts in the following terms: 'A sortal universal provides a principle for distinguishing and counting the particulars it collects. It presupposes no antecedent principle or method of individuating the particulars it collects. Characterizing universals . . . whilst they supply principles of grouping, even of counting particulars, supply such principles only for particulars already distinguished, or distinguishable, in accordance with some antecedent principle or method' (Strawson (1959), p. 168). Wiggins rightly criticises the suggestion here that countability is a necessary condition of a concept's qualifying as a sortal concept, but it seems plausible if taken as a sufficient condition. However, if so, resistance to the relative identity thesis must be unmotivated. For, as Geach has made plain, and is now generally accepted, we can count by relations weaker than absolute identity. Moreover, as Wiggins has made plain, a relation may be such that it cannot hold between two objects which are simultaneously spatially distinct without being an absolute identity relation. The thesis that a sortal concept supplies a principle for

counting particulars thus does not require that identity under a sortal concept be Leibnizian. It is only when the notion of a criterion of identity is included in the account of a sortal concept that opposition to thesis R becomes comprehensible.

2 It has been suggested to me that case (β) can be interpreted differently, in such a way that the 'is' of composition is needed to show that it does not illustrate thesis R. Think of a situation in which a speaker does not know which came first, the coffee-pot or the jug. Such a person might say 'the coffee-pot is the same collection of bits as the jug' meaning 'the coffee-pot is or was the same collection of bits as the jug is or was'. Is the embedded sameness relation here not reflexive? Consequently, do we not need the 'is' (or 'was') of composition to deal with this case? However, this line of thought is incorrect. 'The coffee-pot is or was the same collection of bits as the jug is or was' is equivalent to 'the coffee-pot is the same collection of of bits as the jug was or the coffee-pot was the same collection of bits as the jug is', and this does not state an equivalence relation between jug and coffee-pot since neither disjunct is true when 'jug' is replaced by 'coffee-pot' and neither is true when 'coffee-pot is replaced by 'jug'.

3 Properties not shared by people who are the same surman cannot be possessed by surmen on either of the accounts given of how names *for* surmen can be introduced. Hence, numerically identical surmen must, as, of course, is required, be indistinguishable.

4 Of course, necessary and sufficient conditions of f-hood cannot be specified in an identity-free way for *every* term 'f' – consider, for example, 'twin' or 'member of a string quartet' – but these are not sortal terms.

3

Persons and Personal Identity

P. F. Snowdon

1 Introduction

David Wiggins has written, a number of times, about the nature and identity of persons.[1] As to their nature, Wiggins has been, like many of us, strongly influenced by P. F. Strawson's famous account of persons in Chapter 3 of *Individuals*, objecting primarily, and, it seems to me, rightly, to Strawson's overly even-handed treatment of the mental and the physical aspects of a person. Part, at least, of Strawson's even-handedness is revealed when he allows that just as a person's body can outlive the person's consciousness, a possibility which is not seriously in question, so a person's consciousness can outlive his or her body. This claim is questionable because it seems to be inconsistent with materialism. The simplest reply to Strawson is that it needs far more than the 'not very great' exercise of imagination, cited by him, to convince us that there is such a possibility. Wiggins himself has gone further and argued that conceptual analysis can reveal what he calls the necessary 'matter-involvingness' of both persons and their psychological attributes.[2]

My concern here, though, is the so-called problem of personal identity. Strawson, in *Individuals*, said little about this problem, and suggested that it should be regarded as 'of relatively minor significance and relatively little difficulty'.[3] This is an assessment which Wiggins, again rightly, does not share, and he has recently proposed, and argued at length for, the thesis that the, or a, fundamental truth about personal identity is that

Earlier versions of this paper were read at the universities of Cambridge and Kent. I am grateful particularly for comments by Tom Baldwin, Jane Heal, and Colin Radford. I have also profited from many conversations about Wiggins's theories with Naci Mehmet. Finally, I am very grateful to the editors for advice and patience.

persons are animals; a person remains in existence so long as the animal which that person is remains in existence.

It is, surely, a very important task for current philosophy to determine what the most plausible defence of this thesis is. Wiggins is not alone in defending it, but his is the profoundest and most developed exposition of it currently available. My aim is to consider some of the propositions which Wiggins has endorsed (or which I interpret him as having endorsed) in the course of presenting his account.[4] I shall argue that a number of them are dubious, and I shall hint at an alternative approach. This exploration is intended to be a tribute to his work on personal identity, and a contribution to the provision of a theory along lines inspired by it.

2 The Accept-All Theory and Some Problems for it

I begin by defining a position in the theory of personal identity, in terms of its attitude to four claims. They are:

(1) I am fundamentally a person.
(2) The notion of a person is a notion of a kind of thing which has certain distinctive requirements for members of the kind to remain in existence.
(3) I am fundamentally an animal.
(4) The notion of an animal is the notion of a kind of thing which has certain distinctive requirements for members of the kind to remain in existence.

(1) and (3) are in the first person, but the idea is that each reader will interpret them as about him- or herself. The sentences are also not precise, and two semi-clarificatory remarks are appropriate. 'Fundamentally' in (1) and (3) tries to express the idea that the predicates in them purport to give the essential and basic nature of the item being spoken about. (2) and (4) are saying about the respective notions of person and animal what Wiggins once expressed thus: they 'afford some principle by which entities of this particular kind . . . may be traced through space and time and reidentified as one and the same'.[5]

What I call the (AA) view (short for Accept All) claims that each of (1) to (4) is true. Why might such a view seem plausible? The simple answer is that considered individually each claim seems worthy of assent. Thus, many of us, adults and children alike, would affirm (1), or something like it. Of (3) the same cannot be said, but many of us, again adults and children alike, would certainly say that we are human beings. It seems reasonable to accept that human beings are a kind of animal, from which (3) apparently follows. Also, amongst our most fundamental self-attributions are some which seem to require thought of ourselves as animals to make sense, for example our overwhelming sense of being a certain sex. Further, (3) would itself be asserted by many educated adults. (2) and (4) are more distinctively philosophical, but there is no doubt that most philosophers discussing personal identity accept them both.

One way to think of Wiggins's recent discussions of personal identity is as an attempt to defend (AA). What are the main problems faced by (AA)? There are, I want to suggest, two main problems. The first arises because many philosophers on reflection find (3) implausible. It is, therefore, necessary to explain why the arguments which cause people to reject (3) are misconceived. The second problem is to avoid a threatened incoherence in (AA). The threat arises because according to (1) and (3) we belong to two kinds, each of which, according to (2) and (4), has distinctive persistence requirements. Clearly (AA) cannot allow that it is possible for the verdicts about our identity which are generated by the requirements associated with the two kinds to diverge in any possible cases. What reason, though, do we have to believe that this is not possible, and what is the explanation for its impossibility?

3 Wiggins's Response

How has Wiggins responded to these two difficulties? Certainly a lot of his discussion bears on the second problem. He has argued in different ways that for an object to be a person it is necessary that it is an animal (of some sort), and if that crucial claim is accepted the second difficulty has been answered. It is, I think, somewhat less clear what Wiggins has offered in response to the first difficulty. One reason for saying that it is not clear is that Wiggins does not provide, in either Wiggins (1980a) or Wiggins (1987b), a substantial unified discussion of the standard type of argument against (3), although there certainly are remarks which are relevant to the assessment of such arguments. By the standard type of argument I mean those which object to (3) on the basis of its inconsistency with intuitions about personal identity which the description of certain cases tends to elicit from us. These intuitions can be inconsistent with (3) in two ways. Some intuitions allow persons to survive in circumstances where there is no longer the same animal – call these 'permissive' intuitions. Others require that there is no longer the same person even though there is the same (human) animal – call these 'restrictive' intuitions.[6] Such arguments have been widely accepted, and acceptance of them has tended to carry philosophers past (3) almost before it is noticed as a possible thesis for discussion.[7] What, according to Wiggins, should be said in response to these objections?

The bulk of his discussion concerns the concept of a person, correcting what he sees as mistaken accounts of it, or correcting mistaken inferences from acceptable remarks about it. In fact, as compared with other recent writers about personal identity, one of the most distinctive features of Wiggins's positive discussions is, it seems to me, the concentration on determining the general conditions for being a person. It seems, therefore, to be assumed by Wiggins that objections to (3) can best be answered by supplying fairly direct support for the conclusion that they deny. Whatever the reason, Wiggins's strategy has had the unfortunate consequence that many writers fail to discuss his account properly because, I conjecture, they are persuaded by the standard arguments that (3) is wrong, and detect no answer to such arguments in Wiggins's writings.[8]

4 Some Questions about the Term 'Person'

Since Wiggins concentrates so intently on determining what it is to be a person, it is worthwhile, at the start, to highlight some of the issues about the concept of a person which any account must address. First, is the term 'person' ambiguous, or can the uses of it be fitted around a single interpretation? Second, what general logical properties does the term have? In particular, is the term 'person' one which if an object satisfies it at any time during that object's existence then the object must satisfy it at all times? If not, can we make sense of the idea of a pre-existent object of some type becoming a person, or of something which is, at some time, a person ceasing to be a person? Third, is the term 'person' an individualistic predicate or not? This is perhaps vague, but I am asking whether it can be relevant to the question whether an object satisfies it how that object relates to other entities. Fourth, in so far as we should refer to psychological features in our elucidation of the term, how should we pick out those features?

It is obviously very difficult to provide a satisfactory elucidation of the term 'person'. People are inclined to say quite different things about it. So, any suggestions must be advanced in a spirit of caution, but, also, some explanation as to why it is so difficult should form part of any theory.

5 The Animal Attribute Theory of Persons

I shall begin with a discussion of the analysis of the notion of a person that Wiggins proposed in *Sameness and Substance*. He calls his account the Animal Attribute Theory of persons, (hereafter abbreviated to AAT). Here, in a condensed form, is the proposal:

> '(Perhaps) x is a person if and only if x is an animal . . . of a kind whose typical members perceive, feel, remember, (etc.) . . . , conceive of themselves as perceiving, feeling, (etc.), . . . (etc.)' (p. 171).

Now, although Wiggins himself has expressed reservations about this, it remains a very interesting and regrettably underdiscussed suggestion.[9] I shall consider it in two stages. The first stage does not quarrel with the restriction of personhood to animals, but asks how satisfactory is its specification of the sub-class of animals which qualify as persons. The second stage considers whether the restriction to animals is correct.

AAT, like virtually all elucidations offered by philosophers of the notion of a person, has at its core the specification of certain psychological capacities and states. However, it specifies (or conceives of) them in a distinctive way, and also relates them to the condition for being a person in a distinctive way. Both of these distinctive aspects merit consideration.

In connection with the first, one thing that is emphasized is the presence of the dots in the analysis. They mark its current incompleteness. However, the point cannot be that the notion of a person is inherently incomplete, since it is obviously assumed that it is already settled what lines of inquiry will remove the gaps. So AAT has the status of a derived or intermediate elucidation, flowing from a more basic interpretation of the notion. The first question is: what is the more basic elucidation? The second is: what is its justification?

The answer to the first question has to be, as far as I can see, that to be a person a thing must belong to a kind the typical members of which have a psychological nature of the sort *we*, humans, have. The dots represent ignorance about the full story as to what our psychological nature is. The second question now becomes rather pressing. Why must the psychological aspects to be alluded to in the account of what it is to be a person be those constitutive of typical human psychological nature? I cannot detect a convincing answer to that in *Sameness and Substance*.

Further, it seems, as it stands, a questionable proposal. Thus, it would be reasonable to count it as part of human psychological nature that we develop through certain stages (which developmental psychologists aim to plot), and also that we have, say, a particular battery of senses and emotions. It is, surely, implausible to suppose that possession of these features is a condition for being a person. But this means that the more basic elucidation cannot simply invoke the idea of human psychological nature. It must, rather, if the general idea is to remain worthy of consideration, be restricted in some way. It turns out, then, that AAT is seriously incomplete as a proposal.

Another very important feature built into AAT is that the psychological features relevant to personhood are to be determined empirically rather in the way the features of, say, gold are to be determined. It is hard to evaluate this suggestion, and I shall restrict myself to two critical remarks. The first concerns the support which Wiggins gives for the claim. He claims that the list of features relevant to being a person are differently related to the sort –person– from the way that the features cited in a standard nominal definition are related to the type being defined. Thus he contrasts the elucidation of 'person' with Aristotle's elucidation of 'house'.[10] The contrast is supposed to be that the relevant list for 'person' is not *transparent* to us. Unfortunately it is not transparent what the meaning of 'transparent' is. Thus, it is not clear that the defining list for house is transparent, and indeed from the quotation it seems not to have been clear to Aristotle.[11] It is important not to exaggerate the transparency of features relevant to nominal definitions. But it is equally important not to exaggerate the non-transparency to us of the list suitable for 'person'. Most people who have written about persons cite rationality, self-consciousness and understanding. So it is not clear that there is any deep difference between those concepts which we all regard as capable of nominal elucidation and the notion of a person. My second comment is that there are possibilities we countenance with relatively empirical concepts which we do not seem to accept for 'person'. We would not countenance the possibility that the elements on the standard list elucidating person might be eliminated given investigation of a wider sample, nor that features with no obvious connection to those already on it might, on investigation, merit being put on the list. Person seems not to be akin to a natural kind notion.

These critical remarks concerned the treatment in AAT of the cognitive capacities linked to the notion of a person. However, AAT relates the capacities to the notion of a person in a distinctive and ingenious way. To be a person is not to have those capacities but, rather, to be a member of an animal kind the typical member of which possesses them. Leaving aside whether the requirement of being an animal is satisfactory, we can ask whether this yields the right extension for the term 'person' within the class of animals.

Because of its interesting structure AAT can be accused of being illiberal. It rules out the possibility of a freakishly gifted member of a kind being a person where the typical members of the kind are not so gifted. But if there were a highly intelligent, rational and self-conscious parrot would we not describe it as a person?

One reply is that the described creature would be a person, but when the case is properly considered it is not a counter-example to AAT since we would have to count the new creature as not a genuine parrot but rather as the first member of a new kind which the experiment had created. This is, though, a rather desperate piece of armchair biology. Why should not a significant cognitive difference be generated by relatively minor neural reorganisation, so lacking in other effects that there is no question of a new kind?

In another respect AAT is liberal. It allows, for example, that brain damaged human beings are persons, whereas an account which requires that the cognitive capacities be possessed by an individual for it to be a person would not allow this. There is certainly something to be said for this consequence. Thus if someone claimed that a person dies each day in a certain hospital, it cannot be replied that the claim is false on the grounds that enough damage had been done to the brains of the patients by their treatment prior to death that they were no longer persons!

6 An Alternative Proposal

We have accumulated some data about our use of 'person' which look inconsistent with those approaches AAT is intended to replace, but other data which seem to be inconsistent with AAT. Prompted by this finding can we be more constructive? Now, it seems to me that the verdict about the parrot cannot be dismissed as wildly alien to our understanding of the term 'person', but neither can the use of 'person' in the hospital deaths example. We could, of course, take this evidence to indicate that we want a disjunctive definition allowing in more cases than AAT does as it stands. But it is worth wondering whether we should not say that the term 'person' has acquired two centres of gravity. It is not true that normal English speakers have a sense that 'person' is lexically ambiguous; however, we seem to have two contrasting uses.

Consider these examples. We are in the desert and see in the distance an object. It is very hard to make out, but someone hazards the suggestion that it is a person. How would we respond to the remark? I think that there is an inclination to say that we would agree if, but only if, the object turned out to be a human being. We would not say, except as a joke, 'You are quite right, because as I can now see using these binoculars, it is a highly intelligent Martian'. Nor would we say, again except as a joke, 'You are quite wrong, for, as I can now see using my binoculars, it is in fact a brain damaged man who has lost his powers of reason'. This is a well established use of 'person' which simply does not fit Locke's famous definition. Nor does it fit AAT. It does not fit AAT because it is simply *equivalent* to 'human being', whereas, for the notion elucidated by AAT, it is a genuinely open question whether its extension is restricted to human beings.

It does seem to me though that there is another use, in which we are prepared to talk of non-human persons, and, indeed, of humans who are not persons. Talking this way seems to be responsive to the psychological endowments of the individual object. The idea that an individual object can qualify in virtue of its capacities rules out AAT as a satisfactory elucidation of this second use. I shall call the first use the 'human' use, and the second use the 'psychological' use. If there are two uses in this way we have part of an explanation why the elucidation has proved so difficult. I shall leave the psychological use unclarified, except to remark that if the aim is for it to be a theoretically interesting notion, interesting, perhaps, to moral and to psychological theory, there will certainly be some room for debate as to how it should be characterised.

7 Persons as Animals

I now return to the question, set aside during sections 5 and 6, whether persons must be animals. In discussing this I shall ignore the suggestion in the previous section and assume, as is normally done, and as is done by Wiggins, that there is a single, unified notion of a person. Two possible sorts of counter-examples suggest themselves to the claim. The first are persons who are, as we might say, present in, or realised by, biological items which are less than whole animals. Could not there be a person who was no more than a brain, or half a brain? If there could be persons like this they are not evidence that persons can be 'non-biological', but it would be wrong to think that animals are the necessary biological unit for their presence. The second possible sort of counter-example are persons who lack any biological nature. The crucial case is that of artificial robotic persons, but other examples would be deities (or God), and angels. At first sight, at least, deities and angels are not animals, but they are (or seem to be) accorded the status of persons by those who believe in them.

To defend AAT against refutation by such cases it needs to be argued that they do not really represent possibilities. How, though, can that be argued? It seems to me that two grounds for such a claim might be advanced. Let us call the battery of psychological capacities which the typical person possesses 'P'. Either it can be argued that the entities in question cannot possess P or it can be argued that although it is possible for such entities to possess P, were they to do so they would still not be persons. The second line of argument assumes that the term 'person' incorporates a restriction on its application within the general range of P-possessors to animals. This assumption seems inconsistent with the evident fact that we have no sense that, for example, someone who does believe that robots satisfy 'P' (or that God satisfies 'P') is misusing the word 'person' in applying it to them (or to him). If it is accepted that such a conception of the term 'person' is mistaken it follows that AAT can be defended only by arguing that it is not possible for the suggested entities to possess P. It needs to be argued, that is, that it is an essential property of (some of) the properties in 'P' that they can be possessed only by animals.

What are the prospects for making a persuasive case for such a claim? In the next section I shall consider the line of argument which, it seems to me, Wiggins regards as the strongest one. After that I shall briefly assess the prospects in the light of further considerations.

8 Persons as Humans

I have assumed that when Wiggins proposed AAT he thought that it is possible for there to be persons who are not human beings. His approach restricted possible candidates to animals, and it is a defence of that claim that is being sought. More recently there are indications (in Wiggins (1987a)) that he does not think that that is possible, or, at least, that he is inclined to doubt that it is possible, for there to be non-human persons. It seems to me that the line of thought Wiggins uses to support this more restricted conception of persons represents his main ground for supposing that non-animal persons are impossible, and so I shall examine it. The crux of the argument is given in the following passage from his 1987 paper:

> Presented with the human form, we immediately entertain a multitude of tentative expectations, unless something inhibits or perverts this response: and that is how it has to be. But faced with a Martian or an automaton, unless this creature is synthesized by procedures that would carbon-copy

the contingencies of human frame and constitution, we should have to be
mad to entertain any of these expectations. What we face is at best an alien
intelligence whose sources of satisfaction are inscrutable, except in so far as
we can make sense of them by imagining ourselves in its place – but that is
a way of proceeding which is excluded by the hypothesis that what we
confront is a Martian or automation. An alien intelligence is not a person.
A person is a creature with whom we can get on terms, or a creature that is
of the same animal nature and psychophysical make-up as creatures with
whom we can get onto terms, there being no clear limit to how far the
process can go. (Though that is not how we define 'person', but simply the
consequence of a certain method of elucidation.)[12]

Now, this line of thought, which I shall call the Interpretation Argument,
is one about which far more needs to be said than can be said here if it is
to be properly evaluated. In outline, it can be represented as having two
premises:

(5)   if an entity is a person then it is interpretable by us,
and
(6)   only human beings are interpretable by us.[13]

There is, it must be conceded, a question whether (6) is a fair representation of what Wiggins wishes to claim.[14] The problem is that Wiggins
seems to allow that perfect human replicas would be interpretable, but it
is questionable whether such a replica would actually be human. This
raises a hard and important issue, which I shall ignore by interpreting
'human' in the more inclusive sense.

Premise (5) can certainly be questioned. In thinking of an entity as a
person I am, of course, thinking of it as possessing psychological states,
beliefs, desires and so on. It seems quite possible, though, that there are
persons with their psychological states whom I cannot interpret at all,
who are, that is, totally inscrutable to me, or whom I cannot interpret
much. Perhaps they are much cleverer than I am, and can block my
efforts to understand them. It is not self-evident that all persons must
fulfil those conditions, whatever they are, which render them interpretable by me.

However, this is a rather blunt response. In the first place, there are
many theorists of interpretation who would think that we should accept
some sort of thesis about the detectability-in-principle-by-us of propositional attitudes in others. In the second place, there is some plausibility
in the intuition that if two persons meet and cooperate in the goal of
mutual understanding they will succeed, which, if true, is enough to link

personhood to understanding in principle by us. I wish to focus, rather, on (6).

The basic problem is that premise (6) is not adequately supported. It is certainly not enough to point out that where the intelligence is manifestly non-human there are certain expectations which we do have in the human case, and which facilitate our making sense of each other, which it would be mad to have as *expectations* in that case. That is no doubt true, but nothing follows unless it can be shown that interpretation is impossible without such prior expectations, and that is certainly not shown. Further, even if we allow that expectations are necessary for interpretation, we have been given no reason for thinking that that degree of expectation which is necessary for interpretation can be legitimate only in relation to whole human beings. Wiggins seems to allow that the expectations (which are, presumably, expectations about the psychology of the object of interpretation) are grounded in the physical nature of the item. If these expectations can be grounded given a more limited physical basis than a whole human being, say given a human brain, the argument cannot show that anything more than that is necessary for personhood. Unfortunately, Wiggins does not say, and certainly does not support any claim about, what exactly is the minimum physical structure necessary to generate (non-insanely) the expectations. Suppose that our synthesised creatures were not quite carbon-copies, but lacked a few bones characteristic of humans. Can we say that they would have to be uninterpretable?

There is another idea in the passage, which perhaps can be expressed in the following argument.

(7)   Interpretation involves putting oneself in the other's place.
(8)   You can do this only if you are of the same basic kind as them.

Why, though, should we accept (8)? We can certainly try to put ourselves in another's position even if he or she is different to ourselves, and thereby attempt to make sense of them. Can it be ruled out *a priori* that it will work? Let us suppose, that as the result of some cosmic accident the aliens speak a language indistinguishable from English. Treating them as speaking English makes perfect sense to us of their communications with each other, and of their attempted communications with us. Surely they would then be interpretable by us. How can we rule out this extremely unlikely but surely possible occurrence *a priori*?[15]

I conclude that premise (6) has insufficient claim to be accepted, and that the Interpretation Argument is unconvincing.

9 Other Grounds

There are levels within what I have called 'P' in §7. Three which can be
distinguished are; (a) having experiences, including perceptual experiences, (b) possessing beliefs and desires (having propositional attitudes),
(c) being self-conscious, capable of thinking of itself as itself. These may
not be, indeed are not, the only ones worth distinguishing, but the points
can be developed with them.

It can be asked, first, how it might be argued that only 'biological' or
'living' entities can possess these? In reply I wish to make two remarks.
The first is that if it is allowed that it is possible for non-biological
creatures to reach level (a) it seems very difficult to suppose that it is
impossible because of the nature of the more advanced levels (b) and (c)
for non-biological creatures to possess them. It hardly seems that there is
anything more obviously biological about (b) and (c) than about (a). On
the contrary, the acquisition by an entity of levels (b) and (c) seems to
require the addition to, and integration with, whatever is necessary for
(a), of more complex cognitive and behavioural structures. There is,
surely, nothing obviously biological in the idea of these structures. So,
unless *experiences* can be shown to be restricted to biological structures,
we cannot restrict personhood to the biological. The second remark is
that no persuasive case exists for accepting such a restriction. One
argument might be that experiences have only been found in biological
creatures, and so they are obviously biological properties.[16] If this conclusion is read as saying that it is in the nature of such states to be found
only in biological entities then the argument is a non-sequitur, illegitim-
ately inferring a 'can only' from an 'has so far only'. Another argument
might be that unless an object resembles us at least to the extent of being
a living creature we cannot know, or have a justification for believing,
that it has experiences. Even if sound, this does not show what is needed.
I think that we should allow that we do not understand the nature of
experience sufficiently to accept that it is restricted to 'living' entities.

The claim just made that levels (b) and (c) are not more obviously
'biological' than (a) will not, perhaps, be accepted by everyone. I am
thinking, firstly, of John Searle's infamous Chinese Room Argument,
which purports to be a reason for thinking that machines cannot have
propositional attitudes or an understanding of language. It is, I take it,
reasonable to be sceptical of the cogency of that argument.[17] There are,
secondly, the arguments, whatever they are, which sustain the research
programme (associated with Ruth Millikan, David Papineau and others)
dedicated to analysing beliefs and thoughts in what are conceived of as

biological terms.[18] It cannot be said that this approach is misguided, but it is neither clearly successful nor mandatory.

I submit, then, that we do not understand psychological states sufficiently to be justified in restricting them to biological items. In contrast there is a positive ground for allowing the possibility of the presence of such states in entities which are less than animals. This ground is the strongly empirically supported idea that the mental processes and states with which we are familiar are localised in the brains of their possessors. If items such as brains are able to function in isolation from the rest of the animal we can have psychological states without animals.

Animals, then, really have no claim to be, of necessity, the unique possessors of mental states, nor, therefore, to be the only persons.

10 Summary and a Suggestion

Wiggins has proposed that persons must be animals. He intends this to be a proposal about what falls under the term 'person' in that sense which we would be inclined to explain, initially at least, by citing distinctive psychological capacities. In §5 some scepticism was expressed about the conception embedded in AAT as to how those psychological features should be specified. I then claimed, in §7, that it would be unsatisfactory to defend the central claim by thinking of 'person' as simply the term we use when these psychological features occur in animals, but not when they occur elsewhere. To defend it it is necessary to show that the psychological features require animals for their presence. I then argued, in §§7–9, that neither Wiggins nor anyone else, has given persuasive grounds for this claim, nor for the stronger claim that persons must be human, and that there are grounds for rejecting it, in that brains can probably sustain such features.

Why is Wiggins inclined to think that persons must be animals? My conjecture is that, in part, it is because he subscribes to (AA), agreeing with philosophical tradition in accepting (1), (2) and (4), but also wanting, for whatever reason, to accept (3). He also accepts, again in accordance with the standard approach, that 'person', as it figures in (1) and (2) is a psychological concept. To reconcile these claims seems to require one to suppose that 'person' at some stage in its philosophical analysis will reveal a restriction to animals.

I have suggested that this project is likely to be in vain, but I also want to suggest that it may not be necessary in order to defend (3). If we share with Wiggins a sense of the truth of (3), a sense, to which he has given eloquent expression, that we are real, natural objects (what else but animals?), but also find it hard to accept his account of 'person', what should we do? An alternative approach is to wonder whether it has not been a serious mistake in the philosophical tradition to accept (1) and (2) where 'person' has, what I have called, a psychological interpretation.[19] Affirming (3) would not then commit us to unearthing anything in particular in the concept *person*. 'Person' in its psychological use should be thought of as a term which can apply to entities of different types, which does not pick out what *we* fundamentally are, and does not pick out a sort sharing criteria of identity.

It then becomes necessary to re-express the question for which the so-called theory of personal identity is seeking an answer, since it cannot be: what are the criteria of *personal* identity? We can ask instead: under what conditions do *we* remain in existence? More, of course, needs to be said, but it seems that we have, or are close to having, a perfectly definite question.[20]

It also becomes possible, once we are thinking this way, to wonder whether there is not strong evidence of a distorting influence on philosophical thought about ourselves as a result of the prominence standardly accorded to the psychological use of 'person'. Philosophers have been lead to claim that certain psychological capacities are essential to us, when those capacities *seem* to be ones we can lose. They have also been lead to suppose that we survive if certain psychological features are preserved in ways which precisely *seem* to involve them being taken from *us*.

I favour exploration along these lines.

In §6 I acknowledged the existence of a use of 'person' which seemed equivalent to 'human being', and in this conclusion have so far said nothing about it. It might be asked whether, despite the apparent disagreements, this is not just what David Wiggins himself is proposing. It is, though, surely not what he is proposing, since the link between human beings and this use is *not* to be established by *arguments* which try to show that certain psychological states are restricted to humans.

NOTES

1 An early discussion is Wiggins (1967), Pt IV. The two discussions I shall consider are Wiggins (1980a), ch.6, and Wiggins (1987b). Some of the same themes, as well as others, are in Wiggins (1979b).
2 See, for example, Wiggins (1987b), pp. 63–66.
3 P. F. Strawson (1959), p. 133.
4 I shall more or less totally ignore five important aspects of Wiggins's treatment, each of which could be the subject of a paper. First, I shall not be concerned

with his attempt to defend Locke's treatment of persons against what he sees as inadequate objections. Second, I shall not attempt to assess the general assumptions about identity which shape Wiggins's approach. Third, I shall not consider the (modified) Fregean semantic theories which also shape his account. Fourthly, I have not attempted to plot the significant differences between Wiggins (1980a) and Wiggins (1987b). Finally, I have not attempted to consider what seems to me to be a very interesting, but not, perhaps, articulated or defended, conception of the geography of the personal identity debate which influences his discussion in Wiggins (1980a).

5 Wiggins (1980a) p. 15.

6 The obvious permissive intuitions are those which allow (successful) brain transplants to preserve persons. The obvious restrictive intuitions are those which require a degree of psychological continuity for the survival of the person beyond anything required for the survival of the animal. I have discussed the former in Snowdon (1991), and the latter in Snowdon (1995).

7 Noonan (1989) is an example. In the introductory first chapter proposition (3) fails to make an appearance.

8 It is fair, I think, to cite Unger (1990) as an example. He treats Wiggins as an exponent of 'a biologically oriented approach' (pp. 120–123), by which he seems to mean an approach which requires that the physical basis for a person's consciousness be living or organic matter. Wiggins's account is, probably, committed to such a claim, but it quite fails to exhaust his central idea, that the person is an animal. Unger argues (perhaps, one should say, intuits) that it is possible to gradually transform the brain into an inorganic structure, and then transplant it, preserving the person. If this simple style of argument were sound then far less *recherché* imaginabilia would refute Wiggins's approach. Unger should have wondered whether Wiggins's conception of persons is consistent with employing such a method of argument.

9 There are similarities between Wiggins's proposal and the conception of persons argued for in Wollheim (1989), ch.1. I hope to discuss Wollheim's approach elsewhere.

10 Wiggins (1980a), p. 173.

11 Wiggins summarises Aristotle's definition of 'house' as a shelter against destruction by wind, rain and heat. This would let in bus shelters, tents, and holes in the ground. Why limit the to-be-avoided causes of destruction in that way? What about cold? Why, anyway, is destruction the thing to be avoided, rather than gross inconvenience?

12 Wiggins (1987b), p. 72.

13 The conclusion that persons must be animals obviously follows if we grant that human beings are animals. I shall grant that.

14 A reason, distinct from the one discussed above, for doubting that (6) fits Wiggins's intentions is that (5) and (6) do not imply that the class of humans and that of persons are coextensive, whereas Wiggins is tempted to say that they are. (See Wiggins (1987b), p. 60). I shall ignore this problem.

15 Colin Radford drew this simple but interesting case to my attention.

16 See Searle (1992), p. 1.

17 See Searle (1984), ch. 2. Searle's vivid example merely refutes the Turing
    test, with its emphasis on linguistic response as a mark of intelligence, but
    gives no reason to think that a properly structured machine, that is one with
    senses and motor responses, cannot also possess linguistic understanding.

18 See Millikan (1984) and Papineau (1987). In Millikan's exposition the crux
    comes on pp. 93–94. Millikan explains that she favours a biological account
    of belief, firstly because we have evolved to acquire them, and secondly
    because if they are biological that explains how they can be defective, that is,
    how they can be wrong. The first point is no better than the argument that
    since our shape has resulted from evolution, shapes are biological. The
    second point is the crucial one, but it requires that no other explanation for
    the possibility of error is available. Why should we accept that? It further
    requires, which is also by no means obvious, that the defects which biological
    accounts ground are the right kind.

19 This is not an outrageous suggestion. Suppose we came across an evidently
    non-human creature which could speak to us. We might well say; 'It *is* a
    person, but WHAT is it?'.

20 We are here at the edge of a very big issue, for which Wiggins's conceptual
    realism might be thought to have implications. Must the account of personal
    identity be linked to a general concept of which it has to be taken as
    elucidatory? Even if that requirement is granted, it does not follow that
    'person' expresses the relevant concept.

4

Ambiguity and Semantic Theory

S. G. Williams

1. A persistent concern in David Wiggins's writing in the philosophy of language has been to elaborate, illustrate and defend in detail some version of the following highly influential proposal: that a correct theory of meaning for a natural language should comprise an axiomatized theory of certain specially chosen or favoured semantic properties of expressions of the language that combines with an appropriate descriptive anthropology to make maximal sense of the shared life and conduct of speakers of the language.[1]

What should constitute the core semantic theory and how this theory should combine with the descriptive anthropology to achieve the required result have been much disputed even by advocates of the proposal.[2] But abstracting from indexical features, most of them would allow, I think, first that for each sentence of the relevant language, the core theory should contain sufficient resources to prove (in accordance with some canonical proof procedure) a theorem indicating, directly or indirectly, the meaning or meanings of that sentence (or one of its indicative transforms); and secondly that the meanings thereby indicated should (*ceteris paribus*) coincide with the contents of speech acts that the sentence (by virtue of its mood) is standardly or characteristically or conventionally used to perform.

Now as it stands such an account says nothing about other semantic notions than those used to generate the meaning-indicating sentences of the core theory. It says nothing about structure or semantic componency, for instance, or about validity or analyticity. It offers no theory-transcendent definitions or elucidations of such notions; nor does it offer any guarantee that the theory will uncover all the structure-determining and

I should like to thank David Charles, Sabina Lovibond and David Wiggins for detailed and very helpful comments on earlier drafts of this paper.

validity- or analyticity-determining properties that speakers' linguistic practices support. To be sure, *some* such properties of expressions will be uncovered as by-products of the search for a core theory which appropriately matches up sentence meaning with speech act content. But it would be an accident at best if all such properties were revealed.

It is evident therefore that the proposal needs considerable supplementation if it is not to leave us in the dark about these additional, meaning-related notions. But while there is scarcely unanimity about how exactly this should be done, we at least have a rough idea how to articulate some of the notions so that core semantic theories may be adequately constrained in the appropriate respects.[3] One suggestion, for example, would be to try to characterize semantic componency – which I shall henceforth refer to simply as *componency* – in something like the following way: by first elucidating what might be termed an exhaustive but non-redundant set of components of an expression of a language, and then taking a component of an expression to be a member of such a set. Or in more detail, where e and e′ are expressions belonging to a language L, and E is a set of expressions belonging to L,

(a) E is an exhaustive but non-redundant set of components of an expression e iff knowledge of the meanings of the members of E in L is, of necessity, *a priori* sufficient for knowing the meanings of e in L, but knowledge of the meanings of the members of any proper subset of E in L is not *a priori* sufficient for knowing the meanings of e in L.[4]

(b) e′ is a component of an expression e iff there is an exhaustive but non-redundant set of components of e of which e′ is a member.[5]

Thus in English {'Mars', 'is red', 'and', 'is round'} is an exhaustive but non-redundant set of components of

(1) Mars is red and Mars is round.

For knowing the meanings of the expressions in the set must be *a priori* sufficient for knowing the meaning(s) of (1), though merely knowing the meanings of those in any proper subset is plainly not *a priori* sufficient. And 'Mars' (say) is therefore a component of (1).[6]

Furthermore, this characterization provides a condition of adequacy against which theories of meaning can be tested. In particular, let M be a semantic theory for a language L, and let the theory which consists of the particular clauses in M governing the members of a set of expressions, E, together with any general clauses in M governing their categories and modes of combination, be called *the subtheory of M for E*. Then M will be adequate only if the following holds: for any expression e and set of expressions E in L, E is an exhaustive but non-redundant set of components of e in L just in case the subtheory of M for E entails the clauses governing e in M, and the subtheory for M for a proper subset of E does not. Such a constraint will clearly rule as inadequate a 'listiform' theory for a finite language[7] – one which contains a distinct axiom for each sentence of the language – when speakers genuinely understand those sentences through grasp of their component expressions.

2. In this paper, I want to consider two further semantic notions not integral to the production of a theory of meaning for a language in the initial sense: the opposed notions of ambiguity and univocality. These two notions are intimately related to that of componency, but they have not received quite the same degree of recent philosophical attention. In part, this is easy to explain, for once the concept of meaning is available, an ambiguous expression can be defined as an expression with more than one meaning, and a univocal expression as an expression with just one. What is more such a definition seems to generate a natural condition of adequacy (additional to the componency condition): an expression of a language L must be assigned n semantic roles in an adequate semantic theory for L just in case it is n-ways ambiguous.[8] (In the limiting case, an L-expression should therefore be assigned a single semantic role just in case it is univocal.)

It seems to me, however, that not only do the concepts of ambiguity and univocality in general deserve greater scrutiny, so in particular does the condition of adequacy. For, first, although it is surely right that genuinely ambiguous expressions should have distinct semantic roles in an adequate semantic theory, the converse claim is much less clear. Why should expressions with distinct semantic roles automatically be treated as ambiguous? Or equivalently, why should univocal expressions automatically require a single semantic role? It is true that the condition of adequacy as a whole can be taken to embody a theoretical precisification of what are in fact looser and vaguer pre-theoretical notions of ambiguity and univocality. (As we shall see, there is certainly something to be said for taking it this way.) And so in this sense at least it is possible to see the converse claim as true. But it is highly doubtful that the condition constitutes a correct account of the *pre-theoretical* notions of ambiguity and univocality. Secondly, if this is right, our ordinary intuitions about univocality cannot be taken (as they often are in semantic theory) to warrant the claim that an expression should be given a unique semantic role. For such intuitions relate for the most part to much looser notions of univocality. (Indeed, even if it is insisted that the condition really does embody a correct account of the pre-theoretical notions, such intuitions become at best a rough and ready guide to univocality.)

3. Now at this stage, it might be wondered why we should be so interested in what at first glance appears to be the very modest question whether a condition of adequacy relating to ambiguity or univocality is correct, or has been correctly applied in this or that case. But the answer is clear. For the condition is used in many areas of semantic theory to warrant quite far-reaching (and sometimes quite implausible) conclusions about the regimentation of natural language sentences. I shall give three examples, all of which presuppose that the relevant core semantic theory is at least partly constituted by a truth theory.[9]

The first example concerns the word 'exists'. Pre-theoretically, many have felt this word to be univocal in such sentences as 'Unicorns exist' and 'Goethe exists'; and consequently, when presented with the fact that it seems to be a second-level predicate in the first, and a first-level predicate in the second, and so has different semantic roles, they have tried to reduce uses of the first sort to those of the second or vice versa. But this has led to some pretty implausible proposals: that 'Unicorns exist' should be construed as 'Some unicorns exist', for instance, where the quantifier ranges over both the mythical and the real and 'exists' is treated as a first-level predicate; or that 'Goethe exists' should be so construed that 'Goethe' is interpreted descriptively and 'exists' treated as a second-level predicate. If, however, we begin to question whether univocality really does imply a single semantic role, or whether everyday intuitions about univocality genuinely warrant the ascription of such a role, it then becomes less clear that either of these implausible reductive proposals is necessary.[10]

4. The second example is furnished by sentences of other moods than the indicative – imperatives, optatives, interrogatives and so on. Because such sentences are not on the face of it truth-evaluable, they pose an obvious difficulty for any purely truth-theoretic core semantic theory. But the difficulty seems easy to deal with, at least in the case of imperatives and optatives, once it is recognised that just as indicative sentences have truth conditions, so both imperatives and optatives have compliance conditions.[11] For the core semantic theory can then be widened so that it embraces this additional sentential value. Unfortunately this seems to have the consequence that certain recursive expressions, like 'and', have more than one semantic role. For they seem able to operate not only on indicatives but also (e.g.) on imperatives – cf. 'Harry, close the door and put the kettle on!' – and so will be given distinct clauses depending on the

types of sentence they operate on. For example, in the case of 'and', we might have:

(2)   for indicatives, ϕ, ψ, '[ϕ and ψ]' is true in L iff [ϕ is true in L and ψ is true in L]; and

(3)   for imperatives, ϕ, ψ, '[ϕ and ψ]' is complied with in L iff [ϕ is complied with in L and ψ is complied with in L].

'And' must therefore have more than one semantic role, and so by the condition of adequacy, it must be ambiguous, when it plainly isn't.[12]

Directly or indirectly, this problem has spawned a whole range of theories, all of which take essentially (2) (or some Tarskian analogue of it) as the only axiom to govern 'and'. Sentences involving other moods are then parsed in such a way that they consist of a mood signifier concatenated with an indicative, the mood signifier being interpreted according to the vagaries of the particular theory.[13] ('Harry, close the door and put the kettle on!', for example, will be parsed as one imperative with an indicative core: perhaps, 'Harry, make it the case that you close the door and you put the kettle on!'.) But although there is a good deal to be said for each of these theories, none (I think) is entirely satisfactory. (One stumbling block is provided by compound imperatives, such as 'Harry, close the door, and George, you put the kettle on', the constituent imperatives of which are addressed to different individuals.[14] It is true that by analogy with imperatives addressed to one individual, we might construe the sentence in this case as a single imperative addressed to the pair of them: perhaps, 'Harry and George, make it the case that you, Harry, close the door and you, George, put the kettle on!'. But I do not think this would be right. For unlike the original sentence, this implies intuitively that Harry could be held responsible for George's not putting the kettle on, and George for Harry's not closing the door.) However, if we begin, as before, to question whether univocality really does imply a single semantic role, or whether everyday intuitions about univocality genuinely warrant the ascription of such a role, it becomes unclear that sentences of non-indicative moods need to be parsed as a mood signifier concatenated with an indicative sentence. Perhaps clauses along the lines of (2) and (3) will do. (And if so, the problems concerning Harry and George clearly vanish.)

5.   The third and final example derives from Tarski.[15] It concerns the provision of a truth theory for a first-order quantificational language, and is the one I want to consider in most detail. So let us suppose that our aim is to provide a truth theory for a first-order quantificational fragment

of English – L, say – including sentences constructible from names and predicates such as 'Mars' and 'is red', connectives and quantifiers such as 'and' and '∀' ('every'), and unstructured sentences like 'It's raining'. If we allow ourselves the concepts of truth and reference, we can easily construct a truth theory for the non-quantificational fragment. Thus a homophonic theory for sentences constructed from names, predicates, truth-functors and unstructured sentences can be built up around such axioms as (2) above and

(4) Ref(L, 'Mars') = Mars.
(5) for each name α in L, 'α is red' is true in L iff Ref(L, α) is red.
(6) 'It's raining' is true in L iff it's raining.

And using a tiny fragment of metatheory, we can then prove standard, meaning-giving T-sentences.

When sentences involving quantifiers are included, however, it appears that truth and reference are not enough. To provide a truth theory for the whole of L, we must be able to derive biconditionals like '∀$\xi\xi$ is red' is true in L iff everything is red' from the assignments of semantic properties to the quantifier and the open sentence 'ξ is red'.[16] But since an open sentence is surely neither a referring expression nor something which can be true or false, we appear forced into assigning it a different semantic property. In the spirit of Tarski, we may take this to be the ordinary concept of *being true of an object*. (Strictly speaking, in order to accommodate n-place open sentences for arbitrarily large n, we need something tantamount to Tarski's generalization of this notion, namely that of *being satisfied by an (infinite) sequence of objects*. For ease of exposition, however, it is convenient to restrict ourselves to the concept *true of*; and we do so by confining ourselves to sentences all of whose subformulas containing free variables are one-place (monadic).) The role of 'ξ is red' may then be given by means of the following clause:

(7) 'ξ is red' is true of an object iff that object is red;

and that of the quantifier by means of something like the following:

(8) for each monadic open sentence ϕ and free variable v in ϕ, '∀vϕ' is true in L iff ϕ is true of everything.

But this generates a problem. For consider the sentence '∀ξ[ξ is red and ξ is round]' ('Everything is red and round'). If we apply the quantifier axiom (8) to it, we will end up saying that it is true iff the complex open sentence '[ξ is red and ξ is round]' is true of everything. And we have no means of evaluating this. For the only relevant axiom for 'and' that we have so far, namely (2), tells us how 'and' functions when the expressions to which it applies are (closed) sentences; it tells us nothing about how it should function when it applies to open sentences, as it does in '[ξ is red and ξ is round]'.

Now it might seem obvious what to do at this stage: we should provide additional clauses to govern 'and' when it is flanked either by open sentences or by closed and open sentences. With our assumption about monadicity, this would yield the following four clauses ((2a) is (2) above):

(2a)   for all closed sentences, ϕ, ψ in L, '[ϕ and ψ]' is true in L iff (ϕ is true in L and ψ is true in L).

(2b)   for all closed sentences ϕ, open sentences ψ in L, '[ϕ and ψ]' is true of an object z in L iff (ϕ is true in L and ψ is true of z in L).

(2c)   for all open sentences ϕ, closed sentences ψ in L, '[ϕ and ψ]' is true of an object z in L iff (ϕ is true of z in L and ψ is true in L).

(2d)   for all open sentences ϕ, ψ in L, '[ϕ and ψ]' is true of an object z in L iff (ϕ is true of z in L and ψ is true of z in L).

But in being assigned three clauses when it forms open sentences, all involving *true of* in different ways, and a further clause when it forms closed sentences, this one framed in terms of truth conditions alone, 'and' is thereby being given a multiplicity of semantic roles. And so by the condition of adequacy it must be ambiguous. But this is surely incorrect. 'And' evidently means the same thing in 'It's raining and it's cold' as it does in 'Everything is red and round'.

The most famous solution to this problem, the one associated with Tarski, is to unify the different roles of 'and' by offering *truth of* conditions for closed as well as for open sentences. For instance, the sentence 'It's raining' will be true of an object iff it's raining. (And 'It's raining' therefore becomes, so to speak, a zero-place open sentence.) This then allows us to say: for all open and closed sentences, ϕ and ψ, the formula '[ϕ and ψ]' will be true of an object iff both ϕ and ψ are true of it. So instead of being assigned four semantic roles, it is therefore assigned one and ceases to be ambiguous. At this point it may be wondered in what sense we are now constructing a truth theory. For the notion of truth itself seems to have been jettisoned. But we may reply by using Tarski's famous characterization of truth in terms of being true of: a sentence ϕ is true iff it is true of all objects. Plainly this will get the right result for 'it's raining'. This will be true iff it is true of all objects; and it is true of all objects iff it is raining. So 'it's raining' is true iff it is raining. And something similar can be shown to hold for all sentences of the language.

Difficulties with this account, however, have not escaped commentators.[17] One objection is that, without an *ad hoc* syntactic restriction to closed sentences in the characterization of truth, it allows all open sentences to have truth conditions. ('ξ is identical to ξ' would be true, for example, and 'ξ is red' would be false.) But in order that open sentences should have truth conditions and so be truth-evaluable, they must express (Fregean) thoughts, and intuitively there is no thought that 'ξ is red' expresses: it doesn't say anything. Secondly, the account treats closed sentences as true or false of objects, when intuitively if closed sentences are true or false of anything, it is surely the world or perhaps some corresponding state of affairs that they are true or false of, not particular objects.[18]

6. Now the most popular line of response to difficulties with the Tarskian approach is to reject the claim that in order to characterize the truth conditions of sentences containing quantifiers, it is necessary to invoke a semantic category of open sentences whose semantic role is given by the concept of *truth of* or *satisfaction*. According to this response, we can get by perfectly well with the concepts of truth and reference alone, provided we employ quantification over referring names.

The basic idea is that a universal quantification will be true if whatever (non-vacuous) proper name is put in place of the variable which the universal quantifier binds, the resulting sentence is true. But to make this plausible we have to be careful which names we use. We could not for example restrict the names to the language in question to give us:

(9) '$\forall v \phi$' is true in L iff for all non-vacuous names, γ, in L, $\phi(\gamma)$ is true in L.[19]

For if everything nameable in L were red such a restriction would result in the L-sentence '$\forall \xi \xi$ is red' coming out true when it should not. The problem is obviously that in natural languages, not every object has a name. (They are rich, but not that rich.) So it has been suggested that instead of restricting the names to the language in question, we use arbitrary possible extensions of it. More formally,

(10) '$\forall v \phi$' is true in L iff for all possible extensions of L, L′, and all (non-vacuous) names, γ, in L′, $\phi(\gamma)$ is true in L′.

Provided every actual object is nameable in some possible language, the truth condition for '$\forall \xi \xi$ is red' will be correct.

This is the so-called Fregean view of quantification, endorsed and argued for in roughly the above way by Gareth Evans.[20] And it is a view which (officially at least) requires neither open sentences to have *truth* conditions nor closed sentences to have *truth of* conditions. However, it is (I think) vulnerable to different objections. For even leaving aside the apparent ontological profligacy involved in quantification over possible language extensions,[21] there remains the question how we can be sure that every object is nameable even in principle. Insofar as we take seriously the notion of referring to something – as a practice that some possible community could in principle take part in – I can see no reason at all to suppose that this is true.[22] (It is extremely doubtful, for example, that each transfinite number is nameable in this sense.)

At this point, it may be objected that we do not, strictly speaking, need the concept of reference in the quantifier clause. We could get by instead with functional assignments of objects to some syntactically distinguished set of singular terms. In particular, let C be such a set and let L′ be the language which results from adding C to L. Then we could display the meaning of the quantifier by means of the following clause:

(11) '$\forall v \phi$' is true in L iff for some term γ in C and all functions f such that $f(\gamma)$ has a value, $\phi(\gamma)$ is true in L′.

And since every object can be assigned to a given term by some function, it does not matter that some objects may be unnameable.

For this response to succeed, however, it is necessary that $\phi(\gamma)$ be an expression which can intelligibly be said to be true or false. But if γ is an expression whose role is exhausted by its merely being assigned an object by a function, this is surely not so. For suppose ϕ is the open sentence 'ξ is red' and the object assigned to γ by some function f is red. Then for the account to be right, 'γ is red' must be true, which in turn means that it must express a thought. But for 'γ is red' to express a thought on any given occasion, γ must present the object assigned to it by f in some way (though not necessarily always the same way); and the mere assignment of an object to it by a set theoretic function does not do this. To be sure, when $f(\gamma)$ has a certain value, the claim ' "γ is red" is true' could be thought of in this context as a misleading way of saying that 'ξ is red' is true of that value. But then 'and' must again be a former of open sentences in 'Everything is red and round'.

7. There are, then, at least *prima facie* grounds for thinking that the Fregean and the Tarskian accounts of quantification are unsatisfactory.

What has gone wrong? Again it seems to me that the root of the difficulties lies in the assumption they both make about ambiguity and semantic role. Both accounts explicitly reject the idea that 'and' should be characterized in accordance with (2a–d), i.e. in terms of truth *and* being true of something. For 'and' (they say) will then be classified incorrectly as ambiguous when it plainly isn't: univocality entails unitary semantic role and 'and' is obviously univocal as it occurs in (say) 'It's raining and it's cold' and 'Everything is red and round'. Again, however, once we begin to question the assumption about semantic role, or at least to question whether our ordinary intuitions about univocality are enough to sustain the conclusions about semantic role, it becomes unclear why axioms (2a–d) are not an adequate account of 'and'. Perhaps the *ad hoc* manœuvrings of the Fregean and Tarskian attempts to achieve semantic unity are unnecessary after all.

8.   These examples show clearly that the correctness or otherwise of the ambiguity condition of adequacy, and of the kinds of intuitions invoked in connection with it, is a question of more than merely local or tangential interest. The use of that condition in arguing directly for substantial theses in the philosophy of language such as the ones we have just seen is widespread and (I suspect) almost universally accepted; but the difficulties which the examples illustrate certainly provide grounds for thinking that it is either wrong or used far too indiscriminately.

So what can be said in favour of the condition, and in particular the claim that expressions with a multiplicity of semantic roles are invariably ambiguous, or equivalently, that univocal expressions always have a unique role? When considering this question, it is tempting at first to appeal to methodological considerations. For suppose that the connections between different uses of a word ('and' or 'exists', say) are sufficiently tight for identity of meaning. Then any theory which ascribes to the word a unitary semantic role will (other things being equal) be simpler than one which does not, since it will employ fewer genuinely independent principles (axioms). But general methodological considerations dictate that where other things are indeed equal we should prefer simpler theories. So in those circumstances, any theory which gives the word a unitary semantic role should be preferred to one which does not.

But without a general argument to show that there are never any countervailing circumstances, these considerations cannot establish the general claim; and it is precisely a consequence of the above examples that sometimes there may be such countervailing circumstances. As we have noted, the most commonly attempted reductions of first-level uses

of 'exists' to second-level, and vice versa, and the accounts of quantification and of other moods than the indicative that attempt to preserve a
unitary semantic role for 'and', all have their difficulties.

A better argument (I think) is grounded in the possibility of learnability
failure. To illustrate this, suppose that 'and' has different semantic roles
in 'It's raining and it's cold' and 'Everything is red and round'. (I here
use the third example; but the argument applies equally well to the
others.) And suppose further that certain speakers fully understand the
first of these sentences, and that 'and' occurs with the same *meaning* in
both. Then by the characterization of componency (§1), the speakers
ought to be able to understand the second sentence if they also understand 'Everything', 'is red' and 'is round'. But this is plainly not necessary. With sufficient imaginative impoverishment, they may fail to
appreciate the role of 'and' in the second sentence and be unable therefore to understand it. So 'and' cannot have the same meaning in the two
sentences.

But even this argument does not compel. For it may be that a complete
understanding of the word 'and' requires appreciation of each of its
different roles in some way. (The roles may be related to its meaning as
species is to genus, for instance.) So if our speakers genuinely do understand the first sentence – and in particular 'and' – then they should be
able to go on to understand the second. And if they cannot, then that just
shows that they did not understand the first sentence fully in the first
place.

9.   These very general arguments, then, fail to show that multiplicity of
role and ambiguity, or univocality and uniqueness of role, must coincide.
And that is surely as it should be. For although the notion of semantic
role is a relatively precise notion, the ordinary notions of ambiguity and
univocality are not. There are many intermediate positions between
chance homonymy and univocality. (A word, for instance, might have
different meanings inherited from a common origin (e.g. geometrical
terms which also represent figures of speech, like 'elliptical', 'hyperbolic',
etc.); or it might have a common component revealed under analysis
(e.g. focal terms like 'healthy'); and so on.) And it can become extremely
vague where close ambiguity ends and univocality begins. Admittedly, it
might be maintained that in spite of such vagueness there will nevertheless be a borderline. But even if that is so (which I doubt), we have yet to
be offered a reason why multiplicity of role should provide that cut-off
point. (And here I leave aside any vagueness in the notion of semantic
role itself.) It seems to me then that if we are to identify ambiguity and
multiplicity of role, or univocality and uniqueness of role, in the way the

condition of adequacy implies, we must do so by stipulation. It has to be the product of a stipulative precisification of the ordinary loose and vague concepts of ambiguity and univocality, made perhaps in the interests of theoretical simplicity.

10. What then of the intuitions invoked in connection with the ambiguity condition? Plainly the above considerations have the consequence that we should be very chary in general of using our negative intuitions concerning ambiguity or our positive intuitions concerning univocality to argue for corresponding conclusions about semantic role.[23] For it is hardly likely that our ordinary intuitions relating to the loose concepts are invariably going to be reflected in a stipulated precisification of them.[24] But it is worth remarking that such intuitions are not an infallible guide even to the loose notions.

This is perhaps best seen by examining a kind of argument which underpins a considerable amount of thinking about univocality and adverts to learnability considerations again. To illustrate it, suppose someone fully understands the English sentences 'It's raining and it's cold', 'Everything is red' and 'Everything is round'. Then he or she will have sufficient knowledge to go on to understand the sentence 'Everything is red and round'. But if this is right (so the argument goes), 'and' must mean the same thing in 'Everything is red and round' as it does in 'It's raining and it's cold'. (Plainly similar arguments, if correct, could be used to establish that 'and' also means the same in 'Harry, close the door and put the kettle on!', and that 'exists' means the same in 'Unicorns exist' and 'Goethe exists'.)

Now for reasons already mentioned, it is evident that this cannot establish that 'and' has a single semantic role in the two sentences. But the point here is that on its own it does not even establish that it is univocal in the ordinary, loose and vague sense. For the argument works only if the reason why someone can go on to understand 'Everything is red and round' on the basis of understanding 'It's raining and it's cold', 'Everything is red' and 'Everything is round' is that he or she can understand the components of those sentences and recombine the subset consisting of 'everything', is red', 'is round', and 'and' in accordance with the characterization of componency (§1). But without further argument it is not clear whether that recombination process really is in accordance with the characterization of componency.

To use an example of Martin Davies's,[25] we can in some sense go on to understand a word like 'hydrophobia' on the basis of our understanding of words like 'hydroelectricity', 'hydrocarbon' and 'narcophobia'. And doubtless this is partly because we can decompose (say) 'hydroelectricity' and 'narcophobia' into their components, including 'hydro' and 'phobia'. But to understand 'hydrophobia' we have to do more than recombine them in accordance with the characterization of componency. For that requires that our understanding of 'hydro' and 'phobia' be *a priori* sufficient for understanding 'hydrophobia', and that seems very unlikely. Rather, in understanding 'hydro' as it occurs in 'hydroelectricity', we appreciate that it means something like *produced from water*, but that 'hydro' in 'hydrophobia' is unlikely to mean this. By comparing it with 'narcophobia', which means *fear of sleeping*, we then reason analogically, rather than by *a priori* means alone, that 'hydrophobia' must mean something like *fear of water*. Similarly, therefore, we need further considerations to show that such analogical reasoning is inappropriate in the case of 'and'.[26]

11. I conclude first then that the best that can be said for the ambiguity condition of adequacy is that it encapsulates a natural precisification of the ordinary concepts of ambiguity and univocality; and secondly that for a given expression, our negative intuitions about ambiguity, or our positive intuitions about univocality, are *at best* first stages in an argument for the univocality (not merely in the precise sense, but even in the loose sense) of the expression. This means that without further argument we cannot be certain that 'and' or 'exists' (say) should each be treated in a unitary way.

That said, however, what the unitary approaches do is provide one explanation of our positive intuitions concerning the univocality of those expressions. And if we are to resist this explanation fully, we must not only construct alternative semantic theories for the expressions – we already have some idea how to do this – we must also provide some alternative account of what brings their different uses together, what makes us think of them as univocal. Only by doing this will we be able to undermine the suspicion that at least variants of the unitary accounts, which aren't vulnerable to the difficulties we have noted, must be constructible. Accordingly I want to examine briefly how we might group together the uses of the expressions in some principled way. This of course brings us to the rich territory lying between chance homonymy and identical semantic role. But although there are consequently many possibilities open to us, what I want to do is explore the single idea that what groups them is a *closely analogous or common conceptual role*.[27] I shall concentrate initially on our third example, where 'and' is apparently functioning as a former of both open and closed sentences, and then indicate briefly how similar considerations may apply to the other two.[28]

12.   Consider the sentence

(12)   Jack and Jill pushed the boulder up the hill.

Is 'and' in this sentence a genuine conjunction? Is it right to group it with
sentential conjunction? It is often argued that it is not by observing that
it cannot be translated, at least straightforwardly, as a sentential conjunction. In particular, it cannot be translated as:

(13)   Jack pushed the boulder up the hill and Jill pushed the boulder
       up the hill.

For although (13) entails both 'Jack pushed the boulder up the hill' and
'Jill pushed the boulder up the hill', (12) entails neither. Here the
thought is that if 'and' is to be a genuine conjunction in (12), it must be
seen to be a conjunction in its correct representation in a semantic
theory. But the most plausible semantic representation of it according to
which it would be a conjunction is (13); and that is incorrect since it
wrongly represents (12) as satisfying the first of the inferential rules
governing the use of 'and' in (13) which are standardly thought to
contribute to a characterization of the conceptual role of 'and':

$$\text{(and-E)} \quad \frac{[\phi \text{ and } \psi]}{\phi} \qquad \frac{[\phi \text{ and } \psi]}{\psi} \qquad \text{(and-I)} \qquad \frac{\phi, \psi}{[\phi \text{ and } \psi]}$$

So 'and' in (12) should not be classifed as a genuine conjunction, since
it does not there have the conceptual role of a conjunction, or at least a
role sufficiently similar to that of a conjunction.

13.   Now I do not wish to examine the merits and demerits of this
particular argument. Its importance for me lies in its deployment of the
notion of conceptual role in grouping uses of 'and'. For it might be
thought that just as we can provide grounds for ruling out 'and' in (12)
as a conjunction by making it plausible that it does not have the right
kind of conceptual role, so equally we can establish that the uses of 'and'
in which it functions as a former of both closed and open sentences are
genuine conjunctions by showing that they have (through their semantic
representations) the same, or sufficiently similar conceptual roles. But
there is an immediate problem in applying this idea to our third example,
where 'and' occurs in such sentences as 'It's raining and it's cold' and
'Everything is red and round'. For the most plausible (even if mistaken)
way of seeing 'and' as a genuine conjunction in (12) is by construing it as
a sentential conjunction in its semantic representation. But in the third

example, we are trying to see how 'and' can be construed *both* as a former of closed sentences *and* as a former of open sentences: we are not trying to reduce one to the other. It follows that we must provide a conceptual role not merely for 'and' as a former of closed sentences, but also for 'and' as a former of open sentences. But how are we to do so?

One suggestion – and in my view the right one – would be to extend the rules so that open as well as closed sentences can straddle 'and'. The conceptual role of 'and' as a former of closed sentences would then be given (in part) by restricting the rules to such sentences, and that of 'and' as a former of open sentences would be given (in part) by restricting the rules to those instances in which one of the premises at least or the conclusion is an open sentence. But again there is a problem. For despite the fact that many logic text books are crammed with such rules, inferences of this sort, at least on the face of it, do not correspond to any ordinary inferences we use. It seems not to make sense, for example, to argue in any way corresponding to the following formal derivation of the sequent '$\forall \xi [\xi$ is red and ξ is round] $\vdash \forall \xi \xi$ is red'.

I   (1) $\forall \xi [\xi$ is red and ξ is round]   Assumption
    (2) $[\xi$ is red and ξ is round] $\forall$E
    (3) ξ is red   and-E
    (4) $\forall \xi \xi$ is red $\forall$I[29]

For (2) and (3) are open sentences, but all steps in any inference must involve closed sentences.

Indeed if this is right, it is hard to see how 'and' can function in any other way than as a former of closed sentences. But this in turn leads to a further problem. For suppose we try to prove the above sequent by restricting the terms in the '$\forall$' rules to names – thereby ensuring that at each line there is a closed sentence:

II   (1) $\forall \xi [\xi$ is red and ξ is round]   Assumption
    (2) [a is red and a is round] $\forall$E
    (3) a is red   'and'-E
    (4) $\forall \xi \xi$ is red $\forall$I

Then for the application of $\forall$I to be assuredly valid, 'a' must be a name which could in principle refer to any object at all. But in discussing the demerits of Fregean quantification we have already seen reason to doubt that all objects are nameable even in principle. And if they are not, then the most we could expect to prove at line (4) would be the claim that all *nameable* objects are red, not that all objects are. To be sure, we could

validate the proof by means of functional assignments of objects to 'a' –
it is surely true that there is no object that cannot be assigned to 'a' by
some appropriate function (cf. §6). But then '[a is red and a is round]'
and 'a is red' must themselves be thought of as open sentences. And so
(II) is really in no better position than (I).

Of course either (I) or (II) *must* be acceptable; and since they seem to
stand or fall together, they both must be. But how can this be when all
steps in any inference have to involve closed sentences? Here I think we
must take care not to mix up what is written at a given line in a formal
proof with how what is written there should be interpreted informally. It
is the informal expression of how the line should be interpreted which
should be a closed sentence, not the formula in the line itself. For
example, line (2) of (II), if interpreted informally, may be taken to
express the thought that with respect to any *particular* object, a, a is red
and a is round. According to this interpretation, therefore, although 'a' is
a variable and '[a is red and a is round]' is an open sentence, the thought
itself is expressed by a closed sentence. (Notice that if this is right,
'and'-E at the next stage in the informal reasoning takes place even
though 'and' is not the major connective. For 'a' will continue to be
bound by the quantifier 'any particular' in the informal expression of line
(3).[30])

14.   The proposal then is to group together 'and' as a former of open
sentences and 'and' as a former of closed sentences, to treat them both
as genuine conjunctions, by construing them as having common or at
least closely analogous conceptual roles. How might we justify this
proposal? An obvious first suggestion would be to treat the above introduction and elimination rules as exhaustive of their conceptual roles.
More precisely, we might say that a particular use of 'and' is a genuine
conjunction in the context '[A and B]' iff it satisfies the above introduction and elimination rules relative to any semantic values appropriate to
A, B, and '[A and B]'. Since truth is evidently a value appropriate
to closed sentences and being true of a particular object is appropriate to
open sentences, this makes the uses of 'and' in 'It's raining and it's cold'
and '[ξ is red and ξ is round]' conjunctions. But there are problems.

First, the suggestion allows in too many semantic values. For example,
falsity is appropriate to closed sentences, but relative to the value false,
'and' certainly does not satisfy the 'and'-introduction and 'and'-elimina-
tion rules. (From the falsity of the sentence '[A and B]', it does not follow
that A is false and B is false, only that one of them is.) And it is no use
amending the suggestion to say that 'and' is a conjunction in the context
'[A and B]' if it satisfies the relevant introduction and elimination rules

relative to *some* semantic values appropriate to A, B, and '[A and B]'. For if certain uses of the word 'and' had been synonymous with sentential disjunction, we would have been forced to conclude that in those uses it was a genuine conjunction. (Again take falsity as the relevant value: if 'and' is interpreted as disjunction, the rules preserve falsity.) Secondly, and more familiarly, the suggestion would allow a truth-functor which meant '. . . and – – and $7 + 5 = 12$' (say) to count as a genuine conjunction. (Even relative to truth, this will evidently satisfy the two rules.)[31]

15. To deal with the first problem, we evidently need to restrict the semantic values that are appropriate. One suggestion would be to restrict them to what the characteristic speech acts of the expressions in question aim at. Thus the characteristic speech act of the indicative is assertion, and assertions undoubtedly aim at truth. (The primary purpose of asserting something is to try to say something true.) But although this would naturally extend to sentences of other moods, it does not apply in any obvious way to open sentences. For open sentences do not possess a characteristic speech act: what they do is systematically contribute to the meanings of expressions – closed sentences – which do.

Better, I think, would be to introduce the idea of a *fundamental* semantic value appropriate to a category of expression. This is the value (appropriate to the category) in terms of which one understands or explains the others. Thus (at least in a classical framework) truth would be fundamental in the category of indicative sentences, whereas falsity would not; and being true of something would be fundamental in the category of open sentences, whereas being false of something would not. In both cases, our understanding of the latter notion would be based on an understanding of the corresponding former notion: falsehood would be untruth and being false of something would be not being true of it. This would then allow us to modify the suggestion, to say that 'and' is a conjunction in the context '[A and B]' if it satisfies the relevant introduction and elimination rules relative to the fundamental semantic values appropriate to A, B, and '[A and B]'. And the difficulties associated with the original suggestion disappear, since falsity is not, in the relevant sense, a fundamental semantic value appropriate to the indicative.[32]

This still leaves the problem of deviant connectives such as '. . . and – – and $7 + 5 = 12$'. And it is a notoriously difficult problem to tackle directly.[33] It seems to me, however, that in order to warrant the general proposal, we do not need to do so: we can find good reason for thinking that uses of 'and' in which it occurs as a former of open or closed sentences should be grouped together as conjunctions by virtue of their possessing common or analogous conceptual roles without stating those roles explicitly. For if what we have said so far is right, the occurrences of 'and' in 'Everything is red and round' and 'It's raining and it's cold' are governed by the same introduction and elimination rules (relative to the appropriate fundamental semantic values). And since the rules governing these occurrences of 'and' will either be partly constitutive of their respective conceptual roles, or at least direct consequences of them, the fact that they are governed by the same rules provides strong evidence, in the absence of grounds for treating one or the other as deviant, that they have the same or closely analogous conceptual roles. We thus have good reason for thinking that 'and' is a genuine conjunction in both constructions, and that there is therefore no need to postulate a unified semantic role to account for our positive intuitions about the univocality of its occurrences in 'It's raining and it's cold' and 'Everything is red and round'. Notice that similar considerations go over to other connectives ('not', 'or', 'if . . . then', etc.), even though the detailed articulation of their conceptual roles, and in particular the inference rules which partly constitute or emerge from those roles, may be very different indeed.[34]

16. What of the other two cases we began with? As far as 'exists' is concerned, matters may well be very similar. Its first-level and second-level uses (if that's what they are) can plausibly be represented as being governed by very similar rules of inference. At any rate, within the free logic necessitated by having a useful first-level existence predicate at all, the obvious introduction and elimination rules for the two uses have a common structure. Thus, where t is a singular term (simple or complex)[35] and ϕ is an open sentence, we would expect the introduction rules for the first-level and second-level predicates to be of the following form:

$$(\text{exists}_1\text{-I}) \quad \frac{\phi(t)}{t \text{ exists}} \quad (\text{exists}_2\text{-I}) \quad \frac{\phi(t)}{\phi s \text{ exist}}$$

– subject to certain provisos. (The second rule is just an introduction rule for the existential quantifier.) And since the validity of both rules depends crucially on the existence of the referent of the when the premiss is true, both will be subject to the same or symmetric provisos relating to t and $\phi(t)$.[36]

The elimination rules have a similar parity of structure. According to the standard rule for the second-level expression, one (in effect) first deduces a proposition from the claim that an arbitrary object has a given property, and then (subject to certain provisos) concludes that the same proposition follows from the assumption that satisfiers of the property exist. The first-level rule simply involves switching property and object. One first deduces a proposition from the claim that a given object has an arbitrary property, and then (subject to analogous provisos) concludes that the same proposition follows from the assumption that the object exists.

The rules, therefore, must have something like the following form. (Here ψ is atomic and t may be complex; while a is simple and φ may be complex. The lines through the assumptions ψ(t) and φ(a) indicate that these assumptions are discharged when θ is inferred from 't exists' and 'φs exist' respectively.)

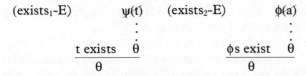

The proviso in (exists₂-E) will be the entirely standard condition that the term a does not occur in φ, θ or in any of the assumptions used in the derivation of θ from φ(a), except φ(a) itself. And the proviso in (exists₁-E) switches term and open sentence; ψ must not occur in t, θ or in any of the assumptions used in the derivation of θ from ψ(t).[37] Notice that the assumptions that ψ is atomic and a is simple, and that both t and φ may be simple or complex ensure that symmetry is preserved.

Since there are again no grounds for thinking that 'exists' in either case has anything like the complexity of content of a deviant operator analogous to the one mentioned in the case of 'and' (§14), we may (I suggest) take the structural symmetry as strong evidence of a common or closely analogous conceptual role.[38] And this means in turn that we may reasonably treat the occurrences of 'exists' in 'Goethe exists' and 'Unicorns exist' as being sufficiently close in meaning (if not synonymous) for intuitions about their apparent univocality not to warrant the postulation of a unified semantic role.

17. By far and away the most difficult case is that of expressions (if there are any) out of which sentences of other moods can be constructed recursively. Plainly, if we were to pursue the parallel with indicative-formers, we could then see such a role as being partially elucidated in terms of their role in non-indicative inference. But there is unfortunately no general agreement that anything could sensibly answer to the description of non-indicative inference.[39]

Now for all I know, it could turn out that the notion of non-indicative inference makes perfectly good sense. But even if it does not, this may not matter. For even those who deny the existence of such inference allow that non-indicative sentences can sometimes be *inconsistent* with one another. 'Harry, close the door and put the kettle on!', for example, is plainly inconsistent with 'Harry, don't close the door': utterance of the corresponding speech acts would obviously result in incoherence, since at least one of the two sentences must fail to be complied with. (Indeed, it is inconsistencies like these which make it highly plausible that 'and' is a conjunction in 'Close the door and put the kettle on!'.) And since the inferential power of the indicative-forming 'and' can equally well be obtained using the *incompatibility* rules made familiar by tableau systems, we may be able to capture what binds together (say) the conceptual role of 'and' as it occurs in indicatives and 'and' as it occurs in imperatives by appealing directly to such rules in the latter case.[40]

To make this more precise, let us call those inference rules which partly constitute an expression's conceptual role the *inferential component* of that role. And let us say that the conceptual role C_1 of an expression e is *inferentially tantamount* to the conceptual role C_2 of e iff the inferential component of C_2 is reformulable in a way that is (*mutatis mutandis*) a component of the conceptual role of C_2 (or vice versa). (Here the *mutanda* are the kinds of expression that e concatenates with and the relevant fundamental semantic values.) Then without grounds for supposing that the imperative-forming 'and' is a deviant connective (of the sort mentioned in §14), we may reasonably conclude that the conceptual role of 'and' as it occurs in imperatives is indeed inferentially tantamount to its role as it occurs in indicatives. For the standard tableau rules for 'and'[41] are deductively equivalent to its introduction and elimination rules, and the tableau rules stated so as to govern imperatives rather than indicatives and relativized to compliance do plausibly constitute a component of the conceptual role of 'and' as an imperative-former. And this (it seems to me) is sufficient to treat 'and' as a genuine conjunction in both. It is fair, I think, not to construe the inferentially tantamount conceptual roles as being instances of a common role. But they are sufficiently analogous (I suggest) again not to require a unified semantic role to account for our positive intuitions about the univocality of the occurrences of 'and' in 'Harry, close the door and put the kettle on!' and 'It's raining and it's cold'.[42]

NOTES

1 See e.g. Wiggins (1965), (1971a), (1976b), (1980b) and especially (1987a), Essay IV. Cf. also Davidson (1967), (1973), and McDowell (1977).
2 Wiggins himself has long favoured a core theory central to which is the notion of a truth condition. His original espousal of the suggestion that

meaning should be understood in terms of truth conditions stemmed from Frege (see Wiggins (1965) and (1971a)). But his subsequent development and illustration of the suggestion was considerably influenced by Donald Davidson's elucidation of it in Davidson, opp. citt. For an elaboration of Wiggins's dissatisfaction with Davidson's overall semantic programme, however, see references in note 3. And for a brief history of the suggestion that meaning should be understood in terms of truth conditions, see Wiggins (1996).

3 Cf. Evans (1981), Davies (1981a), (1981b), (1987), and Wiggins (1980b), (1985/6) on structure; and Evans (1976) and Wiggins (1980b) on validity.

4 Note that in (a) the language parameter must take wide scope with respect to the *a priori* operator. For otherwise in knowing the sense of an expression, one would end up knowing the meanings of all expressions of the language – at least given the most direct sense of knowing which language a language is.

5 Using these notions we can also characterize what it is to be a *semantic primitive*: e is a semantic primitive in L iff e has one and only one component in L. (This would be e itself.)

6 Notice that the second conjunct of (a), the conjunct that expresses the non-redundancy of the components of e, really is necessary: otherwise the union of the above set and {'Julius Caesar'} would be an exhaustive but non-redundant set of components of (1), and 'Julius Caesar' itself would be a component of it. Notice also that the qualifier 'of necessity' is needed in the first conjunct. For understanding a complex expression can – and mostly will – involve structured knowledge of the meanings of its components, and so without the qualifier the set {'Mars is round and Mars is red'}, say, would be an exhaustive but non-redundant set of components of (1). (With the qualifier, of course, it won't be, since it would always be *possible* for someone to have unstructured, or mere 'phrase-book', understanding of the sentence.)

7 See Evans, (1976) §2.

8 The notion of semantic role is itself somewhat vague. But we may take it that an expression has distinct semantic roles (in a given theory) just in case it is governed by non-trivially distinct semantic axioms or theorems of the theory (axioms if it is a semantic primitive, theorems otherwise).

9 I.e. an axiomatized theory of truth the axioms of which entail putative meaning-indicating sentences of the form 'S is true (in L) iff p' (or *T-sentences*). The concept of truth employed in any such theory I take to be the ordinary concept of truth, or at least thoroughly grounded in it; likewise, such concepts as reference and satisfaction. (I reject therefore the idea that reference and satisfaction should be thought of as internal to a theory. Perhaps the most attractive reason for taking them this way is to avoid having to give them a reductive analysis, perhaps in terms of causality (cf. McDowell, op. cit. pp. 183–5). But to think of them as notions not internal to a theory, but essentially our ordinary notions, is not necessarily to think that they admit of a reductive analysis. On the contrary, the notions may be primitive (though doubtless partly elucidatable in terms of other semantic notions).)

10 I do not say that all accounts which try to assimilate these apparently different uses of 'exists' are implausible. Cf. Wiggins's uniform treatment of 'exists' as a second-level predicate in Wiggins (1994a).

11 I shall here ignore interrogatives, since it is still very much an open question what semantic values (analogous to truth and compliance) are appropriate to them.

12 See Dummett, (1981a), ch.10 and (1991a), ch. 5, and McGinn, (1977) for versions of this argument.

13 See Lewis, (1983), McGinn, op. cit., and Dummett, opp. citt.

14 Though, interestingly, not for Davidson's paratactic theory (see Davidson (1979)). According to this theory – simplified somewhat – the imperative 'Harry, close the door' is tantamount to two indicative sentences, 'I command that. You, Harry, close the door.' But then the compound imperative above involving more than one addressee may be taken to be tantamount to three such sentences, 'I command that and I command that. You, Harry, close the door. You, George, put the kettle on' – where the demonstratives refer respectively to the first and second sentences which follow the conjunction. Davidson's theory, however, is implausible on independent grounds, most notably that when one issues a command by uttering an imperative, one is hardly *saying* that one is (cf. McGinn, op. cit. and Segal (1991)).

15 See Tarski (1983), ch. VIII. My presentation below of the argument owes much to Gareth Evans's in Evans (1977), §2.

16 Throughout this paper, I shall refer to open sentences explicitly as open sentences; when I omit the adjective 'open', I shall mean a closed sentence.

17 See e.g. Evans (1977), p.262 and Davies (1981a), pp.121–2.

18 Notice that the second objection presupposes that the notion of *true of* involved is the ordinary notion, not one that is internal to a theory (cf. note 9). Notice also that it may be possible to motivate the syntactic restriction in the first by pointing out that it is only *closed* sentences that are truth-evaluable.

19 '$\phi(\gamma)$' is the result of replacing v by γ in ϕ.

20 See Evans (1977), §2; cf. Davies (1981a), ch. 6.

21 It may be possible to overcome this problem using a modal truth theory; but the difficulties are prodigious. For a modal Fregean truth theory for a quantified modal language, see Davies (1978). Thomas Baldwin presents an alternative Fregean account of quantification which avoids possible language extensions. But the price of his account – perhaps easier to pay – is an ontology of *possible contexts of utterance*; see Baldwin (1975), pp. 72–76.

22 Baldwin's account also requires it to be true, and so is equally vulnerable. (See Baldwin, op. cit., p. 75.)

23 Nothing in what I say here should cast doubt on the general reliability of our positive intuitions concerning ambiguity.

24 Indeed, even if there is a borderline between close ambiguity and synonymy, and it lies in the difference between multiple and single roles, it is scarcely going to be reflected fully in our ordinary intuitions.

25 See Davies (1981b), §5.

26 The absence of contrary intuitions would certainly be one such consideration.

27 For attempts at detailed elucidation of the idea that the meanings of logical constants such as 'and' and 'exists' might be articulated in terms of their conceptual role, see Harman (1986) and Peacocke (1987).

28 I should say that in exploring the possibility that the notion of a closely analogous or common conceptual role may be one factor in explaining the univocality or apparent univocality of certain kinds of expression, I am not thereby committed to advocating what is sometimes called conceptual role semantics, that the 'ultimate source of meaning or content is the functional role symbols play in thought' (Harman (1982), p. 255.) All I require is that certain expressions – here 'and' and 'exists' – have such roles and that one way of understanding the expressions exploits them. Nor (I should add) do I mean to imply that such an account cannot be brought under the umbrella of more traditional approaches. I am still unsure, for instance, whether it can be understood in terms of focal meaning.

29 The '$\forall$' rules used here are: ($\forall$E) $\forall v \phi / \phi(t)$ (where t is a name or variable); and ($\forall$I) $\phi(t)/\forall v \phi$ (where t is a name or variable subject to the usual restrictions).

30 The complete description of the step from line (2) to (3) would then read: with respect to any *particular* object, a, a is red and a is round, and so (the object) a is red.

31 Cf. Peacocke (1976) p. 229.

32 It is a good question *why* truth (or being true of something) is explanatorily or epistemologically prior to falsity (or being false of something). And the answer (I suspect) is intimately related to the question why assertion is correspondingly prior to denial. But I shall not pursue either question here. (For some pertinent remarks, see Dummett (1981a), pp. 316–21.) It should be noted that which values someone counts as fundamental may vary with the general assumptions about semantics that he or she is making. For instance, although truth is fundamental in a classical framework, it may not be if the framework is anti-realist: something like proof may then be fundamental and truth derivative.

33 For help with it, see Peacocke (1987), §2.

34 For more on the differences, see Peacocke (1987), esp. §§3–4.

35 By a complex term, I mean one that involves a definite description operator.

36 In workable logics, these provisos will embody conditions relating (e.g.) to the scope of such and such connectives in ϕ. ('It's not the case that Fa' will obviously not entail 'a exists' or 'Fs exist', whereas '[Fa and Ga]' will.) But it is doubtful that rules stated in those terms can be of the right form to capture in general the conceptual role of the different uses of 'exists', since such conditions will vary greatly from language to language. One way around this would be to see the introduction rules for the two uses of 'exists' as mutually dependent, so that the first-level predicate would be used in the proviso in the

introduction rule for the second-level predicate, and vice versa. The proviso in the second-level rule would then be that $\phi(t)$ should entail 't exists' (i.e., in effect, that the referent of t exists); and the proviso in the first-level rule would be that $\phi(t)$ should entail 'ϕs exist' (i.e., in effect, that satisfiers of ϕ exist). For the most part, these rules would be unable to figure in workable logics – if only for the reason that the provisos will not in general be decidable. But they can nevertheless act as constraints on what can count as a workable logic with respect to a given language. (Notice that one cannot refute this proposal by arguing that the first-level use is prior to the second just *because* it is first-level. Doubtless second-level predication cannot be grasped without having first grasped first-level predication. But that does not entail that *every* first-level predicate is conceptually prior to any second-level counterpart it might have.) I should emphasize that for present purposes nothing hangs on this proposal. All that matters is that the same or symmetric conditions apply in both cases.

37 'If ψ is permitted to occur in t, then any conclusion will be derivable from 't exists': take t to be 'the thing which is not F' and ψ to be 'Fξ'. If ψ is permitted to occur in θ, then 'Fa' will follow from 'a exists': take t to be a, ψ to be 'Fξ' and θ to be 'Fa'. And if ψ is permitted to occur in the assumptions used in the derivation of θ from $\psi(t)$, then 'Ga' will follow from '[Fa→Ga]' and 'a exists': take t to be a, ψ to be 'Fξ' and θ to be 'Ga'.

38 Given that the provisos for the elimination rule are not identical, but merely symmetric, and that the same will almost certainly be the true of the provisos for the introduction rules (cf. note 36), an *analogous* role is much more plausible.

39 Someone notably antagonistic towards the idea of imperative inference is Bernard Williams (see Williams (1973)).

40 See e.g. Hodges (1977). Indeed, we might even characterize the meanings of certain indicative-forming logical constants (particularly 'not') *directly* in terms of the notion of incompatibility (see Harman, op. cit.). Peacocke exploits the idea in detail in his (1987).

41 These state that if either A or B is incompatible with a set of sentences, then so is '[A and B]'; and that if both 'not A' and 'not B' are incompatible with a set, then so is 'not [A and B]'.

42 These considerations go over straightforwardly to optative conjunctions, which will be governed by entirely analogous tableau rules.

5

Paradoxes of Content Monism

Julie Jack

In this section*, I claim that content-monism should be rejected and outline a version of content-pluralism. The ground on which I urge rejection of monism is its role as a crucial assumption in deriving three paradoxes about discovery potential.

I Deduction

1 If inference from A to B is informative (non question-begging), A has a content not containing that of B.
2 If inference from A to B is correct (valid), A has a content containing that of B.
3 An unambiguous sign has only one content.
4 Ambiguity apart, inference from A to B cannot be both informative and correct.

II Definition

1 If analysis of A in terms of B is informative (non-circular), B has a content not containing that of A.
2 If analysis of A in terms of B is correct (permissible), B has a content containing that of A.
3 An unambiguous sign has only one content.

---

* *Editors' Note*: Julie Jack's contribution arrived at a point when Essays and Replies were already close to our word limit. In the circumstances, we publish an extract from the submitted article, which is itself an extract from a larger scale work in progress.

4   Ambiguity apart, analysis of *A* in terms of *B* cannot be both informative and correct.

III Equality

1   If *a is b* is informative (non-trivial), *a is b* has a content which is not the same as that of *a is a*.
2   If *a is b* is correct (true), *a is b* has a content which is the same as that of *a is a*.
3   An unambiguous sign has only one content.
4   Ambiguity apart, *a is b* cannot be both informative and correct.

Monism is the theory that a non-ambiguous sign has only one content. Being committed to 3, it must reject 1 or 2 in each of the above explicit derivations or accept 4, the sceptical conclusion. Rejection of 1 or 2 poses a threat to realism about informativeness or correctness, by severing it from content relations. We should hold on to 1 and 2. And rejection of 1 or 2 poses a threat to realism about content relations, by severing negative claims from consequences for informativeness or correctness. Objectivity in the areas of deduction, definition, and equality requires the constraints which these conditionals impose.

What then of 4? Accepting it entails that unless ambiguity is appealed to, correctness and informativeness will not be simultaneously available. But this is untenable. Admittedly, we can try to dispense with actual correctness or actual informativeness, but that is a counsel of despair. Or we can try to embrace ambiguity. However, consider the implications of this strategy for the case of deduction. Here the strategy maintains, in the spirit of Wittgenstein's *Foundations of Mathematics*, that a new proof alters meanings. Thus x, representing the premise-conjunction, could *come to* contain y, representing the presumptive conclusion, through meaning-change in x or y (or both). But while ambiguity might account for the illusion of answering the question with which we started, it can't account for the reality; deliberately relying on it would be irrational, because self-defeating. The strategy of making ambiguity essential to deductive discovery dooms deliberate discovery-projects to failure.

A less disastrous course is to retain 1 and 2 but prepare to reject 4. That means resisting the attractions of monism and rejecting 3. If we abandon the assumption that there is such a thing as 'the' content of a sign, we are left with nihilism or pluralism about content, pluralism being the theory that a non-ambiguous sign can have more than one content, nihilism the theory that content does not exist. Nihilism is absurd, unable to confess its desire to maintain a theory distinct from others. Content pluralism, however, is worthy of consideration.

For 4 to be correctly derived, 'content' should have the same use in 1, 2, and 3. Rendering this as 'kind of content', we can reject 3. So we can reject 4: the antecedents of 1 and 2 are jointly satisfiable without ambiguity. Now we need to prevent the re-emergence of the paradoxes by showing that the appearance of contrariety between the consequents of 1 and 2 is illusory. A better interpretation than contrariety is that different criteria of containment or sameness are to be deemed relevant in moving from 1 to 2, because different factors are mentioned in their antecedents. Thinking of 'containment' and 'sameness' as determinables under which determinate categories fall, the process can be described as 'category-shift'.

At I, 3 of *The Concept of Mind* Gilbert Ryle describes conjunctions which span categories as absurd, instancing 'She came home in a flood of tears and a sedan chair'. Within this useful analogy, that which is absurd is not category-shift, rather it is the grammatically fostered temptation to perceive 'in' as having the same relevance to both tears and chair. When 1 and 2 are conjoined, their grammar encourages a similarly absurd 'seeing single' or category-merging; but category-switch is not absurd.

Without restricting the number of admissible categories, content-pluralism requires a respectable endowment of criteria of sameness and containment for each; otherwise nihilism triumphs. As a first step towards accounting for category-shift in discovery-projects relevant to I–III, I would like to mention five distinct semantic categories. Each is recognized in practice, and each has been recognized in theory. They are: Import, the intra-categorical sameness conditions for which are framed in terms of the Fregean conception of necessary co-extensiveness; Acceptation, the sameness conditions for which are based upon Carnap's notion of intensional isomorphism; Perspective Type, reflecting David Kaplan's account of character; Purport or subject-matter, derived from Peter Strawson's conception of statement; and Hidden Connotation, which is the content (by one of the above) of the defining expression from a suitable definition of the term in question, e.g. from a stipulative reference-fixing definition of the kind described by Saul Kripke.

6

Ethical Upbringing: from Connivance to Cognition

Sabina Lovibond

1. An idea which provides the starting-point for much current discussion in ethical theory is that moral judgements seem to possess two features, *objectivity* and *practicality*, which 'pull in opposite directions' from one another.[1] Their objectivity is attested by our sense of being accountable, as moral thinkers, to standards of sound judgement that we may fail to meet.[2] Their practicality reveals itself in the feature emphasized by ethical non-cognitivism – that of being so related to action that, in the absence of coercion, persistent failure to act in the way indicated by one's professed moral opinions tends, logically, to discredit the sincerity of those opinions.

The reason these two features are believed to 'pull in opposite directions' is that awareness of how things stand in a reality independent of the thinking subject is presumed to be compatible, indifferently, with any conative attitude towards the reality apprehended (including, of course, a simple lack of interest). The very idea of objectivity is presumed, in other words, to be in tension with that of an internal relation between judgement and action. (Objective reality is, as it were, public property: it presents the same face to every competent enquirer. How then could it make any practical claim on private individuals?)

A position is emerging in moral philosophy which promises to resolve this tension – to demonstrate the possibility of combining 'internalism'[3] with ethical cognitivism. This position has both a psychological and a metaphysical aspect. On the psychological side it offers what might be called a *Bildung* ('formation') model[4] of value-experience. This would be a corollary of the more abstract thought that, in general, the experience

I would like to thank the following people for their helpful comments on earlier drafts of this paper: Roger Cash, Howard Caygill, Mark Larrimore, Sarah Richmond and, especially, Stephen Williams.

of language-users brings into play conceptual capacities acquired in the course of socialization – that where such capacities are present, they should not be thought of as imposing a grid or 'scheme' on the manifold of pre-conceptual 'content', but rather as playing an ineliminable role in the identification of what is experienced. Applied to the evaluative, this yields the idea of a *culturally constructed perspective* to which value (including ethical value) discloses itself. The process of construction involved here is one among the many that turn us out as potential subjects of the various kinds of experience we can reflectively attribute to ourselves. More concretely, it is a matter of initiation into a system of linguistic practices – those which provide admission to the mentality of the morally aware. As learners, our goal is to become qualified to exchange thoughts about the new subject-matter with those already versed in it; hence we have to get into a position in which we and they, in using the relevant vocabulary, are *thinking of the same objects* (and/or properties). This is a process both of cognitive development (one learns to place things correctly with respect to current value-concepts) and of psychological adjustment: the 'spirit' of such practices consists as much in a pattern of concern as in a habit of thought. So within any given practice involving a value-term, a fully finished participant will be someone who has achieved a thorough-going identification with each of these things.

This model is balanced on the metaphysical side by a critique of the affectless conception of reality built into the modern ('scientific') worldview: only by rediscovering the idea of the factual, or real, as laden with evaluative significance can we make sense of a kind of *cognition* that would preclude indifference on the part of the knower. Once we admit the ineliminable role of the conceptual in articulating what is there to be experienced, and so in bringing it about that there is anything to discuss under the heading of 'objective reality' (since 'a nothing would serve just as well as a something about which nothing could be said',[5]) we shall no longer be alarmed by the seemingly relativist overtones of the term 'perspective'[6]. For this admission implies that the *normal* occupation of an aspirant to knowledge consists in exploring what is to be seen from a certain perspective – one into which he or she has previously been, or is even now being, initiated with more or less difficulty. Since no item of distinctively human knowledge is accessible without such initiation, the enabling role of *Bildung* in the case of ethical (and other) value-experience cannot be cited as evidence of any specific defect in the cognitive status of that experience.[7]

The distinguishing feature of evaluative (as opposed, say, to perceptual) *Bildung* is that it renders us sensitive to considerations with an inbuilt (positive or negative) *appeal* which will be registered, however selectively, in deliberation. And the role of ethical *Bildung* is to sensitize us to a particular sub-set of such considerations – a sub-set whose members not only tend to claim deliberative priority[8] but are also especially apt to be hostile to natural impulse (to 'demolish our self-love', as Kant says).[9] For example, it implants a sense that there are certain things we cannot do because to do them would violate the legitimate claims or expectations of others. Consequently, although initiation into the perspective of the conscientious person is not the only branch of learning that is 'advanced' and difficult to entrench (think for instance of scholarship, connoisseurship or specialized technical skills), it can perhaps be regarded as the only one that is both 'advanced' and *mandatory* for the purposes of social existence. (This would explain why it constitutes a zone of collective anxiety: 'civilization and its discontents' . . .)

The *Bildung* model, then, responds to complaints about the 'queerness' of the idea of objective value by reassembling some of the less familiar elements of the Platonism which originally supported it.[10] It maintains, with Plato, that culture (i.e. education in a broad sense) should terminate in a discipline of *desire* for the beautiful or noble,[11] where 'desire' means – as it does pre-philosophically – something with a propensity (not of course indefeasible) to express itself in action. One consequence of this thought is that in so far as such desire is absent from your experience, your individual cultural formation must be imperfect or imcomplete. Another, obtained by counterposing the first, is that in anyone whose formation *is* complete the appreciation of evaluative features of the world will be constituted (in part, or under one aspect) by a desire for the realization of the relevant species of value.[12]

These remarks bring us face to face with the slightly uncanny figure of the *virtuous person*, the settled inhabitant of the perspective to which ethical considerations reveal themselves. The virtuous person represents the limiting case of success in the production of a subjectivity for which the objective and the practical elements in moral judgement cease to 'pull opposite ways'; as such, he or she provides a concrete resolution of the theoretical tension outlined at the beginning of this paper, and is the natural focus of attention in the dialectical context established there. However, discussion of the ideal outcome of *Bildung* is of limited interest unless it sheds light on the relationship between ideal and actuality – the latter comprising what John McDowell elsewhere in this collection calls the 'ordinarily "good" person' as well as, *a fortiori*, the ordinary mediocre or morally unsatisfactory person.[13] My aim in what follows will be to bring out the permeability of the boundaries between these conceptually distinct identities (that is, the moral identities behind such labels as 'virtuous person', 'good person', etc.), and so to display the fragile and problematic character of the ethical cognitivism yielded by our model – a cognitivism I nevertheless wish to defend. Objective value (including ethical value) is that which discloses itself to the evaluatively informed person; but the perspective that defines the 'evaluatively informed' person is one that can be occupied with no greater security of tenure than we possess, in general, on our identity as social beings.

2. A natural point of entry to the discussion of this notion of permeable boundaries is the phenomenon of akrasia, or weakness of will, in its ethical variant. This phenomenon gives rise to a problem for the attempt to combine cognitivism and 'internalism' in the way I have outlined, and it is by exploring a certain proposed solution to that problem that we can gain access to the territory that interests me. The question is how to discharge the obligation to render plausible, in the face of what looks like abundant evidence to the contrary, the Socratic thesis that where person A is sufficently strongly motivated to comply with the demands of virtue and person B is not, there must be some relevant cognitive difference between them – some difference in the way they understand their situation. The solution I want to consider takes the form of an argument in favour of the Socratic thesis, or perhaps I should say a sympathetic reinterpretation of it. This interpretation maintains that when you display moral weakness, you retain a capacity for correct *judgement* as to how you should act in a given situation (indeed, if you had never entered the mental world of the virtuous, the conflict constitutive of akrasia could not have arisen), but your *perception* of the situation may differ in being no longer 'clear' but 'clouded by desire'; in the moral as in the aesthetic sphere (*mutatis mutandis*), failure to recapture the full subjective power of the experience may prompt the thought that on the later occasion 'the fault lies in me, not in the music'.[14]

The above ('clouded perception') proposal is undeniably in keeping with the kind of ethical cognitivism suggested by the *Bildung* model. And before venturing any criticism of it, I would like to add what I take to be a word of elucidation. This has to do with the conditions that permit A's cognitive state to be regarded, by contrast with B's, as one of *clear* perception. Classical Platonism expresses in its notorious demands for cultural closure[15] a vivid awareness of one such condition, namely the requirement that *Bildung* be sufficiently homogeneous in content to yield something – anything – that will *count* as a state of attunement to objective moral demands. Only where this condition is met will there be a stable point of view with which we can identify for the purpose of talking about the 'demands' of, say, courage, and of the courageous person as 'responding' to these; and when we do talk in this ethically loaded way (as opposed to saying simply that A faced the danger while B ran away), we demonstrate our investment in the forces that direct *Bildung* and that designate certain behaviour-patterns as the ones flowing from a 'clear perception' of the ethical. In other words, we take the side of (a certain kind of) authority.

Now, it is at this point that one may be struck by a certain tendentiousness in the way the 'clouded perception' proposal represents our allegiances: an implicit decision to speak on the assumption that these allegiances are in reality what they are officially, or ideally, supposed to be. This observation is, of course, unsurprising in so far as the *Bildung* model is something we have inherited from the idealist tradition in Greek philosophy – the tradition which teaches that the ideal *is* the real (Plato), or that the good man is the measure of what is genuinely pleasant or worthy of pursuit (Aristotle). However, for anyone not already committed to this style of thought, it is natural to say that in practice (or 'really') the authorities that address us through the demands of the moral virtues do not enjoy our unqualified loyalty.

Perhaps, then, the worm's-eye view should also be taken into account in developing the *Bildung* model. Plato at any rate finds it instructive by way of contrast. In the *Protagoras* (352d) he makes Socrates say that acquiescence in the idea of akrasia, i.e. acceptance that under the influence of immediate feeling we sometimes act against our better practical judgement, is characteristic of the 'vulgar' outlook for which reason is not assured, simply *qua* reason, of a commanding role in the mind.[16] This attitude is 'vulgar', by Platonic standards, in that it represents as natural (and as such unpuzzling) the state of affairs in which practical judgement and actual motivation fail to coalesce; it sees a judgement of the form 'I ought to . . .' or 'I must . . .' as one that can be made without that wholeness of affective involvement that would rule out acting in contempt of whatever value the judgement recognizes, for present purposes, as salient.[17] Such a view indicates that the holder sees 'reason', or for our purposes the cognitive content of value-judgements, as essentially something emanating from an external authority. The attitude in question is therefore appropriate not to a fully autonomous being, but to one who retains something of the cognitive detachment that marks the recipient of *Bildung* (the person who is still in the process of being initiated into the moral perspective). Whereas the Socratic rationalist assumes, 'aristocratically', that the source of correct judgements cannot be other than himself, the 'vulgar' person pictures a correct judgement as issuing from elsewhere – as it were, from 'those who know'. It is this absence of full identification with the voice of 'reason' that reduces the latter to something not inherently 'commanding'.[18] In particular, the occupant of the 'vulgar' perspective will presumably take it for granted that there is a component of our evaluative thinking – the 'difficult', instinct-denying component – in which our participation always retains something of the character of adaptation to *other people's* usage.

One might be tempted to think of this kind of adaptation on the part of the less-than-virtuous as a matter of *feigning* (some of) the ontological commitments characteristic of the virtuous. This diagnosis would bring the adaptive behaviour within the scope of Gareth Evans's account of fictional reference.[19] The parallel would be with the case of discourse about novels, films, etc., where, according to Evans, speakers join in a practice that *mimics* the activity of transmitting information about particular individuals – of recording or recounting actual events in which those individuals have figured. In so doing, the argument continues, they *connive* with the author(s) of the artefact in using names or other referring devices to make statements that can attain to truth only within the context of the shared pretence (sc., because of the presence in them of names which are vacuous outside that context). 'Conniving' thus entails appropriating the available make-believe information in such a way that, when you exchange thoughts about a fictional character with other readers (viewers, etc.), you and they can be truly described *within the pretence* as 'thinking of the same object'; or as Evans puts it, you 'must be so related that, had the pretence been real, [you and] they would actually have been thinking of the same thing'.[20] What happens here might be seen as a pragmatic suspension of disbelief: on entering the game we consent to proceed, if only at the level of attention and memory, on the supposition that something rather than nothing is being represented.

I think this part of Evans's work has much to contribute to the development of a position in moral philosophy that is both cognitivist and 'internalist'. Specifically, I think it can help meet the previously noted need for mediation between the actual (imperfect) and the ideal product of ethical *Bildung*.

We might begin by distinguishing two different ways in which linguistic behaviour can be deficient in ontological 'seriousness'.[21] There is, on one hand, fictional discourse as envisaged by Evans, participation in which takes place against the background of a quite definite ontological attitude: if questioned outside the context of the practice, we reply without hesitation that the 'objects referred to' within it do not really exist (even if this thought can itself be expressed only by means of referential 'connivance', i.e. by 'making a move within a pretence in order to express the fact that it is a pretence'.[22] On the other hand, some situations in which we are invited to connive in the use of a vocabulary apparently denoting real objects and properties admit of no definite answer to the question whether our participation (if we allow ourselves to be drawn in) rests on belief or disbelief. It is possible to connive with other people's talk about things for which, while not necessarily viewing them in the light of outright fictions, one would be unwilling (as it were) to take full ontological responsibility.

This latter phenomenon, as far as I can see, has not received the attention it deserves in the context of the *Bildung* model. Perhaps the best way to reach a proper appreciation of its importance in ethical *Bildung* is through reflection on the experience of *not knowing whether one (really) means what one is saying*. Think of the following exchanges: 'Doesn't the bride look beautiful?' – 'Yes, gorgeous.' 'A nice man, hard-working, but I don't believe he has a first-class mind; he lacks the killer instinct.' – 'Well, perhaps you're right.' Now consider the various circumstances in which it might be said that the second speaker in each of these exchanges was insincere. In order to single out the case that interests me I need to distinguish it from two others:

(1) The first case is that in which you, as the second speaker, privately *think the contrary* of what you say, i.e. think that the bride looks unattractive or that the student does have a first-class mind. I mention this case only to set it aside for present purposes: your lack of candour here relates not to your ontological attitude to the concepts employed in the conversation, only to your view about whether certain objects fall within the extension of those concepts.

(2) The second case is like the first in that here again you, as the second speaker, have undergone or are currently undergoing the standard exposure to the relevant linguistic practice, and are thus in some degree a qualified participant in it. Now perhaps in this capacity you have no quarrel with what is being said to you. In general, you and your interlocutor agree (outwardly) in locating instances of the beautiful/gorgeous, the first-class mind and the killer instinct; so the behavioural (conversational) phenomena here may be typical of those found in exchanges between competent observers about the incidence of an objective property. The occurrence of such phenomena is consistent, though, with the possibility of a more radical moral evasion on your part, namely the sort where you know as well as anyone else in your linguistic community what counts as a first-class mind, etc., but regard the concept itself as a vacuous one (cf. 'phlogiston') and perhaps also as a pretext for evil (cf. 'witch').[23] Where this is so, your continued participation in the practice will be analogous from your own perspective (though I suppose

not normally from that of your interlocutor) to the conniving participation of an intelligent novel-reader in discourse 'about the novel', i.e. it will be functionally adequate but ontologically disengaged. (Compare R. M. Hare on the 'merely descriptive' use of terms whose normal use is *both* to describe *and* to prescribe or commend.)[24] This case resembles the one that interests me in so far as it involves a lack of candour about your attitude to a concept; note however that the dissembled attitude here remains quite clear-cut.

(3) Finally, the interesting case: repeat the foregoing scenario, but change the second speaker's ontological attitude from one of outright disbelief to one of agnosticism. Is there – really – such a property as 'beauty', as people currently understand the term? Are there such things as 'first-class minds'? A frank answer might be: sometimes I talk (and think) as if I believed in these things and sometimes not; it depends, at least in part, on whom I am talking to. To that extent my participation in the practices, when I do participate, tends towards the character of Evans's 'conniving' participation in the use of a vacuous name; but it does not fully assume this character, since I cannot say categorically that I regard the terms in question as vacuous. What is true is that my attitude to them exhibits something ontologically sceptical, tentative or irresponsible.[25]

Would it be correct in these circumstances to say, as provisionally suggested, that I am *feigning* certain ontological commitments, namely those corresponding to the particular value terms I use? In the end, this account of the situation seems inaccurate. For if we agree with Elizabeth Anscombe that pretending in general consists in 'trying to appear what you are not',[26] then my performance under the third scenario will fail to qualify on at least two counts. In the first place, my behaviour probably exhibits more of passive compliance than of purposiveness: I do not so much try as *allow myself* to present a certain (ethical) 'appearance'. And in the second place, it is not clear that a person with the relevant ontological commitments is 'something I am not'. Why should nothing less than an unequivocal instantiation of the property of being such a person be held to count? (Why should we think that anything short of perfect ontological engagement renders an utterance null and void as an expression of the ethical personality of its author?)

The idea of pretence is too crude to capture what was posited in the third scenario. By inviting us to construe the situation as one in which my real ontological commitments in the sphere of value are belied or misrepresented by my behaviour, this suggestion implicitly credits the hidden reality – the way things really stand in respect of those commitments – with a degree of definiteness or determinacy equal to that of the behavioural signs with which it is to be compared. But in fact we have no business to assume that the hidden reality possesses that degree of determinacy. Wittgenstein was right to be impressed by the laboriously constructed dimension of inwardness that makes it possible for an adult human being to be a hypocrite;[27] vanity may incline us, though, to exaggerate the difference between the actual adult condition and that from which it emerges, namely a condition of psychological inchoateness which tends continually to subvert the distinction between *what one really is* and *how one presents oneself to others*.

3. This 'decentred' condition is no doubt a mark of imperfect rationality. It is certainly unbecoming in anyone pledged to the Russellian view that there is 'only one world, the "real" world',[28] and it shows a lack of respect for the 'alternately platitudinous and mysterious principle that anything that is true (however we come by it) is consistent with anything else that is true (however we come by it)'.[29] Still, I want now to take a fresh look at the seemingly unsatisfactory state of affairs illustrated by my third scenario – a state of affairs which shows how inconclusive our identification with the demands of virtue may actually be. I shall suggest that our 'decentredness' can after all take on a positive aspect for ethical cognitivism, since it is indispensable to the kind of subjective change in which evaluative *Bildung* consists; the idea will be that the same considerations can tell a story both of deficiency and of potentiality.

Recall from §1 the account of value-experience as involving an exercise of conceptual capacities. If this account is right, then our openness to such experience will be due to whatever course of events may have placed the necessary conceptual resources at our disposal; for it will depend on a sensitivity to certain facts, or features of the world, which would be nothing to us if we lacked the resources to express an awareness of them. According to the *Bildung* model, the acquisition of these resources depends upon a discipline of 'learning correct judgements'[30] – a discipline which, carried far enough, instils an acceptance of the ontological implications of the judgements learned.[31] But the first step is simply to draw the learner into outward conformity with a linguistic practice or practices; and this means that learners, as such, have to pass through a stage in which the linguistic behaviour they exhibit cannot (yet) be seen as expressive of any ontological commitment. The imitative behaviour on which the process depends is, to begin with, *mere* behaviour: only as it becomes progressively infused with subjectivity or intentionality can we begin to read such commitment into it.

This is not a criticism of anything that takes place at the pre- or proto-intentional stage, for that stage is a necessary precursor to intentionality proper. The promiscuity of the sign is something on which *Bildung* positively relies. That is, it relies on the fact that signs are, as it were, silent with regard to the spirit of any given speech act in which they may occur – in particular, the degree to which that spech act is 'really meant', or is an authentic expression of the speaker's personality. It is precisely because a sign is equally apt for communicating a certain content, irrespective of the burden of 'seriousness' that it carries, that someone who fails to qualify as a 'serious' discursive agent (e.g. a child learning to talk; someone joking or teasing) can execute a speech act that lacks nothing as a communication of the content in question.[32] Hence the ontologically agnostic or frivolous deployment of conceptual resources, though sometimes associated with a loss of faith under the impact of critical reflection (as e.g. in the 'beauty' example), belongs no less fundamentally to a context of growth and creativity.[33]

Now if our primitive relation to the ontology of ethical value is characterized in this way by externality, it should not be surprising if something of the same externality is still present in the thinking of the initiated person. In fact, granted the indebtedness of sincere or 'serious' value-judgement to a historical background of less than fully responsible linguistic performance, the more natural ground for surprise (or for a sense of the uncanny,[34] as I put it earlier) is that anyone should ever definitively emerge from this background. And this is encouraging from the point of view of the *Bildung* model, since it supports the claims of that model to be able to solve the problem identified earlier for our attempt to combine ethical cognitivism with 'internalism'. The problem was: how can we make sense of the phenomenon of moral weakness in someone who, by hypothesis (since they 'know'), has been successfully initiated (i) into a conceptual repertoire whose point is to articulate a scheme of concerns with a bearing on action, and (ii) into the habit of thought ('practical reasoning') whereby such concerns are synthesized into an all-things-considered judgement as to how they should act in any given case?

Suppose for the sake of convenience that the 'better judgement' against which the akratic acts is a judgement expressed verbally. (This assumption is harmless, since if the relevant state of mind has been correctly characterized it must always be possible in principle to *elicit* something on the lines of 'I know it would be [e.g.] a betrayal of trust, but . . .') Then the solution to our problem – prefigured, arguably, by Aristotle, who is well aware that one can talk like a virtuous person at the very moment of acting otherwise[35] – will be to see akratic behaviour as expressive of a state of mind in which the 'outer' and the 'inner' (linguistic behaviour and subjectivity) have failed to achieve complete fusion; that is, a state of mind that falls short of *(really) meaning what you say.* Interest centres here not so much on the point being made about akrasia, considered in abstraction[36], but rather on the corollary that levity or opportunism in relation to current linguistic practices – the posture attributed to the akratic – is to be seen not as an aberration but as an empirically *normal* condition. The process of ethical formation can then be understood as one intended to emancipate its subject from this condition by constructing in him or her a unified system of practical commitments.[37]

The normality of the condition just described is what lends colour to 'externalism' – the view that you can be aware of an ethical fact which, by your own lights, is such as to make a certain course of action necessary, yet still fail to act in the way indicated. This view takes for granted some version of the mentality that counted in Platonic terms as 'vulgar'. That is, it presumes that one will relate to judgements of value – or to the concerns they express – as issuing from a standpoint that is not exactly one's own (even though one may be able to muster a high degree of empathy with it). By contrast, 'internalism' presumes that our attitude to such judgements will in principle be one of *authorship*, and hence that we shall take full ontological responsibility for the concepts proper to them. So while the former theory is true to life in a state of incomplete ethical formation, the latter reflects the experience of the fully finished ethical subject. It follows that anyone who regards the fully finished condition, pessimistically, as a mere 'regulative idea' will be obliged by the same token to regard internalism as an exercise in *merely* ideal, not actual, psychological description.

4.   It may be felt that the view I have been developing concedes too much to ethical 'irrealism'.[38] What, after all, can be left of ethical *knowledge* if (firstly) we make its subject-matter a correlate of the existence of certain linguistic practices to which we acknowledge a commitment, but then (secondly) we represent this commitment as itself a fugitive thing, about whose presence in our thinking there may be no 'fact of the matter'? Doesn't the second part of this account concur for all practical purposes with the deconstructionist picture of the subject as a recycling point for available fragments of discourse, none of which, as momentarily appropriated for the purposes of a speech act, has any more claim than the next to be seen as the expression of his or her 'real self'? And isn't that picture the psychological counterpart of scepticism about the familiar distinction, drawn within the class of declarative utterances, between

those that do and those that do not refer to an objective reality?[39] The two scepticisms seem to go together in that if we cannot explain the difference between referentially 'serious' and 'unserious' language, it makes little sense to look for the different modes of subjective involvement associated with each.

The first point to note in response to this challenge is that nothing I have said about the loose ends of the *Bildung* process need be read as a contribution to any systematic critique of realism. Instead we have been conducting an enquiry, against the background of the familiar assumption that declarative speech acts succeed most of the time in recording aspects of reality, into the phenomenon of referential 'connivance'. Our introduction to this phenomenon was provided by the case of proper names: here the traditionally stark contrast between fact and fiction (and accordingly, between the presence and absence of ontological commitment) remained essentially unquestioned, and the role of 'connivance' was to shed light on the apparent possibility (otherwise, on anti-Cartesian premises, a puzzling one) of communication about admittedly fictional objects. In the separate case of value-predicates, by contrast, we were concerned with discourse not 'about' something objectively unreal but about a subject-matter whose reality could not be brought home to learners all at once: here, therefore, 'connivance' on the part of the learner was a dynamic intermediate stage *en route* to the state of affairs in which teacher and learner could do something analogous to *exchanging information* about a single array of objects. In drawing attention to the vagueness we sometimes experience in this latter context about the extent of our ontological commitments, I have not taken myself to be offering an answer to the question of how language as such relates to reality.[40]

Still, the point might be pressed by someone with 'irrealist' designs on moral discourse in particular: if we admit to often lacking a clear sense, even at the level of inward conviction, of whether or not we are talking about something real when we use a value-predicate, then aren't we in effect endorsing the non-cognitivist picture of evaluative discourse as an inherently expressive (rather than representational) *genre*, unable to stand on the same footing as those linguistic practices in which there is a clear division between mere referential connivance and genuine reference?

One of the first philosophical lessons I can remember learning from David Wiggins was that a distinction can be *non-absolute* – that is, it can admit of doubtful cases – without therefore being *unreal*. This is how I think matters stand with the contrast between being, and not being, ontologically committed to the objects or properties denoted by the

value-expressions we use. Thus, the method of introspection may leave
many questions unanswered as to how far such usage is supported by
attitudes of genuine esteem for the values concerned (if *meaning* is not a
mental process, one might say, neither is *really meaning*).[41] Yet that we do
believe in a contrast between the presence and absence of such commitment is evident from the distinctions we draw empirically[42] between
degrees of practical or ethical seriousness, where this attribute stands
opposed to the linguistic opportunism of the uninitiated. And although
our subjective grip on the boundaries of the 'serious' may waver, the
objective property of 'seriousness' or sincerity in others (the fusion of
transient linguistic behaviour and enduring evaluative dispositions) has
an interest for us that is guaranteed by the demands of communication.
More precisely, it has a guaranteed interest for anyone with a stake in the
kind of linguistic activity that is 'oriented towards mutual understanding'
and towards the co-ordination of action.[43] This interest is grounded in
the natural need to distinguish, for our own deliberative purposes, between those in whom the use of evaluative language is a reliable indicator
of future behaviour and those in whom it is not.

Hence we can look favourably on the view of F. H. Bradley[44] that a
general account of the opposed terms *play* and *earnest* should invoke the
idea of *limit*. The 'unserious' in our lives is that which we recognize as not
to be pursued, practically, beyond a certain point (witness the contrast
between playful and genuinely aggressive fighting, or between flirtation
and seduction);[45] the 'serious' is that which is not so circumscribed. Now
some of our uses of language are underpinned by a clear perception both
of the existence of such a limit, and of where it lies. Thus when we
connive with a fictional proper-name-using practice we understand, for
instance, that visiting the public record office to investigate Sherlock
Holmes's ancestry would be outside this limit: it would show a failure to
appreciate the proper place of talk about Holmes in the general context
of getting on with our lives. But there are also linguistic practices such
that although our participation in them is marked, as in the fictional case,
by a kind of reserve – an unwillingness to take full ontological responsibility for our subject-matter – still we could not make any *a priori*
statement as to where the limit will come: that is, we could not say at
what point we might make a mental gesture analogous to the one that has
to be made in connection with the ancestry of Sherlock Holmes ('Look,
this is just *words*').

One might say, by way of the proverbial footnote to Plato, that our
perspective on the language of ethical value is 'vulgar' in proportion to
our readiness to take refuge in the thought that it is just a matter of words
– the characteristic thought, or so I suggested earlier, of those who

experience the habit of mind of the virtuous as something originating outside themselves. However, *pace* Plato, this thought is not necessarily a contemptible or even an inaccurate one. For in so far as the virtuous (or should it be 'virtuous'?) habit of mind has been superimposed incuriously and with violence on the human material it encounters, the 'vulgar' perspective – that of the *vulgus* or *demos* – will have a kind of justice on its side; it will express, in its potential recalcitrance, an intuition of the underlying foreignness of what it may nonetheless have come to acknowledge as *correct* judgements of value.

Those who reason pessimistically, in the sense of §3, may comment that this is the universal human condition and that the fully integrated subjectivity that would definitively exclude akrasia represents a level of culture (a spiritual 'aristocracy') about which rationalist philosophy is best left to fantasize. Without taking sides in this debate, we can note that even if the pessimists are right in their totalizing claim, that will not diminish the significance of differences in the democratic credentials of actually existing moralities. For these will also constitute differences in the extent to which it is (morally) understandable that at moments of stress, the ontological commitment of their bearers should falter. The study of such differences will be an exercise in critical social thought. This critical dimension follows logically upon the naturalism of the *Bildung* model – that is, upon the model's understanding of ethical formation as the work of historically situated human beings.

NOTES

1 Smith (1991), p. 402; cf. Mackie (1977), ch. 1.
2 Cf. Wiggins (1991a), Essay III, §5 (one of whose targets, incidentally, is the idea that this sense of accountability might be a delusion which we could surmount through philosophical critique).
3 Cf. McNaughton (1988), p. 22: 'The view that a moral conviction, coupled with suitable beliefs, is sufficient to supply the agent with reason to act, and thus to motivate him to act, is often called *internalism* because it postulates an internal or conceptual connection between an agent's moral attitude and his choice of action.'
4 For more on *Bildung* see Lovibond (1989/90), esp. at §§V ff; McDowell (1994), pp. 84 ff. The label '*Bildung* model' is intended to pick out a body of thought in moral philosophy to which various writers – notably David Wiggins – have contributed: see especially Wiggins (1991a), Essay V, which develops a conception of the evaluative as a system of reciprocally adjusted 'property-response pairs' whose refinement both depends on *and* feeds into a 'process of interpersonal education, instruction and mutual enlightenment' (p. 196). See

also McDowell (1978), esp. p. 21 and context on 'moral upbringing'; (1979); (1981); Burnyeat (1980). My debt to this literature will be obvious, though I cannot begin to do justice here to the subtlety with which it addresses traditional questions in the 'metaphysics of morals'.

Moretti ((1987), p. 26) sees a conflict between the teleology of *Bildung* (which 'is truly such only if, at a certain point, it can be seen as *concluded*') and the ever-changing social demands of capitalist modernity, whose tendency is to withhold from the individual 'the quiet happiness of "belonging" to a fixed place'.

5 Cf. Wittgenstein (1967), §304.
6 Cf. Wiggins (1991a), pp. 113; 335, note 19.
7 I say 'any *specific* defect' because the sort of reply to ethical relativism envisaged here is one that proceeds by pointing out that the indebtedness of ethical judgement to social learning does not distinguish it in any radical way from judgement about any other subject-matter. Such a move will not, of course, satisfy those who think that once we recognize the socially situated character of *everything* that goes by the name of 'knowledge', the appropriate response is to adopt a global relativism; I comment on a position of this kind in Lovibond (1992).
8 I say only that such considerations 'tend' to claim deliberative priority because I wish to leave open the question whether it is of the essence of the ethical to take precedence over all other structures of concern. For argument to the contrary see Williams (1985), p. 188: ' . . . practical necessity is in no way peculiar to ethics. Someone may conclude that he or she unconditionally must do a certain thing, for reasons of prudence, self-protection, aesthetic or artistic concern, or sheer self-assertion . . . a conclusion of practical necessity is the same sort of conclusion whether it is grounded in ethical reasons or not.' For my purposes it will be enough if ethical considerations are recognized as *a* ground of practical necessity. (This may be the place to point out that my occasional use of 'moral' rather than 'ethical' in the present paper is not meant to evoke Williams's 'morality system', which is a technical term explained by reference to the moral philosophy of Kant.)
9 Kant (1948), p. 67, note. Note that in order to focus more sharply on the particular concerns of this paper I am abstracting as far as possible from the point, rightly emphasized by Wiggins (e.g. (1991a), pp. 95–6), that evaluative judgements are not *in themselves* practical but impinge on action only through the integrative function of practical reason (cf. (1991a), p. 258). I shall be interested primarily in value-judgements *qua* expressions of what we take to be the *salient* feature of a situation (cf. (1991a), p. 233) – the feature that deserves to be reflected in our practical response to it. It is when this feature belongs to the range that figures in Aristotle's ethical theory under the generic description *kalon/aischron* (noble/base), i.e. when we are called on to meet the demands of moral virtue in contrast to those of ordinary personal advantage, that the success of *Bildung* in socializing or 'civilizing' individual motivational dispositions will be most severely tested. For discussion of the *telos* of this

socializing process cf. McDowell (1978), §§9–10; (1979), §3; also his contribution to this book.

10 Cf. Mackie (1977), p. 23: '. . . the main tradition of European moral philosophy from Plato onwards has combined the view that moral values are objective with the recognition that moral judgements are partly prescriptive or action-guiding . . . In Plato's theory the Forms, and in particular the Form of the Good, are eternal, extra-mental realities . . . But it is held also that just knowing them or "seeing" them will not merely tell men what to do but will ensure that they do it, overruling any contrary inclinations.' For the famous 'argument from queerness' see ibid., p. 38.

11 *Rep.* 403b6–7: *dei de pou teleutân ta mousika eis ta tou kalou erôtika.*

12 Cf. *Rep.* 500cd.

13 McDowell, p. 103 below. Alasdair MacIntyre ((1981), p. 52) complains of post-Enlightenment moral philosophy that it has nothing to say about the relationship between actual and ideal human nature; I hope to show that the *Bildung* model is well placed to make good this defect.

14 McNaughton (1988), pp. 129–30. (This is based on McDowell (1979), p. 334–5, where the crucial suggestion – following Aristotle – is that 'the incontinent or continent person does not fully share the virtuous person's perception of the situation': 'incontinent *or continent*' because for Aristotle these two types, although they behave differently, are alike in needing to overcome an inclination that is threatening to make them flout the requirements of virtue.)

15 I mean 'closure' as in 'closed (rather than 'open') society'. Cf. *Rep.* 424d1–2: 'It is there, in *mousikê,* that the guardians [of the ideal city] must build their citadel.'

16 'Vulgar' here stands in for 'typical of *hoi polloi,* the many'.

17 For the term 'salient' see note 9 above.

18 That is, it reduces 'reason' to something whose power to motivate will be contingent, in any given situation, on the absence of countervailing natural motives (fear, lust, greed, etc.) strong enough to make us think 'So much the worse for *reason*'.

19 Evans (1982), ch. 10.3; for the word 'conniving' see p. 366. Note that this appeal to Evans's work pays no particular regard to him as a philosopher who 'reverses the priority, in the order of explanation, of language over thought' (Dummett (1993), p. 4).

20 Evans (1982), p. 368.

21 The theme of 'ontological commitment' which will be prominent in the remainder of this paper originates for me, at least in its application to ethics, in Wiggins's remark about the need for an interpreter of moral discourse to be 'ready to put his mind where his mouth is at least once for each sentence *s* of the object-language' ((1991a), p. 113: cf. note 6 above).

22 Cf. Evans (1982), ch. 10.4; for the words quoted see p. 369.

23 Thus Naomi Wolf in *The Beauty Myth* (1991), p. 12: 'The beauty myth tells a story: The quality called "beauty" objectively and universally exists.

Women must want to embody it and men must want to possess women who embody it . . . None of this is true.'

24 Hare (1963), ch. 10.1–2.

25 Something analogous can perhaps occur in relation to proper names, especially those of putative supernatural beings. Evans ((1982), p. 365, note 37) sees Greek mythology as comprising stories 'not involving any pretence on the part of the original tellers', whereas *we* know that these stories are false; but it may be that in the intervening period there have been speakers who used the mythical proper names in a spirit of genuine ontological ambivalence. (A former pupil writes to me that scenario (3) corresponds to his own experience of 'believing in God' and of taking part in conversation about religious matters.)

26 Anscombe (1981), vol. II, p. 85. The phrase quoted is Anscombe's own simplified version of something more carefully worded. (Note also that she opens her discussion by distinguishing 'real pretences' from 'mock performances', as in imaginative play.)

27 Wittgenstein (1967), Pt II, p. 229.

28 Russell (1967), p. 169.

29 Wiggins (1991a), p. 152.

30 Cf. Wittgenstein (1967), Pt II, p. 227.

31 'Acceptance' in a dispositional sense, of course: the model does not allow, at this early stage, for anything as voluntaristic as a *decision to accept* a particular concept as part of one's repertoire.

32 This is the phenomenon of 'iterability' insisted on by Jacques Derrida in support of his account of the sign as 'a possibility of functioning cut off, at a certain point, from its "original" meaning . . . What would a mark be that one could not cite? And whose origin could not be lost on the way?' (Derrida (1982), pp. 320–21). It is also noted by Donald Davidson in the context of a discussion of Frege's assertion sign: '. . . before Frege invented [this] sign he ought to have asked himself why no such sign existed before . . . the plight of the actor is always with us . . . there cannot be a convention that signals sincerity' (Davidson (1984), pp. 269, 270, 274). (I owe these references – and their juxtaposition – to the unpublished University of Oxford D. Phil. thesis of Sarah Richmond ('Derrida and Davidson', 1992).)

33 Cf. Aristotle, NE 1142a 16–20.

34 I believe it is possible, therefore, to agree (if only in a formal way) with Mackie's view that there is something 'queer' about the notion of objective value. What is correct about this view is that the perspective to which the requirements of virtue are disclosed is a 'queer' one – an unlikely one for human beings, *qua* animals, to be capable of occupying. However, this thought is not destructive of the ethical provided we remain willing to admit that that perspective is, at least in some measure, *ours*.

35 Cf. NE 1147a 19–24; b11–12 (the 'verses of Empedocles' analogy).

36 No philosophical *explanation* of akrasia is being offered – not at any rate if an 'explanation' necessarily involves descent to a level of description that is

epistemologically more basic. Akratics are people who sometimes act in accordance with their sincerely expressed practical convictions and sometimes not; to say of such people that their behaviour displays an incomplete fusion of 'inner' and 'outer' is simply to redescribe them.

37 Cf. Wiggins (1990/1), p. 82, note 14: 'Writers of the rationalistic persuasion fail to see someone's conformity in act to his best considered finding as the hard-won achievement that it is. They fail to see it as something not to be taken for granted.'

38 For this term see Smith (1986), p. 289: 'A moral realist is one who holds that certain moral judgements, valuations of the form "x is good", say, are correct, and that their correctness consists in the fact that they describe the way the world is (or, perhaps, the way the world vis-a-vis the judger is); in this case, correctness requires that x has the property of moral goodness. An irrealist is one who denies this.'

39 Cf. Rorty, R. (1982), p. 127: 'Consider the following examples: "2 plus 2 is 4"; "Holmes lived in Baker Street"; "Henry James was born in America"; "There ought to be more love in the world"; "Vermeer's straightforward use of light is more successful than La Tour's trickery". These are all warranted assertions, and all true in exactly the same sense. On this view, the notion of "reference", as a relation satisfying (1) [sc. 'Whatever is referred to must exist'], is pointless, a philosopher's invention. All we need is the commonsensical notion of "talking about", where the criterion for what a statement is "about" is just whatever its utterer "has in mind" – that is, whatever he *thinks* he's talking about.'

40 For what it is worth, the metaphysical attitude of the present paper has been 'quietist' in the sense canvassed by Crispin Wright ((1992), ch. 6).

41 Cf. Wittgenstein (1967), Pt II, p. 218. Stewart Candlish ((1991), p. 224), commenting on the radicalism of Wittgenstein's later discussions of the will, notes that 'the impression that particular actions are *essentially* voluntary is very deep-rooted in our thinking. It can seem just inconceivable that our voluntary movements do not have some special origin which gives them their voluntary character . . .' In so far as the same is true of our *seriously intended* judgements of value (i.e. in so far as it seems inconceivable that they do not have some special origin which gives them their 'serious' character), the same philosophical remedy is indicated: 'seriousness' should be seen as belonging to an act of judgement (viewed, now, under the aspect of linguistic performance) not in isolation but in virtue of its place in a behavioural pattern or *Gestalt*.

42 Again, though, not on the basis of *isolated* behavioural or psychological episodes. Cf. C. C. W. Taylor ((1980), p. 516) on the truth-conditions of 'A ranks the doing of x by him on this occasion higher than he ranks the doing of y by him on this occasion', and (analogously) of 'A ranks the doing of actions of type E higher than he ranks the doing of actions of type F'. (He thinks the truth of such propositions is 'loosely linked, in the way characteristic of cluster-concepts, to the satisfaction of an open disjunction of conditions'.)

43 Habermas (1987), p. 204. In the end, I think Habermas is right not to
capitulate to Rorty's irony about 'the need for a distinction between "responsible" and "irresponsible" discourse – that need to distinguish sharply between
science and poetry which makes us distinctively Western' ((Rorty 1982),
p. 132).
44 Bradley (1914), pp. 57–64.
45 Bradley's examples ((1914), p. 59; p. 62, note 2).

7

Incontinence and Practical Wisdom in Aristotle

John McDowell

1. David Wiggins has written important and deeply perceptive works in an impressive array of fields. In this paper, I shall try to show my admiration and affection for this best of teachers and colleagues by airing one of my few disagreements with him. I hope this will not seem strange; it should not seem strange to anyone who knows how philosophy proceeds.

Wiggins has written illuminatingly on Aristotle's understanding of practical thinking, and, although only a couple of his papers deal directly with Aristotelian texts, an Aristotelian spirit informs his own conception of practical reason. But although Wiggins applauds and exploits Aristotle's reflections about the intellectual excellence that is operative when excellence of character is put into practice, he sees just about nothing to be said for Aristotle's treatment of cases where there is an approximation to the thought that would find expression in virtuous behaviour, but that thought is not realized in action: cases of *akrasia* (incontinence).[1] In Wiggins's view, this is a missed opportunity for a satisfying completion of the Aristotelian picture: Aristotle is equipped to be aware that we can acknowledge our rationality without playing down the possibly recalcitrant elements in our make-up as rational animals, but here he lapses into a primitive 'Socratic' faith in the controlling power of the intellect.

I think this criticism rests on a rare failure of charity. We can find Aristotle's picture of *akrasia* attractive without losing the insights that drive Wiggins's negative estimate of it.

2. When we consider thinking directed at what to do in general, and its expression in behaviour, realism dictates a healthy sense of how human beings can fail to live up to the results of their practical intelligence. This is where Wiggins begins his discussion of 'weakness of will'.

The first aim of practical thought is to equip a prospective agent with a focused awareness of which considerations speak rationally for or against the options he contemplates, and with what force. Practical thought may or may not resolve the reasons that come to its notice into a conclusion to the effect that one thing rather than another is, all things considered, the thing to do. But even when practical intelligence cannot effect such a resolution, it aims at a decision to do something that is backed by a reason for doing that.

Now even when practical thought does arrive at a view of how the balance of the reasons points, it is another question whether the agent will act on that verdict. No doubt the very idea of lively awareness that reason speaks in favour of some action would lose its intelligibility if we tried to abstract it away from the idea of a propensity, at least, to be motivationally swayed by that thought. But why should we expect a guarantee that when different motivational propensities are in the offing, associated with reasons that point in different directions, thought's resolution of the competing reasons into a judgement as to where the weight of the reasons lies – if thought manages such a thing – will ensure that a corresponding motivational force beats out all competitors for control of the agent's behaviour? Still less does it seem realistic to expect decision, the product of practical thought, to eliminate the possibility that a competing motivation might control action in the other sort of case, where thought has to settle for a decision to follow one set of rational considerations rather than others without managing an 'all things considered' judgement. Thus: even though the very idea of thought directed at action requires more than merely external connection to motivational susceptibilities, it shows a strange confidence in the intellect's capacity to control the life of an intelligent animal – of which much else is true besides that it is intelligent – if someone supposes that the internal connections are perfectly rigid, so that an agent's best judgement as to how the reasons lie, or his decision in the absence of such a judgement to follow one set of reasons rather than another, is sure to reach expression in action.

All this is simply accentuated if there is a temporal gap between decision and action. Considerations that shone vividly for prior thought may lose motivational efficacy when the time comes to put a decision into effect.

It seems common sense, then, to suppose that even the perfect operation of a perfectly tuned practical intelligence is not enough to ensure that action will accord with its results. If an agent is to act in accordance with his own best judgement, or to execute a reasoned decision made in the absence of a best judgement, he needs executive virtues like firmness of will. (That is to be distinguished from pigheadedness in the face of possible grounds for rethinking one's decision.)

Now consider Aristotle's characterization of *akrasia* in *Nicomachean Ethics* VII. 3. As he remarks (1147b13–17), it concedes a great deal to Socrates' reported doctrine that there can be no such phenomenon. Aristotle allows for incontinence only where something has gone wrong with the agent's practical thinking. He does not acknowledge cases where the thinking is in good order, but there is a failure of executive excellence between the thinking and the action it endorses. Indeed the opposite condition, continence (*enkrateia*), figures in Aristotle not as an executive virtue that anyone needs, however excellent the disposition and activity of his practical intellect, but, like incontinence, as a falling short of true virtue: that is, a falling short of temperance, for the paradigmatic cases of continence and incontinence. So far from needing what Aristotle discusses under the head of continence, a temperate person does not have the bad appetites that a continent person has to strain to keep unsatisfied (1151b32–1152a3).

Aristotle makes great contributions to our understanding of practical reasoning. But he does not complete his reflections by explicitly noting the space between thought and action, and the consequent need for executive virtues to ensure that excellent deliberation finds expression in behaviour. This is the ground for Wiggins's disappointment with what Aristotle says about incontinence.

3. In the account of incontinence that figures in the central sections of VII. 3 (1147a24–b5), Aristotle seems to be aiming to represent a state of motivational conflict. The conflict lies in the opposition between a practical syllogism not acted on, capturing the thought that would be operative in the behaviour of a temperate person placed as the incontinent person is, and the appetite, embodying a motivationally active thought of pleasure, that is actually operative in the behaviour of the incontinent person (1147a35–b3).

But Wiggins reads the remarks with which Aristotle introduces this passage in such a way that they rule out such conflict. The result is that Aristotle looks seriously confused. Wiggins finds in the introductory remarks a claim that when the premises of a behaviour-directed syllogism are put together in the mind, the action they enjoin follows of necessity. If this were Aristotle's view, he would be committed to supposing that, since the action (abstention) that would be characteristic of a temperate person is not forthcoming from a person who displays incontinence, the thought (the practical syllogizing) that would be characteristic of a temperate person cannot be in the person's mind either. The premises can be

there, but only separately, not understood together in their rational
bearing on what the agent is to do. As Wiggins remarks (p. 250), this
would abolish the struggle that Aristotle elsewhere associates with incontinence.

In Wiggins's 'translation-cum-paraphrase', the relevant lines
(1147a25–8) go like this (pp. 248–9):

> The one premise [the major] is universal, the other premise is concerned
> with the particular facts, which are the kind of thing to fall within the
> province of perception. When a single proposition results from the two
> premises, then [in the case of scientific or deductive reasoning] the soul
> must of necessity affirm the conclusion; while in the practical sphere it
> must of necessity act.

But as the brackets signal, the allusion to scientific or deductive reasoning is an importation; and 'in the practical sphere' may be a mistransla-
tion.

What Aristotle actually says, in the second sentence here paraphrased,
is this:

> When a single opinion results from them, there is a necessity that the soul
> in one kind of case [or perhaps: at once][2] affirm the conclusion, and, in the
> case of premises concerned with production, that it immediately act.

Wiggins's reading finds here a contrast between theoretical reasoning,
where the result is an affirmation by the soul, and practical reasoning,
where the result is an action. But there is no explicit allusion to theoretical reasoning. (Indeed, the announced overall topic is reasoning that
combines universal and particular premises, and Aristotle's official account of theoretical reasoning does not even accommodate this structure.) Moreover, 'in the case of premises concerned with production' (*en
de tais poiêtikais*: not *praktikais*) is strange wording for practical reasoning
in a general sense, behaviour-directed thinking of any kind, set in contrast with theoretical reasoning. This wording might do in an informal
and context-free mention of practical as opposed to theoretical thinking.
But here, soon after 1139b1–4 and 1140b6–7, it is more naturally taken
as a reminder of the contrast, *within the sphere of the practical in a general
sense*, between production (*poiêsis*) and action in a strict sense (*praxis*). In
that case the passage restricts the claim that action (in the general sense)
must ensue to one kind of behaviour-directed thinking, the productive,
and allows other cases *of behaviour-directed thinking* where the most that
is necessary if the premises are put together is an affirmation.

Thought directed towards production posits an end that is instrumentally remote from anything the agent can do here and now, and seeks a means. It may select among means that are merely practicable, on the basis of ease of achievement and other desiderata (1112b16–17). No doubt practical thinking can solve a problem of this kind without issuing in the action that constitutes the solution. But this can happen only if the agent decides after all not to pursue the posited end. Perhaps he revises his view of its desirability when he realizes what it will cost to achieve it. This decision revokes the major premise of the reasoning, that such-and-such is to be achieved. If, however, the elements of the reasoning stay in place, then the agent's motivational orientation, for purposes of this reasoning, is simply defined by the posited end. In that case, barring phenomena like paralysis or forcible prevention, the completion of a piece of practical thinking of this kind cannot but lead to realization in action. If what happens is under the sway of the agent's motivations at all, it will be controlled by the nisus towards the posited end; if considerations that appeal to some other motivation are allowed any relevance, besides the subordinate one of selecting among different ways of satisfying the primary motivation, that just means that the terms of the agent's practical problem are not as given by the elements of the productive deliberation.[3]

On this reading of what Aristotle means when he says that certain completed reasonings issue of necessity in action, the remark reflects no general prejudice about the efficacy of practical intelligence. Aristotle does not claim, implausibly, that when any behaviour-directed thought is brought to completion, it necessarily finds realization in action. His thesis simply registers, innocuously, that in deliberation directed to a problem of production, the very terms in which the predicament is conceived eliminate all motivations other than pursuit of the posited end.

But it is not problems of production that are solved by the intellectual excellence operative in acts of virtue. For this case, all that Aristotle's remark insists on is that if the premises of the syllogism that a virtuous person would act on are put together in an agent's mind, there must be an affirmation of the conclusion. This precisely leaves room for the premises to be put together without issuing in appropriate action. And Aristotle exploits this later in the central passage of VII.3. In setting out the opposition between the syllogism of temperance and the incontinently felt appetite, he says (1147a34): 'the former says to avoid this, but the appetite drives'. Strictly speaking, 'the former' should refer to the universal premise that prevents tasting, mentioned at 1147a31–2. But a universal premise can 'say to avoid *this*' only if what it says is mediated by a minor premise, directing the universal prohibition at a particular object.

So it is really the whole syllogism that Aristotle must mean to describe as 'saying to avoid this'. Contrary to Wiggins's reading, we can see the point of the introductory remarks as being precisely to make room for syllogisms that do such saying (which requires that the premises are present and put together), but get no further than that towards realization in action.

4. But this reinterpretation at most removes what looks, in Wiggins's picture of Aristotle, like a blemish of exposition; it does not address the central issue. Given this reading, Wiggins is wrong to suppose that Aristotle commits himself to a doctrine that practical thought of necessity achieves realization in action, a doctrine that would have the effect of eliminating any possibility of weak *akrasia* (as opposed to the rather uninteresting impetuous variety: 1150b19–22). Still, Aristotle does take it that, if the premises of the syllogism of temperance are put together in the mind of an agent who nevertheless pursues some pleasure that he should not pursue, that calls for special explanation. The drift of VII.3 seems to be that something must have gone wrong with the agent's purchase on the minor premise of virtue's syllogism, so that although the agent in a way sees things as a temperate person would, the match between the relevant part of his practical thought and that of a temperate person is imperfect. If the match in thought were perfect, there would also be a match in behaviour. We need not saddle Aristotle with a doctrine that would commit him to concluding, from the failure of match in behaviour, that the premises of the syllogism of temperance can be present only in blank separation from one another, so that there is no room even for an approximation to a match in respect of the practical conclusion that a temperate person would draw. But Aristotle still implies that in cases of weakness there can be at most an approximation to such a match; and in Wiggins's view this is evidently an insufficient acknowledgement of the possibilities of failure to put thought into practice:

> [T]he *Nicomachean Ethics* . . . describes, elucidates, and amplifies the actual concerns of human life, and makes transparent to theory the way in which these concerns necessitate, where they do necessitate, the actions or decisions in which they issue. Those who find that this is enough in practice to retain their interest in the subject will discover that they can drop Aristotle's doctrine of the akrates' ignorance of the minor premise . . . (p. 261).

'Ignorance of the minor premise' may need to be nuanced, if we are to avoid all risk of overstating what Aristotle envisages. (Aristotle indeed speaks of ignorance, for instance at 1147b6, but it is clear that he is straining to avoid alleging an outright failure of grasp.) But no toning down, so long as it leaves in place the basic idea that there is some breakdown in the incontinent person's practical thinking, will help to meet Wiggins's point. Wiggins's idea is that Aristotle ought to have allowed that even perfectly executed practical thinking may need executive virtues if it is to show itself in action; the thought alone does not suffice. In that case it cannot be correct to infer a defectiveness in thinking (whether we call it 'ignorance' or not) from a defectiveness in behaviour.

I think it is quite wrong to object to Aristotle on these grounds, and the materials for seeing that it is wrong are all in Wiggins's paper.

5. The essential thing is to realize that Aristotle's aim in connection with *akrasia* is to characterize a person whose practical thought comes as close as possible, consistently with a failure of action, to matching the practical thought, not of a possessor of just any kind of practically oriented intellectual excellence, but specifically of a person who has 'practical wisdom' (*phronêsis*). Aristotle's conception of the relations between practical wisdom, continence, and incontinence reflects a deeply attractive view of the efficacy of a quite specific kind of practical thinking, when present in its perfect or ideal form. There is no implication that practical deliberation generally, regardless of its type, flows smoothy into action without any need for executive virtues: that is, no unrealistic conviction of the power of practical thought in general to eliminate recalcitrant motivations and control action. This undercuts the basis for Wiggins's disappointment.

Practical wisdom is the intellectual excellence that is operative in the behaviour of a fully-fledged possessor of virtue of character, a possessor of virtue of character in the strict sense (see VI.13). It is a correct conception of the end of human action (1142b31–3). Aristotle does not believe that such a conception can be spelled out in general rules of conduct (1094b11–27, 1109b12–23). We cannot encapsulate the content of practical wisdom in a general formula that could be abstracted away from the concrete details of life. A correct conception of the end is accordingly inseparable from a kind of perception (1142a23–30, 1143a5–b5), which Wiggins helpfully glosses as 'situational appreciation':[4] a capacity to discern which of the potentially action-inviting features of a situation is the one that should be allowed to call into operation one of the standing concerns whose being put into practice on the appropriate occasions constitutes living out a correct conception of the sort of life a human being should live.

Now consider a situation that calls for the most striking sort of exercise of temperance, namely abstaining from an available but excessive bodily pleasure. That the pleasure is available is within the awareness of a temperate person no less than anyone else. And facts of that shape, that there is an opportunity for pleasure, can engage a motivational suscepti-bility that is one of the standing concerns of a virtuous person. (Too little interest in the pleasures of appetite is a defect of character: see NE III.11.) But on this occasion what matters about the situation, as the practically wise person correctly sees it, is not that the pleasure is there to be had, but whatever it is that marks out this potential pleasure as excessive.

By separating temperance from continence as he does, Aristotle im-plies a picture on these lines: on an occasion like this, what is charac-teristic of a practically wise person, which a possessor of temperance in the strict sense must be, is not simply that he counts as irrelevant to the question what to do an instance of a kind of consideration (the potential for pleasure) that is relevant to that question in other circumstances, but that his counting it is irrelevant is completely realized in how his motiva-tional make-up responds to the situation. It shows in his feeling no appetitive pull towards the potential pleasure. So he stands in sharp contrast with people who are continent or (weakly) incontinent. Such people in such a situation would in a way share the practically wise person's view of the status of the opportunity for pleasure as a candidate reason for acting, namely that it counts for nothing in the face of the fact that the pleasure is excessive. But in them the opportunity for pleasure would trigger an appetite, which would need to be overcome to yield continent behaviour, and would issue in incontinent behaviour if not overcome. Fully-fledged practical wisdom is a 'situational appreciation' that not only singles out just the right one of the potentially action-invit-ing features of a predicament, but does so in such a way that none of the agent's motivational energy is enticed into operation by any of the others; he has no errant impulses that threaten to lead him astray, so that he would be at best continent even if he managed to avoid being led astray. His 'situational appreciation' is such as to insulate the attractions of competing courses of action from generating actual urges to pursue them.

This picture simply requires the thesis that a person who is continent or incontinent can achieve at most an imperfect approximation to the 'situational appreciation' of a person who is temperate in the strict sense, in a situation where temperance requires refraining from an opportunity for pleasure. The picture is that full achievement of that 'situational appreciation' would prevent the attractions of competing courses from actually exerting any motivational force. If the attractions of competing courses do exert a motivational force, as they do in cases of incontinence or continence, it follows that the 'situational appreciation' that is characteristic of fully-fledged practical wisdom cannot have been fully achieved. The most we can find in such cases is something less: something that yields a similar selection of what matters about the situation, but without the singleness of motivation that fully-fledged practical wisdom would achieve.

There need be no implication that the attractiveness of the competing course goes dim, in the view of the situation that the practically wise person achieves. The pleasure is there to be had, by the practically wise person no less than by anyone else.[5] He can be completely aware of the attractiveness of the competing course; it is just that he is not attracted by it.

If the course that is not to be followed retains its attractiveness, there is nothing surprising in the fact that ordinarily 'good' people are liable to feel an appetitive attraction towards it, so that their action will be continent at best. This is especially unsurprising in the young; there must be stages in ethical upbringing at which it is too soon to hope that a correct conception of how to live can have been perfectly ingrained into someone's motivational make-up, in the way that is characteristic of fully-fledged practical wisdom.

The picture leaves this kind of lapse looking only natural. No thesis of Aristotle's clashes with a common-sense recognition that most people do not achieve the singleness of motivational focus that figures in his picture of the ideal. What he insists is that where such singleness of motivational focus is not achieved, there cannot be a perfect cognitive match with the ideal case. But this leaves plenty of room for approximations to the ideal, falling short of the unobstructed transition to action that the ideal would guarantee: cases in which the undimmed attractiveness of the course that, with his approximation to practical wisdom, the agent sees is not to be followed generates a felt temptation to follow it. Aristotle's picture leaves plenty of room for cases where continence might figure, not exactly as an executive *virtue*, but as an executive disposition that is required if the agent is to act as, in a way, he realizes he should: this realization being, from the terms of the case, less perfectly meshed with his motivational susceptibilities than in the ideal case.

6. Wiggins appreciates the beauty of this conception of practical wisdom. As he puts it, someone who fully appreciated the end that practical wisdom has in view would find the associated reasons for acting '*distinctively compelling*' (p. 254). It would be impossible to make sense of someone's fully possessing a practical understanding so conceived, and

grasping what it dictates in a particular situation, but nevertheless allowing himself to be moved by the attractiveness of some different course of
action.

But this special compellingness figures in Wiggins's treatment of Aristotle only by way of diagnosis of a supposed failure on Aristotle's part to
leave *any* room for gaps between fully achieved results of practical
thinking and action in accordance with those results. Wiggins's Aristotle
extrapolates from the distinctive compellingness of the considerations
that appeal to practical wisdom in particular, to the idea that *any* fully
achieved conclusion of practical thought must flow smoothly into action
without any need for executive virtues.

But there is no need to saddle Aristotle with this extrapolation. Aristotle's point about *akrasia* need not be anything over and above a corollary of the fact that he credits the conclusions of practical wisdom, in
particular, with that distinctive compellingness. This leaves him no option but to suppose that if someone in a way achieves one of those
conclusions but does not act accordingly, what he achieves can be at
most a flawed approximation to the conclusion. But that implies nothing
to the detriment of the picture that Wiggins gives, and supposes that
Aristotle is committed to rejecting, of the gaps between practical thought
in general and action. Aristotle does not botch the general case, as
opposed to the special case of practical wisdom, as Wiggins suggests. The
general case is simply off-stage as far as Aristotle is concerned; his
interest is in the special case, and there is no particular reason for him to
bother with the general case at all.

In 'Deliberation and Practical Reason', Wiggins extracts a convincing
picture of practical reason in general, at least outside its merely technical
employment, from things Aristotle says about the operation of practical
wisdom. Here extrapolation to the general case yields treasure. But that
should not make us forget that it is extrapolation. Aristotle's chief concern, at least in the *Ethics*, is – as is appropriate there – with the
deliberation that is characteristic of practical wisdom; he is interested in
other manifestations of behaviour-directed intelligence only in order to
differentiate them from practical wisdom, or perhaps, in the case of
technical deliberation, in order to get as much as he can out of modelling
the operations of practical wisdom on it. We are bound to do him an
injustice if we forget the restrictedness of his topic, and read his insistence, *for that special case*, that failures in action must betray flaws in
thought to imply a denial that there is a role in the explanation of action
for anything besides the way the agent thinks – a denial of any role for
factors like firmness of resolve, in an account of how practical thought in
general flows into action.

That is just how Wiggins reads Aristotle. This shows when he writes (p. 251) of 'the distinction that Aristotle is obliged to postulate between the continent man's and the incontinent man's knowledge and perception of a situation'. Reasonably enough, Wiggins is sceptical of such a distinction: 'How . . . can it be maintained, even in the face of all the phenomenological findings, that the continent and incontinent man see different things, or *must* see things differently?' But the supposed obligation to postulate this difference is a product of not allowing Aristotle his restricted topic. From Aristotle's insistence, *for the special case of practical wisdom*, that a clear seeing of a situation in the light in which practical wisdom casts it leaves no room for defective action, Wiggins has inferred a doctrine that the quality of an agent's vision is *always* a complete explanation of how he acts. Thus, since a continent person and an incontinent person act differently, there must be a difference in how they see things. But there is no such doctrine, and no obligation to invent a cognitive difference between the continent and the incontinent person. The only cognitive difference that Aristotle is obliged to postulate is a difference between, on the one hand, a possessor of practical wisdom and, on the other, indifferently, a continent or an incontinent person, who are alike shown not to see things exactly as the practically wise person does by the fact that they feel an appetitive pull towards action other than what, as they in a way realize, virtue requires. Once we have in view the lapse in vision that allows conflicting motivations to be felt, so that the best that can be achieved is continence, it is quite another matter, on which Aristotle leaves his options open, what determines whether the agent acts continently or incontinently.

7.   The end of human action, of which practical wisdom is a correct conception, is what Aristotle also refers to as 'the good and the chief good' (1094a22) and identifies, in Book I of *Nicomachean Ethics*, with *eudaimonia*: that is, living well and doing well (1095a14–20). Modern commentators often suppose that Aristotle conceives this end of living well in terms of the optimal combination of a bundle of intrinsic goods, marked out as such by their natural appeal to human beings. This style of reading is partly sustained by Aristotle's claim that *eudaimonia* is self-sufficient (1097b6–20), in the sense that 'on its own it makes life worthy of going in for and lacking in nothing' (1097b14–15); this is read as saying that nothing that human beings are naturally disposed to find worth pursuing can be missing from a life of *eudaimonia*. It is also partly sustained by a wish to equip Aristotle with a way to establish the pursuit-worthiness of a life of virtue from first principles, by claiming that it optimally secures what human beings are anyway bound to regard as

worth securing, without any need for this justification of virtue to exploit the tendencies to delight in virtuous activity as such that the members of Aristotle's audience have acquired in their ethical education (see 1104b3–13, 1095b4–6).

On this sort of reading, the thesis that *eudaimonia* is self-sufficient would risk making it especially difficult to understand how someone could act contrary to what he sees that *eudaimonia* requires, in order to enjoy physical pleasure. This would be to pursue something that would have to be an element in the bundle of goods that is supposedly all that can make life worth living at all, but at the known expense of a better arrangement of that very bundle of goods. The conception of practical reason that is operative here risks looking like a less crude version of the conception that, in the closing pages of Plato's *Protagoras*, serves to obliterate the very possibility of acting contrary to knowledge of how the reasons for acting lie.

But we should not take the claim of self-sufficiency like this. No doubt the valuations of actions that are characteristic of the propensity to delight in virtuous activity for its own sake cannot simply cut loose from dispositions to find things worth pursuing that human beings have any-way, independently of ethical upbringing. That would make a mystery of how ethical upbringing, whose prospects must be conditioned by the prior nature of its recipients, can impart such a scheme of values. But it does not follow that the scheme of values that is characteristic of delight-ing in virtuous activity for its own sake must be a construct out of the idea of an optimal combination of goods that naturally appeal to human beings as such, so that the genuine pursuit-worthiness of such activity can be defended as conducive to the best arrangement of those goods. These acquired values can have a sort of autonomy with respect to what naturally appeals to human beings. And the claim that *eudaimonia* is self-sufficient can be read in terms of standards for pursuit-worthiness set by these acquired values. So, as Wiggins puts it (p. 260):

> In the definition of self-sufficiency, we need not take 'lacking in nothing' to mean 'lacking in nothing at all that would be found valuable by anybody pursuing whatever course', only 'lacking in nothing that a man who had chosen the great good of eudaimonia would regard as worth bothering with'.

This takes us completely away from the idea that the attractiveness of the course that the incontinent person pursues is merely an inferior quantity of some single kind of attractiveness, of which the virtuous action pos-sesses a superior quantity. It allows us to see that the incontinent person can be tempted by a 'peculiar or distinctive charm' in the course he follows: something that cannot be regarded as merely a smaller amount of the very same kind of worth-whileness that he denies himself when he declines the virtuous action. This rejection of what Wiggins calls 'the principle of compensation in kind' (pp. 259–60) is essential if we are to make room for a common-sense picture of incontinence, a picture that is immune to the difficulties concocted in the *Protagoras* passage.[6]

But this leaves untouched the thesis that incontinence is possible only on the basis of a flawed approximation to the view of a situation that practical wisdom would achieve. What dictates that thesis is the distinctive compellingness of the verdicts of practical wisdom; the argument needs no help from the principle of compensation in kind. Wiggins suggests that when we see our way past the difficulties that the *Protagoras* passage extracts from an unrealistically monolithic conception of reasons for acting, we thereby see how we can 'drop Aristotle's doctrine of the akrates' ignorance of the minor premise' (p. 261, already quoted above). But if we allow Aristotle the restricted scope of his doctrine, this rebuke stands revealed as misplaced.

8.   Wiggins is admirably hostile towards pictures of practical reasoning in terms of weighing quantities of a homogeneously conceived worth-whileness. But I think he understates the distance between this sort of thing and Aristotle's conception of deliberation with a view to *eudaimonia*. He takes Aristotle to hold that

> wherever a man has to act, he can subsume the question at issue under the question of eudaimonia and discern which course of action is better from that point of view (p. 258).

He bases this on *De Anima* 434a5–10, which he paraphrases like this:

> Sensory imagination is found in other animals but deliberative imagination only in those which have reason. For whether one shall do this thing or do that thing it is the work of reason to decide. And such reason necessarily implies the power of measurement by a single standard. For what one pursues is the greater good. So a rational animal is one with the power to arbitrate between diverse appearances of what is good and integrate the findings into a unitary practical conception.

But there are two things wrong with this as a basis for the attribution.

First, the passage does not say that a rational animal can *always* integrate its conceptions of the apparent good, in a given situation, into a unified practical verdict, but just that rational animals can do that (perhaps only in some cases), whereas non-rational animals cannot. The passage is consistent with supposing that some situations may defeat the integrative efforts of practical reason. This is a good thing. As Wiggins reads him, Aristotle would here be casting doubt on the very possibility of tragic predicaments.

Second, the passage does not mention *eudaimonia*, and I doubt that that is its topic. This passage is about practical rationality in general, and I have already suggested that we should distance that from the kind of susceptibility to reasons that is characteristic of practical wisdom in particular. When a situation calling for temperance is seen in terms of doing well, the agent's decision what to do does not supervene on a judgement that sets one apparent good, seen as greater, against another, seen as smaller. The pleasure promised by the course that the agent realizes is not to be pursued is recognized, indeed, as an instance of something that is in general a good. But the prospect of pleasure is not taken to be, here and now, a good, on the dimension of goodness marked out by the idea of *eudaimonia*, but a smaller one than the virtuous action; it is not taken to tell in favour of pursuing the pleasure, by the lights of *eudaimonia*, but more weakly than the reasons for abstention. Rather, by the lights of *eudaimonia*, the prospect of pleasure does not speak at all in favour of pursuing it in these circumstances.

If we conceive the correct practical verdict, on which the incontinent person fails to act, as based on allowing the apparent good constituted by the promise of pleasure to tell in favour of pursuing the pleasure, but not as strongly as the considerations that speak in favour of abstention, we make it harder to comprehend incontinence. On this picture, the attractiveness of the promised pleasure is allowed to count towards the agent's practical judgement; it is simply outweighed. On the different picture I am urging, that attractiveness is not conceded any relevance to the question what to do, and it becomes easier to understand how, denied any bearing on the question of reason, it should insist on making itself felt by triggering an appetite.

9. As I have remarked, Aristotle notes a convergence between the view of incontinence that he is led to and the view that Socrates took (1147b14–15). This convergence encapsulates Wiggins's complaint (p. 251):

> When what I might almost venture to call a more Aristotelian account than Aristotle's promises to be possible . . . , why did Aristotle give such a Socratic account of the phenomena of weakness?

Calling Aristotle's account 'Socratic' means that it is too optimistic about the power of practical thought to unify motivational direction, and about the control of practical thought over what people do.

I have urged, however, that Aristotle's concern in his discussion of *akrasia* is exclusively with a special kind of action-directed thought, whose perfect operation Aristotle has good reasons for associating with a perfection of moulded character that leaves no room for the agent to be pulled by conflicting motivations. There is no slighting the way reasons for acting, in general, can resist resolution by thought into an overall verdict as to how one should act, and no slighting the way motivational propensities can resist control by thought. Even when *eudaimonia* fixes the nature of the practical attention that an agent directs at a situation, there is no assurance that his practical thinking can resolve the relevant considerations into an overall verdict: no assurance that an action is available that will count as doing well (*eu prattein*, that is, *eudaimonein*). And even where a correct conception of *eudaimonia* does yield a clear identification of one action as doing well, Aristotle allows for cases where an agent approximates to such thinking without acting accordingly. There is no naive intellectualism here.

This raises the question whether we can exploit the coincidence with Socrates the other way round, to begin on a rehabilitation of Socrates from the common charge of unrealistic intellectualism.

It is at worst a salutary exaggeration to say that all we really *know* about Socrates – apart perhaps from something about his method – is that he propounded the famous puzzling theses: that virtue is knowledge, that no one does wrong 'voluntarily', and that virtue is one. Our best sources, the early dialogues of Plato, do not lay down slabs of moral theory; they come across, rather, as undoctrinaire explorations of those evidently dark sayings, and of obviously cognate issues such as whether and how virtue can be taught, and in what sense one has a reason for right conduct.

Many modern commentators have counted the closing argument of the *Protagoras* as authentically Socratic, not on the basis of any compelling textual ground, but rather because it fits a philosophical reconstruction: this is supposed to be the sort of thing Socrates *must* have thought if he was to connect knowledge with virtuous action as he seems to have done. The result is to saddle Socrates with a pitifully unrealistic picture of the connection between reason and motivation.[7] But if I am right about Aristotle, who notes his own convergence with Socrates, there is no 'must' about it.

In that case, what is going on in the *Protagoras* argument?

The apparently Socratic idea that virtue is a kind of knowledge that ensures living well can be interpreted in two contrasting ways. The first we can associate with the sophists (at least as Plato pictures them). According to this interpretation, the advantages that virtue brings are recognizable as such independently of the special propensities to value and disvalue courses of conduct that are acquired in ethical upbringing, so that a claim to be able to teach virtue holds out a promise of something that anyone, whether virtuous or not, will count as living well. The second is the one that I believe we should associate with Socrates. According to this interpretation, the attractions of a virtuous life are real, but recognizable only from within a commitment to that life. What we find in the *Protagoras* is a version of the first of these. At the end of the dialogue (361a3–c2), Socrates suggests that he and Protagoras have changed places; we can take this to tell us, almost in so many words, that the position propounded in the closing argument is not the authentic Socratic view, but a sophistic travesty of it.[8]

Perhaps what Aristotle does in his discussion of practical wisdom and its expression in action is simply to recapture what Socrates was really driving at. If I am right about Aristotle, this can liberate Socratic moral psychology from the strange want of realism that much recent commentary has found in it.

NOTES

1 See 'Weakness of Will, Commensurability, and the Objects of Deliberation and Desire', as reprinted (with revisions) in Wiggins (1987a), pp. 239–67. Unless otherwise stated, all subsequent page references are to this paper.

2 Sir David Ross (Aristotle (1954)) translates '*entha men*' by 'in one type of case', and glosses this as an allusion to scientific reasoning. This matches Wiggins's interpretation. The suggestion that '*entha*' means 'at once' is due to Anthony Kenny (1966), pp. 163–84; and again in (1979), p. 157. It is not crucial to decide between these: contrary to what Kenny implies, we can take the structure, with Ross, to be 'in one kind of case . . . in another kind of case . . .' without saddling ourselves with what Kenny wants to avoid, 'an irrelevant contrast between theoretical and practical reasoning'. On Ross's translation of '*entha*', everything turns on what the contrast between the two kinds of case is supposed to be; and Aristotle's specification of the second case casts doubt on the Ross/Wiggins gloss on the first (see the text below).

3 Admittedly the example Aristotle offers, to illustrate his claim about the case in which action must follow (1147a29–31), is (to say the least) not a clear case of a syllogism of production. But the point of singling out production here is not that the posited end is instrumentally, as opposed to specificatorily, remote from what the agent can immediately do, but rather that, if a practical problem is of the productive kind, the agent's motivational stance, for the problem's purposes, is defined by the posited end. What matters is not the mode of

remoteness of the end from the agent's immediate possibilities of action, but the fact that the major premise can appropriately contain 'must', whereas if a major premise says merely that something is good, we do not need to regard it as revoked if the agent ends up pursuing some different good. The point about production is that productive deliberation, by its mode of focus on an end, defines a deliberative situation in such a way that a 'must' is appropriate in the major premise. That *is* exemplified in Aristotle's illustrative example.

4 See 'Deliberation and Practical Reason' in Wiggins (1987a), p. 231. My sketch of how practical wisdom should be conceived closely follows that beautiful paper; I want to bring out how easily it can be separated from what Wiggins takes to be its natural continuation, his negative evaluation of Aristotle's treatment of *akrasia*.

5 At 1151b34–1152a2–3, Aristotle says: 'Both the continent person and the temperate person are such as to do nothing contrary to the *logos* on account of bodily pleasures, but one of them has and the other does not have bad appetites, and the latter is such as not to be pleased contrary to the *logos*, whereas the former is such as to be pleased but not such as to be led.' The third part of this three-part comparison restates the claim that the temperate person, unlike the continent person, lacks the bad appetites that respond to opportunities for pleasure that are not to be pursued. He lacks any active motivation that would be gratified by pursuing such a pleasure, so there is nothing to make it true that he would take pleasure in that action. But this is surely consistent with supposing that the physical pleasures of such action are there to be had, for him as much as for anyone. It seems ridiculous to suppose that a temperate person is such as simply not to feel the physical pleasures of, say, illicit sex. There is a difficulty about imagining him engaging in such activity, and that is a way of putting Aristotle's point here. But if we contrive to imagine that, what we contemplate is a possible world in which he feels those pleasures, though no doubt he is not pleased to be doing so. David Pears offers a different reading of this passage ((1978) p. 276, and (1980), p. 173); but Pears's reading is based on a gratuitously assumed connection between potential feelings of physical pleasure and awareness of opportunities for physical pleasure, on the one hand, and felt appetites, on the other.

6 Wiggins suggests (p. 260) that Aristotle may have 'some occasional slight tendency to believe something rather like the principle of compensation in kind'. But this is gratuitous. Nothing like the principle is needed in order to make sense of Aristotle's taking the line he does about incontinence. The Aristotelian thesis (see for instance *De Anima* 433b8–10) that 'even the purely pleasurable appears to us under the aspect of good', which Wiggins cites as perhaps resting on the principle, simply says, rightly, that pleasurableness appears as a reason for acting, something to be said in favour of courses of action that promise it. The idea of apparent goods no more implies the sort of homogeneity that the principle affirms than does the idea of reasons for acting.

7 In Terence Irwin's version (1977), the picture purports to depict human beings as they are. In Martha C. Nussbaum's variant (1986), the picture depicts how human beings should aim to be, in order to allow reason a

prospect of carrying them safely through life. Nussbaum's Socrates is not blind to plain facts as Irwin's Socrates is, but just as unrealistic, though in a different way. Both versions leave Aristotle's 'Socraticism' quite mysterious.

8 This undercuts Gregory Vlastos's suggestion ((1956), p. xl; cited by Nussbaum (1986), p. 451) that the argument is likely to be authentically Socratic, since it argues to a Socratic conclusion. It is questionable whether the conclusion is Socratic, even though the words that express it can also express a Socratic thought.

8

Naturalism and Non-Naturalism in Ethics

Roger Crisp

The truth is that the scientific way of looking at a fact is not the way to look at it as a miracle.

Wittgenstein, 'A Lecture on Ethics'

1. In his well-known book on ethics, John Mackie put especially clearly a long-standing objection to the view that the world contains what he called 'objective values'.[1] The objectivist – the evaluative realist – is committed to something like Platonic Forms, in the sense that goods must instantiate 'to-be-pursuedness', and wrongs 'not-to-be-doneness'. And to explain how we detect such dimly understood properties, the objectivist can appeal only to the yet more obscure notion of intuition.

Mackie accepts that moral phenomenology is problematic for his view. It does capture an important aspect of the appearances to say that the action of the hoodlums we catch setting fire to a cat somehow has 'not-to-be-doneness built into it', and that we can see this.[2] But to take the phenomenology as veridical, Mackie believes, would commit us to too much. His suggestion, of course, is that we understand ourselves to be in systematic error, and that we replace the notion of moral qualities in our explanations with that of a subjective response causally related to certain natural features.

John McDowell has shown how much of the attraction of Mackie's proposal lies in its enabling us to retain what might be called the

This essay is dedicated to David Wiggins with affection, admiration and gratitude. I wish to thank the following for extremely helpful comments on previous drafts: the editors, William Child, Strefan Fauble, James Griffin, Brad Hooker, Martha Klein, Michael Martin, Andrew Mason, Andrew Moore, Ingmar Persson, Paul Robinson, David Wiggins, Geoff Willis and Nick Zangwill. I should like to acknowledge the support of a British Academy Postdoctoral Research Fellowship during the writing of this paper.

'scientific' view of the world, that is, a view of the world in which *everything* is ultimately fully explicable in scientific terms.[3] The phenomenology of value, taken straightforwardly, asks us to give up that world view; the world view asks us to give up the straightforward understanding of the phenomenology. The phenomenology asks too much, since it will leave us with many more questions unanswered than it can itself answer; while the scientific world view sweetens its demand by promising – in time – to answer all questions, including that which remains after the denial of the straightforward understanding of the phenomenology.

Recently, however, several philosophers have thought it worth trying to meet both demands, interpreting the phenomenology as access to evaluative aspects of the world which can themselves be scientifically understood.[4] Realist naturalism about values in general may be taken as the thesis that genuine evaluative properties are natural properties. The most widely accepted form of ethical naturalism at present invokes the notion of moral theory: the fullest account of moral properties will emerge from our best moral theory alongside our best theory of the rest of the natural world.[5]

It might appear that this form of naturalism is inherently unstable, in that our best moral theory may conflict with our best theory of the rest of the natural world (since ethics, like everything else, will be part of the scope of such a theory). Our best moral theory may involve, for example, the postulation of supernatural properties. But, naturalists will claim, such conflict is unlikely. Because of the weight attached to the requirements of generality and simplicity put on us by the scientific world view, pretty well any moral theory which is consistent with that world view will be held to be superior to a theory not so consistent.[6]

My aim in this paper is to contrast these naturalistic views with the non-naturalistic position adopted by David Wiggins. Wiggins's account represents a third option: Mackie suggests dropping the claims of phenomenology and keeping the scientific world view; naturalists recommend keeping the claims of phenomenology, making them consistent with the scientific world view; while Wiggins proposes retaining the claims of the phenomenology as self-standing, understanding the world in terms of the autonomous discourses of ethics and a non-comprehensive science which will allow talk of moral properties without seeing them as part of its purview. My first task, then, must be to formulate a clear distinction between naturalism and non-naturalism.

2. (i) According to the scientific world view, properties which are candidates for inclusion within that view must pass the 'causal explanatory test'.[7] To pass this test, properties must play, in explanations of

phenomena that demand explanation, a role which cannot be played by certain other, perhaps 'lower-level', properties.

We might attempt, then, to differentiate between naturalism and non-naturalism using the *causal criterion* of a property's being natural. According to naturalism, explanations must employ reference to only those properties that pass the causal explanatory test, and non-natural properties will be those that fail the test. The non-naturalist position will then be that talk of these properties need not be eschewed despite their failing the test.

The problem with using the causal criterion here is that avowed non-naturalists, including Wiggins, will allow a role in causal explanation to what they take to be paradigm non-natural properties.[8] One mark of the concept of truth for Wiggins is:

> If x is true, then x will under favourable circumstances command convergence, and the best explanation of the existence of this convergence will either require the actual truth of x or be inconsistent with the denial of x.[9]

Consider the question of why I believe that a certain object has some apparently non-natural property. A non-naturalist explanation of my arriving at this belief will 'vindicate' the belief if it turns out that the most plausible account involves postulating the existence of that very property. If I believe that P. G. Wodehouse is amusing, that the conversation I had with my friend was reassuring, that the hoodlums' treatment of the cat is disgusting, the best explanation of these beliefs is more than likely to be that those objects do indeed have those properties. In these cases, things appear to me in such a way that there is 'nothing else to think', just as there is nothing else to think but that $7 + 5 = 12$, and that seven plus five's equalling twelve vindicates the judgement that it is so.[10]

(ii) An alternative approach to distinguishing the notions of natural and non-natural properties, in the hope of characterising the debate between naturalists and non-naturalists as a genuine one, involves the *discipline criterion*.[11] Wiggins refers us to G. E. Moore:

> By nature then I do mean . . . that which is the subject matter of the natural sciences, and also of psychology.[12]

Natural properties might be understood to be those properties 'dealt with' either as they stand, or in terms of other properties, by the natural sciences or psychology.[13]

Let us allow naturalists to postpone answering internal questions about the reducibility of one science to another. We might then say that their position will be at its strongest when it is based on the widest possible array of natural properties.[14] So for the sake of the present argument, we might permit further additions to the list of disciplines dealing with a single natural world, in particular, social theory and economics, which are bound to rear their heads in naturalistic accounts of justice.[15]

If the debate between naturalists and non-naturalists is to be of real philosophical interest in moral philosophy, naturalists will not attempt to characterise their position, on the basis of the discipline criterion, as the view that natural properties are those postulated in scientific explanations and that these properties are the only properties. For on this use of the discipline criterion, moral properties are not natural. The very reference to moral theory in the kind of ethical naturalism on which I have focused would be sufficient to rule out that theory as a form of naturalism.

A further option is to introduce the notion of first order theory at the start, recognizing the naturalist view that natural properties include those dealt with indirectly by the natural sciences. A moral example used by naturalists is hedonistic utilitarianism.[16] If hedonistic utilitarianism were the best moral theory, goodness would be constituted by pleasurableness, and rightness by its maximization.[17] Pleasure, and the commensurability of pleasures, we must assume to be notions dealt with directly by the natural science of psychology. It is, I presume, a consequence of this brand of naturalism that the rightness of actions will not turn out to be, say, their being performed in such a way that the agent treats humanity as an end in itself – unless that property can itself be dealt with indirectly by natural science. According to this use of the discipline criterion, then, naturalism is the view that genuine properties are, or are constituted by, natural properties, where natural properties are those identified by the discipline criterion.

There are two versions of this view. One is that what is natural is what is the actual, historical subject matter of the natural sciences. But this view places unwarranted weight on the contingent fact of what has been of interest to natural scientists. Those psychologists who have studied happiness, for example, have not generally done so out of any conviction that utilitarianism is correct. And even if that had been their motivation, it would surely be odd to allow the fact that one small group of human beings was committed to utilitarianism to confer the respectability on that theory which comes from consistency with the scientific world view.

The second version of the view is that what is natural is what is potentially the subject matter of natural science.[18] But this begs the very question to which we are seeking an answer. Again, then, we have failed to find a way of construing naturalism and non-naturalism which will provide ground for a substantive debate in moral philosophy.

(iii) The final thesis considered in the previous subsection begged the right question. What we require is some account of what is central to the scientific world view which does not rest too heavily on the history of science itself. We might expect that a scientific world view could be stated using scientific concepts. But these concepts should not be identified merely by reference to the discourse of contemporary scientists. An account of the scientific world view is best developed in terms of something like what Bernard Williams has called the 'absolute conception' of the world.[19] The aim of science is to offer a full explanation of what happens in the world in conceptual terms which are not restricted in their use to those occupying a particular local standpoint; this full explanation should include an account of why things appear as they do to those occupying such local standpoints; and scientists operate on the assumption that an explanatory account of this kind is theoretically available.

The best interpretation of ethical naturalism, then, is as the claim that moral properties – those which would be identified by the best moral theory – are natural properties – those which would be identified by the best scientific theory, and which can be described in the conceptual terms available to a being occupying some non-local point of view on the world.

Which concepts do I have in mind? Those, perhaps, which could be employed without Davidsonian interpretation through engagement.[20] Consider the following example. Assume, for the sake of my argument, that the correct moral theory consists *only* in the principle that travelling at more than 30 miles per hour is wrong. The notion of what it is to travel at this speed could plausibly be said to be graspable by some being occupying a non-local or non-anthropocentric point of view. Naturalists would argue that, were this moral theory correct, naturalism would be vindicated. Of course, the reason I chose this implausible example is that any more plausible case would immediately raise the questions of which properties can be understood from a non-local point of view, and of what kind of understanding is at stake. But I shall put those issues aside for the present in the hope that the *standpoint criterion* allows me to put naturalism in its best light, and to distinguish it from non-naturalism in such a way as to clarify what is at issue between naturalists and non-naturalists in ethics.

3. Let me now move on to examine some of the problems Wiggins finds in ethical naturalism, and to consider his own non-naturalistic and 'subjective' alternative.[21]

In Wiggins's view, naturalism cannot explain the action-guiding nature of moral judgements, that is, cannot in fact retain the straightforward understanding of moral phenomenology as a confrontation with 'to-be-pursuedness'. The reason for this – which is evident once we employ the standpoint criterion – is primarily that naturalism omits from its account of moral properties our sentiments and responses. Once they are introduced, there is no puzzle about the 'magnetism' of value terms, or values.[22] But they are not to be introduced purely as a solution to any such puzzle.

According to Wiggins, the stress he places in various but connected ways on reactions and responses entitles him to the name of 'subjectivist'. This, however, does not make him what Warren S. Quinn calls a 'mentalist', that is, a philosopher who believes that our responses to evaluative features are prior to the features themselves, and that what might be taken as a cognition of the feature is in fact something noncognitive.[23] There are two sides to Wiggins's story about the relation between properties and responses to them, and the first side can be told to discredit the mentalist.

The best hope for a subjectivist attracted by the scientific world view might be thought to be an account of the property–response relation which takes as much as it can from (one interpretation of) Hume's essay 'Of the Standard of Taste'.[24] This form of subjectivism envisages an external world which though devoid of value can be assessed by a competent judge. By honing the criteria for competence, the subjectivist can attain standards of correctness without postulating the existence of external evaluative properties.

The problem with this Humean account is, Wiggins suggests, threefold.[25] First, there is no aesthetic or moral 'sensory organ'. Second, discrimination between responses will require reference to the properties themselves. Third, there is an explanatory lack. Not only do the Humean criteria of competence appear to claim for themselves the same sort of objectivity as the pre-theoretical judgements being explained, but there is an obvious explanation available to a non-Humean of why competent judges are to be listened to, viz. they get things right. And the best account of getting things right will involve the notion of properties to which the judge is competent to respond.

Here, of course, the naturalist will claim that natural properties suffice. The heart of the debate between the naturalist and the non-naturalist, as Wiggins sees it, concerns this issue:

> Our subjective reactions to objects or events will often impose groupings upon them that have no purely naturalistic rationale . . . That, in a way, is the point of subjectivism.[26]

The illustrative example Wiggins chooses is that of 'the funny'. Since this might appear to be something of an *a posteriori* matter, a naturalist may try to disprove Wiggins's claim by attempting just what he denies is possible. Such a naturalist will not hit on just one natural property which, as a correlate to funniness, might on its own provide the basis for a full account of the funny. Rather some disjunctive set of properties will be found, such that funny properties can be said to be constituted by natural properties $p^1, p^2, p^3, \ldots p^n$.

This proposal suffers from an explanatory lack similar to that found in the Humean account.[27] The set of disjunctive properties will be, from the natural point of view, *shapeless*, in the sense that the only way of making organizational sense of it will be by seeing it in terms of the very predicate of which it purports to be an elucidation.[28] A being with no grip on the funny, but with a full grasp of the disjunctive set, would perhaps be able to identify clear cases of instantiation of one of the members of the disjunctive set. But unless the set were so large that it could no longer be said to be picking out the natural properties corresponding only to the funny, new cases would probably arise where matters were not so clear. A sense of humour is quite different from a scientific interest, and it is not obvious that the latter alone would be sufficient to enable the scientific being to go on in the right way in its employment of the evaluative terminology at home in the sphere of humour.

But even if the scientific being could go on in the right way, the problem remains. The scientific being would not see the point of the predicate, that is, it would not see objects *as funny* so much as *something-described-(who can tell why?)-as-'funny'*. This is the point Wiggins makes when he distinguishes 'the ethical or aesthetic interest in value and the theoretical cum explanatory interest in the prediction and control of natural or social processes', and when he speaks of the *engagement* required in understanding various human practices.[29] An analogy with colour is illuminating. Without visual apparatus, our scientific being could nevertheless measure the relevant subjacent properties and accurately predicate redness of objects. But it would be doing so blindly, in more than one sense.[30]

Our use of the standpoint criterion enables us to see how the point here can be put in terms of radical interpretation. Wiggins shows how noncognitivism fails to provide us with the resources to understand ourselves, emptying of content the inner view we take on our lives to the extent that it becomes incomprehensible.[31] By depriving themselves of the notions of engagement, participation and perspective, naturalists run into a similar difficulty, one which would be faced by our purely scientific being. Radical interpretation requires us to minimize inexplicable irrationality in our understanding of those interpreted.[32] The scientific being might be able to predict when we shall laugh, but it would not have any full-blooded explanation to offer of why we laugh or of why we describe what we are laughing at as funny. The objection to naturalism, then, is that it will make radical interpretation of propositional attitudes and behaviour impossible in cases where explanations invoke concepts the point of which can be seen only from an anthropocentric perspective. It is of the essence of non-naturalism, of course, that it can employ such predicates. Particularly important here are vindicatory explanations. Naturalists may claim the resources for these;[33] but in fact they are ruled out by shapelessness.

We can now see that the issue here is not *a posteriori*. The shapelessness objection in ethics is *a priori*, as would be an analogous argument in the philosophy of mind. The Davidsonian argument suggests that, because we are guided in our ascription of propositional attitudes by normative principles and holism, organizational sense of such ascriptions will not be available at the level of materialistic explanation.[34] The argument against the ethical naturalist is also *a priori*: given the essentially normative or evaluative character of moral properties, natural analogues (the sheer existence of which any moral theorist will of course permit) must be shapeless.

At this point, naturalists will attempt to deal with shapelessness. The naturalists I have been discussing do not claim that moral predicates will or even may be expunged from our explanations. Rather moral theory is allowed a self-standing role, such that genuine moral properties will be those identified by the best moral theory. In the case of the funny, genuinely funny properties are those identified by the best theory of the funny. These properties will then be identified with, that is, said to be constituted by, natural properties. There might be an analogy here with biological theory: biological properties are those identified by the best biological theory, and these can be identified with lower-level physical properties. There is no reason to assume that we would be able to grasp the organizational sense of any grouping of lower-level properties under a biological heading without reference to biological theory.

If, however, it is accepted that the best account of natural properties involves the absolute conception in something like the way I outlined above, this sort of response is not open to naturalists. It seems at least plausible to suggest that biological predicates will feature in an absolute conception. But surely moral predicates will not, partly because of the essentially normative or evaluative nature – the 'to-be-pursuedness' – of the properties to which they refer.[35] For this reason, the naturalist's appeal to moral theory cannot provide a solution to the problem of shapelessness. Further, if naturalists stretch the natural to the point where the moral can be accommodated without any difficulty, naturalism becomes so anodyne that any genuine debate will dissolve.

4.   Noting the various uses to which the subjective/objective distinction has been put in ethics, Wiggins attempts a position incorporating both subjectivity and objectivity, where subjectivity amounts to moral judgements' being 'answerable to what registers upon the critically-regulated object-involving responses of human subjects', and objectivity to certain of these judgements' being 'such as to have been determined by circumstances not extraneous to the facts'.[36]

Wiggins's position is elucidated partly in terms of evaluative properties and responses to them being 'made for one another'.[37] McDowell has elaborated the idea that one way to understand the metaphysical status of values would be in terms of an analogy with secondary qualities such as colour.[38] Assuming that a plausible view of the world will be relaxed enough to allow its contents to be coloured, McDowell softens the Mackiean charge of Platonism against realism. Values can be understood in terms of our sensitivity to them in such a way that they are internally related to motivation.

It might be thought that this is the route which Wiggins is taking,[39] and indeed ought to be taking, when he speaks of properties and responses being made for one another. But this thought would be incorrect. First, Wiggins ought not to take the route for the reason that the analogy fails, and at a central point. McDowell noticed the problem, speaking of values being such as to *merit* certain attitudes.[40] Crispin Wright has spelled it out further.[41] In the case of primary qualities, the extension of the truth predicate among statements ascribing such qualities is determined independently of our best opinions, while there is no such independence in the case of secondary qualities. Here, since we should want to avoid making moral truth dependent on our beliefs, we should if anything seek an analogy with primary qualities. But that, of course, is just what the secondary quality analogists are trying to avoid.

Second, Wiggins anyway does not overwork the analogy. His use of it in 'Truth, Invention and the Meaning of Life' – the text most often referred to in this context – is merely to remove from the scene an ill-judged objection. All Wiggins wishes to maintain is the uncontroversial claim that colours and values are conditioned by human sensibilities. And, as regards the relation between properties and responses, the response or reaction is not to be taken as constituting the evaluative property in question, nor as a criterion of it, nor even as an indicator.[42] The sheer existence, if I may put it like that, of the property need not depend on any response or possibility of response in humans as they now are. When we respond to cruelty, for example, the cruelty of the object in question is independent of that response, or human responses in general.[43]

The response to cruelty, then, is made for the property 'cruel' in the sense that it is that property to which it is a response and that property which, in many cases, explains particular responses. How, then, is the property made for the response? Let me refer here to a central passage in 'Truth, Invention, and the Meaning of Life':

> Surely it can be true both that we desire x because we think x good [sc. that desiring is made for goodness], and that x is good because x is such that we desire x [sc. that goodness is made for desiring]. It does not count against the point that the explanation of the 'because' is different in each direction. Nor does it count against the particular anti-non-cognitivist position that is now emerging in opposition to non-cognitivism that the second 'because' might have to be explained in some such way as this: such desiring by human beings directed in this way is one part of what is required for there to be such a thing as the perspective from which the non-instrumental goodness of x is there to be perceived.[44]

When evaluative properties which are *there to be perceived* are introduced into the story as part of an alternative to Humean subjectivism, 'the point of calling this position subjectivism is that the properties in question are explained by reference to the reactions of human subjects'.[45] Some mentalists – Humean subjectivists, for example – claim that to say that something has some evaluative feature is to say that it would elicit a certain response under certain conditions.[46] Wiggins's account is richer, in that the properties are to be seen as independent of the responses to them. It is just that *understanding* the properties requires reference to the responses.[47]

From the point of view of the debate between naturalists and non-naturalists, the metaphysics of Wiggins's subjective non-naturalism is best seen as going hand in hand with its epistemology. Non-natural properties are as real as natural properties, and can be adduced in explanations of why objects are valuable. But for any plausible characterisation of the perspective from which natural properties are discernible, non-naturalists will insist that evaluative properties are not (all) discernible from that perspective. Some evaluative properties will be *sui generis*, in the sense that they will not be identifiable with properties discernible from a perspective which is not informed and shaped by an internal grasp of the values in question. The metaphysical claim about non-identification rests on the epistemological claim about perspective, which itself involves a view about the grasp of concepts. Wiggins's position, then, is a version of what Jonathan Dancy calls a 'stronger' form of moral realism, according to which real properties are those not constituted merely by the availability or possibility of a characteristic human response.[48]

Let me return to the case of the funny. Wiggins claims that 'there is no saying what exactly the funny is without reference to laughter or amusement or kindred reactions', and asks, 'Indeed how could there be? By hypothesis, the linked properties and responses we are speaking of are arrived at by a historical process'.[49] Now part of a satisfactory account of the funny can and should employ non-naturalistic concepts – absurdity, bathos, wit, irony, slapstick, whimsy, pun, joke – without any reference to reactions. This is all of course on the understanding that such an account will make little sense to somebody utterly insensitive to the qualities under discussion, that is, somebody with no access to the humorous perspective. Important reference to responses will be made in an account not of the properties but of the nature and history of the epistemological perspective in question. Here, agreement in reactions will be important in the establishment of the evaluative language required for evaluative judgements,[50] though agreement in reactions amounts only to the joint occupation of a perspective, not to agreement in the specific reactions had in, or judgements made from, that perspective. To think that reference to the responses here commits one to reference to them in giving an account of the properties judged from the perspective would be to be guilty of an error similar to that of confusing the genealogy and content of morals.[51]

Quinn distinguishes realists into those who believe that the response is logically separable into some pure cognition of the relevant property and some noncognitive correlative state, and those who deny this.[52] Non-naturalists would do well to ally themselves with the first group. For they can then make sense of those cases where a person can see from an anthropocentric perspective that certain actions will be described approvingly by some as, say, straightforwardly 'macho', 'chaste' or 'pious', and grasps the point of those descriptions, but herself fails to approve of or disapproves of these actions. The anthropocentric perspective required for the discernment of evaluative qualities should not be characterised in every case by the presence of some single capacity to respond in a particular way to a particular property. Rather a whole range or human interests, desires and concerns is required.

When offering an account of why evaluative judgements have *pro tanto* motivating force, we shall of course refer to the positions of the evaluators. Evaluations are made from an anthropocentric perspective, and this perspective will be characterised in terms of those occupying it having the capacity to desire, react and respond in various ways. The non-naturalist is nevertheless entitled to claim that specific responses are 'made for' their respective properties – that of laughter for a good joke, abhorrence for cruelty, and so on. And non-naturalism retains the advantage over naturalism that it can use evaluative concepts as they stand, with all their proprietary magnetism.

5. Let me end with some questions for Wiggins, to some of which I shall suggest possible answers.

(i) *To-be-pursuedness*. I began this paper with an account of Mackie's charge that realism about values – what he calls 'objectivism' – cannot avoid an implausible Platonism. How good a response to that charge does Wiggins's non-naturalism represent?

It might be thought that, like McDowell, Wiggins can avoid any mystery which might attach to an account of to-be-pursuedness which was perforce offered without reference to human sensitivity to value. But if Wiggins follows Wright in his rejection of the secondary quality analogy at the relevant point, whether or not he attempts analogies with primary or mathematical qualities at that point, is it not the case that his cosmos will be so constituted that to-be-pursuedness is in fact 'built into it', that funniness, for example, is a property of the world quite independent of us which we have developed in such a way as to be able to detect and to respond to?[53]

(ii) *Intuitionism*. The other component of Mackie's charge is epistemological: a realist must be an intuitionist.

Wiggins may be able to deflect this part of the charge by claiming that there is nothing obscure, nothing to be explained in reductive terms, about the perspective from which we *discern* what is valuable – at least, nothing obscure to *us*.[54] If it makes sense to speak of levels at which the world may be conceptually carved up, the move from lower to higher levels can be seen as a move to ever more anthropocentric perspectives. Chairs will not seem mysterious to beings that sit; nor will the discernment of chairs. The same everyday story might perhaps be told about cruelty or beauty.

(iii) *Directions of fit*.[55] Crudely speaking, the concern of beliefs is how the world is, while that of desires is how the world should be. Why should we accept that beliefs about values – that is, beliefs about how the evaluative world is – require certain conative capacities – that is, capacities directed at how the world should be?

Wiggins's answer here might depend on conceptual capacity. There may be certain concepts one can be said to have grasped only if one responds in the right way: a child who is apparently managing to identify central cases of cruelty as such, but who finds them randomly funny, beautiful or just plain boring, might be said by someone – perhaps with Wittgensteinian sympathies – not to have mastered the concept of cruelty. To be sure, part of teaching children what cruelty is involves teaching them how to react to it.

But if we stretch the notion of perspective to account for those cases of machismo, chastity and so on, in which we can see things from another's point of view and yet dissociate ourselves from their attitudes, why should the wayward child not be said to have grasped the concept of cruelty? And as reactions begin to appear ever more distantly related to properties, we might ask what is to prevent our imagining some intellectually powerful but emotionally quite stunted creature grasping evaluative concepts.

(iv) *Kant.* Kant plausibly suggests that morality represents itself to us as supplying reasons to act which are independent of our desires and inclinations.[56] Has Wiggins left sufficient room for such independence in his account?

Wiggins might stress the fact that reactions play an epistemological role in his account. Morality does indeed supply us with reasons to act which are independent of desires we have to act upon them, but these reasons can be discerned only by those with the capacity to react to them. This would commit Wiggins to what Williams calls 'externalism' about reasons.[57] Note that the form of externalism I have described here is compatible with what we might call 'weak internalism':

WI: *P* can have a reason to φ iff *P* has some motive to be served by φ-ing.

It is incompatible only with a strong version of internalism, according to which:

SI: *P* can have a reason to φ iff *P* has some motive to be served by φ-ing *for that reason.*

Wiggins might then be an externalist without being committed to the view that I could have a reason to do something which *nothing* could motivate me to do. But even the amoral psychopath might be said to have a reason to stop being cruel to the child if, for example, he could be threatened into stopping. Reasons which could never *explain* an action can nevertheless *justify* it.

Alternatively Wiggins might reject the Kantian position by further linking moral properties and responses, or moral reasons and desires, in a strong internalist account of reasons. And this may bring us back to the response to the question asked in §(iii) above: if it is in some sense part of discerning that the burning of the cat is cruel to discern also that one has some reason to act in some way in response to that cruelty, then a non-conative being cannot discern that such an action is cruel in the same way as we do.

(v) *The nature of Wiggins's project and the relation between levels of explanation.* Wiggins might see himself as doing either or both of the following: (a) developing a principled and systematic account of the metaphysics and epistemology of value; (b) showing what is wrong with other such accounts which are at odds with common sense. He holds that the main issue here is that of whether evaluative claims can be true or false. This might suggest that he believes a debate about realism can be avoided because the Mackiean charge can be rebutted immediately as resting on the mistaken assumption that the world as it is must be identified with the world as it is characterised by science.[58] If so, that raises another question: what *is* the relation between natural and moral properties? Or is my mistake to think that this question can be answered, when it can be answered, in anything other than a piecemeal way?

NOTES

1 Mackie (1977), pp. 38–42.
2 This now standard example comes from Harman (1977), p. 5.
3 McDowell (1983).
4 See e.g. Sturgeon (1984), (1986); Railton (1986); Lycan (1986); Boyd (1988); Brink (1989).
5 Sturgeon (1984), pp. 59ff.
6 See Sturgeon (1984), p. 61, where the possibility of supernaturalism is countered with a reference to the existence of naturalistic theories.
7 See Harman (1977), ch. 1; McDowell (1985), p. 117.
8 Wiggins (1991a), p. 355.
9 Ibid., p. 147.
10 Ibid., pp. 128; 149–60; 164ff.; 199ff.; 204–6.; 330, note 14; 340; 344–8; 354–6. Cf. Railton (1986), p. 171, who finds the notion of causal interaction with a non-natural reality 'intolerably odd'.
11 See Brink (1989), p. 22.
12 Moore (1903), p. 40. See Wiggins (1991a), p. 193, note 12; (1993b), pp. 303–4.
13 See Brink (1989), pp. 157–9; Wiggins (1993b), pp. 330–1.
14 See Griffin (1992), p. 306.
15 Sturgeon (1984), p. 60; Railton (1986), p. 184; Brink (1989), pp. 157ff.
16 Sturgeon (1984), p. 61; Brink (1989), p. 176.
17 It is an interesting question whether the best moral theory is that which we have strongest reason to believe or that which is true.

18 Notice how Moore continues in the passage already quoted to say that the subject-matter of the natural sciences includes all that has existed, exists or will exist.

19 Williams (1978), pp. 245–9. Something like the absolute conception is often adduced in the philosophy of mind by physicalists. But we must allow the moral analogue to encompass more than physical properties, since ethical naturalists tend not to make their case in physicalist terms and physicalists tend to reject the notion of moral properties. See Sturgeon (1984), p. 60; Stroud (1986/7), p. 265. (On analogies and differences between positions in the philosophy of mind concerning the relation of mind and brain and positions in moral philosophy concerning the relation of values and the world, see Snowdon (1989), esp. p. 139.)

20 See Davidson (1973).

21 One objection Wiggins makes to certain naturalists can be put aside immediately, viz. that they confuse the genealogy and the content of morals: a naturalistic account of the origin of morality, such as sociobiology, does not *commit* one to a naturalistic account of its content. The naturalism under discussion here rests on the scientific world view, not on any thesis about the source of morality. See Wiggins (1991a), p. 353; (1990/1), pp. 69–70; (1993b), pp. 310–11. The moral objection to naturalism – that attempts to reduce the complex language of political evaluation represent a danger to freedom ((1991a), p. 328) – can also be laid aside. The naturalists under discussion do not commit themselves to linguistic reduction; see Sturgeon (1984), pp. 59ff.; Sayre-McCord (1986), p. 16; Brink (1989), p. 177.

22 Wiggins (1991a), pp. 198ff.; (1990/1), pp. 81–2; (1993b) pp. 307–9. The term 'magnetism' is of course C. L. Stevenson's ((1963), p. 13). It is worth comparing Wiggins's arguments with those of R. M. Hare in e.g. (1952), ch. 5.

23 Quinn (1978), p. 257.

24 See Wiggins (1991a), pp. 186ff.; 190ff.

25 Wiggins (1991a), pp. 188; 192–5.

26 Ibid., p. 193; cf. pp. 195; 330, note 14.

27 It is found also, for example, in Railton's naturalistic account of well-being ((1986), pp. 171–84) as consisting in what a fully-informed agent would want herself to want. Why would such an agent have the desires she in fact has? The answer to this question will appeal to evaluative properties the naturalistic understanding of which is likely to be shapeless. Wiggins ((1993b), pp. 303–6, 311) claims that Railton's naturalistic utilitarianism likewise fails to account for the normativity of ethical judgements.

28 'Shapeless' is Simon Blackburn's term ((1981), p. 167); see also McDowell (1981), pp. 144ff.; Charles and Lennon (1992), pp. 7–8; Wiggins (1993b), pp. 332–3.

29 Wiggins (1993b), pp. 329–32. Cf. Sturgeon (1984), p. 75, note 14, who suggests that there is nothing objectionable in taking talk of moral virtues to be part of psychology.

30 Wiggins (1991a), p. 107.

31 Wiggins (1991a), pp. 92–108.

32 Davidson (1973); Grandy (1973); Wiggins (1991a), pp. 111ff.
33 Sturgeon (1984), pp. 63–73; Brink (1989), pp. 182–97.
34 Davidson (1970), (1973).
35 Michael Martin pointed out that there may be *other* ways of appreciating the shape of moral properties from within the absolute conception. Presumably the non-naturalist reply will be that the normativity of moral properties, and hence the properties themselves, would remain unexplained.
36 Wiggins (1991a), p. 346; cf. pp. 201ff. The latter phrase Wiggins takes from Peirce's essay 'On the Fixation of Belief'; see (1991a), p. 342.
37 Wiggins (1991a), pp. 107; 194.
38 McDowell (1985).
39 This interpretation of Wiggins is surprisingly widespread. See e.g. McGinn (1983), p. 146; Wright (1988), p. 1, note 1; Brink (1989), p. 231, note 9. The latter reference claims that Wiggins's position – interpreted as Humean subjectivism – is lacking in explanatory power.
40 McDowell (1985), p. 118.
41 Wright (1988), pp. 14–25.
42 Wiggins (1991a), pp. 205; 207. This is missed by M. R. DePaul in his Critical Notice of *Needs, Values, Truth* (DePaul (1990), p. 630).
43 The responses I have in mind are primarily those to cruelty inflicted on beings other than the responders.
44 Wiggins (1991a), p. 106. Note that the point is made more clearly in the second edition.
45 Wiggins (1991a), p. 195.
46 Quinn (1978), p. 258.
47 It is important to distinguish Wiggins's subjectivist thesis from the view, taken from Wittgenstein, that agreement between human beings must play its part in fixing the sense of a predicate (Wiggins (1991a), pp. 349ff). For if this is what is meant by the claim that a subjective judgement is 'one that is *however indirectly* answerable for its correctness to the responses of conscious subjects' (Wiggins (1991a), p. 201; my italics), then all judgements will be subjective.
48 Dancy (1986), pp. 167–70. According to the weaker form, moral properties are independent of any particular experience of them. Wiggins believes that moral concepts are 'subjective' in Dancy's sense, that is, such that they cannot be grasped by a being that does not share in characteristic human concerns. See ibid., p. 168.
49 Wiggins (1991a), p. 195, incl. note 16.
50 See note 47 above.
51 See note 21 above.
52 Quinn (1978), p. 258.
53 See McDowell (1983), p. 4.
54 See Wiggins (1991a), p. 197.
55 This notion – originating from Anscombe – is well elucidated in Platts (1979), pp. 256ff.

56 Kant (1948), ch. I.
57 Williams (1981), ch. 8.
58 See e.g. Wiggins (1992a). Wiggins's metaphysics provides us with another
    way of dissociating 'the two notions, of the world as it is scientifically
    understood and of the world as it really is' (Williams (1978), p. 239). What
    Wiggins calls 'real science' ((1991a), p. 355) is not inclined always to assert
    precedence or to exceed its boundaries. See also McDowell (1983), pp. 9–16.

9

Of the Standard of Taste

Anthony Savile

Hume's essay on taste has come in for attention recently, not least from David Wiggins, both on its own account and for the light it sheds on general questions of value. Going by the literature, it is anything but certain whether, looking strictly at what he writes, we should see Hume as over-confident about the essay's outcome or as rather more of an ironist than he openly admits to being. There is also a third, generally unexplored, possibility, namely that his confidence is well placed and quite untouched by irony. Which reading do we best adopt? Appearing in the present volume, the question could be phrased: Just how sensible is Hume's subjectivism?

1. What is wanted is a manner of resolving differences about taste that would avoid the extremes of a scientistic conception of aesthetic reality and of radical subjectivism. The one treats critical assertions as verified by the existence of 'real qualities' in objects, an almost technical term, I think, whose compliants would be straightforwardly non-relational properties; by contrast, the other assimilates them to assertions about or expressions of the judging subject's own sentiment concerning their

It has been my very great good fortune to have been first a pupil of David's, when he started teaching at New College in Michaelmas Term 1960, and then a colleague, when he came to Bedford College, London a little less than a decade later. Quite apart from the exciting philosophical lessons that came my way in those two fine places, I learnt from David humane things. As a pupil, I saw how an outstanding teacher attends to the peculiarities and foibles of the minds before him closely, patiently and at their own pace; as a colleague, I learnt how, with good humour and persistent prodding, impersonal seeming institutions can sometimes be brought to take seriously the idea that they exist to serve individuals, rather than the other way about. I also learnt another, more important, humane truth: that at their best, the relation of pupil and that of colleague are continuous with that of friend.

subject matter. In place of these unsatisfactory rivals, Hume holds out 'a *Standard of Taste*, whereby differences of men may be reconciled, or at least the one confirmed and the other opinion condemned' ('Of the Standard of Taste' (in Hume (1987)), para. 6).

'Reconciliation' here does not consist in the discovery that the parties in some dispute are mistaken about the relation of their views to one another, the standard somehow enabling them to see behind merely verbal differences to an underlying agreement between them. Hume makes this plain well before floating his own proposal, remarking that although such illusory disputes regularly occur in the sciences, in matters of taste genuine disagreements are far more common. Rather, a reconciliation of divergent views takes place by those in disagreement applying the proffered standard and then coming to see that at least one of them has to abandon his or her earlier way of thinking (together with the sentiments integral to it), so that in the end their judgements and sentiments fall into accord.

Furthermore, application of the standard is to reconcile critical differences by bringing sentiments into accord with a *correct* view of the matter. This is evident from Hume's thought that while we may indeed find it impossible to get some critics to agree, at least when we are uninvolved in the dispute, we can see how the standards should be applied, and then 'a decision [is] afforded condemning one sentiment and confirming another'. Plainly, condemning and confirming would only make sense if we take the change of view that is looked for to be in the direction of correctness, and not falling just anywhere.

Notoriously, the standard consists in the joint verdict of true judges, those who have a rare combination of 'strong sense, united with delicate sentiment, improved by practice, perfected by comparison, and cleared of all prejudice . . . This can alone entitle critics to this valuable character [i.e. that of being true judges]; and the joint verdict of such, wherever they are to be found, is the true standard of taste and beauty' (ibid., para. 23). When it is asked why appeal to the true judge should impress contending parties, the answer is presumably to be found in the relation between the judge's verdicts and what makes one of the disputed assertions true. The sentiments that the verdicts of true judges express are, it may appear, simply *constitutive* of these truths, and, since disputing parties are in search of truth, once they come to recognize the constitutive relation that the standard establishes, the assumption is that they will be moved to follow it without demur. The main trouble is practical, and it comes in discerning what the true judges' verdicts in fact are. But about that Hume is fairly sanguine: 'In reality', he reports, 'the difficulty of finding, even in particulars, the standard of taste, is not so great as it is represented . . . Just expressions of passion and nature are sure, after a little time, to gain public applause, which they maintain for ever.'

The constitutive reading of the standard is largely fuelled by passages from earlier writings. So, in the *Treatise*, the idea of *vice* is accounted for in terms of a sentiment of disapprobation, which arises in us towards particular actions (e.g. wilful murder). 'Here is a matter of fact; but 'tis the object of a feeling, not of reason. It lies in yourself, not in the object. So that when you pronounce any action to be vicious, you mean *nothing*, *but* that from the constitution of your nature you have a feeling or sentiment of blame from the contemplation of it' (Hume (1888), p. 468). Likewise, in 'The Sceptic', composed fifteen years or so before the taste essay, we find: '[Deformed, odious, beautiful, amiable] . . . those qualities are not really, in the objects, but belong *entirely* to the sentiment of that mind which blames or praises' (Hume (1987), p. 163); a little further on, and directly on aesthetic judgement, Hume says: 'Beauty is not a quality of the circle. It lies not in any part of the line whose parts are all equally distant from a common centre. It is *only* the effect, which that figure produces upon a mind, whose particular fabric or structure renders it susceptible of such sentiments' (ibid., p. 165).

These claims are already so well represented in the earlier writings that when we now find Hume claiming that 'beauty and deformity, more than sweet and bitter, are not qualities in objects, but belong *entirely* to the sentiments' ('Of the Standard of Taste' para. 16, emphasis added here and above), it is entirely natural to suppose that the idea is central to the view on offer and that a perfect community reigns between earlier and later views. The constitutive interpretation of the standard looks solidly enough anchored in Hume's thought, though looking forward somewhat, I say that it is far from the only thing that we find anchored there.

While the larger part of the essay is given over to finding a sufficiently sensitive specification of the true judge, towards its very end, Hume raises a number of queries that he professes to find no more than marginally irksome. Yet they ought to give him pause, because unless circumvented they will show that the proposed standard cannot work. There are four of them, and they are interesting enough to set out in some detail.

First, there are two issues of 'inner frame'. 'A young man, whose passions are warm, will be more sensibly touched with amorous and tender images, than a man more advanced in years who takes pleasure in wise, philosophical reflections, concerning the conduct of life, and moderation of the passions. At twenty, Ovid may be the favourite author, Horace at forty, and perhaps Tacitus at fifty' (ibid., para. 29). We are to assume that our attention is fixed on true critics of the already specified kind. If we demand joint (uniform) verdicts from them, that is, agreement in their sentiments, the very differences of frame deriving from their variously mature mental habits will ensure that there are none, or at least that there are far fewer than we might like to think. Hume infers that there is nothing to choose between these authors if what we are seeking is a ranking. 'It is almost impossible not to feel a predilection for what suits our particular turn and disposition. Such preferences are innocent and unavoidable, and can never reasonably be the object of dispute, because there is no standard by which they can be decided' (ibid., para. 30).

Since it seems so eminently right to refuse to rank Ovid, Horace and Tacitus, it is tempting to approve Hume's dismissal of the query. Yet any such sympathetic response ignores a greater threat, one which Hume also fails to notice, or else too cavalierly brushes aside. If we fix on good judges who are distinguished from one another only in ways to which no exception can reasonably be taken and find their voices discordant, or otherwise failing to sound in unison, there just are no 'uniform verdicts' that their divers sentiments propose. Since such verdicts is supposedly constitutive of the valuationally central aesthetic qualities of the writing under scrutiny, assertions that invoke them cannot be correct. In the situation described, Ovid will precisely not be amiable, Horace not elegant, Tacitus not estimably judicious and terse.

Parallel remarks may be made about the second issue of internal frame Hume mentions, this time built around those natural dispositions that distinguish people at the same stage of their maturation and which tend to stay with them throughout their lives. 'One person is more pleased with the sublime, another with the tender, a third with raillery' (ibid.), and their sentiments are correspondingly diverse. There is no clear limit to such peculiarities, but if we look for uniformity among well-chosen critics to determine whether, say, the sublime Milton merits that title, more has to be said than that we are concerned only with innocent differences between good judges. Since Hume fares no better with this version of the difficulty than the last, one may begin to suspect of a measure of irony lying behind his apparent confidence.

This suspicion grows as we turn to issues of 'external situation', and introduce material that bears on the standard's diachronic aspect. We are to consider our approach to foreign or temporally distant cultures (our own included, of course). Given our particular background, it is not easy for us rightly to appreciate, say, Terence or Machiavelli. Over time, evaluative responses to these and other authors vary, since in different ages the very same features of their writing take good judges in different and sometimes estranging ways. Here, Hume is more openly aware of the threat to his project than before. In response, the description of the standard-setting good judge is refined: we are to fix attention on such as are learned and reflective in addition to possessing the qualities already listed. These will then be the judges best able to abstract from matters that might otherwise inhibit favourable response, and so serve as suitable guides, whose voices will coincide with the finest critics of the past (learned and reflective ones too, we may presume). Despite hailing from a different background than their predecessors, they are unlikely to be upset by conventions that are, critically speaking, neither here nor there. The learned will be best placed to know what the assumptions of natural-ness were for earlier ages and what apparent unnaturalnesses were func-tioning as merely formal conventions; the reflective will fix which responses to the conventions are appropriate, determining which are acceptable and which strain the imagination too far.

If this is how Hume reasons, he is unduly optimistic. Judgements of the learned and the reflective may themselves be expected to differ at differ-ent times. What it is that such people see in the past as being of interest and not distressingly strange will itself be liable to vary as their own conceptions of what is natural and what is far-fetched are tempered by their own experience, where, inevitably, this is experience that is different at different times. The objection reaches far. Almost any aesthetically interesting property may be encountered in a setting that makes it diffi-cult for a later audience to appreciate and sharply identify. But under the last consideration, even when the ideal critic is more closely charac-terised than before, the constitutively construed standard for that property, namely uniform response among accredited judges, will be certain to break down once diachronic considerations are allowed to surface.

Hume handles his final hesitation in a curiously asymmetrical way. Our estimation of literary works is not independent of their moral tenor and revolutions of morality lead good judges from different periods to dis-agree about them. One expects to find him dealing with the point by refining the character of the good judge yet further, and holding out to us the prospect of a uniformity that we do not notice because of the way in which important constancies of sentiment get lost among the many dissenting but irrelevant voices that make up the motley of critical history. He does nothing of the kind. Instead, he appeals to the sound moral judges of his own day and insists that we are bound to follow them. 'A very violent effort is requisite to change our judgments of manners, and excite sentiments of approbation or blame, love or hatred, different from those to which the mind from long custom, has been familiarized. And where a man is confident of the rectitude of that moral standard by which he judges, he is justly jealous of it, and will not pervert the sentiments of his heart for a moment, in complaisance to any writer whatsoever . . . nor is it proper for us to do so.' (ibid., para. 33).

By the end of the essay, then, it may appear that Hume has to all intents and purposes abandoned his proposed standard, even though he presents what he offers to his reader as no departure from it. Since he introduces these four objections of his own accord, yet plainly cannot answer them in accordance with his programme, it can easily seem that his attitude is more equivocal than at first it looks. So, one may well wonder whether beneath the calm surface of the writing, Hume surmises that there just is no safe passage between the Scylla of a purely non-relational conception of aesthetic reality and the Charybdis of radical subjectivism. In that case, the best-advised position to take in critical disputes will be that of the ironical sceptic.

2.   To stave off defeat at this stage, we need do little more than draw out something implicit in Hume's remarks about the development of the tastes of the ideal critic, one, it will be recalled, who has developed his natural inclinations and sentiments by means of *practice* and *comparison*. Plainly, it would be unreasonable to expect the very same person to guide our judgement in just any area. Rather, we shall think that one who makes himself expert in one particular field will be a good guide for it, and when we look in another direction we shall seek advice from someone else. Similarly, we shall expect Hume to think, in accordance with his dictum that we turn our attention most readily to matters that resemble us, that the practised eye that is perfected by comparisons will best be able to make judgements of a limited kind, in areas in which it is naturally inclined to exercise itself.

Once this is granted, the original proposal might be better understood as specifying the true judge not with respect to just any area of interest, as Hume seems to envisage, but to an area *appropriate to his interests, his character and his background*. Then we shall not require the older man to serve as standard for Ovid (*interest*), though maybe he will serve well for Tacitus. Equally, the person with a penchant for the sublime (*character*) will not be well chosen as an appropriate standard to judge *Candide*. Nor shall we expect the home-grown judge (*background*) to be well placed to provide the best critical assessments of writing of foreign provenance.

This refinement of Hume's rougher specification is only to be seen as a refinement of the standard itself. Identifying the most competent critic for the judgement of Ovid by reference to the interests of the young and so forth, will do nothing to prevent the greying sage from sharply appreciating Ovid's merits, nor, *mutatis mutandis*, prevent the precocious

youth from enjoying a well-founded admiration for Tacitus. As far as the
standard itself goes, however, it is a different matter. There the criterion
of good taste in respect of one author or another will be the sentiment of
someone whose interests, temperament and background naturally draw
him to works of the kind in point and whose responses are most appropriately chosen for the writer in question.

With this adjustment made, greater warmth might greet the proposal.
The standard does now yield a much more uniform response to literary
works up for evaluation than it could hope for before. Many divergencies
of taste that previously made for trouble emerge as innocuous. Not only
can absolute questions such as 'Is Ovid a fine poet?' sometimes receive a
clear answer, as before they did not, and as Hume did not always allow;
also, we can appreciate, as before we could not, why it is right to say there
is no evident ranking to be made of Ovid and Tacitus, or of Addison and
Milton. The standard, as now formulated, just does not cater for comparisons between writing of significantly different sorts.

If this move avoids the first three hazards, what shall we now say of the
licence Hume surprisingly grants to abide by our own moral standards as
against those of the culture from which an alien work proceeds? 'Where
the ideas of morality and decency alter from one age to another, and
where vicious manners are described without being marked with the
proper character of blame and disapprobation, this must be allowed to
disfigure the poem, and be a real deformity. I cannot, nor is it proper that
I should, enter into such sentiments' (ibid., para. 32).

Notice, first, that this passage makes no mention of *our* moral sense as
opposed to any other. The contrast is simply between a sensibility that
takes pleasure in what is vicious and one that does not. When, a little
later, Hume does speak with satisfaction of our moral superiority (as in
the preference he expresses for the moderns against the ancients), that
too can be taken as a contingent, factual, matter, reflecting the good
fortune that we have of being able to judge more easily in accordance
with the well-developed ethical dimension of the standard than did some
of our predecessors. Hume is, after all, perfectly entitled to believe that,
as it happened, that refined standard was happily realised in mid-eight-
eenth-century French or enlightened and liberal Scottish and English
society and not in the culture of classical times. Putting it like this will
help him avoid the charge of moral chauvinism or of parochialism.
(Nothing has been said about the reason for insisting on the place of such
a dimension within the standard, but let us just take that on trust).

Then, second, just as the relativizations of the standard that resolved
Hume's earlier worries grew out of a more precise sense of what commitment to practice and comparison amount to, so also here we may reflect

that the concern for *humanity* that sets itself against barbarity and in-
decency is itself a natural outgrowth of the *strong sense* and associated
reflection that Hume has built into the specification of his standard at the
outset. A man of strong sense can scarcely fail to be a person of developed ethical sensibility. So, if we think of foreign (or subcultural)
material that offends that sensibility, even if as a matter of fact in the
culture from which it stems the best local judges approve it, there is room
enough to think that we should not take them as fully compliant with the
standard. It is not in the least condescending to think, on reflection, that
our standards must prevail here. As Hume observes, it is a truth of fact
that we can not easily set aside standards of which we are confident; what
is more, by those very standards themselves, there being no others
available, it is not proper that we should.

3.   The passage last cited touches on a normative strand in Hume's
thought, also rooted in his earlier writings, but one which sits most
uncomfortably with the present reading. When he demands that the
sound judge mark the moral deformities of the literary work with their
proper measure of blame and disapprobation, this is no stray remark.
Elsewhere, he observes that 'the good qualities of an enemy', though
'hurtful to us' nonetheless '*command* esteem and respect' when we consider them without reference to our own particular interests' and that
'tho' 'tis certain a musical voice is nothing but one that gives a particular
kind of pleasure; yet 'tis difficult for a man to be sensible that the voice
of an enemy is agreeable, or to allow it to be musical. But a person of fine
ear, who has the command of himself, can separate these feelings and
give praise *to what deserves it*' [emphasis added] (Hume (1888), p. 469).
   All that has yet been said to motivate anyone to emulate the sentiments
of the true judge, when they are initially in disgreement with them, has
been that good judges speak true and that we have an interest in truth.
But this is unimpressive, because as soon as we come to see that truth in
these matters is constituted by the sentiments of good judges, its motivation will crumble. That good judges' sentiments differ from our own
cannot by itself lead us to exchange our judgements and feelings for
theirs. If, in addition, we are now told that it is *proper* to be moved by this
or that, in the way that good judges are, one is bound to ask what it is that
makes it proper *for the good judges themselves* to respond as they do. This
question the constitutively-read standard cannot answer; but it is fundamental, and without a satisfying answer to it the standard collapses.
   This point underscores an objection of David Wiggins's to Hume's
proposal, namely that his standard is unfaithful to our understanding of
what a good judge actually is, in particular for its having 'insufficient

regard for the properties attributed to objects within the critic's or judge's sentiment of approbation' (Wiggins (1987a), p. 192). The idea of the good judge needs to be far richer than anything the constitutive picture of him can provide, because, without something more the normative idea of the propriety of his responses, as indeed that of the centrality of practice and delicacy of discrimination to the good judge's character, must remain so much eyewash. The proposal sounds in order by mimicking our practice, but at the same time it removes from it anything that might give these ideas the substance which they purport to possess.

Earlier I said that the constitutive interpretation of the standard is very largely rooted in Hume's earlier writings, but there will be those who discern in the taste essay's account of critical discourse additional underpinning for it. That is, while allowing that Hume's position is ultimately untenable, whether he recognised it or not, they will say that it is one from which he is theoretically unable to detach himself. A passage from the start of the essay, embodying a general claim about evaluative discourse, might be cited in support.

> The sentiments of men often differ with regard to beauty and deformity of all kinds, even while their general discourse is the same. There are certain terms in every language which import blame, and others praise; and all men who use the same tongue must agree in their application of them. Every voice is united in applauding elegance, propriety, simplicity, spirit in writing; and in blaming fustian, affectation, coldness, and a false brilliancy. But when critics come to particulars, this seeming unanimity vanishes; and it is found, that they had affixed a very different meaning to their expressions. ('Of the Standard of Taste', para. 2).

Here Hume is less concerned with overall comparative judgements of the kind on which I have so far focused than with finer-grain verdicts, those that must provide the bases underlying any serious overall critical evaluations. Going by these lines, one might possibly come to think that, at the level of fine grain, our aesthetic language works for Hume in the following fashion: a particular term, 'elegance', say, or 'fustian', comprises two distinct elements, one that is quite neutral with regard to sentiment and the other of which is sentiment-involving. Now, what we find in practice is that, although people say that they approve of elegance, in fact they often call something elegant of which they disapprove. This is where disagreements typically lie. People agree readily enough about the applicability of a term's neutral element, but differ in the sentiment they attach to it. And just because, in our ordinary meaning 'elegant' *analytically* implies favourable response, these divergent judges, in so far as they employ that word, must be using it in a different sense than do the rest of us.

Bipartite models of evaluative language are familiar enough, and their origin is sometimes traced back to Hume. If this view really were Hume's own, there would indeed be no satisfactory explanation of how the wisdom of true judges can legitimately be brought to bear in disputes of taste. Since they are cast in the role of reconciling sentiments in the way outlined at the start, their main task will not be to get people to agree on the neutral element of their aesthetic vocabulary's terms. That is here presented as a relatively uncontentious matter, and where there are differences of opinion we may presume them to be quickly resolvable. Rather, the true judges serve to get arguing parties to feel the same sentiments, hence, on this particular vision of the matter, to agree that the poet the parties disagree about has produced truly fustian verse or truly elegant rhymes or, alternatively, to agree that the work is fustian or elegant only under the 'ambiguity' that reverses the usual response and leaves the neutral element untouched. Yet all the established critics have to rely on to achieve this is an appeal to snobbery or ungrounded exercise of intellectual muscle, since their exercises of practice and comparison are not permitted to have any reference beyond themselves.

Two examples that illustrate the passage show beyond dispute that this picture of critical discourse is a travesty of Hume's own. In the one, we are to image Homer and Fénelon disputing the virtues of their respective heroes. Fénelon opines that Achilles' deeds are too mingled with ferocity to count as estimably heroic; and as for Ulysses' prudence, that contains an undue degree of cunning and deceit to merit the epithet. Plainly, the disagreement here is not simply one of attitude to something that is uncontroversially agreed between the two authors. Rather, what is in question is whether Achilles is genuinely heroic and Ulysses genuinely prudent. As Hume envisages it, the true judge will be best placed to decide the matter, not in the sense of stipulating the answer or forcing approval or disapproval upon us, but in the light of his greater sensitivity to the details of the cases.

The brief discussion of the Muslim and the Christian that follows supports the diagnosis. The former 'bestows praise on such instances of treachery and inhumanity . . . as are utterly incompatible with civilized society . . . Every action is blamed or praised, so far only as it is beneficial or hurtful to the true believers' (ibid., para. 4). Here the disagreement in evaluation of some deed does not stem from disagreement of attitude to an acknowledged treachery; rather, one party is so insensitive to what the case actually shows up that he does not even judge the deed to be a treacherous one. Prejudice blinds the Muslim to what is before him. The imagined Christian, purged of prejudice, recognizes what the Muslim does not.

These examples do, I think, make the normative aspect of the judge-ments quite comprehensible. The good judge is sensitive to something about the situation that makes it one to which a certain evaluative attitude is, in Hume's terms, proper, and one that commands the associ-ated sentiment. And this way of seeing the illustrations provides the basis for thinking that the true judges' attitudes are ones which have weight for me. For I have an interest both in what is present – making my reaction to the work a reaction to what it has to display – and in making my reaction one that is called for by what is on display. As Hume points out, we cannot drive a wedge between seeing what is on display *for what it is* and our reaction to it, as if it were just up to me to react as I will once my judgement of the facts is made (as is suggested by the bipartite account). Seeing and judging Ulysses' prudence for what it is cannot be divorced from my estimation of it, and any aberrant evaluative response will itself call in question whether I do see it *for what it is*. Hence the observation that 'in every language there are certain terms which import praise, and others blame'.

What counts decisively against the constitutive reading of the standard, however, is less that it can not achieve its ends, which Hume might simply have failed to spot, than that it entirely neglects the story of Sancho Panza's kinsmen and their function in the essay. The anecdote is told to illustrate the importance to the good critic of possessing delicacy of taste, where 'the organs [are] so fine, as to allow nothing to escape them, and at the same time so exact as to perceive every ingredient in the composition' (ibid., para. 16). Clearly, one who possesses such delicacy must only make distinctions *where there are distinctions to be made*, and not be one simply to draw distinctions among things that come before him. This is explicitly a world-sensitive delicacy, and that it is so central a characteristic of Hume's true judges ('whether their taste be taken liter-ally or metaphorically') is itself a powerful reason to believe that their verdicts cannot be constitutive of the truth of critical claims.

The gloss on the story that Hume proposes bears this out. The taste-vins' seemingly absurdly conflicting fine judgements are verified not by reference to their rare character, their practice and delicacy and lack of prejudice, but by the presence of the iron key with the leathern thong at the bottom of the liquid they are sampling. The relevance of this for criticism is plain: 'Though the hogshead had never been emptied, the taste of the one [i.e. the pair of experts each of whom is sensitive to something particular in the wine] was still equally delicate, and that of the other [i.e. the scoffing onlookers] equally dull and languid: but it would have been more difficult to have proved the superiority of the former to the conviction of every bye-stander' (ibid.).

A question of accommodation has to be acknowledged here. The key and its leathern thong are used by Hume as analogues of rules and principles, conformity to which supposedly evokes the sentiments of good judges, and not of the qualities themselves for which sound judges are claimed to serve as standard. And it is at this precise point that Hume so roundly asserts that 'it is certain that beauty and deformity . . . are not qualities in objects, but belong entirely to the sentiment' (ibid.).

However, proponents of the constitutive reading of the standard cannot make anything of this. In context, the most this textual observation will yield is that beauty is constituted by the joint verdict of practised judges as they manifest sensitivity to some feature of the objects which they confront (viz. their conformity to rules and principles) – one which is liable to elicit a corresponding approbation. Yet, since this formulation has it that the sentiments of true judges only enter the picture if they are responses to what is present in the object, it is not discernibly different from saying that beauty (for example) is a property that objects have in virtue of being thus and so conformed, to wit, the property of being liable to elicit such and such responses in sensitive and practised judges. This is a far cry from the claim that 'beauty and deformity . . . belong entirely to the sentiment', but it is worth noticing that it is entirely continuous with a strand of the *Treatise* that I obliquely alluded to before, but made nothing of (cf. Hume (1888), p. 299).

What Hume needs but does not quite succeed in articulating, or retrieving from this section of the *Treatise*, is unabashed reference to something in the world for the good judge to detect distinct from the sentiments, yet distinct also from any supposed rules and principles that might be specified without reference to our sentiments and responses (different from key and thong, that is). Significantly enough, not finding such an articulation to hand, Hume himself goes on to speak of 'methodising the beauties of writing or *reducing* them to general principles' (emphasis added), though quite how self-consciously he uses the phrase may be queried. Nevertheless, if we pick up the hint this locution does suggest that Hume has it in mind to minimize the sort of one-sidedly internalist account of the valuational properties that he proposes elsewhere. For what gets methodized or reduced cannot be the sentiments themselves, but at best what produces them, viz. the beauties of the writing. That Hume is sensitive to this thought comes out sharply at the very end of the same paragraph, where he explicitly enough identifies the individual work's conformity to a rule or principle as a beauty of the writing that the bad critic wants the delicacy to be sensible of.

However, eschewing reductionism in the aesthetic domain as much as in the case of sweet or bitter and the other sensible qualities, we are bound to advise Hume not to say in the explication of his anecdote that it is the key and the leather that the tastevins taste. Rather, it is the taste of leather and iron that has infiltrated the wine that their expertise makes them sensitive to, and he will preserve the force of his tale by saying (in line with his theoretically-induced belief in rules and principles) that by parallel it is their conformity to the rules of good writing that endows the poet's lines with the liability they have to evoke the positive sentiments of good judges, but that that liability is what it is in objects that 'is naturally fitted to produce the feelings'. It is on this, not on the supposed rules and principles, that he really needs to concentrate. In mitigation of the lapse, we may recall just how difficult Locke, so much less drawn than Hume to run the two together, found it consistently to keep apart qualities and our ideas of them (cf. e.g. Locke (1975), II.viii.19). It is not absurd to think that Hume has made a similar slip here in conflating a liability to produce feelings on the part of some object with something 'belonging entirely to the sentiment', and, still looking for something in the object to call forth the sentiments, feels obliged to talk of rules and principles to supply the need. As soon as the conflation is remedied, rules and principles become superfluous and can be entirely dispensed with, or else treated on their own merits as a matter of merely peripheral interest.

4.   Two issues remain. To be content with this way of reading the essay, we still have to find a role for Hume's standard to play in critical practice. We also need to be clear how it is to do so. Now, even when taken constitutively, the standard's working would have required amplification. All the abandoned reading really proposed was a thesis about the truth-conditions of certain assertions central to critical discourse. It had nothing at all to say about how the parties might be brought to recognize the truth in any given case of critical dispute. This can be seen by reflecting that the good judge is essentially only a hypothetical, not a categorical, figure. An optimal response to some drama of ancient times that had never been performed would have been what fixed its literary worth, and that to which disputing parties would have been directed; but what should they do to identify it?

The answer is clear: they must look to actually existing, well-trained judges for guidance, and now judges whose responses are certainly not constitutive of literary worth, nor proof against error. Such guides will (unsurprisingly) have just the character that Hume originally specifies in elaborating his standard; and they will have this character for just the reasons that Hume gives. They will provide the surest indication we could have of what those hypothetical optimal responses might be, and they do this because they come as close as any actual evidence can bring us to what such a response to a given work would be.

What this suggests is surely that, once true judges no longer act hypothetically and criterially for the truth or falsity of critical claims, but categorically and evidentially for literary works' possession of valuation-ally interesting critical properties, we should simply shift our conception of the standard from the former back to the latter because the very same epistemological issue arises here as there. The standard is properly, and, I surmise, for Hume always was, conceived of as evidential for sound criticism, not constitutive of it. If you like, 'Of the Standard of Taste' is a contribution to the theory of aesthetic evidence, not to the theory of aesthetic nature.

Once we see it in this way, we can look back at the sources of variation in response that occupied Hume before, and recognize that his reaction to them is entirely appropriate and not one to criticize. They do not strike him as difficultes because they are not difficulties, despite the fact that, on the abandoned reading, we should have expected him to have found them more troublesome than he did. So as far as evidence goes, uniform verdicts may be ideal, particularly when culled from a wide range of people, but, for the reasons that Hume notes, they are not very frequent among those whose judgement we think is likely to be trustworthy. On the other hand, we can certainly tolerate a degree of divergence among such people before we begin to think that they have nothing to tell us about what we find baffling. That is, under the constitutive reading of the matter, the standard operated in an on/off manner, but, when it is taken evidentially the question at issue is largely a matter of degree: How well supported is the judgement that this work is thus and so? Here, a less than uniform response will only rarely lead to a downright negative assessment.

Further, speaking evidentially, there is very good reason not to narrow down the specification of the true judge in the way previously envisaged. The impact of widely (if not uniformly) shared responses among people of different temperaments and different humours is far more impressive than any uniform verdict among a narrowly-chosen band would be. Likewise, when we consider diachronic matters. For the most part, the evidence of good judges available to us will be of those in our own culture, sharing many of our moral assumptions, and it should not surprise us that Hume thinks primarily of them. But even when we can appeal to culturally and temporally distant critics, there too we shall be well advised not to neglect the insights of those of our own place and period. This is all the more legitimate as we recall the store Hume sets by persons of learning, taking care thereby that our own local guides should be ones best able to understand the foreign material they come to scrutinize.

Anyone brought up under the tutelage of Kant will suspect that even if there remains a role for Hume's standard to play, the idea of evidential appeal to good critics is thoroughly wrongheaded. It suggests, that in forming my aesthetic views and critical opinions my own responses to an object may simply give way to those of someone I recognize to be a good critic, even when my own responses are entirely at odds with what that person tells me. I am just encouraged to 'grope about empirically among the judgements of others', as Kant disdainfully put it, rather than 'pronounce my judgement *a priori* and not as a mere imitation because the thing gives universal pleasure' (Kant (1952), §32.3). (The term 'a priori' here only means that the judgement is made on no other basis than the subject's own response to the object of his attention.)

There is certainly one way of thinking about Hume's programme under which this accusation would be justified, and maybe it chimes with what Kant himself believed was amiss with empiricist aesthetics. Let Peter and Paul disagree in some critical judgement they make, yet be willing to settle their difference by consulting good judges, on whose identity they happily agree. Further, let these persons' sentiments concur with Paul's view of the matter. The idea might then be that Peter should accept what they say and, as a result, come to think that the work in question is as Paul claims it to be and not as he, Peter, is inclined to judge it. Now, given that reconciliation aims beyond mere agreement to agreement on what is correct, appeal to good judges should be capable of transmitting knowledge in such cases, so the view that Peter comes to form must leave him knowing that the work is indeed as Paul sees it and not as he does.

This situation, Kant will protest, is incoherent – and rightly so. But what goes wrong with it is not, surely, that aesthetic judgements cannot express knowledge. Certainly, admirers of David Wiggins's writings on these matters will concur, the kind of subjectivism that connects aesthetic judgements with the discerning of phenomenally-elusive subjective properties of things should not deny that. Nor can it be that aesthetic knowledge cannot be transmitted from one person to another. Reading Homer will, on certain suppositions about his claim to expertise in the matter, enlighten us about Helen's charms. So why not here? Well, in the case of Helen we are at least presuming that if only we could be confronted by her and not merely by her wraith (as Euripides had Paris beguiled, and Mephistopheles Faust) we should enjoy the sentiment that Homer himself (or, better, his ultimate ancestral informant) enjoyed. And while that counterfactual's holding may not be sufficient to make Homer's putative knowledge transmissible to us, it does, with some qualification, seem to be necessary. However, in the case which we are considering, the condition is not fulfilled, for we are trying to imagine that appeal to the true judges will settle the issue for Peter, even while he does *not* share their enjoyment of the work in question. So any attempt to by-pass the subject's own experiential response by appeal to expert witnesses will fail.

When Kant makes his hostile remarks about 'heteronomy' he does so in the course of rejecting any appeal to rules and principles by way of securing proof in critical disputes. But this merely inserts another cog in the argument. To be told by a good judge that this work conforms to certain rules and principles and so should carry my approbation cannot provide me with knowledge here for just the same reason as before. We are supposing that even if I could see the work conformed to some rule, it would still not move me. The argument proceeds as before.

However, if this is how Kant did understand Hume, he misunderstood him. In the first place, Hume's standard reconciles varying *sentiments* rather than just *judgements*, and this could only come about by people sharing their experiential responses to something rather than somehow sincerely agreeing in their judgements while differing sentimentally *in petto*. Nor will it do to suppose that Hume thinks that such agreement of sentiment comes about as a result of some prior agreement in judgement secured by consulting good critics first. What he makes plain is that the good judge tries to show the disputing parties what to see. He operates not by enouncing what Peter is to believe, but by getting him to respond to the poem with which he is having difficulty in the light of suggestions about what to look for. Belief is concurrent with response here; it does not precede it. The evidence of the good judge is, properly speaking, indicative, not inductive.

Textually, Hume says:

> When we show the bad critic an avowed principle of art; when we illustrate this principle by means of examples, whose operation, from his own particular taste, he acknowledges to be conformable to the principle; when we prove to him that the same principle may be applied to the present case, where he did not perceive or feel its influence; he must conclude on the whole that the fault lies within himself and that he wants the delicacy which is requisite to make him sensible of every beauty and every blemish in any composition or discourse. ('Of the Standard of Taste', para. 16)

Against this background, we see now more precisely how a successful reconciliation can be expected to take place. The party whose response to a given poem changes has found that the true judge is able to *show* him something he had not been aware of before, and so comes to make the judgement (incorporating the correct sentiment) that had up to then eluded him. The convert does not just agree verbally and keep quiet about his own unchanging response. His response changes as a result of commerce with the good judge *in the face of the work itself*. If 'imitating another's judgement' were all he did, then his utterance would be insincere; but there is no reason whatever to suppose that Hume has that sort of case in mind.

Kant himself should be content with this suggestion. For one thing, he shares Hume's respect for critics: as he puts it 'they correct and expand our judgement' ((1952), §34), but they only do this by enabling us to respond appropriately to things to which previously we were not responsive. Second, he is adamant that the young poet – even when mistaken about the value of his work – should not just take the good judge's word for it. He has to be persuaded in the face of his own writing, and the way in which Kant, like Hume, supposes this to come about is by critics alerting him to the presence of some defect in his writing which he can then recognize, probably not something he would have achieved without their help. Knowing what to look for enables him to see it.

Finally, it would be perfectly in order for Hume to point out that discussion of aesthetic knowledge here can well be sidestepped. In the aesthetic domain it is not so much *knowledge* that concerns us as *appreciation*. And appreciation, which though it may well provide knowledge, cannot bypass the experiential response. We all know of Helen's beauty; appreciation, alas, is beyond us. And when Hume's poor critic modestly supposes himself insensitive to things that the good judge tries to point out, what he regrets is absent appreciation, not present ignorance. Hume brings out these points well; he could only do so on assumptions about the role of good judges that view them evidentially, not constitutively; and evidentially in such a way as to give no toehold to Kantian objections.

10

Logic, Truth and Moral Judgements

Wilfrid Hodges

There is an unkind saying that philosophers specialize in whatever they are bad at in real life. Thus experts on space and time arrive late for their lectures, logicians try to get their way by personal abuse, weak-kneed people write papers on 'The Will', and moral philosophers are often not. (There was a specialist in ethics, whose name I genuinely forget, at the Hebrew University in Jerusalem. His students had good reason to ask him 'Dr So-and-So, would you agree that a person who aspires to teach moral philosophy should be of virtuous character?' 'No,' he answered, 'no, no, not at all. Look at Abraham Fraenkel. He teaches mathematics, and is he a triangle?')

Since we are going to be examining the views of David Wiggins on truth and morals, I had better say at once that he is very definitely the exception to the rule. He is in philosophy exactly what he is in real life – nobody could slip a knife between them. Even if fate had forced him into a totally different profession (say, an Air Commodore or a manufacturer of soft furnishings), I believe he would still have been a philosopher, thinking much the same thoughts and saying much the same things as he thinks and says today.

David and I first met in 1960, when he became my tutor in Greats. Later he gave me my first permanent job, in the Philosophy Department at Bedford College, now sadly disbanded for the sake of Efficiency. We saw less of each other when I moved into mathematics. But we keep in touch; he even comes and gives philosophical talks to my computer science students and colleagues, which they much appreciate. I am most enormously in his debt, both for his teaching and for his help towards me in my early career. I salute him for his integrity, for the courage of his convictions, and for his personal warmth and thoughtfulness. As I said, he is exceptional.

1 The Marks of a Style

In a moment I shall be more critical of some of David's philosophical arguments. But before we come to that, let me recall four distinguishing marks of his philosophical method, as I remember them from two or three decades ago. Some of them will reappear in the essay that we shall be studying.

1 *Be prepared to change the question as you go.* There are arguments for this which apply in any field of study. After you have considered a question for ten hours or ten pages, you know more about it than you did at the beginning, and so you may well be able to phrase the question better. But philosophers have a special reason for adopting this precept. Many philosophical problems revolve around the analysis of concepts from everyday life (pain, needs, promises, identity etc.) These concepts carry a heavy load of experience and custom, far more than we could hope to express in a simple definition. To a great extent, philosophical debate must draw on things which are simply not there in the first formulation of the question.

It is sometimes said that a skilful legal draftsman knows just how much incoherence to build into a law in order to create the right amount of freedom for interpretation. The same may apply in philosophy too: pose your problem in a way which forces the philosopher to question the formulation. This may be a good way to start a discussion and get it headed in the right direction.

2 *Go at the question indirectly.* For example, start with something which you understand better, even though it may not seem relevant. One can dismiss this advice with easy jibes about the drunk looking for his keys under the streetlamp (he lost them somewhere else, but it was too dark to look for them there). These comments overlook several things: (i) the power of analogy, (ii) the problem that we get stuck in old formulations and need to be prized out of them, (iii) the need to get moving.

3 *Keep a store of unsolvable problems.* This is a point which I remember David making explicitly; at the time he was giving hints on how to run a tutorial. The point was straightforward: we have to be puzzled about something before we can start to do philosophy. I guess the same is true for any field of study, but philosophy is a special case. In chemistry we solve one problem and move on to the next; in German there are always new authors to study. The philosopher is still fretting over the same problems which exercised Plato, Aristotle, Chrysippus and Augustine. If these problems had been solved, there would be nothing left to do. The

only reason we are still at work on the same problems is that they have nuggets of unsolvability scattered through them.

4   *To make a thesis definite before you discuss it, formalize it in some appropriate logical language.* David used to do this rather more than he does now. The merits of a sharp formulation hardly need stating. Also logical languages are good for sorting out ambiguities in the placing of quantifiers. On the other hand, many of the theses that David deals with today are just not well adapted for formalizing in elementary logic. Take for example his fourth 'mark of truth' in the essay we shall be studying:

Every true belief . . . is true in virtue of something.

How on earth is one to formalize this, bearing in mind that 'true' here is the term under scrutiny? The phrase 'in virtue of something' has to operate either on 'true' or on a formula '*x* is true'. The first route leads us into the minefields of higher order logic; the second is philosophically suspect (I would have said) and lands us in the snares of *de re* modality. I don't say it couldn't be done, but a useful formalization would have to come at the end of a discussion, not at the beginning.

To be personal for a moment: as a student of David's, and then a beginning lecturer in his department, I found some of these precepts quite hard to accept. The most serious stumbling block was Number One. It's right for the subject, no doubt about that. But not everybody is temperamentally inclined to keep moving the goalposts; it seems too much like cheating. I think it was this as much as anything that led me away from philosophy and into mathematics – a field where questions are posed exactly and then answered once and for all. (Of course there are people who try to do the same in philosophy, but it makes it harder for them to be good philosophers.)

2   Formal Logic versus Meaningful Philosophy

I turn to the main question on the agenda: How can formal logic and methodology contribute to meaningful philosophy? The documents in front of us will be David's essay 'Truth, and Truth as Predicated of Moral Judgments' in his book (1991a), which should be read together with Postscript 3 at the end of the book, and Alfred Tarski's famous paper on truth ('The Concept of Truth in Formalized Languages' in his (1983)[1] which David has called in evidence.

Forgive a little more autobiography. When it was suggested that I might like to comment on his essay and its relation to Tarski's work, this

seemed to me a splendid idea. I understand a few things about Tarski's
paper, including some which are perhaps not generally understood; and
so I wrote a first draft in which I described the framework of Tarski's
paper, and then discussed how far David's paper fitted this framework.
The result was altogether unfortunate. Starting from Tarski, I came
nowhere near Wiggins. So I abandoned the first draft and wrote a second,
which is partly a reflection on why the first went wrong. If a philosopher
and a mathematical logician found it hard to understand each other, that
might say something about the ways in which philosophy can interact
with mathematical logic.

We turn to David's paper. His opening question is: Do moral judgements admit of plain truth? Let us call this the *prime question*. Eight
pages later, he sets out five 'marks of the concept of truth', and the rest
of the paper is about the question whether any moral judgements 'can
have all the marks of truth'. These marks of truth, David maintains, are
characteristic of the notion of truth as we apply it to 'sentences that
are perfectly unproblematic candidates for truth and falsehood' (1991a),
p. 142).

I believe David will confirm that the theses of this paper are part of
a larger agenda. David has a longstanding interest in understanding
what meanings are. He has some sympathy with the Quine–Davidson
approach, which asks how we could work out the meanings of the
utterances of some newly-discovered community that speaks a strange
language. He also has a strong sympathy with Davidson's view (and I
put it in my own words) that the only *semantic* facts we would need to
know about this community in order to unravel their language are facts
of the form

Sentence *s* is true.

From this angle it's very natural to ask whether value judgements can be
counted directly among the true sentences, or whether their meanings
have to be uncovered in some less direct way. This question leads quickly
into thorny old issues about the objectivity of ethics; but it is also a fresh
way of approaching those issues.

David proposes to approach his prime question by a 'detour through
the concept of truth itself'. The detour begins by pointing to a relationship between truth and meaning:

(1) Sentence *s* has as its literal use to say declaratively that *p* (henceforth
    for short, s means that *p*) just if whether *s* is true or not depends upon
    whether *p*.

Now Tarski in his paper on truth offers a criterion for the 'material adequacy' (or 'material correctness') of definitions of truth, namely his Convention T. This says that a definition of truth (restricted to a language L) is adequate if and only if the following holds:

(2) If *s* is any sentence of L then the definition of truth implies

  '*s* is true if and only if *p*',

  where '*p*' is replaced by the (canonical) translation of *s* into the metalanguage.

David recasts the last line of (2) as 'where *s* means that *p*', and then he rearranges (2) as follows:

(3) If *s* is any sentence of L and a correct definition of truth implies

  '*s* is true if and only if *p*',

  then *s* means that *p*.

Running (2) and (3) together, we get an alternative to (1):

(4) If *s* is any sentence of L, then *s* means that *p* if and only if it is a consequence of a correct account of truth in L that s is true if and only if p.

Here David notes that (4) is not going to be any use to us unless we have some independent criterion of what is a correct account of truth. He proposes what one might call an anthropological criterion, replacing 'correct account of truth' by

(5) [theory of truth] that combines with a descriptive anthropology to make sense of the shared life and conduct of L-speakers and that makes better sense than any rival combination consisting of a variant theory of truth and variant descriptive anthropology.

He goes on to say that he has in mind that 'the definition of truth in L and the descriptive anthropology it is paired with will be brought into being simultaneously, adjusted simultaneously, and tested simultaneously against rival pairs'. David then asks what constraints we should put on the notion of truth in L in order for (4) to work when 'correct account of truth' is read as in (5). His answer is the five 'marks of truth'. After stating these five marks, David gives arguments for them. (The arguments don't seem to be related at all closely to (5), but I think it is intended that eventually they will be.)

It will be clear that David's trek from the prime question to the marks of truth runs neither by logical deduction nor by free association, but somewhere in the space between these two. It will also be clear that some recent writings on meaning have had a strong guiding influence; David says in a footnote that he draws particularly on papers of Davidson, Grandy and McDowell. The end result – the list of marks of truth – stands or falls on its own merits, regardless of how we got there. What I want to comment on is the way in which logical theory, and in particular Tarski's highly formal methodology, weaves itself into the much looser tapestry of David's argument.

In §§3 and 4 I comment on two things which David has taken from Tarski, namely the notion of translation and the provability requirement in Criterion T. In §5 I turn to the correspondence theory of truth, which is something that David is very anxious *not* to take from Tarski. §6 describes one way in which Tarski's paper has not been a good influence on David. §7 leaves Tarski on one side for a moment; I make some formal comments of my own on David's argument. Then §8 notes a pleasant use of Tarski's paper in another paper by David. I sum up in §9.

3 The Notion of Translation

First let me review the relevant part of Tarski's paper. Tarski supposes that we have a formal language (call it L), probably designed for carrying out some kind of mathematics or exact science. Thus the language L has an exact grammar, and the expressions of L all have precise meanings which the users of L are expected to know. Doubtless the users of L agree on some axioms which they accept in their reasoning in L, and Tarski assumes that these axioms (together with suitable rules of inference) come with L as part of the package.

The problem is to write down a formal definition of the set of those sentences of L which are true. 'Formal' means 'within a suitable formal language', and so Tarski supposes also that we have a formal metalanguage (call it L') for talking about L. He invites us to make sure that L' contains the following equipment: (a) logical and set-theoretic symbols, (b) symbols which are intended as translations of the symbols of L, and (c) symbols which are intended as names for the expressions of L. We should suppose that L' has suitable axioms to accompany these symbols.

In this setting, Tarski's aim is to find a predicate $Tr(x)$ of the metalanguage L', which picks out all and only those sentences of L which are true.

Tarski notes that it's clear what this predicate $Tr(x)$ should do. Each sentence of L has a name in L', say s, and a translation in L', say p. What is required is that for each such sentence of L the following sentence of L' holds:

(6) $Tr(s)$ if and only if p.

Tarski says that a predicate $Tr(x)$ of L' is a *materially adequate* definition of truth for L if the axioms of L' prove (6) for each sentence of L. This is his Convention T. He proceeds to illustrate how we can construct materially adequate truth definitions in various cases. The well-known recursive definition in terms of satisfaction by sequences is one of these illustrations.

(A technical note in parentheses: Tarski slightly complicates things by first choosing the predicate which is to pick out the true sentences, let us now write it $\phi(x)$, and then introducing Tr as a symbol which is defined to be an abbreviation for ϕ. What Tarski requires in Convention T is that each instance of (6) should be a consequence of the formula which says that Tr stands for ϕ. In context he must mean: a consequence of this formula together with the axioms of L'. My formulation makes the formula unnecessary, by reading 'Tr' as the predicate ϕ itself and not as the new symbol defined in terms of it. Please ignore this if it confuses you; but it will be important that the proof of each instance of (6) uses the axioms of the metalanguage.)

Tarski's Convention T was (2) above. Compare it with (3) to see what David has done to it. The first step is to read 'the translation' as 'a translation', so that we can phrase the relationship between s and p as 's means that p'. (Yes, I know that Tarski first wrote this paper in Polish, which is a language defective in definite articles. But Tarski is known to have checked the translation of this paper very carefully, at a time when he had become fluent in English. The paper consistently says 'the translation'.) The second step is to switch the order of the clauses in (2), so that 's means that p' becomes the conclusion instead of a hypothesis.

The first step here seems to be an unintentional distortion of Tarski, and I shall come back to it. The second change is certainly intentional, and it's a neat example of a time-honoured way of breaking new ground. Namely, we take an implication which is agreed to be true, and we ask in what circumstances it can be read backwards. Mathematical advances often have this form. In logic a famous example is the laws of identity.

Everybody can see that if *a* equals *b* then every property of *a* is also a property of *b*; it took a Leibniz to ask whether the converse holds too.

To return to the first step: what David is after, by combining (2) and (3), is a necessary and sufficient condition for *s* to mean that *p*. So it's important for him that Convention T uses the notion of translation full-bloodedly. Both in the paper and in the Postscript, David makes the point that Tarski is allowed to use the semantical notion of translation even though it is not in general expressible in the metalanguge L′, because Convention T lives at the meta-metalevel – it's a condition on expressions of L′, not a condition expressible in L′.

Unfortunately Tarski seems to have meant much less than David attributes to him. At this date, Tarski's notion of setting up a formal language was in some ways remarkably naive. He supposed that we describe the syntax of the language, and then we just say what the symbols are intended to mean, in a way that seems to us to make sense.

(7) We shall always ascribe quite concrete and, for us, intelligible meanings to the signs which occur in the languages we shall consider. (Tarski (1983), p. 167.)

One naturally asks what role these 'for us, intelligible meanings' are supposed to play in scientific methodology. The answer seems to be simply that the meanings suggest 'axioms [which] seem to us to be materially true' (Tarski, *loc. cit.*). (Maybe for a physical science the meanings also suggest applications.) For all his clarity and precision in describing the formal properties of languages, Tarski was sometimes quite sloppy in what he said about meanings. For example his own statement of Convention T ((1983), p. 187) begins 'Using the symbol '*Tr*' to denote the class of all true sentences . . .'. But if we look at what the Convention actually says, it's clear that the symbol '*Tr*' might as well denote a pot of jam; the denotation of the symbol plays no role whatever in Convention T.

For the matter in hand, Tarski instructs us to put into the metalanguage L′ some symbols which are translations of the symbols of L (see (1983), pp. 170, 210). He must mean that we stipulate that they are to be translations of the symbols of L. Declaring 'I shall use X to mean Y' is much less than having a notion of synonymy. Tarski never requires that we should have any way of telling whether or not a given expression of L′ is a translation of a given expression of L, or even that we should know what it means to say that one expression is a translation of another. (Tarski's footnote on p. 188 of (1983) makes the same point. He says there are 'no great difficulties' in exactly specifying the meaning of 'the translation of a given sentence [of the object language] into the metalanguage'. He would certainly not have said this if he had meant it to involve defining synonym.)

In principle this could be quite a serious flaw in Tarski's account of truth. It means for example that we have to be more careful than Tarski was when we use a metalanguage which already exists – we can't simply stipulate the meanings of its expressions if they already have meanings. This is our situation if we use English as a metalanguage to talk about truth in Bulgarian. I had not seen it pointed out until I read David's use of Tarski.

4 The Role of Provability

To modern eyes, one feature of Tarski's Convention T is rather odd at first sight. Most logicians today would prefer to say that a definition $Tr(x)$ of the predicate 'true' for sentences of L is correct if and only if it does in fact pick out just the true sentences; in other words, if and only if all the equivalences (6) above are *true sentences of the metalanguage*. Tarski requires instead that these equivalences are *provable from the axioms of the metalanguage*.

The reason for this discrepancy is not far to seek. It lies in the views that Tarski had, and with him virtually all the logicians of the 1930s, about what is a proper activity for a logician. Logic is a formal art, and we move forward in logic by making proofs from our axioms. If we want to establish that some formal definition correctly captures a certain idea, there is nothing gained by you and me sitting down together over cups of black coffee and comparing our introspections. We need to agree on some axioms and then use them to prove the correctness; Tarski's Convention T says exactly what it is we need to prove in the case of truth.

There is some irony (but not much) in the fact that Tarski's own work has encouraged us to be more robust nowadays with the notion of truth, so that we talk freely of statements being just *true*, as opposed to *provable in such-and-such a formal system*.

David suggests a quite different reason why the equivalences (6) need to be provable. Suppose all we asked for was the truth of each instance of (6), not its provability. Suppose also that $Tr(x)$ is some materially adequate truth definition for L. Let q be your favourite true sentence (for example Fermat's Last Theorem, or the proposition that John Selwyn Gummer is a member of the British Cabinet, assuming these are in fact true). Let $\psi(x)$ be the conjunction '$Tr(x)$ and q'. Then any instance of (6) has the same truth value as the corresponding instance of

(8) $\psi(s)$ if and only if p.

So it would follow that ψ is also a materially adequate truth definition.

But what is the harm in counting ψ as materially adequate? Here David makes two claims. First, he says,

> . . . whatever else [a definition of truth for L] is or does, it must fasten down the extension of the predicate 'true-in-L' both non-accidentally correctly and in a way that does not depend on any particular object-language sentence's being true. ((1991a), p. 143.)

The predicate ψ will generally fail this test. (David words it as two tests, but I rather think that his final phrase about depending on a particular object-language sentence is meant to be an illustration of accidental correctness, not a further requirement.) But if we add the provability condition, the truth of (8) will no longer be an accident.

And second, if ψ does pass this test, then it follows that in all true instances of (8), s will in fact mean that p. Thus:

> The general condition that will determine the extension non-accidentally correctly for each and every arbitrary x is this:
>
> True x iff p, where the sentence for which 'p' holds a place *translates* or *means the same as* the sentence x. ((1991a), p. 337.)

Perhaps this is not so much a second claim as an explanation of what David counts as non-accidental correctness.

Leaving Tarski's intentions on one side for the moment, how do these two claims stand? If we run them together, they assert that the provability condition in Convention T is sufficient to guarantee that s means that p; hence they justify (3). But this is certainly false, as David himself records in a footnote on page 145; we get a counterexample by taking q to be an irrelevant logical truth. David's footnote suggests that we can make a repair by limiting the means of proof allowed. Using only relevance logic might be an example of the kind of restriction he has in mind. (And of course we would also have to restrict the axioms of the metalanguage in a corresponding way.)

This is an interesting suggestion. But it needs a lot more working out before we can judge it. In some recent unpublished work, Ruth Kempson argues that speakers of a natural language can be thought of as using a certain kind of proof procedure to parse sentences. She claims that in this setting, standard proof rules give a more natural explanation of some phenomena covered by Chomsky's government and binding theory; she can support this claim in some detail.

I am reading David's claims as arguments that some appropriate provability condition in Convention T is both necessary and sufficient for (3). He may well be right, and this could be an important discovery if he is. But of course (3) is Wiggins and not Tarski. It would be totally wrong-headed to claim that Tarski himself put in the provability requirement for any reason along these lines.

In fact Tarski devotes several pages of his paper to proving the material adequacy of what he himself calls an 'accidental' truth definition for the calculus of classes in an infinite domain (Theorem 28, (1983), p. 208). The truth definition is completely syntactic; it says that sentences are true if and only if they can be proved in a certain proof calculus. He comments:

> . . . it must be strongly emphasized that the possibility of constructing a definition of such a kind is purely accidental. We owe it to the specific peculiarities of the science in question . . . as well as – in some degree – to the strong existential assumptions adopted in the metatheory. . . . we have here no general method of construction which could be applied to other deductive sciences.

In short, the provability condition in Convention T provides *no guarantee whatever* that the truth definition will be non-accidentally correct, either in Tarski's sense (accidental = not generalizable) or in David's (accidental = not giving the meaning of the sentence). This is obviously so, for the reason which Tarski himself refers to: we have not put any restrictions on the axioms of the metatheory. (The point applies *a fortiori* if these axioms contain a descriptive anthropology.)

Nor is this the slightest embarrassment to Tarski. Far from it. Proving the material adequacy of 'accidental' truth definitions for various mathematical theories was one of the central themes in the research of Tarski himself and his students from 1926 to the late 1930s. He continued to publish in this vein right up until 1978. His most famous mathematical result, the decision algorithm for first-order sentences true in the field of real numbers, is precisely an 'accidental' materially adequate truth definition.

All of this makes it astonishing that anybody should seriously have suggested that Tarski requires truth definitions to be 'intentionally correct', or that the provability condition in Convention T was meant to ensure this. I fear it says something about the lack of contact between philosophical and mathematical logicians.

5 The Snare of Correspondence

David's argument in this paper makes no use at all of Tarski's recursive definition of truth in terms of satisfaction. Nevertheless David is very concerned that nobody should read Tarski's paper and set off in a different direction under the influence of this definition of truth. Above all, David wants to save us from reading into Tarski's definition of truth some form of correspondence theory. A section of his Postscript is devoted to this ((1991a), pp. 331–339).

One thing that Tarski constantly insisted on was that a definition of 'true' has to be relative to a fixed language. (See (1983), p. 153 for example.) His reason for this was not at all subtle; it was simply that the same string of symbols may occur in two different languages, and be a true sentence in one language but a false sentence in the other. Curiously, I remember David himself giving an example of a sentence like this in a philosophy tutorial at New College in the early 1960s. The sentence was 'Jam dies', which serves both in English and in Latin.

David picks up Tarski's insistence, but he does something different with it. He believes that some writers have been misled by a clause of Tarski's recursive truth definition:

(9) s is true if and only if every sequence of objects satisfies s.

One could carelessly read (9) as saying that s is true if and only if 'reality' satisfies it, i.e. if it corresponds to reality. Thus the notion of satisfaction by every sequence of objects would be 'a wonderful winnowing of precisely what needed to be preserved from "correspondence" ' (Wiggins (1991a) p. 333). To forestall any such reading, David insists that (9) is only a clause in the definition of truth for one particular language.

> . . . unspecified for language, [satisfaction] is not any relation at all. Satisfaction is defined separately for each object language L. And the attempt to define it generally would make it impossible for any truth definition to meet the criterion of adequacy that Tarski imposes on such definitions . . . ((1991a), p. 334).

Is this convincing? In the first place, one would have to read (9) *very* carelessly in order to get any kind of correspondence theory out of it.

In the second place, the distance between truth and satisfaction is not so great. Tarski saw that for the languages he was interested in, there was no hope of giving a definition of the notion 'true' by recursion on the construction of formulas, but he could get round the problem by giving instead a recursive definition of the notion 'true of'. The phrase 'x satisfies s' is only a technical refinement of the intuitive notion 's is true of x'. If there is a property of truth, unspecified for language, then certainly there is a relation of satisfaction, unspecified for language. (Tarski himself speaks of 'the usual meaning of [the notion of satisfaction] in its customary linguistic usage', adding a remark to the effect that it forms a natural generalization of the concept of truth; see (1983), p. 189.)

Incidentally when Tarski himself wanted to relate his theory to the correspondence theory of truth, it was Convention T that he pointed to, not clause (9). (See (1983), p. 404.)

This might have been a case where David took a thesis from Tarski and put it successfully to a new use. But it is not entirely clear from the paper what view David is attacking, or why it matters. I suspect that this part of David's argument is a move in some battle that I don't know about.

6 The Notion of Assertibility

There is one way in which I tentatively suspect that Tarski's setup has been a bad influence on David's argument. Turning once more to those 'sentences that are perfectly unproblematic candidates for truth and falsehood', it does seem reasonable to say that there is one primary criterion for accepting or rejecting them, namely whether they are true or not. But with moral judgements it is not at all clear to me what 'the primary dimension of assessment' (p. 148) should be. Take the statement

(10) X is to blame for Y's death.

As we ordinarily understand the terms, there is a world of difference between saying that (10) is 'assertible' (Wiggins (1991a), p. 109), that (10) is 'worthy of being affirmed' ((1991a), p. 141), and that (10) 'stands for acceptance' (p. 141 again). Tarski's account of truth is resolutely one-dimensional; a sentence is either true or not true, and that's all there is to be said. If – and I only say if – part of the problem about moral judgements is that they can be assessed on more dimensions than straightforwardly factual judgements, then David's scheme of argument has kept this fact well hidden.

7 The Marks of Truth

David says several times that there is no question of giving an 'analysis of
truth' (e.g. (1991a), p. 142). This puzzled me at first, and I wondered if
David was reading something extra into Tarski's theorem on the undefi-
nability of truth. (This theorem says that under certain mild conditions
on the language L, no materially correct definition of truth for L can be
given in L.) But from conversation I gather that David means something
much more empirical: experience shows that it's hopeless to try to reduce
the notion of 'true' to more basic components.

But, says David, for the matter in hand we don't really need an analysis
of truth anyway.

> All we need in order to answer our question about ethics is to determine
> what properties are possessed by every sentence that expresses a truth, or
> the *marks* (as one might say in Frege's terminology) of the concept *true*.
> ((1991a), p. 142.)

This is not Tarski territory, but there are some points I think I should
make. Here are David's marks of truth, with the numbers changed to
letters to avoid confusion.

(a) Truth is a primary dimension of assessment for beliefs and for
sentences that can express or report beliefs;

(b) If x is true, then x will under favourable circumstances command
convergence, and the best explanation of the existence of this convergence will either require the actual truth of x or be inconsistent
with the denial of x;

(c) For any x, if x is true then x has content; and if x has content then
x's truth cannot simply consist in x's being itself a belief, or in x's
being something believed or willed or . . .;

(d) Every true belief (every truth) is true in virtue of something;

(e) If x_1 is true and x_2 is true, then their conjunction is true.

When David says that these are 'properties possessed by every sentence
that expresses a truth', I think he means that each of these marks can be
written in the form

(11) For all x, if x is true then $F(x)$.

This is clear for (b)–(e). We can bring (a) into this form, with some loss of information, by writing it as 'Every true sentence comes high in the primary dimension of assessment for beliefs and for sentences that can express or report beliefs'.

I think David also means that what he calls 'truths uncontroversially agreed as such' all have these five properties. Once we have fixed these marks for uncontroversial kinds of true sentence, we can then 'see in a new way what it *turns on* whether moral judgements have these marks or lack them' ((1991a), p. 142), and this in turn will tell us what it turns on whether moral judgements are true.

There are serious problems here, which come to light if we look at the logical structure of these marks, never mind their meaning. The first is a point of elementary logic. If all true sentences have property F, and the moral judgement j also has property F, nothing whatever follows about the moral judgement j being true. The same holds if we replace F by five properties, one for each mark. The point is that a property which all truths have will in general be a property which some falsehoods have too.

Did David intend that these five marks between them should somehow *exhaust* the concept of (unproblematic) truth, in the sense that any unproblematic sentence which has all five marks must be true? Possibly; but it is not what he says, and he presents no argument in this direction. (There is quite a bit to be argued. He needs to give reasons why his five marks not only exhaust the concept of unproblematic truth, but also can be expected to stay exhaustive when we move to problem cases.) Before he sets out his list of marks, he says 'I think we ought to expect that among the marks of the concept of truth will be the following'; this hardly suggests that he thinks of them as exhaustive.

Second, suppose we agree that these marks are to be taken as exhaustive. Then we face a second problem, which would spring to the eye if we tried to symbolize the marks. David speaks of the marks as properties, and asks whether moral judgements can have them. This is meant to give a clue to whether moral judgements can be true. But if we look at the properties F described by the marks, we see that at least in cases (b)–(e), these properties explicitly involve the notion of truth. Thus with (d), it looks as if we are being asked to judge whether a moral judgement j might be *true* by asking first whether j might be *true in virtue of something*. Clearly this is circular. From the logical structure of the marks, it is conceivable that one could mount an argument showing that no moral judgement could have the property F. But no possible argument could go the other

way and show that *j* does have *F*, because it would first have to show that
j is true, which is precisely the point at issue.

Something has gone seriously wrong with David's statement here. I am
going to guess what he meant. It is a guess, but it seems to make good
sense of what follows.

I don't think that these five marks should be read as properties of true
statements at all. I think they should be read as properties of (unproblematic) *truth*. This is clearly so for mark (a); our attempt to read it in the
form (11) was never convincing. In fact read this way, the five marks
seem like a set of characteristic properties of truth. The question then is
whether there is some feature that some moral judgements can have,
which itself shares these five properties of truth.

Here I do believe that David is hampered by the problem mentioned in
the previous section. I think that in his later discussion in this paper, he
does have in mind some such feature of moral judgements. It's probably
not assertibility; justified practical commitment might be nearer the
mark. If he had faced the question of the different dimensions on which
one can assess moral judgements, he would have said outright what
feature he has in mind. As it is, we have to read between the lines, and I
apologize if I have read wrong. David's discussion of the difference
between evaluation and practical judgement, later in the essay, can be
seen as distinguishing between possible candidates for 'truth' in the case
of moral judgements; likewise his thoughts on 'the right thing for me to do'.

Incidentally I am not convinced by David's statement that in Frege 'A
mark of the concept F is a property that anything has if it falls under F'
((1991a), p. 142 note 5). As I read Frege, his marks of a concept F are
the separate conjuncts of a conjunctive definition of F. He almost certainly takes the notion from Kant, for whom the 'analytic marks' of a
concept are those partial concepts through which we recognize the concept
and which we 'already think therein' (Jäsche Logic, Kant (1992), p. 565).
For Kant the marks of a concept are the 'grounds of cognition' of that
concept; in other words, we recognize (say) gold by perceiving that the
object has the marks of gold, such as heaviness. So it is inconceivable for
Kant, and I guess also for Frege, that the marks of a concept F could
themselves contain F. This reading of Frege would have saved David
from the second problem about his marks, and maybe also from the first.

8 Translation and Empathy

Let me close with a beautiful example of how to draw morals out of
formulas. It appears on pp. 112ff. of David's earlier essay 'Truth, Inven-

tion, and the Meaning of Life' (also in (1991a)). David imagines a moral philosopher trying to analyse the meanings of moral utterances in English. Using Tarski's setting as a paradigm, David gives this philosopher a metalanguage which must include English (or at least translations of all sentences of English). If the philosopher is to explain the meanings of moral sentences of English, he must be able to say in his own words what those sentences mean, and so he must be able to translate them into his own language.

> It follows that the possibility simply does not exist for the theorist to stand off entirely from the language of his subjects or from the viewpoint that gives this its sense. He has to begin at least by embracing – or by making as if to embrace – the very same commitments and world-view as the ordinary speakers of the object language.

It seems to me that David's argument in these two pages flickers between two different points. First, if you want to say what the sentences of L mean, you have to be able to translate the sentences of L into your own language. This is a formal requirement that Tarski very properly imposes. And second, if you want to understand what the sentences of L mean, you have to put yourself into the same world-view as the speakers of L. This is a much more contentious point. For example, do we really have to believe in God – just a little bit – in order to understand statements made by religious moralists? Do we really have to have racist opinions in order to understand jokes about the Irish?

David's move from Tarski to *Weltanschauung* is a subtler analogue of the move that many people make from a theorem of Arthur Prior's logic of time:

$CFpFp$

to its English translation: What will be will be.

9 Envoi

The opening pages of David's essay on truth and moral judgements are a rich pattern-book of ways to use formal equipment in support of an informal argument. From our discussion above, we can pick out at least four kinds of interaction between logic and philosophy.

The first interaction is the traditional one: you sharpen your arguments by translating them into symbols. I'm ashamed to realize that in §1 of this essay I accused David of having taught this precept to undergraduates, and in §7 I accused him of not following it himself.

The second interaction goes in the opposite direction: you show up the weakness of a formal argument by applying it to a real situation. Whether he intended it or not, I think this is what David succeeded in doing to Tarski's use of the notion of translation.

The third is to use a formal situation as an analogue of something real and more complicated. We do this when we teach by drawing diagrams. When David uses the relationship between language and metalanguage to make a point about the need for understanding from inside, he is drawing an abstract diagram.

The fourth is to use a formal argument, not to prove anything, but to set the creative juices flowing. (Referring back again, it is one way to follow the injunction to go at a question indirectly.) David is a past master of this art, and his 'detour through the concept of truth' is an archetypal example.

NOTE

1 The Analytical Index added in this edition is particularly valuable.

11

On There Being Nothing Else to Think, or Want, or Do

A. W. Moore

1. Four lines up on page 127 of 'The Sense and Reference of Predicates: A Running Repair to Frege's Doctrine and a Plea for the Copula',[1] there is a sentence by David Wiggins which has the air of self-parody. It opens with a conjunction; it is annotated twice; it contains one pair of dashes and four pairs of parentheses (in one case nested); and it runs to 215 words. I mention it partly out of a sense of mischief but partly also because its characteristic excesses call to mind everything that can make Wiggins (in fact) such a pleasure to read, as well as a wonderfully rewarding philosopher to study: his painstaking attention to detail; his delicacy of touch; his feel for instructive and salutary examples; the unhurried and unflustered way in which he describes familiar phenomena, injecting just enough theory here or there to cast philosophical light on them, never so much as to distort them; and the way in which he manages, through all the convolutions, to keep track of what is important. People say that he is hard to pin down. He is. But I cannot help thinking that he is hard to pin down not because he is so vague, but because he is so precise.

I think his writing skills, and with them his unique brand of philosophical acumen, are especially well suited to his work on ethics. And it is an idea that has cropped up a few times in his work on ethics that I want to use as a basis for this essay. There will not be much exegesis. I want to remould the idea. I hope that Wiggins, with his philosophically inquisitive instincts, will approve. If I end up with something quite different from what he originally had in mind, perhaps this will serve to illustrate the depth in his writing. If so, then I shall be satisfied that I have provided a fitting tribute.

I should like to thank the editors for their extremely helpful suggestions.

The idea (incongruous, some would say, in the context of such prodigious sentences, with their subtle qualifications and their labyrinthine structure) is that of *there being nothing else to think*. Here are two quotations:

> [Sometimes we can say that] there is nothing else to think . . . [And] sometimes, when we do, it will be possible for someone else to say that we think what we think (and that some of the others who think this may think this) not accidentally, but precisely because there is nothing else to think – with a 'because' that simultaneously vindicates and, by vindicating, explains.[2]

> [Suppose] one comes to believe that p precisely because p . . . [Then] the best full explanation of one's coming to believe that p requires the giver of the explanation to adduce in his explanation the very fact that p. What follows from this is that his explanation will conform to the following schema: for this, that and the other reason (here the explainer specifies these), there is really nothing else to think but that p; so it is a fact that p; so, given the circumstances and given the subject's cognitive capacities and opportunities and given his access to what leaves nothing else to think but that p, no wonder he believes that p.[3]

Now the example that Wiggins adduces most frequently is an arithmetical one: there is nothing else to think but that $7 + 5 = 12$. This, combined with the fact that his ultimate concern is with ethics, suggests that he is trying to draw a boundary round the non-empirical (or the non-contingent). It suggests that he is trying to formulate something which sets arithmetical truths and ethical truths apart from those of geology, say, or from a truth about where someone has left his spectacles. This in turn would chime with an interpretation of the sentence 'There is nothing else to think but that $7 + 5 = 12$' whereby it meant that having any other view about whether or not $7 + 5 = 12$ was literally impossible – and in the most stringent sense. For, arguably, though one can have all sorts of contingently mistaken thoughts, one cannot think something which is itself impossible. This idea has in fact had wide currency, in different forms. Wittgenstein, in the *Tractatus*, writes that 'whatever is thinkable is possible too.'[4] Quine writes that 'when [a deviant logician] . . . tries to deny [a doctrine of logic] . . . he only changes the subject.'[5] True, there is, in each case, a complicating sub-text. Wittgenstein's views make him equally hostile to the idea of thinking something necessary,[6] and Quine is sceptical about the very idea of a necessary/contingent distinction.[7] Still, it is not hard to envisage an argument to the effect that a necessity, unlike a contingency, is such that nothing would strictly *count* as believing its negation (or perhaps even as doubting its truth). And that would yield one particularly strong interpretation of the formula 'There is nothing else to think but that p'.

It is clear, however, not least from the second of the two quotations above, that this is not what Wiggins intends. He wants the formula 'There is nothing else to think but that p' to be interpreted in a much weaker sense, and to have a much wider application.[8] Furthermore, he intends it indexically. While there may be nothing else to think about a certain issue, here and now, there might once have been and there might still be in circumstances where the issue presents itself in a murkier light or less is known about it. Perhaps, then, Wiggins intends the formula to apply, in any given context, not to simple necessities, but to the necessary consequences of whatever shared background knowledge can be presupposed in that context? That is nearer the mark. It would mean that Wiggins was essentially concerned with the drawing of conclusions, or with the ruling out of hypotheses. In fact, however, his idea is more subtle than that. The presupposed shared background is not just a range of propositions from which other propositions follow. It also includes commitments; sentiments; ways of understanding; canons of rationality determining what hangs together with what. In saying that there is nothing else to think about an issue but that such and such, one is presenting anyone who thinks anything other than such and such with a challenge. The challenge is to come up with an alternative story, in full and coherent detail, without at any point straining intolerably against the bounds of credibility which must be acknowledged by anyone aspiring to keep a sane grip on the situation.[9]

There is much more to be said about this. But I want now to indulge in my first bit of remoulding. I want to suggest that we reconstrue Wiggins's formula non-indexically. For whenever the formula correctly applies, it is true, even outside the context, that *not* having the thought in question means paying a price: in particular it means not assimilating, perhaps not being able to assimilate, whatever in the context makes having the thought mandatory. Insofar as a single schematic account can be given of this,[10] there is a viable, elliptical, context-independent reading of 'There is nothing else to think but that p': there is nothing else to think which does not involve paying the price. The propositions to which the formula then applies are precisely those which, given a suitable presupposed shared background of the sort indicated above, come within the ambit of Wiggins's conception. Viewing the matter in this way will, I think, direct us back to his own main interest in introducing the formula.

Which, then, are these propositions? They are those whose acceptance can be given the kind of vindicatory explanation schematized in the second quotation above. (Both quotations, along with many other passages, reveal the direct connection which Wiggins recognizes between applying his formula and giving such an explanation.) Let us call such propositions 'objectively true'. The question immediately arises whether objective truth, on this understanding, is (simply) truth. This is another of those issues on which Wiggins is maddeningly but justifiably hard to pin down. But we can be clear about two things. First, it is the ordinary, familiar, mundane concept of truth, in its full generality, that ultimately interests him. (One of his primary aims is to discover whether there is such truth – pure and simple – anywhere in the realm of ethical thought.[11]) And secondly, he regards objective truth as at the very least the kernel of that concept.[12] We shall not stray far from his concerns, then, and we shall in any case start down an interesting avenue of exploration, if we adopt the following policy: to treat the formula 'There is nothing else to think but that p' (on our context-independent reading of it[13]) as equivalent to 'It is true that p'. Hence any attempt to define it, or to explicate it, or to expand on it, must issue in a formula 'T(p)' such that every instance of the schema

(1) It is true that $p \leftrightarrow T(p)$[14]

is true.[15]

Here is another way of putting the same point. If we say that the formula 'There is nothing else to think but that p' *denotes* those propositions to which it applies, then our policy will be so to understand the formula that it denotes, quite simply, truths. Hence we must rule out a stringent interpretation whereby it denotes necessities. And at a somewhat different extreme, we must rule out a psychological interpretation – 'It is psychologically impossible to think anything other than p' – whereby the propositions denoted might include some falsehoods.[16] Either of these, combined with an argument that the formula applied within the realm of ethics, would have opened up some interesting possibilities. The first, for example, would have opened up the possibility that (certain) apparent disagreements in ethics must really be linguistic disputes or disagreements about non-ethical facts. The second would have opened up the possibility that we are so psychologically constituted that we cannot face (certain) truths about how to live. But neither of these is an idea that Wiggins has bequeathed to us; and neither has anything especially to do with our understanding of the formula.

Now in order to consolidate that understanding we must say some more about the ellipsis. What is the price that someone pays for having an incorrect thought?

This question can be turned round. For in saying that, when things are thus and so, anyone who does not think that things are thus and so pays a price, we are in effect saying that, when things are thus and so, anyone who satisfies a certain condition has no choice but to think that things are thus and so.[17] The question can therefore be put in the form: what is this condition? Or rather: what is *such* a condition? (It is clear, or it should soon become clear, that more than one condition fits the bill.)

Putting the question this way round can give shape to the project of specifying 'T(p)'. We first assume that 'T(p)' takes the following form:

(2) Any thinker who . . . is bound to think that p.

We then put our efforts into filling in the dots.[18]

I shall not myself defend any particular way of filling in the dots. I want to operate at a higher level of generality than that. But it is important for me to say something about the constraints that must be met if the project is to be carried out in a satisfactory and philosophically illuminating way.

I list three such constraints.

(i) The guarantee that every instance of (1) comes out true must be *non-trivial*. We would be violating this constraint if we filled in the dots with 'knows whether or not p'.

Comment: 'Non-trivial' is a vague and slippery term, and (i) is itself correspondingly vague and slippery, as well as being context- and purpose-relative. But very roughly, how non-trivial our guarantee is will be inversely proportional to how quickly and with how few repercussions we are able to satisfy ourselves that we have it. I shall not try to say any more than that, beyond issuing the following warning: non-triviality is quite separate from non-circularity. We should be involved in some sort of circle if, for example, we specified a condition which used the concept of truth. Whether we wanted to avoid that would depend on what our purposes were. If we were trying to analyse truth, we should want to avoid it. But as Wiggins has continually reminded us, if we were trying to *elucidate* truth – as indeed he is – we should not.[19]

(ii) The guarantee that every instance of (1) comes out true must be (to the extent that we are prepared to think in these terms) *a priori*. We would be violating this constraint if, having discovered some oracle, we filled in the dots with 'arrives at a belief about whether or not p by consulting the oracle'.

Comment: The reason for (ii) is simply that the illumination we seek is philosophical illumination.[20]

(iii) The condition specified when we fill in the dots must be such that everyone has a reason to satisfy it (or to satisfy any instance of it, subject to having a view about the matter in hand). We would be violating this constraint if we filled in the dots with 'has been sentenced by God to die as soon as she acquires a false belief, and has acquired a belief about whether or not p'.

Comment: The reason for (iii) is that we need to do justice to the idea that anyone who does not satisfy the condition, and who may thereby think something false, pays a price. This in turn reminds us of the alternative route into carrying out the main project, which I shall call the 'contrapositive' route: to focus on what someone must *fail* to be, or must fail to do, in order not to have the belief in question (or more specifically, perhaps, to think the opposite).

Let me gesture towards four possible ways of carrying out the project, each of which seems to meet these constraints. (But note: although different, they are not incompatible.[21] The constraints still do not force a unique answer.)

(a) We could stick as closely as possible to the genesis of our context-independent understanding of Wiggins's formula. This means turning to the kind of thing whose assimilation, whenever it is available, makes having a true thought mandatory. And this in turn suggests filling in the dots with some suitable embellishment of 'can recognize the reasons for or against its being the case that p, attends to them, and forms a belief about whether or not p on that basis'. This would certainly tie in with what Wiggins says in the second quotation above, where he talks about a subject's 'cognitive capacities', 'opportunities' and 'access to what leaves nothing else to think'.[22]

(b) We could take a leaf out of Peirce's book. We could fill in the dots with some suitable embellishment of 'has a belief about whether or not p which is "fated to be ultimately agreed to by all who investigate"'.[23]

(c) We could take a leaf out of Ramsey's book, as adapted by Hugh Mellor. We could fill in the dots with some suitable embellishment of 'has a belief about whether or not p which, in conjunction with all his other beliefs, makes his desires cause actions that succeed in achieving what is desired'.[24]

But more interesting than any of these, for my purposes, would be to explore some variation on the theme of the unconditioned. I deliberately use that word with its Kantian resonance. I have in mind a quasi-Kantian Idea,[25] a rational idealization of what we took from Wiggins in (a). An unconditioned thought would be a thought whose (objective) explanation and (subjective) vindication came together. It would be a thought *whose best explanation included the fact that the subject's own reason for having it, or continuing to have it, was a result of rational self-conscious reflection on its best explanation.*[26]

That this is an uncompromising ideal can be made clear by considering how a familiar kind of justified, true thought will fail to exemplify it. Wiggins writes that all the children in his son's class at school think that $7 + 5 = 12$; and he says that the best explanation for their thinking this is that '(i) as can be shown by the use of calculating rules (and could in the end be rigorously demonstrated), it is a fact that $7 + 5 = 12$ . . . [and (ii)] they are going by the calculating rules'.[27] I doubt this. At least I think I doubt it. A lot depends on how exactly Wiggins's proposed explanation is to be spelt out. But I suspect that these children first acquired the belief that $7 + 5 = 12$, and have since retained it, less because of arithmetical reflection and more because of inculcation than a straightforward reading of Wiggins suggests. At any rate, there will be elements in the best explanation of their belief which play no part in informing any self-consciously formed *reason* they have for it. It would be absurd to call a typical nine-year-old's thought that $7 + 5 = 12$ unconditioned, in the sense defined. (Wiggins could agree.) The same is true, I submit, of most of our thoughts. Unconditioned thought sets a very demanding standard.

Conditioned thought is correspondingly commonplace. But one feature of conditioned thought is that critical self-conscious reflection is always liable to unsettle it. For it is always liable to locate something in the explanation of the thought – some psychological, sociological or cultural factor – whose discovery militates against the subject's original reason for having the thought (however mildly, however briefly, and however easily that reason can be reinstated).[28] Unconditioned thought, on the other hand, is already rationally reflective, which means that it is, by its very nature, impervious to critical self-conscious reflection. Now:

(d) We could fill in the dots with 'has an unconditioned belief about whether or not p'.[29]

Here no doubt someone will protest that we would thereby be violating a fourth constraint which ought to have been mentioned earlier. The constraint is that the condition specified when we fill in the dots must be

one which thinkers stand a good chance of satisfying, and typically do
satisfy, otherwise we shall be pulling away from Wiggins's original concern with actual explanation.

But I do not share that concern, at least not in the same form. I have
already indicated that I want to remould Wiggins's idea. I am interested
in certain ideals of rationality which may thereby be illuminated. This
interest in turn connects with an interest in parallel projects for volition
and agency. It is to these that I now turn.

2. People certainly use formulae like 'There is nothing else to
want/wish for/hope for but that p' (sometimes with 'any more' inserted at
an appropriate point), or again, a little more idiomatically, 'There is
nothing else to do but X/There is nothing else for it but to do X', 'There
is no other way to live but Y' and the like.[30] There are numerous
questions about how instances of these formulae would ordinarily be
interpreted – what implicit relativization, for example, would naturally be
assumed. But I want to put these questions to one side. I shall simply
appropriate the formulae, however artificially, as (context-independent)
analogues of 'There is nothing else to think but that p', in a quest parallel
to the one which we have just been inchoately conducting. My question
is this. Is there any way of filling in the dots in either

(2w) Any wanter who . . . is bound to want that p

or

(2a) Any agent who . . . is bound to do X,

which, satisfying (counterparts of) the three constraints outlined above,
makes every instance of a suitable analogue of (1) come out true; and, if
so, what is the analogue (or more specifically, what is on its left-hand
side)? I am particularly interested in what we might learn from exploring
further variations on the theme of the unconditioned. (So my quest,
though parallel to the earlier one, runs in the opposite direction.)

What then would it mean to say that a want was unconditioned, or that
something had been done in an unconditioned way? Following the account given for thoughts, we can say that an unconditioned want is a
want whose best explanation includes the fact that the subject's own
reason for having it, or continuing to have it, is a result of rational
self-conscious reflection on its best explanation; while something done in
an unconditioned way is something such that the best explanation of why
the agent does it, or continues to do it, includes the fact that the agent's
own reason for doing it, or continuing to do it, is a result of rational
self-conscious reflection on that best explanation. And, as in the case of

thoughts, we are led to the idea of wants, acts, habits, ways of living, . . . , which are by their very nature impervious to critical self-conscious reflection. All of this raises some very large questions. Where, for instance, are we allowed to pin the label 'rational'? Can we talk about 'rational wants'? How and why can recognizing certain constraints and influences on one's habits and desires mitigate them? How do wants that can withstand critical scrutiny interact with, or relate to, their cognitive counterparts? Does it make sense to talk of 'false pleasures'?[31] What does any of this have to do with Kant? Or with Aristotle?

Some of these questions we shall come back to. But my immediate concern is this. With such an account in place, what does it mean to fill in the dots in (2w) with 'has an unconditioned want as to whether or not p', or those in (2a) with 'does X, or refrains from doing X, in an unconditioned way'?

An extreme reaction would be to say that it means nothing; or rather, that in each case, we get a formula every one of whose instances is false. For a want, and similarly *mutatis mutandis* a thing done, is not answerable to anything except the wanter; and he or she is not *bound* to want anything.

But borrowing from Kant, and also no doubt from Aristotle, we have the wherewithal to construct a more interesting answer, as follows. (I shall put the answer in terms of wants. But it can be extended to things done.) There are certain norms of rationality to which any want is answerable.[32] But some wants, given their content, cannot answer to these norms. So some wants, given their content, cannot survive rational self-conscious reflection, let alone rational self-conscious reflection on what explains them. An unconditioned want as to how things should be in such a case would therefore be bound to have the opposite content. Some instances of the formula, then, are true. In our abbreviated form: there is nothing else, in such a case, *to* want. As for what this comes to, let us be bold and try out the equation of 'There is nothing else to want but that p' with 'It is right that p' or 'It is wrong that~p' (as the case may be); and 'There is nothing else to do but X' with 'There is a categorical imperative to do X'. These proposals, together with the original proposal concerning 'T(p)', I shall refer to as the 'core proposals'.[33]

Before we assess the core proposals it will be worth ranging them against a strain in Kant's thinking whereby unconditioned agency is the only true agency: anyone who does not obey a categorical imperative does not act rationally, and so does not act freely, and so does not, in the true sense of the word, act.[34] I do not know of anywhere in Kant's writing where he explicitly commits himself to this. Indeed there are places where he explicitly repudiates it.[35] But it may well be implicit in other things he says.[36] And it has the interesting consequence for the core proposals that, if there is a categorical imperative to do something, then there is literally, and non-elliptically, nothing else to do: any apparent instance of an agent not doing that thing shows him or her to be at the mercy of some passion (say) and out of rational control.[37] To put the same point somewhat differently, the proposed filling in of the dots in (2a) – 'does X, or refrains from doing X, in an unconditioned way' – contains a pleonasm.[38] There might even be a radical conception of thought along the same lines, whereby nothing less than an unconditioned thought counts as a thought; and similarly for wants. On that conception, we could revert to the extreme interpretation of 'There is nothing else to think but that p', discarded towards the beginning of §1, and still see the formula as denoting truths, not just necessities.

But to return to the main issue: how are we to assess the core proposals? *Are* there such links between the unconditioned (on the one hand) and the true, the right and the categorically required (on the other)? Our philosophical heritage is replete with attempts to substantiate links of precisely this kind. But there is an obvious problem for such attempts. There is a circularity that threatens to make substantiation impossible. We cannot understand rationality, as it occurs in the definition of the unconditioned, except in terms of the true, the right and the categorically required. (Likewise, conversely, we cannot understand what prevents certain conditions on a person's thinking or wanting or acting – such as the weight of received opinion, the power of advertising, or the force of habit – from entering into a rational vindication, except in those same terms.)[39] I commented earlier on the important difference between circularity and triviality. But I also commented that whether we want to avoid circularity depends on our purposes. If we are interested in putting these links to any work in settling actual disputes, then we shall, it seems, want to avoid it. It is in that sense, in the sense that we seem not to be able to put the links to this kind of work, that we seem not to be able to give them any substance.

Suppose, for example, that there is a dispute about whether or not it is right that something is going on. What progress can we make by considering what somebody with an unconditioned want would want? That will very soon become a matter of determining whether the thing is right or not. Nor is it likely to help to consider people's actual wants about the issue. If we agree that these are conditioned in various ways, that will cut no ice: it is not precluded that somebody should have a conditioned want for what is right. If, on the other hand, someone claims to have an unconditioned want that this thing should be going on, then those who think this impossible are unlikely to get anywhere just by pointing out why and how they take the want to be conditioned: she may well refuse to accept their diagnosis, because of what her opponents will see as a similarly conditioned false belief. This is typical of how the two cases of belief and desire will interact, as indeed both will with that of agency. Such interaction may enlarge the circle, but it scarcely makes it any the less problematical.[40]

This example shows how the circle is liable to get traced when the truth of a particular thought is in dispute. Wiggins has shown how essentially the same circle is liable to get traced when the status of a whole family of thoughts as true *or* false is in dispute (in other words, when there is dispute about their very status as thoughts). His special concern is with evaluative thoughts. He has argued that we cannot set standards for having a true evaluative thought, and in particular, presumably, we cannot spell out what it would be to have an unconditioned evaluative thought, except, question-beggingly, in evaluative terms. For whether somebody is equipped to be a sound judge of evaluative matters is itself an evaluative matter. As Wiggins says, 'the criterion for a good judge is that he is apt to get things right'.[41]

The circle will be a problem, then, if we want to use any of the core proposals to settle actual disputes. And if the disputes are deep and radical enough, as they very often are in the moral sphere, it will reinforce that distinctive sense of vertigo which makes us wonder about the very possibility of contact with the true, the right, or the categorically required. But, again quoting Wiggins, 'whatever difficulties there are in the possibility of irresoluble substantive disagreement, no position in moral philosophy can render itself simply immune from them'.[42] That distinctive sense of vertigo may be there to be reckoned with anyway.

There are other purposes relative to which the circle will pose no threat. And one of Wiggins's greatest achievements is the brilliant way in which he has drawn some of these out.[43] If we are less interested in conversion than in understanding (both of ourselves and of others), then there is enormous value precisely in tracing such circles, elucidating our concepts as Wiggins would say,[44] trying to cast philosophical light (where others, in different ways, have cast so much literary light) on some of the myriad impediments to rational self-conscious reflection – impediments to the integration of the objective with the subjective – which, according to the core proposals, allow us to think what is false, to want what is wrong and to do what we are categorically forbidden to do. And in the grip of actual disputes, we can continue to trace those circles, not, admittedly, as a way of settling the disputes, but as a prelude to seeing how a healthy combination of conviction and open-mindedness might bring us to such a settlement.[45]

Where does all of this leave the core proposals then?

Well, circularity at any rate is no objection to their correctness.[46] But I shall not now go much further than this in my ground-level assessment of them. Instead I want to step back up a level, and return to the question of how these proposals (or any others) might satisfy (iii), the third of the constraints that I outlined earlier. This was the constraint that the condition specified when we fill in the dots in (2) – likewise (2a) and (2w) – must be one which everyone has a reason to satisfy. Investigating this question will lend further support to the core proposals. But it will also, more importantly, give us insight into the nature of the overall project and thereby, I hope, help us to say something in response to a very old philosophical puzzle. The puzzle is to explain the special force that attaches to the recognition that something is true, right or categorically required. How can such a recognition *impinge* on us in the distinctive way that it does? Wittgenstein alludes to this puzzle in the *Tractatus*, when he says, 'If an ethical law of the form, "Thou shalt . . .", is laid down, one's first thought is, "And what if I do not do it?" '[47] What we need, he says, is some account of the 'punishment' that 'resides in' not doing as one ought – some account of the price one pays.[48] Providing this will be part and parcel of showing that (iii) is satisfied.[49]

3.   Filling in the dots by making some sort of reference to rationality, as we actually did and many others have effectively done, certainly helps in this connection. But there is still a question about what reason one has to be rational, or to avoid being irrational. (I am assuming that rationality is not defined in such a way that this question answers itself.) Again, suppose we were able to endorse the suggestion made earlier, that there is literally, and non-elliptically, nothing else to do but what one is categorically required to do, so that agents who disobey a categorical imperative are forfeiting their own agency and so in some sense not being true to themselves. There is still a question about why they should mind.[50]

As soon as we start pressing questions of this kind, about people's most basic reasons for doing things, we find ourselves in an area of fierce debate. The principal issue is this. Can there be a reason for anybody to do anything (whether adopted by them or not) which is not grounded in some element of their 'subjective motivational set', as Bernard Williams calls it – in some *conative state* of theirs, for short?[51] I seem to be prevaricating on this issue. For on the one hand, just by urging (iii), I am suggesting an affirmative answer. (I am suggesting that there is a reason which everyone has, or perhaps even must have, irrespective of what happens to motivate them.) On the other hand, by admitting that there is a question even about what reason one has to be rational, I am suggesting a negative answer.

But I do not wish to prevaricate. In fact, I believe that the answer to the question posed is no.[52] (I shall say something below in response to the opposite intuition.) The point about (iii) is this. Everyone can share some reason if everyone shares some conative state. And that is what I think we should be looking for.

This conative state may extend to all possible thinkers, wanters and agents. Or it may be confined to those satisfying some condition which everyone (in fact) satisfies. Either way we can regard ourselves as back with our familiar pattern of enquiry, looking for some suitable way of filling in the dots in

> (2c) Any thinker, wanter or agent who . . . is bound to be in conative state c.

But of course, this quest differs in two important ways from the earlier quests involving (2), (2w) and (2a). The first difference is the very fact that we now insist that the condition be satisfied by everyone. (So we should immediately drop the temptation to fill in the dots with another reference to the unconditioned. Reference to the unconditioned should rather come when we specify the conative state – if the core proposals are on the right lines.) We even allow for the limiting case, where the dots are filled in with 'is a thinker, wanter or agent' and the condition specified imposes no restriction at all. The second difference is that, unlike in the case of (2), (2w) and (2a), we are not interested in determining what the schema is equivalent to: we are interested in finding some suitably explanatory instance of it.

So what is such an instance?[53]

Our answer to this question will be more or less ambitious according to how much of a restriction we impose when we fill in the dots. Most ambitious would be to argue for some instance of the limiting case. More interesting, perhaps, would be to argue for some instance where it was a philosophically open question whether or not it was equivalent to the limiting case, for example by filling in the dots with 'is finite'. Into this category falls an answer that we can extract from Bernard Williams. He has argued that any rational agent must want to be free.[54] Here we fill in the dots with 'is a rational agent', and we replace 'be in conative state c' by 'want to be free'. Whether this is equivalent to the limiting case depends on whether thinkers and wanters must also be agents, and on whether agents must be rational. However that may be, this answer ties in extremely well, I think, with the core proposals. Unconditionedness, as I understand it, just is a kind of freedom.[55]

Another way of answering the question (perhaps equally ambitious) is by means of what we might call a 'conative' transcendental argument. Its conclusion would be (say) that it is a necessary condition of being able to engage in the kind of reflective enquiry in which we are now engaged that one recognize the value of critical self-conscious reflection and that one be minimally motivated to live in a way that can answer to it. This too would deliver a suitable instance of (2c), tying in well with the core proposals.

But I shall draw this essay to a close by gesturing – no more than that – at the answer (or the kind of answer) that attracts me most. Part of its appeal is the way in which it connects with two important intuitions, one which I share and one which I do not. The first is the (very common) intuition that there is something about ultimate value, the value of thinking what is true, wanting what is right and doing what is categorically required – more specifically, there is something about its allure – which is beyond words.[56] This is the intuition that I share, and I shall make some very sketchy remarks about why. The second intuition (no less common) is the one which tells against what I said earlier. It is the intuition that ultimate value is a source of reasons that are *not* grounded in conative states, not even in conative states that are universally shared: ultimate value is 'inherently motivating', and therein lies the special force that I have been trying to explain. I disagree, and I shall try to combat this second intuition by saying something about why there is an impulse to think and talk in these terms.

The basic idea, which I shall not now try to defend, is that human beings are finite, but have an aspiration to be infinite.[57] Unconditionedness is a mark of infinitude.[58] So the dots can be filled in with 'is finite, but aspires to be infinite'; and 'be in conative state c' can be replaced by something like 'want to be (or have an urge to be) unconditioned'. This would be suitably explanatory, and it would tie in with the core proposals.

But how would it connect with the two intuitions? Via the core proposals, together with a development of the basic idea – again, I shall not now try to defend it – which runs as follows. Human finitude involves having insights which cannot be put into words. In fact such insights are acquired by rational self-conscious reflection.[59] But self-conscious reflection being what it is, they include insights into its own nature (that is, into the nature of self-conscious reflection), and thus into the nature of the unconditioned. So there *is* something about ultimate value (the value of thinking what is true, wanting what is right and doing what is categorically required) which cannot be put into words, namely whatever is revealed by these insights into the unconditioned. However, the aspiration to infinitude, and the attendant motivation to be unconditioned, involve an urge to express one's inexpressible insights; for having insights which cannot be expressed is a mark of finitude.[60] So if anyone did try to express their inexpressible insights, in particular their inexpressible insights into the essence of ultimate value – something we are all tempted to do – then ultimate value, or rather what gives ultimate value its allure, would itself be what was motivating them.[61] It would be motivating them to try to say something about it beyond the (mere, effable) fact that it was motivating them. They would be liable to cast it as *inherently* motivating.[62] The first intuition is vindicated, the second accounted for.

These last few paragraphs have of course been highly schematic: I have left out all the arguments. Decency might dictate that I stop there. But I cannot resist mentioning a final twist. Trying to express the inexpressible means wanting unconditionedness, not only in the sense of being motivated to have it, but also in the sense of lacking it (at least in certain respects); for no-one, in the full light of critical self-conscious reflection, could (continue to) attempt the impossible. So anyone trying to put into words the ineffable essence of ultimate value would also be liable to know, and to feel, that they had not attained it. It would present itself to them as an unrealized ideal (very much as in Kant's system, where the 'I will' of a purely rational being becomes the 'I ought' of a conditioned, finite being[63]). Our very reflection on how there can ever be nothing else to think, or want, or do is thus set to become an example of how guilelessly we can think, want and do otherwise.[64]

NOTES

1 Wiggins (1984).
2 Wiggins (1987a), 'Postscript', p. 348, emphasis removed.
3 Wiggins (1990/1), p. 66. Cf. Wiggins (1987a), Essay IV, §7 and Essay V, §10; (1991b), §9.
4 Wittgenstein (1961), 3.02; cf. 5.4731.
5 Quine (1970), p. 81.
6 Wittgenstein (1961), 2.225–3.001.
7 Quine (1970), p. 9.
8 See e.g. Wiggins (1990/1), p. 68, note 7.
9 Cf. ibid., §XII.
10 . . . which is not to say that 'a price' has wider scope than 'whenever', as I hope will become clear.
11 See e.g. Wiggins (1990/1), pp. 64–5.

12 See e.g. ibid., pp. 65 ff.
13 Henceforth this qualification will be taken for granted.
14 Here and hereafter I use standard logical notation.
15 One might think that there were two distinct ways in which the left-hand side
   of an instance of this schema could be false: as a result of 'p's' being replaced
   by something false; and as a result of 'p's' being replaced by something
   neither true nor false. The latter would raise some fascinating questions
   about how far (and how) there might be alternative things to think when truth
   was not involved, questions that are certainly pertinent to Wiggins's concerns. However, I am simply going to bypass those questions by stipulating
   that 'p' must be replaced by a proposition, or by something that stands for a
   proposition; and I shall understand by a proposition something that is true or
   false.
16 Cf. where Wiggins distances himself from a certain kind of relativism in the
   'Postscript' to Wiggins (1987a), p. 348.
17 This is not, of course, to embrace the kind of relativism from which Wiggins
   wants to distance himself (see above, note 16), nor to disregard the difference
   upon which he thereby insists between saying that there is nothing else to
   think and saying that there is nothing else *for us* (or *for me*) to think.
18 But we should beware here of a hasty drive to formalization. It would be
   natural to cast 'T(p)' as follows:

   (2*)∀S ∀t [X(S, t, p) → S thinks at t that p],

   where 'S' ranges over thinkers, 't' ranges over times, and 'X(S, t, p)' picks out
   the relevant condition. Cf. the formula in Wright (1988), p. 18. (Not that I
   intend any criticism of Wright in what I am about to say. He is certainly alive
   to the kind of problem that I raise in this footnote; see ibid., p. 14, note 26.)
   (2*), however, lacks the element of necessity in (2)'s 'bound to' – in a way
   that matters. It leaves us at the mercy of false propositions with respect to
   which no thinker ever satisfies the condition, something which, pending an
   account of what the condition is, we must acknowledge as a possibility
   (unless, say, we believe in a supreme being who constantly satifies the
   condition with respect to every proposition). In such a case, given that '→' is
   purely truth-functional, the relevant instance of (2*) is true, and that of (1),
   therefore, false. On the other hand, we cannot reinstate the necessity simply
   by putting (2*) within the scope of a necessity operator. Given any reasonable
   spelling out of 'X(S, t, p)', that leaves us at the mercy of contingently true
   propositions, for which the relevant instance of (2*), thus supplemented, is
   false, and that of (1), therefore, again false. With sufficient ingenuity we could
   probably circumvent these difficulties. But we might as well stick with the
   informal version (2). What we must do is to take note from these efforts at
   formalization that (2) is not just an abbreviation either of (2*) or of its
   necessitation.
19 See e.g. Wiggins (1987a), Essay IV, p. 142, note 4; Essay V, p. 188, note 4.
   (Cf. Johnston (1989), pp. 147–8; also Wittgenstein (1961), 3.263.)

20 But I concede that the matter is much more complex than this suggests. See Wiggins's admonishment at the bottom of p. 79 of Wiggins (1990/1).

21 Nor are they by any means exhaustive. Any familiar theory of truth could be pressed into service here. We could fill in the dots with some embellishment of 'has a belief about whether or not p which corresponds to reality'. Or we could fill in the dots with some embellishment of 'has a complete and coherent set of beliefs'.

22 Somewhat later ((1990/1) p. 71) Wiggins makes comments that are more pertinent to the contrapositive route. He suggests that, sometimes anyway, thinking something false may mean '[opting] out altogether from the point of view that shall be common between one person and another'. This too might lend itself to suitable generalization and embellishment.

23 Cf. Wiggins (1987a), Essay III p. 120. The phrase in quotation marks is extracted from the passage by Peirce which Wiggins himself quotes, same page, note 34.

24 Mellor (1988/9), p. 86. (This proposal satisfies the third constraint particularly clearly. To see why the others satisfy it one must first see why there is reason to believe what is true.)

25 For the Kantian use of the term 'Idea', see Kant (1933), A312–20/B368–77 and A409/B435.

26 The 'loop' in this definition is important. (It means that the definition could just as well have been turned inside out; an unconditioned thought would be a thought such that the subject's own reason for having it, or continuing to have it, was a result of rational self-conscious reflection on its best explanation, where this explanation included the fact that that was what the subject's reason for having it was a result of.) This loop is designed to ensure that the objective and the subjective are fully brought together. Cf. (but only cf.) certain currents of thought in Spinoza (1959), e.g. Pt III, Prop. I and Pt V, Prop. VI. Note: nothing in the definition guarantees that an unconditioned thought shall involve responsiveness to 'the facts'. It may be the result of a creative act of will on the part of what Kant would call an infinite being; see Kant (1933), B72 and B138–9. Indeed there are elements in Hegel which suggest that this is what it must be; see e.g. Hegel (1975), IV, II, esp. §§44 ff. (Maybe there are such elements in Kant too; see again Kant (1933), B72 and the surrounding material.)

27 Wiggins (1990/1), pp. 67–8.

28 Bernard Williams has argued (i) that reflection can locate something whose discovery actually prevents the thought from any longer being *formed*, and (ii) that this can happen even when the thought in question is knowledge; see Williams (1985), pp. 148 and 167–9. I disagree with (i). (That is, I disagree if the thought is a genuine one, i.e. capable of being assessed as true or false; of course reflection can expose incoherence in the case of a putative thought.) But I do not mind admitting a counterpart of (ii). That is, I do not mind admitting that reflection can unsettle knowledge *in the way I am envisaging*; see Moore (1991), Appendix. Cf. here the material from Peirce quoted by

Wiggins in Wiggins (1987a), 'Postscript', p. 342; and Wiggins's own surrounding text.

29 Is there a problem here if unconditioned thoughts include the creative acts of
    will of an infinite being, or indeed *only* include these (see above, note 26)?
    For such a being would have had the power to decree that things stand
    differently from how they actually stand with respect to the proposition in
    question. – In fact, this is not a problem. Cf. note 18 above; the resultant
    schema is to be understood in such a way (and can be understood in such a
    way) that we may disregard those unrealized possibilities.

30 See e.g. Wiggins himself, in Wiggins (1987a), Essay I, p. 26, end of §14.

31 See Lovibond (1989/90). Cf. Plato (1974), 585d–7a.

32 If a wanter is essentially rational, this may not be incompatible with saying
    that the wanter's wants are not answerable to anything except the wanter.
    There is in any case the question, to which we shall return, of what reason a
    wanter has to have wants that can answer to whatever they are answerable to.
    For the idea of wants that answer to norms of rationality, see further Spinoza
    (1959), Pt IV, Prop. LXI.

33 For the idea of there being nothing else to want (or to will), cf. Kant (1948),
    pp. 86–7. Note that Kant says there are two ways in which willing that things
    be thus and so can be literally, and non-elliptically, impossible: this is remi-
    niscent of the extreme interpretation of Wiggins's original formula discussed
    near the beginning of §1 and it ties in with what I am about to say in the main
    text. As for my bringing in the categorical imperative at this point, that
    connects with the idea that an unconditioned act would be an act whose
    vindication and explanation came together, which in turn seems to be what
    Kant has in mind when he talks about an act done from duty, as opposed to
    an act done merely in accordance with duty (the former would be bound to
    conform to any categorical imperative, the latter would only happen to); see
    ibid., pp. 65–7. For a contemporary discussion of (if not the core proposals,
    then) proposals which have the same shape as the core proposals, see Smith
    (1989); Lewis (1989); Johnston (1989).

34 Cf. Moore (1990b), §II. Note: to say that someone, in acting, does not obey
    a categorical imperative may mean either that they disobey a categorical
    imperative or that they do something outside the jurisdiction of reason
    altogether.

35 E.g. Kant (1956), p. 32.

36 See e.g. Kant (1933), A538–41/B566–9; ibid., 'Transcendental Doctrine of
    Method', ch. 11, §1; Kant (1948), the beginning and end of ch. III; Kant
    (1956), the beginning of the Introduction; and ibid., Pt I, Bk I, ch. I, §6. (All
    that Kant strictly commits himself to, however, is that a free will is a will
    subject to its own rational laws; it does not follow that for the will to be
    exercised freely is for it to be exercised in *accordance* with those laws. Note: the
    Willkür/Wille distinction, which is often invoked in discussion of these issues,
    is especially prominent in Kant (1960), but there is much greater emphasis
    on it in the introductory essay, 'The Ethical Significance of Kant's *Religion*',
    by John R. Silber, than there is in Kant himself.)

37 Cf. St Paul's letter to the Romans, VII, 15–25. And cf. note 33 above.

38 A further interesting consequence is that deliberation about how to act can be understood on the model of (typical) deliberation about how to avoid a catastrophe – not as a matter of choosing between different ways of doing it, but as a matter of trying to find any way of doing it at all.

39 *Cannot*? I think not. I think that if we tried to set up canons of rational vindication which did not beg any questions, for example suitable canons of induction, our guarantee that every instance of (1) should come out true would no longer be *a priori* – if indeed every instance of (1) did come out true. (What about taking a Kantian line and trying to define rationality in terms of some thin notion of consistency? – This might help us to avoid the circularity, but, in common with almost everyone else, I doubt that it would deliver the right results.) Cf. parts of Johnston (1989).

40 Cf. Williams (1985), pp. 40 ff.

41 Wiggins (1987a), Essay V; the quotation occurs on p. 194. Note: one of Wiggins's aims is to explore analogies between evaluative concepts and other concepts that involve human sensibilities, for example colour concepts; but as he and other writers have emphasized, the circularity here highlights an important disanalogy. See §6 of his paper. Cf. various currents in Blackburn (1985); McDowell (1985), p. 118; Wright (1988), esp. §V; Johnston (1989), p. 144.

42 Wiggins (1987a), Essay V, p. 210.

43 See e.g. *ibid.*, §4.

44 See above, note 19.

45 Cf. Wiggins (1990/1), §§VII–VIII; (1991b), §5.

46 Again see above, note 19; and cf. Wiggins (1987a), Essay V, pp. 188–9.

47 Wittgenstein (1961), 6.422. Cf. Wiggins, ibid., pp. 198 ff.

48 Wittgenstein, ibid.

49 If, furthermore, we can show that it is satisfied in essentially the same way in each of the three cases, as of course we should have to if the core proposals were correct, then we may also be able to acknowledge an interesting degree of subsumption. Thus, at one extreme, there may be a categorical imperative to think the truth. That is, it may be that when there is nothing else to think, this is because there is nothing else to do but think it. (Do the core proposals have this consequence? Not quite. They entail that there is a categorical imperative not to think what is false. Unconditioned agnosticism is not ruled out. This of course is more plausible – cf. the Cartesian view of error as involving a misuse of the will (Descartes (1970), 'Fourth Meditation', pp. 98–100) – though I am well aware that many will regard it as still not plausible enough to stave off the sense of a *reductio ad absurdum*. I cannot now enter into the many issues that would be involved in rebutting that sense. But suffice to ask: why should there not be a categorical imperative to attain an ideal?)

50 Cf. Williams (1981), ch. 2, note 1; Smith (1987), pp. 42–3.

51 Williams (1981), p. 102. Some contributions to the debate are: Hume (1888), pp. 457 and 462; Hume (1975), pp. 170–2 and 294; Foot (1972);

McDowell (1978); Smith (1987) (pursued in Pettit (1987) and Smith (1988)); Thomson (1987), esp. pp. 50 ff; Lewis (1989); Wiggins (1990/1), esp. §XV. Note: many of the writers distinguish between 'motivating' reasons and 'normative' reasons (this is the terminology which Smith adopts in Smith (1987), p. 38). The question I posed in the main text concerns normative reasons.

52 Cf. Williams (1981), p. 109.

53 In Wiggins (1991b), there is a beautifully worked out answer (of sorts) to this question. But it would hook up with different responses to the earlier quests. I shall suggest some very different answers.

54 Williams (1985), pp. 55–8. Cf. Kant's idea that a rational agent cannot act except under the Idea of freedom; see Kant (1948), pp. 108–9.

55 Cf. again the currents of thought in Spinoza; see above, note 26. Cf. also Hookway, (1990), ch. VIII. And, of course, cf. Kant, e.g. Kant (1933), A419/B447.

56 See e.g. Wittgenstein (1961), 6.4 ff. Cf. also Wittgenstein (1965).

57 I have tried to say more about this in Moore (1990a), ch. 15; and Moore (1992), esp. §III. Cf. Hegel (1977), pp. 104 ff.

58 Cf. Kant (1933), A322/B379 and A411–20/B438–48.

59 This is something for which I try to argue in Moore (1987), esp. §3; and Moore (1992), passim.

60 Again, I try to argue for this in Moore (1992), §III.

61 And insofar as we can see ourselves as trying to express these insights, there is room here for another conative transcendental argument.

62 But they might also see clearly enough to want, at the same time, to regard it as grounded in some conative state. Cf. Wittgenstein's remarks on the 'deeper conception of the essence of the Good', in Wittgenstein (1965), p. 15; and Wittgenstein (1979), pp. 79–80. Such tensions are characteristic of attempts to express the inexpressible.

63 Kant (1948), p. 114.

64 Much of this I take to be a variation on a familiar Biblical theme. See Genesis, III, 1–7; and cf. Paul's letter to the Romans, VII, 7–11.

12

Rescuing Protagoras

Edward Hussey

1. 'Socrates, we are running my friend too hard', protests the nice old mathematician Theodorus, in Plato's dialogue *Theaetetus*, when he is unable to defend the position of his old associate Protagoras against the onslaught of Socrates' criticism.[1] The time and energy Plato's Socrates spends on the refutation of Protagoras is a measure of the seriousness with which Plato took the Protagorean challenge. Plato's Socrates, behind the barrage of jokes and irony, treats Protagoras, alive or dead, with marked respect. Long years after the time of Protagoras' zenith in Periclean Athens, the *Theaetetus* pays close attention to Protagoras' fundamental thoughts on knowledge and truth, and offers fundamental criticisms.

By an agreeable irony, Plato has thus been instrumental in preserving for us some knowledge of the opinions he wanted to refute. Without the evidence of the *Theaetetus*, we would be unable to do more than guess at the form that Protagoras' thoughts took. With the *Theaetetus*, supplemented by the *Protagoras* and by snippets of further evidence, there seems to be a real chance of rescuing Protagoras, both from oblivion and from misunderstanding (and perhaps incidentally from Platonic criticism).[2] We must not simply assume, though, that Plato's testimony will suffice to elucidate everything. Plato was not writing a thesis on Protagoras, and the dialogue form effectively demanded that much must be left in the background (readers of his own time could be reasonably expected to supply it). Plato's exposition of Protagoras is therefore concise, summary and allusive.

This essay confines itself to the *Theaetetus*, as the necessary first step towards a better understanding of Protagoras. The reconstructed Protagorean theory that emerges is of interest, apart from anything else, because it contains the first recognizable version of pragmatism. This is an area which in recent years David Wiggins has explored and illuminated.[3] I am glad to have the opportunity of offering him this study, which suggests connections between Protagoras and his own explorations, as some acknowledgement of the debt I owe to his teaching and friendship since the time when, as an undergraduate of New College, I was introduced by him to the *Theaetetus*.[4]

2. Plato takes Protagoras together with others who, he says, held that 'sense-perception is knowledge', and that sense-perceptions are always true. The discussion of this thesis takes up a large part of the dialogue. Within the wider discussion, the special treatment given to Protagoras looks logically superfluous, since, as Plato's Socrates admits (*Tht.* 179c1–d1), the criticism of Protagoras' special theory, even if successful, goes no way towards refuting the general thesis allegedly common to all.[5] The section on Protagoras and related theories seems to be a digression.

The criticisms offered of Protagoras are, as Plato's Socrates also seems to admit (*Tht.* 171c10–d5), not necessarily successful as against the real Protagoras. Socrates admits, that is, that what he is criticizing as 'Protagoras' is a straw man who may or may not have the same theories as the historical Protagoras, who cannot be there to defend himself.

This admission may seem to bring into disrepute the whole project of recovering Protagoras from the *Theaetetus*. But it is restricted by Socrates to apply to the criticisms he is making, and by implication does not apply to the original exposition of the theory. Anyone who looks for the historical Protagoras in Plato (and there is hardly anywhere else to look) must therefore remember Plato's self-confessed limits as a historian. The original exposition (*Tht.* 151e8–152c7), though not as complete as might be wished, has to be taken as truly representative of the real Protagoras, in default of convincing evidence to the contrary. Similarly, the 'speech of defence' put hypothetically into the mouth of Protagoras (*Tht.* 166a2–168c2) should be taken (at least provisionally) as roughly historically correct. It is not until the middle of Plato's attempted refutation (*Tht.* 169d3–171c7 and 177c6–179b9) that Socrates makes his caveat about historicity.

The following proposed reconstruction respects the evidence of Plato's text. It is not forced to attribute (implausibly) elementary misunderstandings, carelessness or dishonesty to Plato. But it does involve supposing (not implausibly) that Plato was, for his own purposes, selective in his exposition, and that there was more to Protagoras' thinking than Plato found it necessary to show.

3.1 'A human being is a measure of all things: of those that are, that/how they are, and of those that are not, that/how they are not.' (*Tht.* 152a2–4) The Greek text of this splendid opening statement is assured.[6] Not so the meaning. We can say at most that it has, *prima facie*, some natural implications. (1) 'A human being', *any* human being, is epistemologically important as a 'measure'. (2) All human beings, in 'measuring', are at least *trying* to do the same thing, to discover or to construct some kind of reality. This emphasis on the teleology of 'measuring' is increased by the explanatory clause, which represents the aim of measuring as establishing what is and what is not. In any case, as the many divergent attempts show, it is hopeless to try to interpret the sentence from within itself. The only secure procedure is to begin by examining the theoretical context within which Plato locates it.

Plato's interpretation takes 'measurement' to denote sense-perception, and in addition the process of formation of opinion ultimately based on sense-perception. He attributes to Protagoras the thesis that 'all opinions are true' (*Tht.* 161d3–7, 179c2 and elsewhere). This is elucidated as meaning that, if some state of affairs S is thought to exist by some person X, then S really does exist *for X*. Or, equivalently, if something is thought to be such-and-such by X, then it really is such *for X* (*Tht.* 152a6–8, 166d2–4 and elsewhere). 'Appearance' (*phainesthai, phantasia*) appears at first to be restricted to the objects or results of sense-perception; but 'seeming' (*dokein, doxa*) includes, as is standard usage, any opinion.[7] Since opinions may change, truth and reality of opinions are also relative to the time of holding as well as to the holder; this point, though important, is not explicitly stated.

Non-controversially, then, it can be said that Plato presents Protagoras as recognizing radically relativized truths and realities; and that, in Plato's view, Protagoras held that *knowledge* is available in connection with the relativized truths. This knowledge is available only to the particular person(s) holding the opinion and only at the particular time(s) when it is held.

3.2 All this does not exclude (a) the existence or the possibility of some absolute truth or reality; (b) the availability or possible availability of knowledge of such reality. What does Plato tell or hint about this?

First, since Plato subsumes Protagoras under the heading of 'knowledge = *aisthêsis*', it is clear that, for Plato's Protagoras, if there is any *knowable* objective reality, it is one known *only* by sense-perception or some other kind of immediate awareness.[8] Secondly, Plato's illustrative example, that of the wind that appears warm to one person and cold to another (*Tht.* 152b2–8), suggests that there must be *some* objective reality involved. The important fact that people disagree implies that there is something objective about which they disagree; correspondingly, in Plato's example, it is expressly stated to be 'the same wind' that is perceived by both.

This suggestion fits with the rest of Plato's exposition, and other evidence independent of Plato, which consistently presupposes that Protagoras assumed a certain minimal objective reality. (1) Plato consistently throws the emphasis on subjective perceptions or opinions about the *qualities* of things (using *hoia*, *toiauta* etc.), not about the existence of those same things. (2) Though the 'secret doctrine' is not Protagorean, and not even pretended to be so by Plato, he does present it as *compatible* with Protagoras' views (*Tht.* 152c8–10). Now the 'secret doctrine', in spite of its protestations that 'any one thing is in itself nothing', clearly assumes some objective underlying physical structure of some sort, even if it is not one consisting of identifiable individuals. (3) The 'modified Protagorean' doctrine of 171d9–172b7 is also not Protagoras' own, nor pretended to be so by Plato; but it is presented as a *minor* modification of Protagoras (*Tht.* 172b6: it is held by 'those who don't totally affirm the thesis of Protagoras'). But this 'modified Protagoreanism' incontestably involves the acceptance of some objective reality. (4) The same pattern is seen in the parallel passage of the *Cratylus*, 385a–386e. Here too it is assumed that there objectively is a certain stock of ontological furniture, which can be perceived by all alike. The question said here to be raised by Protagoras' doctrine is whether the pieces of furniture which make it up 'have any firmness of being (*ousias*), themselves of themselves' (386a3–4, cf. e1–4), independently of how they appear. The context shows that the doubt as to 'firmness of being' is a doubt about *the way in which* they exist, not about whether they exist at all.[9] (5) Precisely the same type of formulation, presupposing the objective existence of the underlying thing, is found, independently of Plato, in Plutarch's report (*adv. Colot.* 1108f–1109a) of Democritus' attack on Protagoras.[10] (6) Finally, one of the few genuine fragments of Protagoras' own works, the beginning of his book *On the Gods*, assumes that it is an objective matter of fact whether or not the gods exist.[11]

3.3 In the face of this strong evidence, it is puzzling that many commentators have sought to attribute to Protagoras (as expounded by Plato) a complete *denial* of the existence of any sort of objective truths and realities.

To support this extreme interpretation, (1) it does not help to point to Plato's initial exposition (152b5–8). Here, Plato's Protagoras simply refuses to pronounce on whether the wind is really hot or cold in itself;

presumably because he thinks there is no means of telling. This does not support the claim that Protagoras denied the objective existence of the wind. It does not even imply, as some recent commentators have claimed, that he held that 'it makes no sense to attribute the property [hot or cold] to the wind in itself'.[12] Strictly, it does not even imply that the wind does not objectively possess sensory properties; only that it cannot be known whether it does or not. True, the 'secret doctrine' does explicitly teach that things in themselves do not have at least ordinary sensory qualities; but, as generally agreed, the 'secret doctrine' is not that of Protagoras. It is presented as a possible extension of his views. So all that can be argued from it is that Plato thought it compatible with Protagoras' views that ordinary sensory qualities have no objective existence.

Nor (2) does the existence of relativized types of truth ('true-for-me', 'true-for-you' etc.) have any tendency, in itself, to show that there cannot be any objective truth. At most, the evident contradictions, between what is true for me and what is true for you, show that it will be difficult to find logical room for an objective truth about *some* matters, namely, those on which our perceptions diverge. The objective truth on such matters, if there is any, cannot be just the sum of all the relativized truths; but then it seems arbitrary to make it consist of some subset of them.

Finally, (3) the 'speech for the defence' of Protagoras (and in particular, *Tht.* 167a6–b4) does not necessarily help the extreme interpretation either. For it is manifestly concerned with matters on which there are, in Protagoras' view, real differences of opinion. If he holds that such matters are outside the realm of objective truth, then nothing said here commits him to a denial of the existence of objective truths.

Indeed, such a denial is unlikely for Protagoras. It is not at all like the Protagoras presented by all our sources to take up any firm position on a question which, on his own showing, was so far beyond human reach. He could have put forward the non-existence of absolute truth not as itself an absolute truth, but only as his own opinion. But, if he had done so, what could he have appealed to, in order to persuade others to adopt it as their opinion too?

4.1 So far, then, the evidence is encouragingly consistent. It shows that Protagoras did not deny the existence of an objective reality, but that on the contrary he affirmed that it existed and could to some extent be known.

Plato's exposition also seems to presuppose some claims by Protagoras about the substantive *contents* of this objective reality. The discussion of the wind (with the other passages already cited) suggests that it contains ordinary physical objects and processes, at least. Further, in the discussions of differences of opinion, the disagreements among perceivers or opiners, and the contents of their respective opinions, are repeatedly taken at face value as objectively real or true. It is nowhere suggested in these passages, for example, that it is only true-for-me, not objectively true, that it is true-for-me that the wind is cold. Hence, both the existence of the individual relativized realities, and their having the particular contents they do have, are for Protagoras matters of objective fact.[13] (This is not to say they are knowable generally; that would clash with the evidence in Plato that knowing is tightly linked to *aisthêsis*. Each person presumably has direct awareness only of her or his relativized reality, and this could count as *aisthêsis*, which is not necessarily confined to sense-perception.)[14]

Plato's evidence goes yet further. It also shows, as already implied, that there must be severe general limitations, for Protagoras, on the contents of any knowable objective reality. It has to be (a) knowable by sense-perception, and yet (b) not subject to the differences of opinion which beset sense-perception of the ordinary sensory qualities.

4.2 All this evidence, if accepted, leaves not much room for choice about the general shape of Protagoras' theory of reality. The difficulty is to grasp the underlying motivation and appeal of the theory.

In a general way, we can see that Protagoras fits here within the tradition of Xenophanean empiricism, modified by the criticisms of sense-perception which had become current in the earlier fifth century.[15] Starting from a 'common sense' outlook, he tries to define a non-controversial area, within which sense-perceptions do not radically disagree, where we may suppose a knowable objective reality. This includes a *schematic* underlying physical reality, consisting of, say, physical objects with spatial properties, and physical processes with temporal duration; but excluding sensory properties. In other words, roughly the same as what his fellow-citizens and younger contemporaries Leucippus and Democritus took to be objectively real.[16] He could have plausibly argued that we do, in fact, have knowledge, via sense-perception, of this schematic physical world, of a sort that is not subject to essential disagreement or doubt.[17] The public reality also includes the existence of minds and their various opinions (but not, of course, the truth of those opinions).

There is no space here to trace in detail the affinities of this theory of objective truth and reality, and to justify further the reconstruction that has been offered.[18] In any case, it was clearly not the part of his thinking to which he himself gave most emphasis, and which attracted the greatest attention. That was reserved for his theory of opinion, in which he left behind the realm of objectivity.

5. Protagoras takes up a position about the non-availability to human beings of knowledge of objective truth and reality about the things which most interest them. Here, they have only opinions, and these have no chance of being objectively true or false.[19]

But he evidently does not embrace total scepticism; on the contrary, he claims himself to be a teacher of wisdom and virtue, and holds that he can give a coherent account, within his theory, of what is normally called 'truth' and 'wisdom' and 'expertise'. There is plenty of evidence, both within the *Theaetetus* and outside it, that Protagoras did think he could move out beyond the apparently severe limitations imposed by his restrictions on the availability of knowledge.

The rejection of publicly available knowledge on the most interesting parts of experience leaves us in a world of opinions. Ordinary life for a human being, in the Protagorean interpretation of it, consists of a perpetual negotiation with one's experiences, including memories and the discovery of the opinions of others (whose existence itself is a matter of opinion). As a result of these negotiations, opinions are reshaped. Any human being X, then, has to see X's own opinions under two different aspects. On the one hand they express truly and infallibly 'the-truth-for-X' at the time when they are held. On the other hand, X will recognise, if X is realistic, that they are only X's *opinions*, and as such are subject to revision and even total rejection in the light of further experience.

This 'double aspect' is an obvious paradox in the Protagorean theory, and Plato, to judge by his criticisms, thought that it pointed to a fatal incoherence at the heart of the theory.[20] But, in defence of Protagoras, it may be remarked, first, that the paradox already exists in ordinary ways of thinking. About any one of our current opinions, we must (if we are reasonable and believe in an objective reality) believe, simultaneously, both that it is true now and that it is possibly not true now. Therefore, on the face of it, we not only can but must have, simultaneously, logically incompatible beliefs. So Protagoras' theory is not unrealistic or wilfully paradoxical; on the contrary, it captures and accepts this puzzling feature of belief, and shows itself, once again, close to ordinary ways of thinking. What is more, it removes the sting of the paradox, by maintaining that the belief in the truth of our momentary opinions should not be understood as a belief that they give us knowledge of an *objective* reality. Since, for Protagoras, we have no access to any objective reality on these matters, it is clear that the knowledge he thinks we do have is of a subjective and momentary reality only; so that 'believing in the truth of our opinions' should be taken as a belief in their subjective and momentary truth.[21]

In the second place, it is not clear that Protagoras' theory is incoherent here. At worst (and even this needs to be shown) it says that, for any human being X, X's way of looking at X's opinions involves X in a contradiction. But why should Protagoras (or X) worry about that? Precisely because Protagoras holds that knowledge about matters of opinion is unavailable, he will have in any case to say that contradictions about these matters cannot be known to be false (though, in cases where there is a practical bearing, they may well be 'undesirable' or 'bad').[22]

Plato's criticisms exploit to the full the 'double aspect' of Protagorean opinions. They seek to show that there are contradictions involved in X's treating X's opinions as *both* infallibly true-for-X-now *and* wholly open to revision in the light of further experience and information. Since, as already suggested, this is not just Protagoras' way of treating opinions but a common-sense way, it is clear that Plato's criticisms are of general interest. No doubt that is why Plato takes trouble over Protagoras' theory in the first place: he recognizes that it appeals to certain persistent common-sense ways of thinking.

6.   If Protagoras' theory is as suggested, he still has, at the very least, a lot of explaining to do. Is there any chance of reconstructing any more of the real Protagoras from the *Theaetetus*? That depends on whether we can make good sense of the opinions attributed to him in the 'speech for the defence'.

We must start from the logical status of the speech as a whole within the context of Protagoras' thinking as so far given. The speech of course states part of Protagoras' own present opinions. In so far as it is merely reportage of what Protagoras happens to think, it does not have to be contradiction-free or in any way persuasive. But of course Protagoras wants his opinions to be found persuasive and to be adopted by others. So it will help if they do not contradict one another.

One way in which contradiction might creep in, and has been thought to do so by commentators, is in the apparent assumption, within the speech, that there are certain matters of objective fact (over and above the 'physical framework'). This appears to be the case, above all and most crucially, where Protagoras speaks as though it were a matter of objective fact that some opinions are 'bad' or 'useful' or 'better' (166e3–167c7). It is made clear, at least, that these properties are not supposed to be dependent on whether or not the opinions are actually held by anyone.

Some care must be taken in specifying the nature of the alleged contradiction. Remember that the whole speech gives the contents of some of Protagoras' own opinions. In saying that some opinions are 'bad' or 'useful' in a sense independent of who actually holds them, might he not merely be giving his own evaluations of those opinions? If so, there is of course no contradiction, since he will not be assuming that there is any objective truth involved.

This defence fails. For though of course Protagoras does imply that he himself shares the view that the opinions in question are 'bad', 'useful', etc. as the case may be, he is trying also to recommend that view to others. And, because we, as interpreters, must impute that practical aim to him, we cannot suppose that he wants to ground that view merely on what he himself may happen to believe. If he wants to be persuasive, he must, it seems, offer us an account (of the meaning of 'bad' etc. opinion) which is logically independent of what any particular person (including himself) may happen to think about the opinions in question.

This is evidently a second-order type of opinion that Protagoras is promoting in the speech, since it is an opinion which seeks to provide a general method of evaluating opinions. It exemplifies and sharpens the phenomenon of 'dual aspect' already pointed out: that is, Protagoras must be prepared to say, in some cases: 'this opinion is not now true for me, but it is (possibly) better than my own opinion'. This is paradoxical, but no more so than the commonsense cases of 'dual aspect' mentioned above.[23]

But not only does Protagoras' account of 'bad' etc. opinion have these paradoxical features embedded in it. Whatever its fine print may have been, it is also of necessity involved in some circularity. For it is implicit in the speech that the evaluation of opinion is a matter for the 'expert' (a transparent cover, in fact, for Protagoras himself and other sophists of his persuasion). But the expert's opinion will have itself to be part of 'better' opinion. So the test of the goodness or badness of any opinion will itself have to assume the goodness or badness of some opinion.

7. All this, though, does not actually show that Protagoras is contradicting himself. But can the nature of 'bad' or of 'useful' and 'better' opinion be explained without, in fact, covertly invoking objectivity?

More than eighty years ago, it was suggested by F. C. S. Schiller, the Oxford pragmatist, that what Protagoras was putting forward was in effect an early (presumably the earliest) version of pragmatism.[24] It is strange that the suggestion has gained so little favour, or even consideration, from scholars since that time. Most recent writers on the sophists, and most recent commentators on the *Theaetetus*, ignore it altogether.[25] Yet to see Protagoras as a proto-pragmatist offers the only real hope of making satisfactory sense of the evidence. Not only does it supply the only hope of making non-contradictory sense of the notions of 'better' and 'worse' opinion, but it rounds out the sense of the slogan that 'a human being is a measure of all things'. It points to something, beyond the actual measuring process, that is being approximated by the measurement; and it also reaffirms the 'democracy of opinions': any human being can contribute to the process of approximation by bringing the evidence of her or his 'measurements' to bear on the (joint) construction of 'better' opinion.

The same conclusion may be reached from a different direction.

A first and fundamental question of interpretation is: if knowing is relative to the particular time and to the particular thinking subject, what claims does Protagoras make for his own theory? According to the theory itself, the theory is, of course, true for Protagoras (assuming that he really believes it) at the time he holds it, but not necessarily for anyone else or at any other time. The question is sharply presented by the dramatically important passage already cited, where Protagoras solemnly (but, as we have seen, ambiguously) proclaims: 'I say that the truth is as I have written'. We need not and must not read this as a claim of absolute truth, of course. But, if we are not to suppose Protagoras a ridiculous figure (and Plato never makes him out to be that), we must suppose that he holds not merely that his theory is (uninterestingly) true for himself, but also that it is capable of having some appeal and some point for others over and above its being true-for-and-known-by-Protagoras. In some sense he must think it both *persuasive* and *worthwhile*. And that in turn means that he is bound to give some general account of how he can consistently suppose that any opinion is genuinely more persuasive, and more worthwhile, than any other.

The same demand is imposed on Protagoras even more insistently by a related point: that of the teleology of belief itself. We do not hold beliefs in a detached or frivolous way. We normally hold them just when, and because, we think them *true*: not true-for-us-now, but absolutely true. Protagoras *must* (on pain of being a mere verbalizer, as even Plato never suggests he was) find some convincing substitute to fill the role we normally take absolute truth to fill in the teleology of belief. But it is not easy to envisage any such substitute except a pragmatist one: we believe things because we think that they are, for all practical purposes, as good as absolutely true.

Protagoras, then, I have argued, on Plato's showing, *must* be something like a pragmatist, if he is not to be contemptible as a philosopher (and Plato never suggests he is that). It is fortunate that Plato, having supplied the evidence that allows us to make the demand, also supplies (albeit incidentally and scantily) the evidence that shows Protagoras meeting the demand.

8. Protagoras, in the 'speech for the defence', does not in fact try to define what he means by 'better' and 'worse' opinion. Nor does he clearly indicate what sort of 'goodness' is in question, and how it ties up with the the rest of human life. The only guidance we get is the simile of the doctor. This seems to show that there is meant to be both a subjective aspect to the matter, and an aspect which is not merely subjective. It must be meant to be not merely subjectively believable of 'better' opinion, that it is better both for the individual who adopts it and for the community where it is accepted. 'Betterness' must become *tangible*, so to say, both in the sense-perceptions of the individuals and in the flourishing of the community. Unless both aspects are present, the Protagorean expert will be like a doctor who wholly disregards either the external symptoms or the feelings of his patients.[26]

Protagoras' two-faced conception of 'better' opinion is clearly pragmatist in a wide sense, in that it appeals essentially to 'what works' for the individual and for society. But there are some points which indicate differences from the best-known modern varieties of pragmatism. First, on the view here taken, it is a partial pragmatism only, applying in the regions where there is no objective truth. But these include almost everything of interest to most human beings. Next, Protagoras is never made to speak of a 'best' opinion. So he is not committed to the thesis that there is some uniquely 'best possible' opinion, which could function as a substitute for truth.[27] Finally, he does not try formally to *define* 'better' opinion in pragmatist style, as 'what works better'. But it is clear that he takes 'working better' to be in practice the essential point about 'better' opinion.[28]

So Protagoras, to overcome the lack of accessible objective knowledge, introduces a theory of 'better' opinion which has a more than merely subjective validation. The question of which opinions are 'better' cannot be one on which *knowledge* is available. It must itself be a matter of opinion. Protagoras is implicitly appealing to his own opinion here; but that only restates the problem, for why should he expect anyone else to follow it? Protagoras is implying, as already remarked, that there can be a 'better' opinion about which opinions are 'better'.

To repeat, circularity is involved. The whole operation of forming 'better' opinion in a pragmatist spirit has to be regarded as a 'bootstrap' operation. There are no foundations. Each part of the house of cards rests tentatively on some other part. Thus, according to the theory of Protagoras, the step from the confines of opinion based on individual sense-perception to the adoption of 'better' opinions involves circularity, if the 'better' opinions are adopted *because* they are better. For, as can be seen, that they are better must itself be a matter of 'better' opinion.

Again, circularity may be found in the theoretical account of 'better' opinion. In giving an intersubjective meaning to 'better' and 'worse' opinion, Protagoras is assuming, in effect, that some 'better' opinion has already been accepted. So we cannot understand what is meant by 'better' opinion, unless we have already accepted it as 'better'. Then again, Protagoras is implicitly claiming his account of 'better' and 'worse' opinion as itself part of 'better' opinion. So again we cannot understand his claim, unless we already accept it.

Such circles do not undermine Protagoras' theory. For he never claims to give an account of 'better' opinion entirely 'from the outside', as it were; nor does he need to do so, in order to be coherent and understood. The circularities will be found problematic only by those who misread Protagoras' aims; or by those who, like Plato, believe that we need rock-like certainties as foundations for all cognitive activity. Protagoras did not. He treats human opinion-holding and opinion-forming, in commonsense fashion, 'as a going concern', an activity which we cannot choose whether or not to enter, which we can never judge 'from the outside', and for which we make and remake the rules as we go along.

More worrying, even for those sympathetic to the Protagorean project here reconstructed, is the pervasive vagueness, and the threat of infinite regress, associated with the circularities, that hangs over the whole business of specifying what counts as 'better' opinion. Yet even this may be partly a side-effect of the fact that Plato's aims in the dialogue do not require him to give Protagoras a full-dress exposition. Considering that Protagoras gets more 'exposure' in total in Plato's writings than any other philosopher (except possibly Parmenides), it would be unreasonable to accuse Plato of being particularly unfair.

9. In any case, the notions of 'better' and 'worse' opinion can only have been the beginning of Protagorean pragmatism. What followed, and how the theory was developed, is a further question, on which the evidence of the *Protagoras* is needed to supplement that of the *Theaetetus*. But that is another story, which there is not room for here.

In a volume devoted to David Wiggins, though, it would be wrong to leave unmentioned the ways in which we can see Protagoras, in the *Protagoras*, extending and applying the notion of 'better' opinion. In that dialogue, too, he is given a great speech, an even longer one, of dazzling rhetorical brilliance, in which he unfolds some of the implications in the realm of social and political theory that he drew from his doctrine. Much more than the *Theaetetus*, the *Protagoras* makes clear the optimism which was an essential part of the system of Protagoras, the concept of a natural progress in the evolution of human opinions.

To be an adequate substitute for objective truth, 'better' opinion will have to possess what David Wiggins has listed as the 'marks of truth'.[29] These are closely connected to important aspects of the discussion in the *Theaetetus*. With truth as the primary dimension of assessment for statements (mark (1)), compare 'better' and 'worse', said of opinions, as indicating the assessment of the sophist-experts. With truths as true in virtue of something (mark (4)), compare the explanation of 'better' and 'worse' in terms of practical usefulness. With truth as possessed or not by statements independently of any one speaker's means of recognizing that (mark (3)), compare the existence of experts and the joint and cumulative construction of 'better' opinion. With the requirement that the conjunction of true sentences must again be true (mark (5)), compare the point made earlier about the practical unworkability of contradictions within opinions. That is not to say that Protagoras' 'better' opinion will be totally coherent *at any given* time (or in any given society). What he perhaps hints at in the *Theaetetus*, and seems to assume in the *Protagoras*, is a natural long-term asymptotic process of *convergence* towards the substantial agreement of all human beings (compare mark (2)). This is a process of which sophists are to be the promoters and sustainers.[30]

10. The theory of Protagoras, as it has here been reconstructed, has a modest complexity. It may be said to have three layers.

At the base, the first layer, is the fundamental objective reality accessible to all human beings: the realm of what can be directly and publicly known. This consists partly of the 'basic physical furniture' that can be not only perceived by the senses but counted, measured and weighed (the realm of 'measuring' in the most basic sense).[31] It includes, also, human minds and their opinions.

The next layer is constituted by the subjective realities with their contents. There is one for each human being (and for any other opining being, if any) at each time. Each subjective reality fits on to the objective base, but there is no guarantee that any two will fit in the same way.

Above these, in the third layer, is the 'better opinion' constructed laboriously, under pragmatist constraints, out of the opinions derived from the subjective realities.

The appeal of the theory was twofold. First, it seemed to stick close to people's experience, to give a sense of what it is really like to go on a cognitive quest and to hold opinions; and it purported to eschew grand theoretical claims of any sort.[32] Secondly, it offered a way of avoiding disputes that seemed otherwise interminable. The appeal of the theory in its own day is attested by Plato.[33] Its lasting appeal is shown by the revival of pragmatist theories in more recent times. More generally, such work as David Wiggins's exploration of the concept of truth, and the claims of 'a sensible subjectivism', can be claimed as 'Protagorean' in spirit and motivation. With all due qualification, I would like to end with one of David's most characteristic remarks, made originally about Aristotle, but perhaps applicable to Protagoras also:

> '. . . it seems to be the misfortune of that particular philosopher that few of the things he said can be understood or believed until they are laboriously rediscovered.'[34]

NOTES

1 Plato, *Theaetetus* (*Tht.*) 171c8, in the translation of M. J. Levett (reprinted in Burnyeat (1990)).
2 Most of the few other pieces of valuable testimony will be mentioned below.
3 See particularly Wiggins (1980c) and Wiggins (1987a), Essay V.
4 This essay has previously existed in various forms and been read to various audiences. I am indebted above all to David Wiggins for his interest in, and encouragement of it, throughout its prehistory; and to the editors of this volume for searching criticisms of the penultimate draft. I hereby recant my earlier published estimate of Protagoras (in Hussey (1972), p. 109) as 'not a systematic thinker', though I would still insist strongly on his wish to stay close to 'common sense', and the primacy he gave to practical over theoretical or systematizing aims (cf. Farrar (1988), pp. 47–53).
5 But see Burnyeat (1990), pp. 7–10 on this.
6 The sources are found conveniently in Diels–Kranz, *Die Fragmente der Vorsokratiker*, 80 (Protagoras) B 1, A 1, A 14.
7 *Tht.* 152a–c; 161c–e; 166c–167b. That opinion must be *derived* from sense-perception (or other direct awareness) exclusively is implied by *di' aitheseôs doxazêi* (161d3).
8 Usually, of course, only sense-perception is in question; but see below on our immediate awareness of our own opinions.
9 *Ousia* here may indicate something like a sum of all properties. If Protagoras' theory denies the 'firmness of *ousia*' of X, that need not be taken to imply that Protagoras' theory makes either the existence of X, or of all properties of X, subjective. It is sufficient, on this reading, that some (important) properties of X should be subjective, for its *ousia* to lack 'firmness'.
10 Aristotle *Met.* IV 5, 1009a38–b11 and XI 6, 1062b12–24 imply the same ontological picture.
11 'Concerning the gods, I have no way of telling whether they exist or not, or what they are like. There are many obstacles to knowing this, notably the obscurity of the matter and the brevity of human life' (Diels–Kranz 80 B 4).
12 The quotation is from Bostock (1988), pp. 43ff.; similarly McDowell in Plato (1973), p. 119: 'It seems obvious that, at least as Plato interprets him,

Protagoras refuses to make sense of questions about what the wind is like in itself'. Yet nothing in the passage itself suggests that such questions make no sense.

13 To say that the contents of the relativized realities exist objectively *as such contents* is not, of course, to say that they are objectively true. Nor is it to say, as a once-popular view had it, that the subjectively perceived properties exist (somehow) objectively as well, as part of a grand total reality. This was the 'Brochard–Cornford' view; for a statement, see Cornford (1935), pp. 34–6; and, against the view, Vlastos (1956), p. xiii, note 26a.

14 It is not clear whether Protagoras could or would have allowed memory to count as *aisthêsis* of one's previous relativized realities. Note that the use of the generalizing singular *anthrôpos*, in 'a man is a measure', avoids committing Protagoras to any claim about the number of relativized realities that actually exist.

15 On Xenophanes' epistemology see Hussey (1990), pp. 17–28, and the works there cited.

16 The demarcation-line between the 'primary' and 'secondary' properties may be hard to draw, but the Atomists certainly worked with some such distinction. (As for the gods, Protagoras, like the Atomists and most Greeks of the time, could well have assumed that they had physical bodies.)

17 This implies that any divergent opinions about the physical framework (e.g. opinions of those asleep or insane) have to be discarded as not giving knowledge of it. That does not, of course, involve denial of the subjective truth of such divergent opinions.

18 Other recent works apparently inclining towards an objectivist interpretation of some kind (though not necessarily wholly accepting either Plato's testimony or the reading of it given here) include Kerferd (1981), Farrar (1988) and Classen (1989). The admirably clear study in Matthen (1985) sees the strength of the evidence for the objectivity of 'basic furniture', and seeks ingeniously to reconcile it with a thorough relativism.

19 Protagoras' book-title *Alêtheia*, 'Truth', was presumably ironically ambiguous. It was a statement of what was true for himself, Protagoras, i.e. his opinions. But it was also his exploration, and practical deflation (not refutation), of the very notion of objective truth as applied to human affairs. Hence the subtitle *Kataballontes*, 'Knock-Down Arguments'. On the title, and Protagoras' use of the word *alêtheia*, see Heitsch (1969).

   With corresponding ambiguity, Plato's Socrates makes his imagined Protagoras say in his own defence: 'I say the truth is as I have written' (*Tht.* 166d1–2); that is, both: 'I say that what I have written is true (sc. for me; i.e. "I stick by my written opinions")' and: 'I say that *truth* is as I have written that it is (sc., in human affairs, and for all practical purposes, purely relative)'.

20 On Plato's criticisms of Protagoras, see esp. Burnyeat (1976) and Burnyeat (1990), pp. 19–31, 39–42.

21 To say that is not to devalue our opinions completely. Protagoras wants at least to insist that they are the nearest thing to an objective reality (about the matters in question) that we can possibly have. The report of Aristotle,

Metaphysics XI 6, 1062b13–15 can be defended on these lines: it says that '... he [Protagoras] said that a human being is a measure of all things, meaning just that, what anyone thinks to be so, definitely is (*einai pagiôs*)'. *Pagiôs* is often rendered by 'fixedly' or 'stably', but 'definitely' fits the usage of Plato and Aristotle at least as well, and is clearly preferable here. It was evidently a word favoured by the 'Heracliteans', and occurs in contexts where their ideas are alluded to: see Plato, *Rep.* 479c4, *Tht.* 157a4, Aristotle *De Caelo* 298b30, *Met.* 1063a33.

22 Compare the remarks of the hypothetical Protagoras at *Tht.* 166b4–5, which may suggest that the real Protagoras was not worried by (the possibility of) contradiction in itself. The contradiction here involved is a purely theoretical one. See also below, §9, on co-assertibility.

23 Of course a question of *sincerity* (not of unreason) would arise, in such a situation, if Protagoras did not hastily start to revise his opinions.

24 Schiller preferred to call himself a 'humanist'. The suggestion was made in his (1912), Essay II, 'From Plato to Protagoras', and in his 1908 pamphlet 'Plato or Protagoras?'

25 Burnyeat (1990), pp. 23–24 is an exception, but even he gives the suggestion no serious consideration.

26 Compare [Hippocrates] *On Ancient Medicine*, which is close to Protagoras in several respects: the subject-matter of medicine is 'the things that are suffered' (*pathêmata*) by people in general (ch. 2); 'bodily sensation' (*tou sômatos tên aisthêsin*) is the only 'measure' by which to judge a treatment.

27 But, for the 'asymptotic consensus' and the cumulative and irreversible improvement of opinion, as a necessary part of Protagoras' theory, see §9 below.

28 Note particularly the words *khrêstos* ('useful') and its opposite *ponêros* ('with bad effects') in 167b–c.

29 On 'marks of truth/assertibility', see Wiggins (1980c), pp. 205–12, and particularly (with application to areas of subjective disagreement, and noting the connection with a Protagorean 'natural consensus'), Wiggins (1987a, Essays IV and V and Postscript. They are here called 'marks of truth', and numbered in conformity with Essay IV, pp. 147–152.

30 The claim about the *Protagoras* made here depends on an analysis, which cannot be given here, of the 'Great Speech' (*Prt.* 320c8–328d2) and of supplementary remarks in that dialogue.

31 Cf. the classic formulation by Socrates at *Euthyphro* 7b6–d5.

32 Protagoras' deflation of theoretical claims is also seen in his attacks on geometry as a theoretical science (Aristotle *Met.* 998a1–4) and on the Eleatics (Diels–Kranz 80 B 2). Compare the polemic of *On Ancient Medicine* against those who 'make use of a *hupothesis*'.

33 For the appeal of the theory, see, besides *Protagoras* and *Theaetetus*, the remarks of Socrates and Hermogenes at *Cratylus* 385e–386a. On the motivation, *Euthydemus* 285d–286c, cf. *Crat.* 429d, *Tht.* 167a; also Aristotle *Met.* 1009a37–b12; 1062b12–24, 1062b33–1063b7.

34 Wiggins (1967), p. vii.

13

Pragmatism, Empiricism and Morality

Cheryl Misak

1 Introduction

In this paper, I shall argue that moral judgements ought to be considered candidates for truth and knowledge. The mistake which has often been made, I shall suggest, is to begin with sensory judgements and require that all others be in some respect similar if they are to be objective. We ought to begin instead with a broad notion of experience and then ask what judgements are responsive to it. It will turn out that beliefs about the sensory and the moral are both responsive to recalcitrant experience and thus are both candidates for truth-values. It is not that there is an *analogy* between sensory perception and moral perception, but rather, that once the relevant standards are set out in a non-question-begging way, both make the grade.

The position I shall advocate is a thoroughgoing epistemological holism, the central thesis of which is a thesis about inquiry. Rather than begin by driving a wedge between various sorts of inquiry, we must first try to identify, in an entirely general way, those features of hypotheses which make them candidates for serious investigation. On the way to arriving at such a holism, many programmatic remarks will be made about ethics and a few will be made about mathematics.

David Bakhurst, David Dyzenhaus, Arthur Ripstein, David Wiggins, the editors of this volume, and audiences at the universities of Toronto, Western Ontario, and Frankfurt made extremely helpful comments on various drafts of this paper. The Social Sciences and Humanities Research Council of Canada and the Alexander von Humboldt Foundation provided generous financial support. The project of which this paper is a part began as a D.Phil. thesis presented in Oxford in 1988. David Wiggins's careful and insightful supervision made all the difference to that thesis and to the way the rest of the project will unfold.

This position is a brand of Peircean pragmatism. It is not a kind of realism which says that our true judgements match or correspond to something which is given prior to conceptualization. Neither is it a relativism which says that there are only various, equally good, conceptualizations and so there is no one right answer to any given question. Pragmatism undermines such dichotomies and paints a more complex picture of truth, knowledge, and morality.

2 Empiricism: Traditional and Quinean

Empiricists have always shown respect for mathematical and logical statements, despite the *prima facie* difficulties they pose. Traditional empiricists (think here of Hume or the logical positivists) maintain that all legitimate beliefs originate in and, if they are justified, are justified by experience.[1] But it seems that this does not hold for mathematical and logical beliefs. These empiricists avoid the conclusion that such beliefs are not meaningful, legitimate, objective, or candidates for truth-value[2] by withdrawing the requirement that they be connected to experience. They do this via the distinction between, in Hume's terms, 'relations of ideas' and 'matters of fact' or, in more contemporary terms, 'analytic' and 'synthetic' statements. Analytic statements are supposed to have a special kind of meaning or legitimacy because when they are true, they are true in virtue of meaning and are therefore unrevisable. Synthetic statements are not true in virtue of meaning and they must prove their legitimacy by passing a rather strict empiricist criterion. Hume argued that they must correspond to sensory impressions and the logical positivists argued that they must entail observation statements or be verifiable.

Quine (1953), in the essay, 'Two Dogmas of Empiricism', rejects the distinction between the analytic and the synthetic but nonetheless retains respect for the statements of mathematics and logic. With Duhem, he argues that no scientific statement is confirmed or disconfirmed on its own. For the statement being tested does not by itself entail an observation statement. Only when taken in conjunction with countless auxiliary hypotheses does a statement entail that 'if we do x, we shall observe y'.[3] Thus, rather than the statement in question, any of those auxiliary hypotheses could be taken to be confirmed if we do x and observe y, or disconfirmed if we do x and do not observe y. It is a whole theory, or a substantial part of one, that faces the tribunal of experience.

One corollary of the Quine/Duhem Thesis is that 'synthetic' statements cannot show themselves to be legitimate by passing an empiricist test. For no statement by itself entails observation statements.

Another corollary is that mathematical and logical statements are on a par with sensory ones. They are part of any scientific theory and so they also face the tribunal of experience – they are not unrevisable. Because of their central place in our fallible, evolving, and interconnected web of belief, they will not be easily overturned. But logically, they are as susceptible to disconfirmation as any other judgement and, practically, inquirers may find themselves in a position where it seems best to revise a mathematical/logical belief. (Think, for instance, of the possibility of rejecting the law of the excluded middle in light of quantum mechanics).

The Quinean empiricist joins the traditional empiricist in taking logic and mathematics to be legitimate branches of knowledge by pointing to the fact that they are a part (the very core) of our system of belief and knowledge. Having a place in that effort to make sense of experience is, in Quine's view, all that legitimacy or objectivity amounts to.

But Quine puts the brakes on holism here. The analytic/synthetic distinction has been a dogma of empiricism and needs debunking. But the distinction which encourages the thought that moral judgements are not candidates for truth-values, the fact/value distinction, is fine as it stands. Moral judgements have no role to play in the Quinean web of belief. They are not a part of science; they do not face the tribunal of experience. Aside from a 'salient marker' or two, there are only 'uncharted moral wastes'.[4]

The traditional empiricist will agree with Quine here. Whatever moral judgements are, they do not enjoy either of the kinds of content that have the traditional empiricist's respect. Thus Hume, on one reading, argued that it is we who spread moral properties onto the world; they aren't there to be found. And the logical positivists argued that moral judgements fail the verificationist test of significance; they merely express feelings of approval or disapproval of situations.

Since Quine rejects the traditional empiricist dichotomy, he ought to be hard pressed to say why the exclusion of moral judgements from the web of belief is more than mere prejudice. If there was anything good about the correspondence theory of truth, which has it that a statement is true if and only if it corresponds to the mind-independent (one might as well read 'physical') world of objects, that theory could be invoked to exclude moral judgements. For the correspondence theory virtually guarantees that only statements which simply assert something about the properties of physical objects will be candidates for truth-values. But Quine rejects this account of truth.[5]

The empiricism that I wish to explore is one which sheds the Quinean prejudice against morals. If, as I will suggest (and as Quine sometimes suggests), we should view truth simply as the best that our inquiries could produce, the best that we could do by way of accounting for and explaining our experiences, there is no *prima facie* reason for denying moral inquiry a place in our search for truth. Scientific theories (with a mathematical/logical core) certainly are a part of our attempt to understand experience. But we shall see that, given a broad enough account of experience,[6] so are moral theories.

There is, moreover, an important consideration against expelling moral judgements from the scope of truth and knowledge: the phenomenology of morality is that it aspires to truth. We argue, debate, and agonize over our moral judgements and choices as if there really is a truth of the matter at stake, something that we are trying to discover. I shall return to the issue of truth below, but first, we need to see how moral judgements could be seen to be objective by the empiricist who embraces holism.

3 Radical Holism

This radical holism takes from Quinean holism both the rejection of the analytic/synthetic distinction[7] and the thought that we must view knowledge, truth and objectivity in terms of Neurath's metaphor. We have developed a body of beliefs for making sense of our experience and we modify these beliefs in light of recalcitrant experience. We are to imagine ourselves as mariners adrift on a ship, making piecemeal repairs as they become necessary. There is no land in sight – no destination that we are bound to reach or even trying to reach. We must merely try to stay afloat the best we can.

But radical holism is more thoroughgoing than Quine's because it does not privilege or prejudice any domain of inquiry at the outset. It does not pronounce that there are separate orders of fact and value or of the causal and the normative and then go on to glorify the factual/causal and denigrate the evaluative/normative.

Rather, it takes from traditional empiricism the thought that, in order for a subject matter to qualify for a place in our system of knowledge, or in order for it to qualify as an objective area of inquiry, it must pass an empiricist test. It must meet a suitably formulated verificationist criterion.[8] – one which demands of a belief that it *answer to something*. The empiricism that I want to argue for undercuts the distinctions between analytic and synthetic and between fact and value by setting up an unbiased account of experience and then seeing what sorts of beliefs respond to it.

Russell's hypothesis 'the world and everything in it, including fossils and memories, was created five minutes ago' will be defective on this account just because nothing could serve as evidence for its truth or falsity.[9] If moral judgements are in some way like that, then Mackie (1977) is right that the common belief that they legitimately aspire to truth is mistaken. But if moral judgements can be shown to be responsive to evidence in the way that the radical holist demands, then they are candidates for truth-values; we are right to think that they aspire to truth.

How, it might be asked, can a holist embrace any kind of verificationism? Verificationism seems to rest on the claim that some statements carry with them their own bundle of empirical content which can be verified or falsified, a claim which is the target of the Quine/Duhem Thesis.

But notice that Quine himself can be described as a verificationist who thinks that the unit which must have empirical consequences is a whole theory. This is why he takes it for granted that physics but not morality is a part of our web of belief. Moral theories do not answer to sensory experience. Despite his arguments against verificationism, Quine seems to hold that a judgement, in order to be legitimate, must be a part of a theory which entails observation statements.[10]

An alternative kind of verificationism for the holist might be as follows. It follows from fallibilism that a judgement must be such that it is *not insensitive* to evidence. For fallibilism holds that any judgement can be toppled by evidence. A judgement which pretends to be above empirical evidence is in fact not so lofty. We can say that it is faulty in that it pretends to be something which it cannot be.

Notice that the thought that no judgement must be taken to be immune from evidence seems to be in tension with Quine's statement that any judgement can be held true come what may if we are willing to make radical revisions elsewhere. But the fact that someone might tenaciously hold on to a belief does not mean that the holist must applaud such an attitude. The holist can criticize someone who is prepared to say in advance that she will not revise a certain judgement, no matter what evidence may come to light against it. Perhaps such a person is not engaging in genuine inquiry, is not aiming at truth, does not, as we shall see Peirce suggests, believe the hypothesis in question, but rather, dogmatically holds on to it, etc. We ought not take any judgement to be true come what may, although people certainly do adopt this attitude towards certain judgements.

The significant point of departure from Quine's position is the radical holist's denial of Quine's belief that the only acceptable kind of evidence is sensory. We are in debt to Quine for the thought that sensory evidence can topple either beliefs which arise from the senses or mathematical/logical beliefs. Presumably, he also thinks that beliefs which arise from the senses justify many of our beliefs. But, unless one takes the unattractive Millian path of holding that sensory evidence justifies mathematics, we require an account of what does justify our beliefs about mathematics. Whatever that is might as well be called a kind of evidence.

We take ourselves to be justified in holding a mathematical or logical belief if either there is a proof for the statement in question or if the statement strikes us as obviously right. We are then pressed to ask whether these sorts of considerations can topple beliefs which arise from the senses. Given his holism, Quine must respond 'yes'.

We have already seen that mathematical/logical beliefs are susceptible to revision if such a drastic change is needed to save beliefs about sensory phenomena. So we can have what we might call mathematical evidence against a belief which arises from the senses and sensory evidence against a mathematical belief. Once we have made this move, there are two sorts of evidence in the field of inquiry. We need no longer perjoratively label what strikes us as right in mathematics as 'intuition', as if to distinguish it from *real* evidence.

This sort of talk may seem to threaten holism, insofar as it may seem to reinstate the analytic/synthetic distinction by distinguishing between mathematical and sensory evidence. But no holist wants to claim that there is no difference at all between mathematics and science. Rather, the holist's claim is only that the distinctions are not hard and fast and that, as far as susceptibility to evidence goes, both sorts of statements are logically on a par. I want to add that recalcitrant experience can be had in the context of a proof, in a clash with a mathematical/logical belief, a clash with a belief which arises from the senses, or, as we shall see, a clash with yet other kinds of belief.

4 Experience and Evidence

Some philosophers have thought that sensory judgements have an exalted status because they are infallible. Even had this idea not pretty much died with logical positivism, it has no place in the fallibilist epistemology articulated here. Nonetheless, sensory judgements do seem to be paradigmatic cases of judgements which have a chance at truth and objectivity. So we need to search for some other feature of these judgements which which enables them to aspire to truth and which provides something for beliefs to respond to.

We must, however, be careful in this search not to beg the question straight away in favour of the traditional and the Quinean empiricist and against the radical holist. If we begin with beliefs which arise from our senses and ask what features they have, we do just that. A non-question-begging empiricist criterion will require beliefs to respond to experience, characterized in a way which identifies the special features of experience minimally and prior to the discussion of various sorts of inquiry.

My suggestion is that we take our cue from C. S. Peirce and characterize an experientially grounded belief as any belief that is forced upon one. Peirce arrives at this conception of experience partly by recognizing that 'going back to the first impressions of sense' would be 'the most chimerical of undertakings'.[11] We do not have access to anything raw, unconceptualized, or 'given' in experience.

Experience, on Peirce's account, amounts to 'perceptual judgements' – our descriptions of the clash between our senses and the world. These can be true or false and are matters of interpretation. A perceptual judgement is a description of whatever hold a person had on what actually impinged on her and is thus subject to error. Peirce says: 'Practically, the knowledge with which I have to content myself, and have to call "the evidence of my senses" instead of being in truth the evidence of the senses, is only a sort of stenographic report of that evidence, possibly erroneous' (ibid.). Experience does not give us an 'accurate' picture of the external world. Sensory perceptions only 'provide positive assurance of reality and of the nearness of their objects' without giving 'any insight into the nature of those objects' (Peirce (1931–5), vol. IV, §530).

But once we stop thinking of the authority of sensory perceptions as arising because they are accurate and infallible, their authority needs to be accounted for. After all, we do (and should) take them very seriously.

Peirce argues that sensory judgements are authoritative in the sense that they force themselves upon us. A perceptual judgement is what we are compelled to accept; we have no control over the matter. And 'it is idle to discuss the "legitimacy" of that which cannot be controlled' ((1931–5), vol. VI, §522). The 'hardness of fact' lies in 'its entirely irrational insistency' (Peirce (1958), vol. VII, §659).

On this view of perception, the senses need not figure in an essential way. The key feature of perception, observation, or experience is its insistency. And that is fully general. Experience is not tied to what our ears, eyes, nose, and skin report. Peirce says:

> . . . anything is . . . to be classed under the species of perception wherein a positive qualitative content is forced upon one's acknowledgement without any reason or pretension to reason. There will be a wider genus of things partaking of the character of perception, if there be any matter of cognition which exerts a force upon us . . . ((1958), vol. VII, §623).

Any judgement that is compelling, surprising, brute, unchosen, or impinging is an experience, regardless of what causes us to feel compelled and regardless of whether we can identify the source of the compulsion. All 'compulsions of thought' count as 'experience' ((1958), vol. VIII, §101).

Peirce argues that there are two kinds of such compulsions – sensory experience and experience in which

> ... operations upon diagrams, whether external or imaginary, take the place of the experiments upon real things that one performs in chemical and physical research ((1931–5), vol. IV, §530).

These diagrammatic experiments or thought experiments figure in mathematical and deductive inquiry.[12] They involve

> experimenting upon [an] image in the imagination, and of observing the result so as to discover unnoticed and hidden relations among the parts ((1931–5), vol. III, §363).

The mathematician, for instance, draws subsidiary lines in geometry or makes transformations in algebraic formulae and then observes the results:

> his hypotheses are creatures of his own imagination; but he discovers in them relations which surprise him sometimes ((1931–5), vol. V, §567).

Since surprise is the force of experience, the upshot of such reasoning counts as experience.

Peirce insists that the distinction between kinds of experience cannot be firmly drawn. External facts are simply those which are 'ordinarily regarded as external while others are regarded as internal' ((1982), vol. II, p. 205). The distinction arises, he says, because the inner world exerts a comparatively slight compulsion upon us, whereas the outer world is full of irresistible compulsions. But nonetheless, internal experience also can be 'unreasonably compulsory' ((1958), vol. VII, §659): 'the inner world has its surprises for us, sometimes' ((1958), vol. VII, §438). He intends to leave the difference between the two sorts of experience vague:

> We naturally make all our distinctions too absolute. We are accustomed to speak of an external universe and an inner world of thought. But they are merely vicinities with no real boundary between them ((1958), vol. VII, §438).

We have seen that traditional empiricists argue that mathematical and logical statements are empirically empty but exempt from the rigours of the test for significance. Peirce is not forced to adopt such an *ad hoc* procedure. In his own debunking of the analytic/synthetic distinction, he suggests that we ought to expose mathematical and logical statements to the empiricist criterion. Experiments performed on diagrams will provide the relevant observable data for such statements. It is not that these observations verify or falsify the statements and thus grant them meaningfulness. Rather, the fact that the statements have consequences in such experiments makes them candidates for truth-values. This is what the empiricism of radical holism amounts to: every legitimate belief must have experiential consequences. It must answer to experience of one kind or another. Let us rest with this sketch of the Peircean notion of experience and see how far it takes us in the domains in which we are interested.

Seeing that a piece of litmus paper is blue clearly qualifies as a perception on this account. A certain view – that the paper is blue – is compelling. There is, to borrow a phrase from Wiggins, simply nothing else to think. Such beliefs are quite fallible (the light may be bad) but nonetheless, there is nothing else for me to believe. Moreover, such a belief is not independent of human perceptual and conceptual capacities. It is in virtue of having the capacities that we do that we call a certain phemomenon blue.

Similarly, when a scientist observes the tracks of an electron, the observation is not a theory-free observation. For one will only identify those black marks as electron tracks if one's background beliefs include a complex theory of physics, if one knows what the cloud chamber apparatus is, etc. But once one has that set of beliefs, there is nothing else to think but that those are the tracks of an electron. Again, this is not to say that the belief is *true*, merely, that it is forced upon those with certain capacities, training and background beliefs.

The Peircean idea thus fits well with sensory judgements, both colour judgements and judgements in more theoretical contexts. The idea that experience is what we cannot help but take seriously captures what goes on in science and yet does not invest sensory observation with the fairy-tale features of being infallible and free from any subjective influence.

Peirce clearly thought that his idea lent itself nicely to mathematical and logical judgements.[13] Proofs and valid deductive arguments are such that we cannot see how we could believe otherwise than what they conclude. If we understand a proof, we have no choice but to accept the result. Indeed, we often do not require a proof in order for a mathematical or logical statement to impose itself upon us. '2 + 3 = 5' and 'Not both P and not P' do so without further ado. But again, understanding here requires much in the way of background belief and again, as both Quine and Peirce insist, such statements are fallible. Although we cannot easily imagine circumstances under which we would revise them, they are in principle subject to overthrow. With respect to mathematical and logical statements, we are taken as far as we need to go by the Peircean idea.

5 Moral Judgements

The tendency amongst those who would like to elevate the status of moral judgements has been to explore analogies between the moral and the empirical or between the moral and the mathematical. Thus McDowell (1985) and Wiggins (1976a) suggest that moral judgements are in some respects just as objective (and just as subjective) as colour judgements. And Wiggins ((1976a), (1987a), Essay IV) suggests that a fruitful analogy can be drawn between the moral and the mathematical.

The trouble with these analogies is that they inevitably seem to attract a certain kind of objection. With respect to colour perception, it is argued that there are physical objects in the world which have properties which interact with our physical sense organs and cause us to have the response we do, whereas there are no such objects and no such organs involved in our moral responses. So the analogy and the attempt to elevate the status of moral judgements fail.

In the mathematical case, the objector picks out a different disanalogy, for the moral and the mathematical are surely similar in that neither is primarily about physical objects. The disanalogy here is the striking absence of agreement in moral matters and the striking presence of agreement in mathematical matters. Again, the attempt to elevate moral judgements, if it rests entirely on a comparison with a 'respectable' sort of hypothesis, is thought to founder because it can seem that there is more dissimilarity than similarity between the two cases.

Rather than try to show how moral judgements are like other sorts of judgements, we would do better, I think, to press the minimal Peircean notion of experience and see whether it extends to the moral realm.

However problematic it can seem to be, a case can be made for perception or experience in the moral domain. We often find ourselves compelled in moral matters and, as in mathematics, this compulsion can take two forms. The first is what has been called 'intuition' – upon observing a certain act we simply 'see' that it is odious. The second is that we find some reasons, arguments and thought experiments compelling and may, in light of them, revise our moral judgements.

As with other kinds of observation, observation in the moral domain is fallible. What is intuitively obvious in any kind of inquiry can be discredited – think of initially plausible stereotypes in the social sciences and the fact that Einstein's relativity theory was taken by some to be intuitively false. Indeed, our very ability to recognize mistakes like these turns on the idea that what strikes us as obvious is subject to further experience. But we need not conclude that obviousness should be given no weight. We *must* take our background beliefs seriously in inquiry; if we did not, inquiry would grind to a halt. We need a body of stable belief against which to judge new evidence and hypotheses. Plausibility, obviousness, or coherence with our other beliefs must speak in favour of hypotheses.

And observation in moral inquiry, as in other domains, is laden with background belief.[14] Indeed, it will seem to some that the sort of experience relevant to morality is so liable to vary from person to person or from culture to culture, that it cannot count as evidence for or against a judgement.

The radical holist ought to admit straight away that morality is such that there will be much disagreement about what is compelling, for there will be differences in people's capacities, training and background beliefs. On the account of truth outlined in the next section, it may be that, as Wiggins has stressed, while moral judgements aspire to truth, not all will attain it. But this thought should simply be taken on board; it should not lead us to abandon talk of correctness in moral matters. For no judgement is free of theory or background belief. We might say merely that the baggage which accompanies the sort of experience relevant to most empirical and mathematical hypotheses is more uniform than that which accompanies most moral hypotheses. That is, the background theories and capacities of scientists and mathematicians seem to be to a greater extent shared. That said, we must be careful also to notice the tremendous amount of underlying agreement in moral matters as well as the diversity of background theory and belief in science and mathematics.

Acknowledging such diversity in moral inquiry, rather than damaging radical holism, indirectly supports it by leading to explanations of some troubling phenomena. Take, for instance, the phenomenon of moral blindness – of the inability to see that some atrocious act is atrocious. On the view offered here, if someone does not have certain background moral views or capacities, then we ought to expect that they will not be able to see that a certain act is wrong. We also have the makings of an explanation of the disagreement so prevalent in morals. Without similar background theories and capacities, one will not be able to see what others can.[15]

We also can explain how it is possible to reasonably change one's mind or discover something about a moral matter, a phenomenon the non-cognitivist struggles with. (If there is nothing to respond to, why do we sometimes revise and improve our beliefs in light of evidence and argument?) I might come to see an act in a different light or from a different perspective. Or someone might point to certain features of the act that have been missed or thought to be unimportant. That is, because experience is a matter of interpretation, not only can (and should) we expose ourselves and others to new experiences, but we can also arrive at better interpretations.

It will also seem to some that moral inquiry is not aimed at truth because moral judgements are self-confirming in a way that scientific judgements are not. But again, there is a parallel here in science – the history of science is full of examples that show that those in the sway of a particular theory will find that their observations tend to confirm that theory. And again, we can see our way to an explanation of the troubling phenomenon on the view offered here. As in science, there is a constant dialectic between perception and the background theory. The theory facilitates certain observations and then those observations have to be squared with the rest of the theory. Through critical reflection, exposing oneself to more experience and perspectives, one's background beliefs can be improved and one's judgements revised, despite being able to see only what one's theory allows.

Thus, while it may seem at first glance that the force of experience in moral inquiry is intolerably variable, moral judgements can be seen to be responsive to experience in a way that confers legitimacy upon them, according to the empiricist criterion set out earlier. Their responsiveness differs, to a certain extent, from that of mathematical and scientific beliefs, but those differences are only to be expected and receive explanation at the hands of the radical holist. None of the differences need be destructive of the general case for morals. And if we pay attention to an important distinction, we will want to retain, against all the obstacles, the thought that moral judgements are responsive to experience.

As Peirce insisted, and as our modified empiricist criterion suggests, there is a distinction between tenacity, or holding on to a 'belief' come what may, and genuine belief.[16] Belief, as opposed to some other state such as choosing arbitrarily what to 'believe' or lying about what one believes, must be sensitive to evidence. If one is committed to never revising an opinion, no matter what evidence against it is brought to light, then that is something like blind dogmatism and not a genuine judgement about what is true. Those claiming to hold a belief, something which has a truth-value, *commit themselves* to being open to evidence and argument. If we are to retain the distinction in moral philosophy between mere tenacity and belief or judgement, then moral judgements must be in principle responsive to evidence and argument.

Another way of putting this point is that if we engage in moral *inquiry*, as opposed to holding on to our moral beliefs come what may, we must take those beliefs to be responsive to new reasons, arguments and experiences about what is cruel, kind, odious, just, etc. Moral discussion, for those who engage in it, is example-driven and argument-driven. Thus those who take a creed so seriously that they will say in advance that they will take recalcitrant experience to threaten only non-credal beliefs, do not engage in genuine moral inquiry. For it is a presupposition of that inquiry that one's views are in principle responsive to evidence or open to revision. And we do sometimes engage in genuine inquiry about moral matters rather than in mere tenacity.

6 The Radical Holist as Pragmatist

All of the judgements under discussion here (scientific, mathematical and moral) aspire to truth and I have suggested that philosophy ought to respect that aspiration. Something must now be said about just what it is that they aspire to.

The view of truth implicit in radical holism is a certain (Peircean) pragmatic account: a judgement is true if it would always withstand the tests of a rigorous and sustained inquiry. A judgement is true if it is the best belief for beings of our kind to have; if, at the end of inquiry, it would be agreed to fit best with all the evidence and argument. There is no prejudice here against the aspiration of non-scientific beliefs, for inquiry has not been spelled out as scientific inquiry. Yet, as might be expected, the judgements of science (as well as those of mathematics) provide the least problematic example of judgements which might be true.

There is much to be said about this account of truth which cannot be said here.[17] A few remarks will have to suffice. First, a methodology is directly provided and justified. The pragmatist will say that inquirers must expose themselves to new evidence, argument, and perspectives. For if truth is that which would be agreed to best fit with the evidence and argument, were inquiry to have proceeded as far as it could fruitfully go, the best way to try to discover what is true is to take in as much as one can. Inquirers must take the experiences and perspectives of others seriously, for truth is what is best for the community to believe.[18]

Those positions which thrive, by accident or design, on discounting the beliefs of others (patriarchy or Nazism, for instance) can be criticized because they adopt a method which is unlikely to lead to the truth.

Secondly, *only* this democratic methodology is justified by the pragmatic account of truth. The pragmatist, at this level of abstraction, must remain agnostic about the details as to how inquiry (of any kind) should go. The specific principles of inquiry which are best will be those standards which would evolve as inquiry progresses. In science the standards will be set by scientists and those historians and philosophers of science who have an impact on actual inquiry. In morals, the standards will by set by those engaged in moral inquiry. This does not mean only, or even mainly, 'experts' who sit on ethics boards in hospitals and the like and those novelists, essayists and philosophers who engage in particular issues. For we are all involved in moral discussion.

Thus, this account of truth is not a version of the ideal spectator position, on which the truth is what a certain kind of ideal spectator, in ideal circumstances, would take to be true. We must be careful with the Peircean notion of the end of inquiry. It is not some God's-eye view, but rather, the down-to-earth view which involves the outcome of our actual human practices, if they were to be informed the best they could by evidence and argument. We cannot fill in the details about what an ideal spectator would be like (impartial, sympathetic, utilitarian, interested in simplicity or whatever) and then settle our debates by asking how such a spectator would settle them. Rather, sensitivity to context will be a primary feature of moral inquiry.[19] We must settle our debates the best we know how, case by case, with the assumption that, were inquiry to be pursued as far as it could fruitfully go, there would be a best answer which would make itself apparent.[20]

The epistemology I have outlined in this paper is as follows. We engage in the practice of scientific, mathematical, and moral inquiry. Each has its evolving standards of criticism and evaluation and each has a kind of experience most relevant to it. This experience, and the possibility of clashes with other sorts of judgements, constitute the domain of evidence that could be for or against a hypothesis. The fact that the branch of inquiry in question is responsive to experience justifies our belief that it aims at the truth.

There are differences, to be sure, between the three inquiries. For instance, the chances of judgements in some areas commanding consensus differ from those of others. But this should not lead us to think that science, say, is the sort of thing that might achieve a correspondence with an independent reality, for no thing is that sort of thing. Scientific hypotheses are theory-laden and are part of our attempt to make sense of what impinges upon us. The same holds for moral beliefs. In both areas of inquiry, we are adrift on Neurath's boat. We have our practices and their standards of success. To borrow an apt phrase from Wiggins, in prosecuting those practices, 'we shall reach wherever we reach, for such reasons as seem good and appropriate'.[21] And if we were to reach a stage where we could no longer improve upon a belief, there is no point in withholding the title 'true' from it.

In addition, and against certain contemporary pragmatists such as Rorty, there is a point in conferring the title upon such beliefs. For, as Peirce argues, a regulative assumption of inquiry into any matter is that there is a hope of reaching the truth. Without the hope that there is an answer to the question at hand, there would be no point in debate or investigation; giving up the assumption places an insurmountable obstacle in the way of inquiry. If we are to leave the path of inquiry unobstructed, we must assume that there is a truth of the matter with respect to the issue we are investigating.

This point is of special importance because it reflects a central goal of the pragmatist. The pragmatist insists that philosophy be connected to practice. In this case, a conception of truth must be able to guide inquiry and deliberation. And one need not be a pragmatist to agree here. Truth, after all, is taken to be the aim of inquiry and the aim of any activity ought to provide a comprehensible guide to the pursuit of that activity. We require an account of truth that the investigator can and ought to adopt.

So those contemporary pragmatists who would replace the notion of truth with that of warranted assertion betray their commitment to taking seriously the practices of inquirers, who take their business to be that of trying to reach true beliefs. The phenomenology of moral inquiry is that it strikes us that there is a truth of the matter at stake in moral debate. On the Peircean view offered here, this thought is preserved – moral inquiry is aimed at finding the truth by improving our beliefs through considering more evidence, argument, and perspective. And we are right to take truth as our aim – we *must* do so in order to keep open the path of inquiry.

It is important to stress that the best belief at any stage in inquiry is to be regarded as fallible. One must assume that there is a right answer to the question at hand, but one should not assume that one has the right answer in hand. The right answer, if there be one, is that which would be arrived at were inquiry to be pursued as far as it could fruitfully go, and thus, *qua* seeker after right answers, one must be committed to pursuing inquiry. If one aims at the truth, one should not be smug about the beliefs which seem best at the moment. Our judgements might be rational – they might be the best beliefs at the current stage of inquiry – yet they might well be false.

In addition, the inquirer ought to see that the assumption that moral judgements have truth-values will not always hold, though it has to be assumed to hold in any case under investigation. Tolerance and humility in morals should not arise out of moral scepticism; they should not arise because one thinks that there is no truth of the matter, as the non-cognitivist would have us believe. Rather, they should arise by acknowledging that the assumption that there *is* a right answer to the question at hand is but a hope.

Thus, the pragmatic account of truth not only fits nicely with radical holism, but it also explains and has a good effect on the practice of inquiry. The pragmatist agrees with Wiggins's advice that philosophers should arrange it so that the theory of truth or objectivity is such that certain classes of belief are not barred at the outset. It may very well turn out, once non-question-begging criteria are articulated, that certain classes of judgement do not meet the relevant standard. But an empiricism, such as the logical positivist's or Quine's, that guarantees this result off the bat is certainly unwise. It is much better, I suggest, to be a pragmatist of the sort outlined here.

NOTES

1 It is difficult to say how beliefs might be justified by experience if experience is taken to be something that is 'given'. As Popper (1959) and Davidson (1983) have argued, only beliefs can stand in justificatory relationships with beliefs. The Peircean account of perception upon which I shall rely avoids this difficulty because it holds that nothing is given to us prior to conceptualization. For elaboration and for how this view is compatible with the thought that there is a mind-independent reality, see Misak (1991), pp. 70–79, 126–137.

2 I ride roughshod at this point over any differences between these notions. It shall become clear that I take the key concept to be 'candidates for truth-value', for what I am concerned with is that minimal requirement which will allow judgements into an inquiry with truth as its aim.

3 This characterization of an observation statement follows the usage of many, but not all, empiricists.

4 Quine (1987), p. 5. See also his (1981), p. 63.

5 He seems to advocate various views of truth at various times, but, as we shall see below, I take him to be committed to some kind of non-correspondence view. Quine of course is a physicalist and this is the reason he ignores moral judgements. My point is that his physicalism is merely tacked on to his holism.

6 Quine's early characterization of observation is probably broad enough: 'A sentence is observational insofar as its truth-value, on any occasion, would be agreed to by just about any member of the speech community witnessing the occasion' (Quine (1974)), p. 39. '2 + 2 = 4' and 'That's beautiful' might be

construed as observational on this definition. Later, however, Quine insists that the assent must be prompted by the stimulation of sensory receptors. See his (1990), p. 3.

7 The distinction I wish to undercut is the distinction between judgements which we might inquire into which are responsive to evidence and judgements which we might inquire into which are not responsive to evidence. That is, it is a distinction drawn within the class of judgements which are the objects of serious investigation. The analytic/synthetic distinction is something that inquirers should abandon. This position might well be compatible with a distinction between judgements which are the objects of inquiry and what Putnam (1962) calls single criterion words and corresponding truths such as 'all bachelors are unmarried', which are not the objects of inquiry.

8 This will not be a criterion of meaningfulness or significance, but rather, a statement that gets by it will be objective or a candidate for a truth-value.

9 At least, nothing could serve as evidence that would not also serve as evidence for a more usual hypothesis. And the usual hypothesis has behind it the weight of being the product of our actual inquiries. See Misak (1991), pp. 91–98.

10 See Quine (1990), pp. 12–13; (1986), pp. 155 ff.; (1975), p. 80.

11 Peirce (1931–5), vol. II, § 141.

12 Peirce himself developed a (quantified) deductive logic based on what he called 'existential graphs'.

13 He did not extend the idea to moral judgements, as I shall.

14 Some take a background moral theory to be analogous to a scientific theory in that we perceive that certain acts are right or wrong and thus confirm or disconfirm general principles which constitute the theory. But again, the trouble with this kind of direct analogy is that, once we squeeze moral inquiry into the scientific mould, the dissimilarities or lack of fit is what tends to strike us. Perhaps we would do better to follow McDowell (1979) and Wiggins (1976a) and take moral inquiry to be based rather on an Aristotelian conception of the virtuous person as possessing a special kind of perceptual capacity or sensitivity, the exercise of which reveals how it is appropriate to act. A moral theory here is not composed of general principles but represents a non-codifiable conception of how to live. What is at stake in moral inquiry is not the scientific goal of better prediction, but a conception of ourselves that will facilitate our becoming the best we can be.

15 This view might be thought to lead to a kind of moral colonialism – since others cannot see what is there to be seen, 'we' needn't take their judgements seriously. But we shall see that, on the view of truth offered below, the contrary judgements of others *must* be taken seriously.

16 See Wiggins (1987a), p. 344 and Misak (1991), pp. 59 ff. for an elaboration of this point.

17 For an elaboration and a response to objections, see Misak (1991).

18 This does not preclude, and it might even require, pluralism. For there might be underdetermination in any area of inquiry – the community might agree that $(P \lor Q)$ is true. That is not the same as agreeing that P is true for one

subset of the community and Q is true for another. What we might agree
upon with respect to morals is that certain views of the good life, with their
practical judgements, are permissible.

19 This view thus has affinities with 'particularism' (see, for instance,
   McNaughton (1988)) and with certain feminist views (see, for instance,
   Minow (1990)). And it is, of course, something Wiggins has stressed.

20 Some issues, especially moral ones, will cease to be relevant, or even understandable, as the context in which they are situated changes. Here, as everywhere, it is important to stress the subjunctive conditional nature of the
   Peircean view of truth: if inquiry were to be pursued on the matter, then H
   would be agreed upon. If, for any reason, the antecedent of this conditional
   is not fulfilled, the Peircean will say that the truth-value of the conditional is
   unaltered.

21 Wiggins (1987a), Essay V, p. 207.

14

Replies

David Wiggins

1 Introduction

1. Early on in the preparation of this volume, the proposal for which gave surprise and pleasure in the season of a birthday now a birthday or two ago, and the making of which has cost so many good friends of mine so much labour – but well before it was apparent to anyone how unconscionably the production of replies would delay the publication of these essays –, the editors, whose patience, skill and unremitting benevolence have put me under a debt I could never discharge, gently inquired if I could say what was the connecting thread that tied together the various questions that I have tried at one time or another to write or speak about.

In response to their question, I looked first for some unifying or underlying thought that had been there all along. But the results of this search were so artificial or so far from the facts that I quickly realised that the only intelligible answer was an autobiographical one.

Long though it proved to be, the answer made in this way to the editors' question eventually took on a philosophical shape. But one is not a flawless judge of relevance in this kind of thing. Only readers who want to know the answer to the editors' question (or have some non-philosophical interest in the stamp that a wartime childhood placed upon the lives of members of the generation I belong to) should read the next eight sections. All others should skip to §10. Let me say immediately that the Replies that begin there are of uneven length. Chance has played a part in this, not evaluation: also the length of time I have been away from the topics treated. The longer the absence, the more there is to say.

2. I was born in 1933 in London. My father was a barrister-at-law, a man of passionate and passionately moderate left-wing political

persuasion. His mother and father had been devout chapel-goers, teeto-
tal, vegetarian and serious to a fault. On Sundays, my grandfather, who
was a coal merchant in Northampton, was a non-conformist lay preacher.
By the time I was born, my father had long since turned sharply against
almost all of the things that his parents stood for, save only two. He was
still a vegetarian, which meant being prepared for the ridicule and
curiosity that this entailed in those days. In the second place, an ideal of
public spirit was second nature to him. I speculate that this was the
secular residue of Christian notions of good fellowship and philanthropy.
But he was an atheist (in the rationalist-cum-bible-quoting mode of those
days), unsolemn, politely irreverent and, by the standards of those days,
liberal and easy-going. After reading law and psychology at Cambridge,
he had been called to the Bar. He was eminently suited to a public life,
sociable, musical, approachable and hospitable. But, personal friend-
ships apart, he had the professional life of an outsider to the Bar,
apparently unaware of how best to deploy his talents. He was not party
to any network that would have brought him briefs when briefs were
scarce. (One of my memories of adolescence is of being alone in the
house when the bailiffs came to cast an eye over the furniture to see what
it would fetch.) My brother and I sought for many years to learn something from his career, but were baffled by it.

My mother, who was the daughter of a Yorkshire schoolmaster who had
come from Bradford to be the headmaster of an East End grammar
school, had met my father when she was secretary to a Liberal MP. She
came to resemble my father in his dedication to the public causes to
which the house was frequently given over, but she had little time or good
will for abstractions. Throughout my childhood, except for the years
1940–45, we lived in Hampstead, London, NW3 – keeping up appearances despite lack of money, anxious about money, but also hostile to
money.

In 1940, when I was seven, because of a near miss by a bomb and
driven also by the din of the anti-aircraft battery 200 yards away on
Hampstead Heath, we migrated to a cottage in Berkshire which was lent
by an absent American friend. It was in the wilderness, on the banks of a
small tributary of the Thames, without gas or electricity. Domestic water
was raised by hand-pump.

As a result of this escape from London, I was swept up from the
silly-progressive Hampstead school which I had hated so much to an
Elementary School in Twyford, Berkshire, which was equally and oppo-
sitely hateful. From thence I went, via the friendly and benevolent
Elementary School at Wargrave on Thames (the other village within
reach), to Colet Court. This was the preparatory school for St Paul's

School, London, but translated in miniature form to Crowthorne, Berkshire. Throughout the war, my father worked in a position unworthy of his talents as an official censor at the Ministry of Information, either travelling daily by the crowded slow train from Twyford to Paddington or camping when he had to in Hampstead, beneath the Blitz and behind the sandbags that replaced the shattered windows of the house and shored up the front wall.

In 1945, at the end of the war and when I was twelve, we returned from the life of bicycles, boats, winter floods and paraffin stoves to London and I was sent as a day boy to St Paul's. This school, a glorious Renaissance foundation from the time of Erasmus reborn in Hammersmith in hectic Victorian red brick, seemed to a country boy like me vast and intimidating; and that is how it continued to seem until I reached the Middle and Upper Eighth forms. (Any other school would say Sixth forms.)

In the Middle and Upper Eighths, one found two masters, one for Latin and one for Greek – they alternated week by week –, who were friendly, eccentric, constantly amusing and genuinely learned. Under their idiosyncratic but highly exigent auspices, there was the possibility at last of happiness, of civilization and of security – all available on one simple condition. The condition, which was cheap at the price, was that, in addition to making some efforts in the study of history, one should be prepared to spend most of the day and a fair part of the night translating constantly, to and fro, back and forth, prose into prose, verse into verse, verse into prose, between English, Latin and Greek (and less frequently French and German), heeding distinctions of style and sense (in English as well as in Latin and Greek) which became second nature but which it is painfully hard now to persuade students to listen to. Day in, day out, whatever other assignments there might be, we prepared for oral translation the next day – cribs being totally and everywhere forbidden – a hundred lines of Homer or Sophocles or Vergil or Juvenal, or some equivalent quantity of prose. I have never worked so hard in my life or been so clear exactly what was expected of me.

In the beginning was the word; and the word (this word) was a training for almost anything.[1] Above all, it was a training for the life of a scholar or lawyer or statesman or other public servant or scribe – the very life into which I was carried another step by being dispatched from school to Oxford, where I passed four years reading Literae Humaniores (Latin and Greek Literature, then Philosophy and Ancient History).

It now seems inevitable that my life should have been of this kind. Yet the life of a scholar was not what I thought at the time that I wanted. From the age of seven or eight, the one thing I always thought I wanted to be was a painter. It was to this pursuit I had always given every moment I could free from the demands of school or family. Painting continued as my chief preoccupation well into my second or third year at Oxford – until the moment, that is, when philosophy started to overtake every other concern whatsoever.

3. To judge from what some philosophers have written about themselves, many of them have been drawn into the subject by some passionate concern with how we get knowledge, either arithmetical or geometrical knowledge, or ethical knowledge or whatever, or by some passionate concern with scepticism.

That wasn't where I began at all. Having absolutely no religious beliefs at all imparted to one by one's parents, one is rarely or never excited by the question of how anyone could know religious sorts of things or know anything else. One is apt to assume – even when certain religious people and works of religion give one such pause – that people *don't* know religious sorts of things. One is also apt to assume that one doesn't know the truth of atheism. Here though one is troubled by the doubts about the bounds of sense that are second nature to the agnostic. Faith may be the substance of things hoped for (though I do not hope for them myself) or the evidence (for those who have it) of things not seen: but there is no temptation whatever for one in the condition I am describing to take faith for knowledge. One is also apt to assume, if my own experience is anything to go by, that there is no particular problem about the ordinary knowing of ordinary sorts of thing. The theory of knowledge, when I came to it as a student, appeared simply as a branch of philosophy – one among many, and far less interesting (I thought) than logic or metaphysics.

What carried me into philosophy was not then any question of epistemology. In fact it was *things* or *substances*. Or, as I might once have put it, it was things-in-their-relation-to-us. It was the question of how the objects we speak of and think about – and must ourselves interact with – are articulated or isolated or found or drawn or formed or carved out in the world. That which then carried me further into philosophy was an idea of Gilbert Ryle's which excited me as soon as I started to study the subject more seriously (for I had begun on it very reluctantly, simply because philosophy was an obligatory part of the degree course I was following). The idea was that it is the attempt to combine radically modes of articulation of objects[2] that gives rise to such diverse and amazing philosophical problems as Russell's paradox and the mind–body problem. I was much preoccupied with Russell's theory of types, therefore, and eager to try to understand Russell's Neutral Monism.

I hazard the guess that there was some temperamental connexion between the sort of interest that the question of the individuation of substances aroused in me, and the preoccupation with painting that had secretly sustained me for so long in Oxford. My recurrent idea about that was still that, after dutifully finishing Lit. Hum. in order to satisfy my parents who were so obsessed with my finding a more dependable calling than that of barrister-at-law, I should try to enlist as an art-student at the Slade School – thus escaping the inky seas of the word with the same ease with which I had already escaped the unpaintably variegated green hues of the Berkshire riverscape. If only the Slade would have me, I could prepare there to try, in a drier and more ochrous world, to make my living as a painter.

Well, that was not how it turned out. By 1955, the philosophical interest in logic and metaphysics, in substances, and in reference and individuation, had smoothly and imperceptibly supplanted painting in the forefront of my life. In continuing deference to my mother's and father's desire that I find a secure occupation, I entered the Home Civil Service in 1957. I was assigned to the Colonial Office and became an Assistant Principal in the Finance Department, which administered the Colonial Development and Welfare Act. I was engrossed by this work (which was sensibly and sometimes imaginatively conducted by the Office, let me say, opposing here some of the criticisms that have been levelled at the public service). Yet my chief reaction to the experience was to want to reflect in a more systematic sort of way about the form and content of deliberation in the public sphere. And all the time I knew perfectly clearly that I wanted to be a philosopher.

Towards the end of 1958, I took my chance. I left the Civil Service and went to the United States for a year to Princeton, on one of those wonderful fellowships for foreigners that were among the glories of that hospitable and open-hearted country. (Already, alas, destroying itself, I noted, by the adoption of the unsustainable modes of production and consumption which shocked anyone of a wartime European formation but were destined to be slavishly imitated in Europe and the British Isles. These were being chronicled and criticized even then, in different ways, by Rachel Carson and Jane Jacobs, who fashioned many of my reactions to these things, and by Alan Altschuler.)

In 1959, preternaturally suddenly and contrary to all reasonable expectation, having no further qualifications beyond a first degree, I was offered the chance to become a professional philosopher at New College, Oxford.

4. What else beside Gilbert Ryle's idea had drawn me into this strange life of ours? Philosophy engaged with two other things I cared about. It

engaged with the interest in grammar and language that had been com-
municated to me by those inspirational and idiosyncratic teachers in the
Middle and Upper Eighths at St Paul's – the semantical interest (or its
practical counterpart) that Donald Davidson hit off so exactly, in another
register but instantly recognizably, some fifteen years later, with his
famous question: 'What are these familiar words doing here?'. I shall
return to this in my reply to Stephen Williams.

Philosophy also engaged – albeit less visibly, so far as my manifest area
of interest was concerned – with another fixation. This was a recurrent
preoccupation with politics, a preoccupation that rested in part upon that
which had seemed so special and vividly memorable and good in the
however temporary condition of society that obtained during my wartime
adolescence. Somehow, regardless of individual vice or virtue or political
orientation, the British people had arrived at an understanding of the
common good *as* the common good, an understanding that was nothing
less than Aristotelian. This is not to say that there was agreement about
the nature of this shared good or that the consensus was other than
temporary and conditional. (I underestimated radically its temporariness
and conditionality. I thought too little how weak was its historical foundation.) Still less is it to say that the direction or content of this shared
interest was Aristotelian – alas, no. But there was a shared experience,
there were common points of reference and the consensus embraced a
much larger range of individual aspirations than can be validated now
before the bar of politics or television in the age of instant information.
What was needed in politics, I thought, if anything was to come of all
this, was a way of thinking that partook *inter alia* of philosophy, could
identify and vary the assumptions it was making, yet could progress
without the vain attempt to make every concern visible and explicit once
and for all. Then as now, I thought of philosophy as the one discipline
that could set us all free from any particular assumptions; that could treat
distinct ideas as distinct and mutually irreducible. Philosophy was the
one thing by whose aid I supposed the consensus however momentarily
achieved could be given expression and vindication and carried further in
politics, rather than be dissipated in the cussedness-cum-sentimentality
that is the real *vice anglais*.

At first this last preoccupation, which took a long time to become
visible in my work, was tacit. It became articulate only as it seemed that
the consensus itself was being dissolved, and dissolved at about the same
speed with which the post-war reconstruction of everything uglified or
destroyed so much of what was so beautiful (if utterly unappreciated by
those who could not see beneath the dust and filth of war) in the city of
brick, glass, cast iron and cream coloured stucco in which I had mostly

grown up and gone to school. I should need a book of photographs – the photographs in S. E. Rasmussen's book *London: The Unique City* would be only a beginning – to show what wonderful opportunities, both social and aesthetic opportunities, were overlooked by politicians of all shades in the scramble that was then beginning for a new industrial, technological and social order – for any old new order, it began to seem, as we moved into the era of shameless corruption and of unsustainable land-use and transport policies. These policies were not adopted in the name of the good or the just or the prudent – for the rhetoric of the new political culture no longer required such a pretext – but simply in the name of an attributed demand (in contrast to a deliberatively tested vital need), a demand itself conditioned through and through (if it was there at all) by the very contingencies that those who made the attributions professed that it was their *métier* to eradicate.

5.   There were these three preoccupations then – things and substances (their individuation and identity), logical grammar, and (in potentiality) the conditions, political, aesthetic and environmental, for something one might sum up for short (though I did not then do so) as a kingdom of ends.

It was identity and individuation I was mostly thinking about when I had the unexpected good fortune to graduate in 1960 from a temporary to a non-temporary appointment in philosophy.

As for philosophical grammar, the linguistic philosophy of the fifties and sixties – a profound project, I still think, but for the most part too amateurishly or modishly executed (or so I thought at the time) – engaged fruitfully with the preoccupation with semantics that I had carried into philosophy. (Some other day, I must try to set the record straight about what linguistic philosophy was, or what it could have been, and why it is integral to any true philosophy. Some day someone must also set the record straight about the marvellous *diversity* of the Oxford philosophy scene around 1960.)

The third preoccupation – for which little time was left by the exigencies of teaching myself, in post, enough philosophy in order to deserve to have that post – I pacified with various forms of political-cum-environmental activity (my (1981) looks back on some of these) and then tried to pacify inside philosophy itself by engaging in circumscribed (even if overambitious) philosophical denunciations of the degradations I thought I saw around us of public practical rationality.

In the last of these connections, I cannot emphasize too much the importance of the necessity (initially resented by me as a painful professional necessity and as a distraction from my interests in logic and metaphysics) to conduct tutorials on the subject of Aristotle's *Nicoma-chean Ethics*. All this eventually issued in my (1975/6), (1978c), (1978/9), (1980a, ch. 6), and then in (1981), (1985), (1987c) and some of the things in (1987a). My general standpoint came to this: that the languages of political decision and political theory were tainted gratui-tously by scientism, by economists' and behaviourists' jargon, and by a fatal manipulation of an (in itself natural enough) ambiguity of intention. Were my political and economic colleagues describing, explaining and lending a hand in the realization of objectives elsewhere and otherwise ratified, or were they recommending? Well, the social scientists arrived saying to themselves it was the first of these things they were doing, mouthing phrases they did not really understand about the distinctness of fact and value. Then, whenever they were safely ensconced, they (or the people they advised) always seemed, without really meaning this, to start upon the second thing, crowding out ends that were deeper or inexplicit, but no less vital for that reason, by the devising of multifarious means to ends that were easy and explicit. Having entered as plumbers, they instantly aspired to the role of proprietors (proprietors, I should add, of very little discernment).

All this would not have been quite so bad, I now think, if the social scientists and those who made use of them or were influenced by them had had the attributes that might almost have made philosopher-kings bearable, namely the capacity to deliberate defeasibly, or if they had had some sensitivity to the real difficulties that there are in the idea of practical reason and the ends of social action, or if they had had an open-ended interest in the full range of political ideas and ideals. (Here, it must be confessed, philosophy should have been a more important force: where were our discursive studies of ideas such as *need, fraternity, culture* or *work*?) The truth was, though, that nobody, least of all these maximizers, knew how to describe the intuitive workings of actual prac-tical reason, still less how to improve it for the individual case or (harder still) the communal case. In so far as they had any political or historical vision, the exigencies of proving themselves to be scientists eclipsed this entirely. They derided older authors who professed or even disclosed such a vision.

To emphasize that which is objectively countable and then, in the 'distribution' of this thing, to pretend to impartiality simply because one is mouthing slogans about equality – how could *this* be objectivity? How could so multidimensional and deep a thing as social justice be brought into being (or even described) along these lines? (And how easily could it be further negated!) Cost benefit analysis (the craze of the sixties, more rarely called that now, but not yet dead or spent), as founded in revealed preference theory and megalomaniacally applied to enormous social questions, both typified and institutionalized everything I stood opposed to. All attempts to speculate publicly about substantive ends were shouted down (and are still shouted down) as dogmatic or as paternalistic or authoritarian in intention (a useful confusion), or simply laughed to scorn – as is the claim that deliberation (private and public alike) should take place under the names of the good and the needed, not under the name of the maximum satisfaction of all desires, however destructive or trivial.[3]

6. Back now to what came philosophically first, namely the preoccupation with things or substances. For a long time after I was turned into a professional philosopher (or given in 1960 all the privileges of one), this was the background to most of what I voluntarily (contrast perforce or in the name of duty) attempted in philosophy at New College.

Experimenting endlessly with problems about identity and individuation, sense and reference, with Leibniz and Frege, and so on (see (1963), (1965), (1968)), I settled down in the end to what was for me the right question. It was this: If there were different ways of articulating and tracing continuants, if all answers to identity questions rested on some prior determination of *the same what?*, then could not two modes of articulation render conflicting answers to the question whether a certain identified object *a* was identical with some object *b*?

It helped that P. T. Geach, for his own reasons and in an alien theoretical framework, was interested in a form of this question. It helped too that he seemed to be interested in answering such questions with a *yes*. I was inordinately excited to find grounds (grounds such that I have to ask myself now whether I was getting it right what the positions were that Geach and his inheritor, Harold Noonan, wanted to oppose to mine) for a definitive *no* to this question. The grounds were that the answer *yes* would conflict with Leibniz's Law, which I should have likened, then as now, to the Rock of Ages.

7. This was for me a marvellous discovery, standing in sharp apparent antithesis to the conceptualism that I had taken in from studying Quine's essays in *From a Logical Point of View* (had imbibed indirectly from Kant, I suppose, as filtered through Whitehead and C. I. Lewis). One could try to modify Leibniz's Law. But I soon decided that that was a hopeless venture.[4] See *Identity and Spatio-Temporal Continuity* (1967), Pt 1. One could abandon the conceptualism that had suggested the question to which my answer was *no*. One could opt instead for some brute form of realism. Or finding it compelling to persist in some sort of conceptualism, for reasons I fortified by rereading Frege's *Foundations of Arithmetic*

and Quine's essay 'Identity, Ostension and Hypostasis' (in Quine (1953)),[5] one could think through to the end the thought that one would not expect that *one and the same thing* would be collected up by different modes of articulation.

The outcome of this was that conceptualism, reformed as I thought it should be reformed, led me to a distinctive ontological outlook, a view with consequences whose capacity to create shock and surprise gratified me, I confess. (See my (1968), cf. (1986a).) It led directly by an *individuative* argument – contrast the *referential* arguments that Kripke presents (see Kripke (1972/80)) – to a certain kind of essentialism (see my (1967), Pt 3), (1974), (1975), (1976e), (1979a), (1980a), ch. 4). It led also to the demand that the philosophy of individuation be of a piece with a sound philosophy of biology. (See (1967), Introduction.)

The corrected conceptualism that resulted from these reflections demanded to be squared with the truth in realism (see (1980a), ch. 5). By involving me in all these questions, it led me to various *reciprocity* theses, about things and concepts of things, about sense and reference and about the formation of concepts that graduate to the condition of scientific concepts. Indeed reciprocity – or two-way flow, as I used to call it in internal dialogue with myself – was part of a more general thought (which was sustained by things I found in writers as different as Heraclitus (see (1982)), Leibniz and Putnam (see (1974), (1980a), (1993a), (1993d)). It seemed integral to the proper understanding of Meno's dilemma (Plato, *Meno* 73d). It seemed indispensable to the proper understanding of what we achieve when we come to know what a thing is. It was integral, in a way still too little-heeded or thought through by the philosophy of science, to our understanding of thing-kind words like 'horse' or 'human being'. And not only that. It was a further generalization of the reciprocity point that helped to make it possible to contemplate new possibilities in connection with questions of value. It began to seem possible to explain the irreducible and *sui generis* character of moral and aesthetic language, to combine the claim that we (communally) 'invent' practices with the claim that we *find* the corresponding values, and then to defuse some of the consequences of the supposed contrast between invention and truth. What we invent is the sense; what we find is the truth-value or the kind or the value property. This was not all. Subjectivism took on a new lease of life, but in a way not inimical (or so I came to think) to moral language's pretensions to truth, or to the public reality of that which is revealed to us when we search for the point of view that shall, in Hume's words, be 'common to one man with another'. See (1976a), (1980c), (1987a), (1987b), (1990/1), (1992a), (1993b), (1995/6a), (1995/6b).

8. But now lo and behold: the third preoccupation had come back into its own, without ever speaking its name. It was coming back into its own in these ways, but in other ways too. For that ever-present interest in substance and identity had long since led me into questions about *conscious* substances, and to questions of personal identity (as in (1967), (1976c), (1980a)). But here there was the possibility of a convergence between ideas about the inter-subjectivity of conscious selves (cf. (1980a), ch. 6, (1987b)), ideas about sense and two-way flow, and certain quite new ideas that Donald Davidson had forced me to take seriously about interpretation.

On two visits I had made to Stanford in 1964 and 1965, Donald Davidson – a philosopher who was then known only to a few British philosophers (mainly I think to Austin, to Dummett, to Quinton, my New College colleague, and to Bernard Williams, whom I had succeeded at New College) – had awoken me from a state of Fregean inattention to the problems of 'radical interpretation'. (The name then was 'radical translation'.)

When I first encountered Davidson, I realized immediately that I found his nuts and bolts approach to grammar and semantics utterly convincing, indeed a perfect vindication of what (in home-made fashion) I had always been trying to do ever since I had begun on philosophy. But precisely because I found that part of Davidson's work so convincing, I had to take seriously the rest of what he did, and more particularly the wholly unfamiliar and entirely unwelcome non-Fregean framework in which he located these things. Up to then, I had more or less ignored, as regrettably misguided, everything that Quine had done after writing *From a Logical Point of View*. But as a result of these two visits to Stanford, I became a convert to Davidson's version of the naturalistic framework for semantics – allowing the semantic platonism that is second nature to me simply to hibernate.

Then, when I got back to Oxford, I started, as young philosophy tutors will, to force the combined Davidson doctrine upon two or three exceptionally gifted generations of New College pupils. In one of these was John McDowell, who later did so much to clarify Davidson's semantical programme. I forced it upon my pupils as the proper resolution I had long wanted between J. L. Austin's way of doing philosophy and the way in which philosophy is done in Quine's *From a Logical Point of View*.[6] Not only did the interpretational framework force one to pay attention to what speakers meant by what they said (even to listen to this with the sort of attention that Austin had shown how to pay to it): not only did the listening have to issue in ideas about how to put one's findings together in the systematic way needed to derive truth conditions for whole classes of sentences involving the same words or semantic devices: but the exploration of the overall constraints upon the exercise of listening, imputing and constructing also seemed to suggest the possibility of conclusions deeply at variance with many received views, not least (it eventually appeared) with the prevalent non-cognitive views of the subject matters of ethics, politics and aesthetics. In the neo-Fregean framework, everything I cared about – individuation, grammatical nuts and bolts, and values – was tied up with everything else I cared about in philosophy or almost everything.

9.   So much for some of the connections that link the themes I have tried to explore as I have gone back and forth at various stages between Oxford and London. I cannot in retrospect regret the utter diversity of the teaching commitments that have fallen to me over the years. They have always shown an unexpected way forward for the concerns that have underlain my work. Nor can I regret the enormous amount of time I have had to spend in one-to-one and one-to-two instruction, not even the time spent under the old fifteen-hours-plus stint at New College, Oxford. Not only has this brought some really gifted people into the profession who might not otherwise have been interested in philosophy. It is also a sure way, if one listens hard to what one is saying, of finding out whatever may be wrong with it. It is here, in the field of the elementary, that the seeds of banality and error are either cultivated or extirpated.

As regards what is still unaccounted for in this reply to the editors' question, I would add this. Liking to think one is working in a subject with a long history – an enterprise that anyone can join in and participate in – and admiring the work of people who find their philosophical identity not by reinventing every silly error that has ever been made in the history of the subject but by recognizing themselves in a shared tradition of speculation, I always wanted to see what strange things one could unearth from what has been written before on the questions one is pursuing. From this desire (but also from out of the terrible labours of becoming a teacher of philosophy before the dawning of the age of specialization), there emerged the desire to make various studies of Heraclitus, Plato, Aristotle, Leibniz, Peirce, Frege and, in morals, of Kant and Hume: also the desire to defend these heroes from interpreters who are not sufficiently interested in philosophy itself to know a good thing when they see one.

Obviously, there is more than one way of studying the history of philosophy. I should still, however, defend this way of studying it. It is not to be confused with the efforts of those who have used modern labels to stun and stereotype the philosophical tendencies of the dead philosophers. Recently, I have tried to rescue Hume's moral philosophy from this fate.

Rescue projects are not rare or special. All I have to say about them is that some of them would only occur to a philosopher with an active interest in philosophical questions themselves. In so far as I have succeeded in drawing attention to anything in Hume that would otherwise have escaped attention, well this is owed to a speculative interest in questions that are a bit like Hume's questions. Of course, it is possible that I am wrong to think that Hume has been grotesquely misunderstood. If so, I have chosen a bad example and it will be vain to hope that the Humean effort will succeed as well as I believe the efforts succeeded in which I participated in the nineteen sixties to release Aristotle from the misinterpretations visited upon him by utilitarian and deontological interpreters. (See (1975/6).)

The general point I am moved to make in conclusion does not depend on the truth about Aristotle or Hume. The general point is that the worst present enemy of philosophy is excessive professionalization, the separation from one another of the constituent branches of the subject, the hiving off of its history, and the progressive reduction of the whole subject's state of awareness of itself. That particular branches should pay close attention to this or that bit of science (or social science or economics) is an important and necessary improvement (whatever my reservations about the capitulation of so much work in ethics and political philosophy to that which a true philosophy should itself have influenced – or annihilated). But, if the subject is to engage with the questions that will not go away, or with the new questions that it ought now to be proposing to itself in political philosophy, philosophy of science, logic or wherever, it is no substitute for the traditional attention to philosophy as a whole, to that part of symbolic logic which came from grammar, dialectic and philosophy and is still our birthright, or to the extensions of the philosophical imagination that are provided in literature and history.

2 Identity, Individuation and Possibility

Reply to Timothy Williamson

10. One of the many pleasures of discovering the work of Timothy Williamson and then of being his colleague when he was elected a Fellow of University College, Oxford, was to find that we were in complete accord concerning 'the depth to be gained in metaphysics from the constraints of orthodoxy in logic'.

Against the background of our consensus concerning the necessity and determinateness of identity, Williamson seeks to bring about our further concurrence over the question of the necessity and determinateness of distinctness, upstaging in this way the sympathetic consideration I was once prepared to give, at the time of writing 'Singling Out an Object Determinately' (1986a), to the possibility of affirming the necessity and determinateness of identity while withholding assent from the determinateness of distinctness.

In the course of working towards this satisfyingly symmetrical result, Williamson furnishes a congenial, elegant and newly exemplary exposition of the whole formal situation.[7] He shows how naturally and inevitably the necessity of the distinctness of distinct things can be gathered up by the accumulation of modal and proof-theoretical ideas and considerations that give us the basic modal logic of equalities, K=, which yields the necessary identity of identicals. The same accumulation of ideas and considerations then propels us towards KB=, which is K= plus the 'Brouwersche' principle,

$$\sim\!A \to (\Box\!\sim\!\Box A).$$

Williamson is very fair-minded and statesmanlike about the Brouwersche principle (B). For some have denied it or denied that it is logically guaranteed. While subscribing to (B) himself, he goes to some lengths not to invoke it in various proofs by which he seeks to convince those who waver about the necessity or the determinacy of the distinctness of distinct things. But I shall simply accept (B), which is equivalent to

$$A \to (\Box\Diamond A).$$

If A holds, how could it *help* but be the case that A is possible? That is many times clearer, in fact, than the question whether the accessibility relation between worlds is symmetrical.[8]

11. Given that it is KB= which delivers the necessary distinctness of things that are distinct and given the modesty of the resources required for this result, Williamson makes me see that in *Sameness and Substance* I ought to have accorded the distinctness principle more or less the same dignity as was accorded to the necessity of identity.

Adding now to KB= the uncontentious principle (T), which says that that which is necessarily the case is indeed the case, which brings in the converses of the necessity of identity and the necessity of distinctness, we arrive at KTB=. Then with the advent of KTB=, we have a basic modal logic of equalities, if ever there was one. And at this point the following metaphysical picture becomes available. Facts about the identity and difference of individuals are part of the necessary structure of reality and are completely invariant across possible worlds. If the objects a and b are anywhere distinct, then there is no possible set-up where they are the same. If a and b are the same anywhere, there is no possible set-up where they are distinct.

12. What flows from the acceptance of this picture? I think there flows the full generalization of a claim to which I have always adhered, in *Sameness and Substance* and elsewhere, namely that it is not an option for us to describe possible worlds in a way that would conflict with any of the identities and distinctnesses that actually hold. For actual identities and differences must condition the specification of any world whatever that is both to contain actual things and to count as an alternative to the real world.

When we construct worlds that are alternative to the actual world, we have to be ready, if anything at all hangs on which actual objects are involved in the construction, positively to specify this – just as we have to be ready, if it matters, to write into the construction of alternative worlds the colours or weights of objects (unless this information happens to be deductively entailed by other facts that are present). If you find it incredible that this specifying should be needed, you are radically under-estimating what identity and difference amount to. You are probably holding onto the illusion that pure properties and relations can fix identities.[9]

To say that, when we conceive of possible worlds that are to contain among their individuals actual individuals, we must specify which things are involved in the supposition we are making, is not to say that we are entirely free in the matter of what roles or parts we assign to actual objects in possible worlds.

What then limits us? We are constrained not only by the requirement of consistency within the world being constructed but also by the question of what the actual objects that are involved *are*. When I speak here of 'what objects are', I use the phrase in the sense of *what it is* to which Aristotle drew attention in *Categories* 1–5 and elsewhere. (See *Categories* 2ᵇ30–7, quoted at the beginning of ch. 1 of *Sameness and Substance*.) If what the actual objects are, in Aristotle's sense, does not constrain us, then we shall commit ourselves to the absurd thought that an actual individual could be or could have been just anything.[10]

But is this last – I shall call it the Aristotelian constraint – the sole constraint on the placing of actual individuals within possible worlds? In

Sameness and Substance and elsewhere, I have been tempted to think so. If I am right, then two worlds w_1 and w_2, each lacking Pontius Pilate himself, but each containing someone who plays his part, may differ from one another just by virtue of the fact that in w_1 it is you not I who play the part that Pontius Pilate actually played and that in w_2 it is I not you who play that part. Neither world violates the Aristotelian constraint. Each is possible. Each of us could play that unenviable part. N.B. I am using 'roles' here to speak of identities and 'parts' to speak of what is done or suffered by those who are this or that person.

13.   By this conception, not only is identity irreducible. It does not even supervene upon the totality of pure properties and their compounds. Why have philosophers supposed otherwise? Why have they underestimated the irreducibility and distinctiveness of the idea of identity? Maybe the explanation lies with the recipe provided by Hilbert and Bernays and publicized by Quine for manufacturing an identity predicate for a first order theory or language from all the other predicates of that theory.[11] To anyone tempted to attach great philosophical importance to this recipe, however, I should recommend the following: to formulate their claim carefully and test it in the light of the fact that the absence or presence of identity can make an all-important difference to the decidability or undecidability of a class of formulae of predicate logic. (See Goldfarb (1984).) Less hazardously, I speculate that it is the inability of philosophers to allow that identity has its own content, and the consequential faith that the other properties of things will fix identities, which explains the perennial freshness of the illusion that there are individualized pure essences of things.[12]

14.   The Aristotelian constraint may seem forbiddingly bare. To say that you or I *could have* played the part (although we could not have played the role) of Pontius Pilate: this is the sober effect of imposing only the Aristotelian constraint upon the construction of possible worlds that include you or me, of thinking of persons simply as human beings and of reading the metaphysical 'could' flatly. You or I – or St Francis – could have played this part. Properly and flatly understood, the claim is true. But someone might want very much to say of St Francis that *he* at least could not have played Pilate's part. And that needs to be provided for too. How?

One way might be to seek to expand somehow the account of what in the Aristotelian sense the saint himself *was*. On some other occasion I might attempt that. But another way would be to unpack the intended sense of this 'could', and with it the senses or uses of some other 'coulds'.

Let us try to find the right 'could' by which to deny that St Francis could have done what Pilate did, postponing the other Aristotelian option.

The point about St Francis is presumably that only under the most extreme conditions might someone as percipient and inventive as he was have acted in the easy way in which Pontius Pilate chose to act. St Francis would have had to have been poisoned or doped. . . . There is a condition one could find under which he might behave thus, even though the condition is (until mentioned) contextually utterly remote. Or, in the language of possible worlds, there *is* a world, e.g. a world where he is poisoned or doped or . . . , where St Francis would have done what Pilate did. But if 'There is some world where he does' is all that the flat or minimal metaphysical *could* or *could have* (*potuisset*) says, then it follows that, when someone insists that St Francis couldn't have acted as Pilate did, he is employing a 'could' different from that flat or minimal 'could'. He is employing a more substantial and interesting *could have* (*potuisset*), which places further conditions upon the world in question.

One reaches various degrees or varieties of this – and one reaches the condition under which it's *not* the case that St Francis might have . . . – when we formulate the claim that there is such and such less extreme or less demanding or less disruptive or less specific condition under which some subject would or might have done such and such. That is the claim that is to be denied of St Francis and that we might aspire to have denied of us. Working from here towards that which is most substantial and closest to reality, we eventually reach the case where the condition in question is simply some continuation or extension of the actual state of the world. Here, at this limit, we encounter the categorical or un-iffy *can* (*potest*) or *could have* (*poterat*). In practice, neither you nor I *are able* (*possumus*) or *have been able* (*potuimus*) to play the part of Pontius Pilate. We have never been put to such a test.

15.   So much then for the working out of one metaphysical picture that suggests itself in the presence of Williamson's convincing claim that identity and distinctness are part of the necessary, and indeed the necessarily necessary, structure of reality. So much for what one might want to do within it, and how one might defend it. But Williamson reports that some who are under the influence of Chandler and Salmon might object to his claim that distinctnesses are part of the necessary (and necessarily necessary) structure of reality. Those of this persuasion will refer to cases where, in a whole array of sequentially mutually accessible worlds, an object that has in one world a supposedly satisfactory modicum of its actual matter (or its actual shape and structure) has less and less of either of this (or these) in each next world in the sequence. They conclude that

the transitivity of accessibility is suspect, and under the influence of Prior's original proof of the necessity of distinctness some will even conclude that this principle is suspect too.

Williamson's response to such cases is first to point out that the necessity of distinctness, on which his picture of identities and distinctnesses as part of the necessary structure of reality depends, rests only upon the Brouwersche principle (B), which is independent of the transitivity of accessibility; and then to demonstrate the possibility of a proof of the necessity of distinctness without (B), in a plain 'actually' logic. Both belt and braces are available then, so far as concerns the necessity of the distinctness of distinct things.

16.   Williamson adjourns consideration of any more general threat to S4 and S5 systems, but here I shall place my own convictions upon the record. First I doubt the claim, which the disproof of the transitivity of accessibility depends upon, that it is impossible for an artifact to have originated from completely different matter. I have already committed myself to the claim that, on a correct understanding of possible world construction, we are free to distinguish between two qualitatively similar worlds, each with two similar tables in it, by identifying my actual table with one and not the other of the two tables. What I now claim is that we can do this even for a world where the other table has the matter that actually makes up my table. What could prevent? Where such a world is envisaged, all that has happened is that we have separated our suppositions about where my actual table is in a possible world and where such and such a parcel of matter is in that world, taking advantage of their independent specifiability. 'But how *can* you, where two worlds are qualitatively distinguishable, make a ruling of identity in defiance of the one thing that remains to distinguish the one table from the other, namely the identity of the matter?' Answer: How can *you* in a world where two tables are qualitatively indistinguishable, insist that one not the other is made from such and such matter? Only surely by allowing *supposition* to settle which pieces of wood there the actual ones are. So 'supposition' is my answer too, though subject to the Aristotelian constraint. As I have already claimed, worlds are the shadows of our suppositions and they take on their identity from these. Suppositions themselves take on their identity from (*inter alia*) the objects they relate to.

Can we learn anything at all from the Chandler–Salmon argument? That which we learn relates not to the accessibility relation or the problem of cross-world identification but to a problem we have about particular things *already* pinned down within one world. Given an artifact which starts with such and such actual matter, what are the limits upon how far it can change in respect of its matter? What material changes would have the effect of extinguishing the object itself? The problem of Theseus' ship dramatizes this question. I shall assume that the reader knows the example.[13] We can allow for occasional disassembly of Theseus' ship at times after its original construction. We can allow for some replacement of parts. We can allow for modifications of function or for structural modification. But the thought we have here is that what we cannot permit, if Theseus' ship is to be what is singled out, is an arbitrarily large amount of all three of these things. Perhaps each change is *pro tanto* insignificant; but what matters at each point is the overall distance of the new condition at that point *from the original condition of* the ship that Theseus built and launched.[14] At some point in a sequence of radical changes, we must be ready to say *no* (or refuse to say *yes*) when the question arises whether the thing referred to by some description relating to some time later than the time of construction is indeed Theseus' ship.

In this adjudication, we do not avail ourselves of the doubtful principle that, if each purported state of a certain entity is possible relative solely to its predecessor state, considered without regard to its subject and ancestry, then the last state at t_{1000} is compossible with the first state, at t_1. A good motto for our approach might be: 'The last straw *will* break the camel's back'. Does it not in *some* way support Chandler's and Salmon's doubts about the transitivity of accessibility? It is not clear to me that it does. The last straw principle bears only upon the change question. It negates *a* transitivity but not the transitivity of accessibility. Worlds in which Theseus's ship has quite other matter are irrelevant to the question of how far the matter of Theseus' ship, the ship being specifically singled out in one world, can be transformed there. I say that, with respect to questions about flat metaphysical possibility, these other worlds are accessible to one another and to the actual world. Their constructibility bears not at all upon the question of how far the given ship can in a given world be transformed from its original condition. I conclude that there is no counterexample to be had from this quarter to the claim that S5 is the right logic for the flat metaphysical 'could'. What we are left with is simply the doubtfulness, which is in any case collaterally evident, of any automatic expectation that the accessibility relation will be transitive for each and every kind of 'could' or 'can' that is less remote than the metaphysical 'could'.

17. In the second half of his paper, Williamson vindicates both the determinacy of identity and the determinacy of difference, dismissing

objections to Evans's argument.[15] He gives an elegant proof of the determinacy of distinctness, on what I take to be an incontrovertible basis.

How can I ever have supposed that one might affirm the definiteness of identity and doubt the definiteness of distinctness? I am afraid that the answer is simple. I accepted too readily that vagueness entailed indeterminacy – so readily that, not practising what I have constantly preached for at least twenty years, I did not mark a proper terminological difference, thus making it almost certain that I would confuse them. The thing that seemed obvious was that I could be perfectly clear which object a was and perfectly clear about all sorts of truths of the type 'a=b', 'a=c', 'a=d' (etc.), without being comparably clear about a similar range of truths 'a≠o', 'a≠n', 'a≠m' . . . . What I had caught sight of was of course the point that, even in the case of one who knows what an object is and has mastered a large sufficiency of the many positive identities that flow from knowing what it is, we ought to expect that there will be many judgements of distinctness concerning it for which he is epistemologically unprepared and epistemologically not clear. But this epistemological finding, which may be expected to create an asymmetry between identity and distinctness judgements in respect of what Williamson himself calls margins for error, showed nothing whatever about the *indeterminacy* of distinctness. I hasten to accept Williamson's invitation to extend to the determinacy of distinctness all the defences that I have mustered at one time or another for the necessity and the determinacy of identity.

Reply to Harold Noonan

18.   Harold Noonan begins his discussion by taking issue with my treatment of examples that seem to lend support to the thesis of the sortal relativity of identity, R. Later on, he seeks to show that the criterion of identity for fs (members of a kind) – the criterion of identity, he means, in the sense of something the grasp of which is essential to the full understanding of the concept of an f – is something that, as he puts it, no absolute equivalence relation like Leibnizian identity can provide. If I understand Noonan rightly, however, his present interest is not so much to defend the R position – indeed he has managed to write a good book about personal identity without resting his case for a single conclusion upon the relative conception – as to set the dialectical position straight.

19.   The absolute conception of identity as I had it in *Identity and Spatio-Temporal Continuity* and *Sameness and Substance* was a prolongation of the thoughts of Aristotle and Leibniz and it went as follows. With

REPLY TO HAROLD NOONAN

respect to any object of discourse singled out and differentiated from other things, there has to be an answer to the question what the object is – an f, a g, or whatever. Suppose that the thing is an ordinary changeable continuant substance. Then, in taking the thing for an f or a g or. . . . , we are committed to conceiving of it as a thing with a corresponding way of coming into being, of behaving and interacting with other things, of developing, and of ceasing to be. What the way is depends on what fs are. But, just by virtue of taking x as an f, we are committed to taking a certain view of *what is at issue* in questions of x's persistence or of x's identity or non-identity with any object y that may be proposed as a candidate to be the same thing as x. That which is the point at issue in questions of identity is something that we arrive at in each case by combining three things, namely: (1) the understanding of what an f is, (2) the general understanding of identity (more of that in a moment), and (3) the grasp of what x is in particular (which grasp depends *inter alia* upon our application to what is in front of us of our grasp of what an f is).

20.   All sorts of questions arise about what it takes for one conscious being – and what it takes for conscious beings collectively – to get to this stage of being able to deal with matters of identity and to understand this ontology. Does it, for instance, presuppose the mastery of a more primitive and supposedly self-sufficient level of thought – the level that Strawson pointed to in his characterization of a language for simple feature-placing and that Noonan invites us to think of as admitting 'crude predications' ('this is sticky', 'this is red', 'this is smooth') which do *not* presuppose the availability of any answer to the question 'this what?'? Noonan says yes. But my own answer would be *no*. In practice, an answer to the question 'this what?' is sometimes available and sometimes not. Where an answer is available, it will fit perfectly well into the Aristotelian scheme, celebrating the successful or incipiently successful singling out of something. When no answer is available, however, I should say that the thinker or the speaker and the companion whom he addresses, are *fumbling* for that completion. And, for that case, there need not be any account of their initial *démarches* as self-sufficient or even coherent. When you are working to achieve something, there does not have to be something else that you have *already* achieved.

Taking this view, I am led to claim that, when I say 'this is a horse' and 'that was a horse', thus preparing myself to ask 'Is this horse the same horse as that horse?', I *am*, and (contrary to what Noonan seems to suggest) I *must be*, making a reference to objects. I am referring to horses, if all is well with what I am saying. Understanding what horses are, I understand *on that basis* what it would be for a pair of references to objects to correspond to the singlings out of one and the same thing. And in that case – here comes the absoluteness – everything that applies to the one item referred to will apply to the other item. That is what makes the question being asked a question of identity rather than a question about some other relation. What distinguishes identity from other relations is that it is both a reflexive relation *and* a congruence relation. Whatever actually applies to either of the objects that identity holds between applies to them both. For they are the same object. Identity is of course a general idea. But its *application* to any x and y depends on what sort of thing x and y each is. The finding of congruence – of the sharing of all properties – is in my opinion *consequential* on the finding that there is present what (specifically to fs) it takes for x and y, which are fs, to be coincident.

21. Let us sum this up before we proceed any further. Informally and up to now, 'f' and 'g' have been schematic letters replaceable by English thing-kind words. Later, they will be again. But for purposes of the present section, they will be variables ranging over fundamental thing-kinds (thing-kinds not arrived at by the restriction of genuine thing-kinds). 'fa' will mean 'a belongs to f'.

Then the first contention of the absolutist is this:

(Thesis D): $a=b \leftrightarrow \exists f(a \underset{f}{=} b)$,

where $\underset{f}{=}$ is the restriction of the relation of identity to a fundamental kind f. Absolutism also stipulates simply and generally

(Leibniz's Law): for any a, b, $(a=b \rightarrow (Fa \leftrightarrow Fb))$,

where the letter 'F' holds a place for anything at all that can be true of a or b. But Thesis (D) and Leibniz's Law entail together

$\forall g \ (a \underset{g}{=} b \rightarrow (Fa \leftrightarrow Fb))$,

which entails (see 1980a), ch. 1)

(Absoluteness): $\forall f \forall g \ (a \underset{f}{=} b \rightarrow (b \text{ belongs to } g \rightarrow a \underset{g}{=} b))$.

Leibniz's Law is therefore inconsistent with the relativity of $=$ or of any of its restrictions $\underset{f}{=}, \underset{g}{=} \ldots$

22. Critics may press numerous questions about this scheme, e.g. about the difference between what a thing is and what it is like or does or

suffers (see Aristotle, *Categories*), and about the difference between fundamental answers to the question what a thing is (*human being* or *man*, say) and answers that presuppose some fundamental answer. (Consider *sailor*, which needs to be unpacked into *human being engaged in the business of navigation*, or whatever.) But, in some shape or form, these are questions for everybody. What then is more specific to the continuing disagreement between the absolute and the relative conceptions of identity?

Well, I think that to engage this argument fully, we should first need to know the relativist's conception of the individuation of substances in order to compare and contrast it with that of the absolutist. I have never known how to supply this need, and the lack of such a thing affects my appreciation of the dialectical situation – because I tend to think of the absolute conception as having already arrived at the point where it can establish its coherence and its title to be *a* conception of identity. For this reason I tend to think that the only outstanding question is how strong its title is to be the *sole* adequate conception.

Secondly, and in the interim, there seems to be something else at issue between absolutism and relativism, concerning what a criterion of identity is. But this takes some hunting down. For Noonan and I do in fact agree that the 'essential element in the idea is . . . that the criterion of identity for fs should be something a grasp of which is essential to a full understanding of the concept f'. This characterization seems to me to have the virtue of suggesting that what Frege had in mind when he used the expression 'criterion of identity' at §62 of *The Foundations of Arithmetic* was a special case of this general thing.[16] It has the further virtue of marking the connection between a criterion of identity (the having mastered which is the understanding what is at issue in questions of identity and difference of fs) and a principle of individuation (the grasp of which gives the capacity to single out fs from among other things and keep track of them). I think Noonan and I agree that to know what a cat is involves being able to draw the boundary round a cat in such a way as to *include* both its head and its tail and to *exclude* parts of what is another cat ('determin[ing] where one cat leaves off and another begins') or is something else altogether. Must we then disagree about whether possession of a criterion of identity involves an understanding of what is at issue when someone claims that this is the same cat as the kitten he rescued three years ago from such and such a branch? I should say that understanding this involves no more than possessing oneself more fully and completely of what boundary drawing *already* involved.

A related question is whether these kinds of understanding can always be reduced to words. Surely not, I should say. Only in the sort of case that concerned Frege would one expect that. But here Noonan and I should need to have a conversation.

23.   Moving beyond these uncertainties, we arrive at our chief stated disagreement when Noonan claims that no absolute equivalence relation *can* answer to the conception of a criterion of identity we agree about, namely 'something essential to full understanding of the concept f'. I do not understand why I should accept that. When I say that Tibbles is the same cat as the kitten found in the tree, what I say is tantamount to saying that Tibbles has to that kitten the relation *same* as restricted to cats, or that

$$\text{Tibbles} =_{\text{cat}} \text{that kitten.}$$

According to me, this relation is an absolute relation. The relation is not itself a criterion of identity or a principle of individuation – of course not. But I have now said how it *stands* to such a thing. So I think an absolute equivalence relation *can* answer to the agreed conception of a criterion of identity.

24.   Noonan says that 'conditions of cat-hood . . . can be specified without explicit use either of the concept of identity *simpliciter* or of the concept of f-identity' – in an 'identity free' way, as he will say – and these conditions 'fix uniquely the conditions of [cat]-identity'. But I would ask: can conditions of cat-hood really be 'specified'? This sounds like defining 'cat' and I think we know that we simply cannot do that. Surely we catch on to the use of the word 'cat' by exposure to instances – and in grasping some of the principles of behaviour and development to which cats are subject. Presupposed to that capacity – according to me – is our general grasp of the absolute relation of identity.

   Now it would be very much to the point to recall here that Geach has questioned the coherence of the concept of absolute identity, because of the problems of specifying without the usual risks of paradox what the congruence of absolute identity is congruence in respect of. But, if I understand him correctly, Noonan himself is not subscribing to Geach's argument here.[17] It is not then the coherence of absolute identity that Noonan is questioning. It is the coherence of the absolutists' rejection of relative identity. But here let me clarify. Absolutists do not reject the equivalence relations that are introduced by the relativists.[18] What they reject is the claim that these relations are relations of *identity*.

25.   Let us move on to another matter. Despite the claims rehearsed in §21, there do seem to be examples of relative identity. In *Identity and*

Spatio-Temporal Continuity and *Sameness and Substance*, I explained away many of these apparent examples by invoking the idea Noonan calls '[Wiggins's] famous 'is' of constitution'. Distinguishing on the basis of what he calls logical form between diachronic and synchronic cases,[19] Noonan says that I do not need the constitutive 'is' for cases like that of the coffee-pot which is the same collection of china clay particles as the jug. For he says 'the coffee-pot is the same collection of bits as the jug only in the sense that it *is* at the later time the same collection of bits as the jug *was* before the accident. But this being so, it is false that the jug *is* at the later time the same collection of bits as the jug *was* before the accident'.

Pace Noonan, I think we do need the constitutive 'is' here. We even need it in order to understand what is meant by 'the coffee-pot is such and such a collection of china clay pieces' and in order to understand why this does not have to be read as committing one who claims it to any congruence in the properties of the coffee pot and the collection of pieces. I hold that there is no such relation as Noonan supposes there is of an irreducibly tensed *identity*. Any genuine relation of identity between a and b holds for every time at which either a exists or b exists.[20]

26. Noonan proposes that the debate about the relativity of identity be shifted to the synchronic case. So let us move to that case. The synchronic case of relative identity that he favours is a case of Geach's, given in the third edition of *Reference and Generality*. In this case, there is a fat cat T, c is the largest continuous mass of feline tissue on the mat, and c_n is that mass of tissue less the hair h_n. Then, according to Geach, we must say, when we sort ourselves out, that c is the same cat as c_{293}, but c is not the same lump of feline tissue as c_{293}.

Noonan correctly predicts that here I shall deny that c *is* a cat and shall deny that $c = T$. He predicts that a defender of Geach will then want to know with what right I say that the modal and historical properties of T are essential to being a cat. But I reply that I do not need to show that they are essential to being a cat, only that they are indeed *properties* of T and that they are *not properties* of c or c_{279}.

27. What then of the claim that each of c, c_1 . . . c_{279} is a cat? Noonan correctly predicts that I shall say that all that means is that c *constitutes* a cat. But then he claims that I have no way of enforcing this solution in preference to other possible solutions.

I think I have already given reasons to prefer my view of the matter. But I shall add just two further remarks.

(1) The constitutive analysis has an appeal that is quite independent of this issue.

(2) It is worth considering what kind of conceptualism is at work in the construction of examples like this.

Geach and Noonan believe that we can stipulate both that c_{279} should be the cat Tibbles and that c_{279} should lack such and such a hair, even though that hair is in fact one of Tibbles's hairs. They believe that one can rule that c_{279} is Tibbles less that 279th hair. But can one really stipulate to this effect? (There is an affinity here with creative definition, already alluded to in note 18.) Geach and Noonan would have to be equally happy to rule that there is such a thing as Tibbles the cat minus her tail, and rule this *even though Tibbles herself has a tail*. Does this not mean that Tibbles, *qua* herself, has a tail and, *qua* herself minus her tail, lacks a tail? This had better not be the truth in conceptualism, I say. It would be better for the truth in conceptualism to be the Aristotelian thesis (D) (see §21).

Reply to Paul Snowdon

28. With characteristic forbearance and good humour, Paul Snowdon reviews the various defences I have offered at various times (in deictic or gestural rather than demonstrative mode, as he justly intimates) of a view that he moves me to redeploy and restate like this:

(A)   That what is at issue when we ask whether x is the same person as y is to be understood in the light of the question of what a person is;

(B)   That among intelligences and other sentient beings which we suppose to have mental states, persons are to be distinguished as follows: they are animals of some kind whose members typically perceive, feel, remember, imagine, desire, think, carry out projects, acquire a character as they age, are happy or miserable, are susceptible to concern for members of their own or like species . . . conceive of themselves as perceiving, feeling (. . . etc, as in the preceding enumeration); have, and conceive of themselves as having, a past accessible in experiential memory and a future accessible in intention, . . . ;

(C)   The dots outside the brackets in (B) above are not (*pace* Snowdon) the dots of a superable laziness or mere procrastination: they hold a place for marks of personhood that we supply in open-ended profusion, and have begun to enumerate, as here in (B), by speculating about what it takes for a being to count not simply as the possessor of consciousness (that matter is simply obscure) but as a fit subject of our interpretation and reciprocity – to count, in short, as one of us (whoever it is that we collectively are) or as a being actually or potentially 'on the same wavelength as we are';[21]

(D) The last clause of (C) makes it explicit that 'person' is covertly indexical;[22]

(E) In this open-ended task of enumeration, the relation between 'person', which is indexical, and 'human being' which is not, is as follows: we shall only count something as a person if it is the kind of thing that we who are human beings can interpret and can make sense of in a manner that is in principle not delimited or circumscribed. Plenary interpretation is by its nature a two-way (or potentially two-way) process that requires those who are involved in it to see one another (on pain of being unable to make sense of anyone or anything) as subject to a norm of substantive rationality that they draw out from within themselves yet never fully articulate. People are creatures of a kind to be the subjects of fine-grained interpretation *by* us, who are human beings, and to be the putative exponents of fine-grained interpretation *of* us;

(F) The human norm of rationality to which, as interpreters, we are jointly subject is not something that we discover *a posteriori*. Nor can it be the same as bare *a priori* universal rationality. (Cf. (1967a).) The thing we are concerned with here is a rationality of ends (as well as of means and the fit of means to ends). For these purposes, our only usable paradigm or stereotype of a reasonable being, or of a rational conscious being whom we can interpret, or of a person, is that of a human being. Our only proxy for a thinking, feeling soul is a striving, symbol using/misusing, embodied human being.

29. If contentions (A)–(F) seem obscure or arbitrary, I hope that they seem less so than ch. 6 of *Sameness and Substance*, which is a chapter I tried hard to clarify by *addenda/errata* that were inserted into the inside back cover of the paperback. Later I made another effort to sort out the claims of ch. 6 in the work from 1987 which Snowdon draws upon in his overview. Part of my tribute to Snowdon's criticisms is to try yet again here.

(A)–(F) diverge at one or two key points from Snowdon's account of my view. For I am not engaged, as he sometimes supposes, in the business of limiting real mentality or purpose or experience or consciousness to human beings.

30. What am I to say about cases where persons are said by many philosophers to survive but to survive in circumstances where there is no longer the same animal? According to Snowdon, in the case of

transplantation of a person's brain into the body of someone else, we no longer have the same animal.

Well, Snowdon and I have both tried[23] to persuade philosophers to think harder about what it would take for all this brain surgery (which it seems everyone thinks they can easily envisage) to issue not in a gruesome mess (made more gruesome by any residual flickerings of the experiential memory mechanisms of the supposed subject), but in proper survival. Suppose, however, that, contrary to these doubts, this sort of survival really is thinkable *as* survival, and is thinkable down to any level of detail that the critic may require. (Suppose also that the idea does not violate any of the presuppositions on which we depend to operate the ontology of persons.) In that case, if I *must* allow survival, I am not sure why I am committed to denying that the survivor who emerges from all these goings on is the *same human being* or *the same animal* as the one who entered them. It is my strong impression that, while I have always refrained from saying or writing that 'person' is itself a natural kind word, I have insisted on the dependence of the concept of person upon the concept of human being.[24] But once you understand what a *human being* is and what the *seat of consciousness* is, surely you will not too readily assume that you know what it would be for a human being to be given a new seat of consciousness. If transplantation really were possible, then would not the person follow the seat of consciousness? In that case, does not the animal that the survivor is follow it too?

31.   Among potential counter-examples to the claim that persons are animals, Snowdon mentions 'persons who lack any biological nature', 'artificial robotic persons', 'deities (or God)' and 'angels'. 'At first sight, it seems that deities (plural) and angels are not animals, yet they are accorded the status of persons by those who have believed in them.' What am I to say to this?

Angels and Homeric gods I think we only understand by reference to the human stereotype. We simply abstract from the gross corporeal body (which in pictorial representation has immediately to be restored).

That leaves God in the singular. Now in so far as there are serious thought of God as a person, surely these are thoughts of a personal God. But this is an idea that has to be grasped (if it can be grasped at all) only by construction and extrapolation and abstraction from reason as we know it, namely human reason. How well do we succeed? I am not sure. But the chief point that needs to be made here is how suspect the attempt would be to exploit for other purposes any philosophical concessions that may be made to the idea of a personal God.

The other case Snowdon invites me to consider is that of robots considered as putative persons. But, in this case, what are we talking about? Things artificially synthesized (as if carbon copied) from human beings? Surely these do *not* lack a biological nature.[25] What then about computers as we know them? Computers are programmed to implement certain designated, finitely specifiable objectives. Is that what we think *we* are?

32. Snowdon writes:

> Let us suppose that, as a result of some cosmic accident, the aliens speak a language indistinguishable from English. Treating them as speaking English makes perfect sense to us of their communications with one another and of their attempted communications with us. Surely they would be interpretable by us. How can we rule out this extremely unlikely, but surely possible, occurrence *a priori*?

I do not believe that even a bare metaphysical possibility is so easily established. As Arnauld pointed out in one of his objections against Descartes (*De Natura Mentis Humanae*[26]), our ignorance can often conceal from us the difficulties that lie latent in a supposition. The fact that there are words to describe a putative set-up without violation of the axioms or theorems of deductive logic creates no presumption at all that the set-up is metaphysically possible or can be coherently envisaged (envisaged, that is, at any arbitrary level of detail). Is the cosmic accident Snowdon speaks of the accident that these aliens have exactly the same sensory range and the same sensibility as we have (with our nervous system tuned as it is), and that they have this because their experience corresponds point by point to our human experience? If so, what sort of thing distinguishes them from us? Or is the accident meant to be that their experience and history are utterly different from ours yet, when the time comes for us to interact, co-operate, etc., they use the same words as we do in the same way as we do, as if on the basis of exactly the same associations as we do? That seems like magic. Or rather it seems like a perpetually renewed miracle.

33. In sum, my real brief, which I am indebted to Snowdon for forcing me to clarify, says that our only *paradigm* or *stereotype* of a person or of a conscious rational being of the kind that we can interpret is a human being: that it is simply not clear – once we refrain from the free-wheeling use of possibility – how far we can reach beyond that paradigm or stereotype. It is clear that not just anything is a person; but it is equally

clear that the class of persons cannot be delimited from within. There is no transcendental argument to be had from the possibility of interpretation to the conclusion that persons *must* be human beings. But do not rush to conclude that they need not.

Am I eating my words here? Fewer words than you may think. What matters is the *trend* of the argument I have tried so long to sustain about the original consilience of the concepts of person and human being.

34. In conclusion, Snowdon makes the important suggestion that the real question we should address is under what conditions we remain in existence. He suggests that for these purposes, *person* may not be the relevant concept for us to subsume ourselves under (if it is indeed a matter of subsumption). The proposal echoes the question earlier in his paper about whether 'person' is an individualistic predicate. It also echoes another worry that I have sometimes felt, independently of his paper. In the classical era, Greeks and Romans seem to have found no need whatever for a term with the general sense or function of the word 'person'.[27] Is there then some question that we can ask or concern ourselves with that they could not? I doubt it.

Abandoning the Cartesian project, or adapting it to Arnauld's insights in the passage that I have already cited, and then adapting the project further to the insights of ch. 3 of Strawson's *Individuals*, let us generalize Snowdon's question and ask first 'What are we?'. In the new framework, the question is not to be answered by assuming that, when we say *cogito ergo sum* or *dubito ergo sum*, everything we need to know is written on the face of *cogito*, or *dubito* – in the shape of 'a thinking (doubting) thing'. The reason why it cannot be answered with the claim that what we are is 'thinking things' is that such an answer depends on our seeking to generalize from the first person, but in a way that is utterly obscure, indeed void for simple ineffectiveness. How can the first person case generate even the possibility of plurality? The possibility of plurality has to be present there from the outset. How could it could ever have been present unless persons represented some potential plurality of continuing things, with M-predicates as well as P-predicates? If we advance within the guide lines of some improved construction, however, and we then ask who we are and under what conditions we persist, then the concepts that will emerge from the inquiry (or so I believe) are the familiar, non-accidentally concordant concepts under which we individuate ourselves, namely those of human being and person. The former gives us our first fix upon our nature and the criterion of our identity. The latter fills out the metaphysical and practical nature of the interest with which we are to determine who is to be *one of us* and what that takes.

3 Semantics

Reply to Stephen Williams, with an IOU to Julie Jack

35. Stephen Williams asks why single expressions with distinct semantic roles or subject to more than one semantic stipulation,[28] should be treated as ambiguous. Or, the same question the other way round, he asks why univocal expressions should automatically require a single semantic role and just one semantic stipulation. He poses this question, which is timely and interesting, within a truth-conditional framework. Then, using a range of philosophically interesting examples, he mounts his cross-examination of the answer that previously went unchallenged, which was that the ambiguity that we attribute to expressions should match exactly the diversity of semantic roles we find that we have to attribute to them in constructing (say) a Tarskian truth-definition for L.

Despite the sustained subtlety of Williams's treatment of all his examples, I have doubts about some of his claims. For instance, I should try, if I had not been so reckless already with space, to enter a long and extended defence of Tarski's ingenious unification of the semantic roles of the predicative and sentential 'and'. I should also try to vindicate the claim that, if 'exists' were a first-level predicate as well as a second-level one (as I think it is not), then a real ambiguity and duplicity of role would be the outcome.[29] But I shall concentrate upon the first thing, namely certain more general points about Williams's question itself.

36. In its general form, Williams's question is an extremely old one. It was asked by Aristotle, for instance. My response to Williams will be to suggest that, before we reach any verdict on any of these semantic matters, it will be well to bring into play Aristotle's answer to Aristotle's version of the question that he and Williams have in common.

With minimal injustice it may be said that the principal preoccupation of Aristotle's philosophical semantics is the giving of glosses or definitions. In Aristotle's kind of framework, it will be highly natural to stipulate that semantic roles have the same multiplicity as definitions, that definitions are tested by the acceptability of the paraphrases that they make possible, and that the multiplicity of definitions of an expression is kept as low as it can be by the maxim of not giving more of these definitions than are really needed in order for the theorist to arrive at an intuitively correct understanding of the various contributions that that expression makes in all its occurrences and combinations to each of the various sentences containing it that he has to paraphrase.

One of the problems that exercised Aristotle in implementing the plan that I describe so anachronistically in this way was that the exigencies of arriving at such a set of definitions and the further exigencies of understanding philosophically the whole variety of uses of (say) *be* or *one* or *good* seemed to produce an excessive variety of definitions/glosses. If each gloss represented a distinct sense, then language would be harbouring much more ambiguity than anyone really wanted to recognize. Aristotle's reservations about this possibility will remind one of Williams's.

37. Aristotle's response to this question can be described, however roughly, readily and anachronistically, as follows: it was to allow the new multiplicity of senses to stand, provided only that their multiplicity did not arise from more definitions being in play than were strictly needed to yield correct paraphrases of anything and everything anyone wanted paraphrased; but then, letting that multiplicity stand, to mark out certain broader groupings of distinct senses, namely grouping of senses that were related to one another either *focally* or *analogically*.

> If the things we have named are good in themselves, the account of the good will have to appear as something identical in them all, as that of whiteness is identical in snow and in white lead. But of honour, wisdom and pleasure, just in respect of their goodness, the accounts are distinct and diverse.[30] The good, therefore, is not something common answering to one idea. But then in what way are things called good? They do not seem to be like things that only chance to be the same. Are good things one, then, by being derived from one good or by all contributing to one good[31] or are they rather one by analogy?

Thus *Nicomachean Ethics* 1096b 21 ff. (trans. Ross). Ordinary or philosophically untutored judgements of ambiguity are usually judgements to the effect that this or that expression has at least two more or less disconnected senses. Philosophical judgements of ambiguity cut finer and see through to differences that speakers do not need to think about. Speakers can be readily induced to see these differences, however. They are brought to see them by the joint instrumentality of (1) paraphrase (a test that nevertheless requires careful interpretation), (2) the question (to which one remembers that Davidson gives his own telling expression, see above §8) of what it is that this or that familiar word brings to the contexts in which it is actually used; and (3) the question whether, even if the word's input is mixed with other things that are local to a context, what it *brings* is always the same.

38. Aristotle's way of answering his and Williams's questions still seems to me exactly right, namely to align a word's ambiguity with its multiplicity of semantic roles, but to mark as non-fortuitous the connections between certain of these distinct roles. The doctrines of analogy and focal meaning *buffer* without contradicting the finding of ambiguity.

When I commend this approach, I seem to be taking Aristotle's side against Williams. But then, at a point near the end of his §11, Williams undertakes to provide some 'alternative account of what brings [the] different uses of a certain expression together, [of] what makes us think them univocal', and he remarks that 'this of course brings us to the rich territory lying between chance homonymy and identical semantic role'. He then introduces the notion of '*analogous* or *common conceptual role*'. When he does these things, I am suddenly led to wonder whether his and Aristotle's accounts are really notational variants. In which case, however, I must urge him to follow Aristotle in distinguishing between analogical and focal explanations of the relations of senses.

It may be then that Aristotle and Williams offer notational variants. But I think there is an unresolved issue between them. The issue is whether there is a good reason to take analogy or community of conceptual role as relieving us of any need to reach a positive finding of ambiguity.

I believe that it cannot relieve us of the need to postulate ambiguity. By reference to health as our focus we can certainly explain the possibility of 'healthy complexion', 'healthy lungs', 'healthy constitution', 'healthy climate', 'healthy drink'. 'Healthy' is clearly not a pun here. There is unity in this diversity of uses, a unity of focus. But, in addition to making us see their affinity or connection, a dictionary maker also needs to record the differences between the various ways in which these uses relate to health. After all, not just any old relation to health will do. If just any old relation to health would do, then we should expect 'healthy hospital', 'healthy cure', 'healthy text-book', 'healthy lecture'. But these are *not* in the intended way available.[32] The dictionary maker needs to record and thereby approve the relations to health that do straightforwardly qualify. Is it not his office then to *document* the various different senses of 'healthy' – just as he would need to document and separate, in precisely the way in which von Wright did in *The Varieties of Goodness*, all the distinct uses of 'good' exemplified in the attributive schema *good + noun*? If von Wright was getting things right, then among these are instrumental goodness, medical goodness, beneficial goodness, hedonic/aesthetic goodness. Indeed, as I once tried to demonstrate, we need – even as we relate them to one another – to mark these distinct uses of 'good' as *semantically* distinct if we are to understand the actual ambiguity of certain sentences. (See (1971a), pp. 29–33.)

39.   So where are we? Williams's question being a variant of Aristotle's, I have ventured to press the claims of Aristotle's answer to that question, taken in its full abstract generality. The answer that Aristotle's examples suggest is at variance with Williams's official answer. It is entirely irresponsible for me to insist on this, however, if the Aristotelian framework will not cohere with the truth-definitional approach to meaning that Williams and I both espouse. So will it cohere?

Let me say at once that the Aristotelian and truth-conditional approaches cannot be *integrated*. The reason for this is that they address such different questions. The truth-definition casts much light on semantical structure and modes of combination, but relatively little on most questions of ambiguity. (It is no accident that the Davidsonians have sought to make a virtue of the fact that their axioms and theorems are 'homophonous'. Nor yet is it an accident that Williams's own examples relate to words that mark structure, namely connectives and quantifiers.) On the other hand, the Aristotelian approach which dwells relatively little on matters of semantic structure, casts a flood of light on the problems of word meaning.

If their preoccupations are different then we do not need to integrate the two approaches. But, to judge by our concern to answer questions like Williams's about word meaning, we do need to *coordinate* the Tarskian and Aristotelian approaches.

40.   To that end, let us first liberate the Aristotelian approach a little by releasing it from its preoccupation with definition as such. Really and truly, most words don't have definitions. But all words, even the most indefinable, do allow of elucidations given in terms of words or concepts that are coeval with that which is being elucidated. Exploiting elucidation, we can say that two words are alike in meaning to the extent that they match in respect of the elucidations that we need to use in explaining their contributions to all contexts into which they make an input. And we can say that a word is univocal to the extent that the same elucidation will serve to characterize all of the word's inputs to all contexts.[33]

With these proposals in place, let us now apply the Aristotelian outlook to 'and'. The Aristotelian approach will say that, if the sentential and predicative 'and' really have the same meaning, then that endorses the theoretical need to which Tarski's unification of sentential 'and' and predicative 'and' was directed. An Aristotelian is also likely to say – as I think I should, and as I see that Williams precisely actually invites me to say – that there is nothing at all artificial in limiting the class of true sentences to sentences that are satisfied by all sequences of objects *and closed*. There is nothing artificial, because we should expect truth to be limited in its application to linguistic expressions that are fully determinate in what they claim of what. Once we dismiss the thought that the Tarskian definition of satisfaction is meant to introduce an ersatz for correspondence, we shall find no fault in the syntactic promiscuity of the relation of satisfaction and shall see Tarski's unification of two uses of 'and' as reflecting the relation holding between atomic sentences and complex sentences built up from them, the abstraction of predicables from sentences and the quantification effected upon the concepts that these predicables stand for.

Finally, an Aristotelian will want to point to the distance between the sentential/predicative 'and', the 'and' that has come to abbreviate 'and then', and the 'and' of 'Jack and Jill went up the hill'. No doubt there is an *analogy* between (1) the way in which the former 'and', as it figures in e.g. 'everything is red and round', picks up two sentences open or closed in such a way that 'everything is red and round' predicates being satisfied by everything of the concept these predicates jointly determine and (2) the way in which 'Jack and Jill went up the hill' picks up two terms and then predicates going up the hill of the couple consisting of the references of the two terms. There is an analogy but no more. Despite the analogy, this 'and' means something different from the 'and' of 'everything is red and round'. A straw in the wind: if you want to translate the sentence about Jack and Jill correctly into Russian or Czech, then you will need to recognize this fact and deploy here not a sentence connective or predicate connective but a preposition ('s', taking the instrumental case, and meaning 'with'). Here or hereabouts, let me remark that with 'and' we have a further task, namely that of differentiating 'and' from another connective with the same truth-table, namely 'but'. For a suggestion which another observation by Aristotle (about 'snub') might help the semantic pluralist to make here, let me refer again to (1971a), p. 26.

41. Here then we have the draft for a flier for a semantic programme, a programme already far advanced through the diverse speculations and observations of linguists, logicians, philosophers and dictionary makers. There is a standing temptation to mistake for utter confusion of aims the diversity and occasionally crossed purposes of the efforts of this army of pioneers, ordnancers, snipers, artillerymen, infantry, observers and the rest. But there is more to be said for seeing the diversity of their efforts as a reflection of the plurality of kinds of meaning, the multidimensionality and many-layeredness of meaning, brought strikingly to our notice by the extract from Julie Jack's deeply interesting work in progress.

4 Value and Will

Reply to Sabina Lovibond

42. Sabina Lovibond's beautiful essay pursues and elaborates in certain necessary ways the thought that, by rediscovering the idea of the factual or real as laden with evaluative significance, we can make sense of a kind of ethical cognitivism that will 'preclude indifference on the part of the knower'.

Conspicuous among the many felicitous strokes by which Lovibond depicts the form of awareness with which she is concerned are two that result from her unexpected putting together of things that have seemed, under present demarcations, proprietary to distinct branches of philosophical inquiry. First – something already familiar from her other work – there is the marrying up and harmonization, in her account of the social formation of an adult person, of the distinct colourations of the ideas of *paideia* and of *Bildung*. Second, there is her clever and illuminating application to these matters of Evans's ideas in the philosophy of logic and language about connivance, fiction and the fiction-to-reality shift.

Despising to concur in the evasions that are a standing temptation to upholders of 'moral realism', Lovibond goes out of her way to emphasize the fragile and problematic character of much ethical cognition. She insists upon the role of 'constructive hypocrisy' or the mouthing of words and phrases that are equally apt for committed or tentative or playful or corrupt employment. On her account, constructive hypocrisy is essential to the process by which we arrive, in doubtful or fitful good faith, yet in a certain way inevitably, at an ethical and aesthetic intersubjectivity, and this intersubjectivity becomes a candidate for the title of an objective mode of vindication, perception and discovery – or a mode of awareness.

The chief aim of this genre of philosophy is to point. The aim, well achieved here, is to point at a thing in a way that will make the reader *see* something, make him see that the thing is *there* and then, by virtue of the reader's grasping its actuality, make him grasp its possibility. Rather than try to add anything to Lovibond's *deixis* or to subtract anything, I shall offer two consequential observations. One relates to connivance, the other to weakness of will or *akrasia*.

43. As Lovibond notes, critics of cognitivism in morals and aesthetics will want to bring out the 'seemingly relativist overtones' – i.e. the non-objectivist overtones? – of the idea that ethical formation is a matter of perspective. Then, spotting a more novel opening, they will want to

make much of the admission that, in catching hold of the culturally constructed perspective and the corresponding patterns of concern, the ethically formed human being may have had to connive in modes of description in which he or she will have felt no confidence and may have had to acquiesce in distinctions of whose point he or she may have felt doubtful in the extreme. Then these critics may seek to exploit further two admissions of Lovibond's by which light is to be cast upon *akrasia*, the first being that, among those who are ethically formed, she counts the fully formed person extremely rare whose subjectivity matches exactly and point by point the culturally constructed perspective; and the second being that the *spoudaios* is really an ideal.

44.   What will it take to defend ethical cognitivism against the taunt that at last it has simply admitted that what it rests upon is largely humbug?

The thing Lovibond wants to emphasize is that those who are finding their way into the culturally constructed perspective, or seeking to construct it or extend it, will need at certain crucial points to be prepared to use tentatively or experimentally or probatively all sorts of forms of words they may eventually reject as repulsive or incoherent. Those who are finding their way will only grasp the sense of certain forms of words if they can play along with the presuppositions and expectations on which the forms depend for their point. Now what has to be emphasized here is that the place where 'humbug' plays its part is in the cognitivist's answer to the question of how such a perspective could ever have been constituted. The cognitivist's question is: How was it possible? Humbug, if the critic must call it that, is simply one of the enabling conditions of the coming to be – and the coming to be grasped – of the sense of the words that the corresponding discourse deploys in the description that it offers of a correlative social reality. Whether that reality and the values the discourse purports to find in it really do exist, either in a particular thing or anywhere, is a different question from the question of the constitution of the sense. It is a question that can only be answered, in my opinion, by an extended examination of the strength and dialectical-cum-vindicatory resources of the discourse that this evaluative language subserves.

Once this difference is recognized, the way is clear to stress that in the vindication or non-vindication of ethical claims, there is no question of pretence playing any role at all. The question of vindication is a question not of sense but of reference or truth-value. You can say, if you like, that collectively we *create* a form of life and corresponding conceptions that invest certain features of people, acts and situations with the status of values. But this is not to say that the values themselves are created. Values are discovered by those who live the form of life that is said to

have been created. They are discovered – even though there is no
question of discovery unless (i) all is well (or well enough) with the
cultural perspective from which those who live the form of life make their
judgements and (ii) these judgements are responsive to the criticisms
that are levelled at them.[34]

Reply to Sabina Lovibond and John McDowell on akrasia

45. Apart from the new verisimilitude that Lovibond's presentation
lends to cognitivism, her essay has other aims – to tell the story (essential
to the defusing of wrong versions of the contrast between cognition and
practicality) of how, as a cultural perspective is constructed, a corresponding range of commitments and concerns is created; then to display
the strength of the Socratic-cum-Aristotelian thesis that a sufficient
difference in A's and B's motivation to comply with an ethical demand –
B being the less strongly motivated, let us suppose – argues 'some
difference in the way they understand their situations'; and to show at the
same time the qualifiability of that thesis. She mentions sympathetically
the thesis that 'B's perception of the situation may differ [from A's] in
being no longer "clear" but "clouded by desire" '. She claims that 'the
same considerations can tell a story both of deficiency and of potentiality'.

In Lovibond's account, the considerations in question relate to what
she calls psychological inchoateness: but they cohere with the So-
cratic/Aristotelian claims and cohere equally well with the comment that
she quotes me as making on the opposite side of the argument about the
failure on some writers' parts 'to take someone's conformity in act to his
best considered finding as the hard-won achievement that it is. They fail
to see [this] as not to be taken for granted'.[35]

46. The issue will become slightly clearer, I think, if we ask what it is
that completes the deficiency that Lovibond speaks of. On her account,
the deficiency is a condition of psychological inchoateness, it is normal,
and the remedy for the incompleteness consists in an ethical emancipation, an emancipation that springs from the formation of a 'unified
system of practical commitments'. On the account I was offering, the
deficiency, which I am content and indeed eager to regard as 'normal',
will involve *inter alia* a deficiency of irreducibly executive virtues like
continence, nerve, perseverance and the capacity to pay attention. Continence is the state of character that Aristotle recognizes, recognizes as
the saving grace of one who lacks temperance but pursues the good, yet
which he resolutely refuses to see as a proper virtue of the fully fledged

phronimos – and refuses for that reason to recognize as a virtue. On the account I offered, it is the presence of executive dispositions/virtues that makes possible the unifiedness of a system of practical commitments and its durability in the face of the plurality and mutual irreducibility of ends.

But are not these 'executive' dispositions/virtues themselves cognitive? – someone may inquire. I reply that they cannot help but be cognitive, and in all sorts of ways. But cognitive is not *all* that they are. Their cognitiveness doesn't account for everything that they are.

There is something at issue here that needs to be pinned down. Let us begin with an ambiguity in the claim that Lovibond makes about the case where B is less strongly motivated than A to comply with an ethical demand. She says that there is 'some difference in the way [A and B] understand their situation'. This sentence is ambiguous. (Let the ambiguity stand hostage for that of thousands of similar Socratic and Aristotelian sentences that have been written in discussion of *akrasia*.) (1) Does the claim mean that the *content* of their understanding is different? Or (2) does it mean that their grasp of that content is different? And, if (2) is the correct line of interpretation, then question (3) is whether the cognitive dimension of the inferiority of B's grasp exhausts the inferiority of that grasp. Does the grasp simply fall short in clarity or distinctness or the like? Or may it be, question (4), that the inferiority of B's understanding is an executive as well as a cognitive inferiority? If so, does this executive inferiority represent the residue of truth in the traditional idea that is conveyed in the claim that the *akratês* is 'weak', i.e. not firm enough, 'in will'?

47. The view that I attributed to Aristotle was that B's grasp is inferior to A's grasp because B has a poorer grasp of some particular point which is integral to the force of the ethical demand. So in the paper that McDowell so scrupulously interrogates, I was going along with the suggestion in question (2) above, as it applies to Aristotle, and I was complaining that Aristotle's gloss on (2) is in line with the suggestion in question (3) when it ought, I said, to have been in line with the suggestion in question (4).

In that paper, I may well have misunderstood Aristotle – to what extent is something to be argued in a moment. The thing that is certain, however, is that, in the comments I made about him at (1991a), pp. 250 ff., I misunderstood McDowell.

My complaint was that Aristotle and McDowell say little or nothing to make it plausible that the difference between the *akratês* and *enkratês* and the difference between the *akratês* and the *phronimos* comes down to a matter of the grasp of the minor premise of the practical syllogism. I asked why Aristotle and McDowell overlook the obvious differences between A and B in respect of executive and not exclusively cognitive character traits like courage, or perseverance, or the capacity for paying attention. As McDowell says, it troubled me that 'Aristotle ought to have allowed that even perfectly executed practical thinking may need executive virtues if it is to show itself in action; [that] the thought alone does not suffice. In that case it cannot be correct to infer a defectiveness in thinking (whether we call it "ignorance" or not) from a defectiveness in behaviour'.

It now appears that these criticisms rested on sheer misunderstanding on my part. I paid too little attention to the fact that McDowell's Aristotle wants to understand *akrasia* by focusing on the case of someone who is as close as he can be, consistently with failure in action, to a certain ideal – the ideal of one who has fully–fledged practical wisdom or *phronêsis* and a correct conception of the end of human action, who has a keen situational appreciation and, in tandem with that, the disposition not to count for anything considerations that in this or that case deserve no hearing. (See McDowell's §5.) He is close to that ideal yet he fails for some reason and in a way requiring explanation, to heed an ethical demand. Once we respect Aristotle's focus on this person, we see that:

> There is no implication that practical deliberation *generally, regardless of its type,* flows smoothly into action without any need for executive virtues: that is no unrealistic conviction of the power of practical thought in general to eliminate recalcitrant motivations and control action. This undercuts the basis for Wiggins's disappointment.

48.   There is something disturbing in the fact that over several years McDowell and I were in a position to talk to one another about whatever we liked on almost any day of the week, yet I still misunderstood him. But the question now is what remains for us to argue about.

49.   The chief textual question relates to the phrase '*en tais poiêtikais*' at 1147a 28, where I followed Ross in finding a simple theoretical/practical contrast and paraphrased 'in the practical sphere'. McDowell distinguishes the practical from the productive and argues that, within the practical (as strictly construed), it is only in the case of the *phronimos* that the results of deliberation flow inexorably into action. (No doubt in the productive sphere, they can do so 'inexorably' but this is for different reasons.) It is in the special case where someone approximates to being *phronimos* but fails to act that the possibility is to be explored that his

grasp of the minor premiss was imperfect. (Though McDowell wants to 'nuance' that.)

The suggestion is an interesting one, but I do doubt that the matter can be resolved independently of the very similar passage at *Eudemian Ethics* 1227b 29–30 or of the questions that flow from the fact that the text of Bk VII is held in common for *Nicomachean* and *Eudemian Ethics*. Ross's justification for translating *poiêtikais* as 'practical' may be assumed to have been the fact that in the *Eudemian Ethics* 'productive' or *poiêtikê* knowledge is imperfectly differentiated from 'practical' knowledge.[36] *Poiein* is a generic verb. Given that our passage lies in a shared book, it is at least problematic to *insist* upon a practical/productive contrast. The point that counts against Aristotle's deliberately invoking the practical/ productive contrast at this point is that, as McDowell remarks, the immediately subsequent example about tasting sweet things is so ill-calculated to sustain that contrast. If Aristotle did have the technical or productive specially in mind, he took no trouble at all to fend off misunderstanding.

50. Is Aristotle's topic as specific as McDowell says it is? When I try to read the text in McDowell's more specific way, I can do it but I stumble in some places. (E.g. at 1147b 10–12. Is this really an approximation to the fully-fledged *phronimos/sophron* that Aristotle is talking about?) But having read the text in W.D. Ross's way for so long, I have no faith in my reservations. The chief question that remains – however oblique it may be to Aristotle's exposition – is how cognitive the difference will be between the *phronimos/sophron* and all the other characters, the various *akrateis* and *enkrateis*. The *phronimos/sophron* is someone who has ethical 'vision' and has 'a singleness of motivational focus' that 'silences' (the verb McDowell used in his other paper) counter-attractions (without obliterating them). It is this person that Lovibond has in mind where she writes of 'a unified system of practical commitments' and McDowell has in mind when he writes of 'singleness of motivational focus' bringing about 'a perfect cognitive match with the ideal case'.

Not myself being (nor understanding from the inside what it is to be) an ideal case, I am left here with one question that I want to ask. Does not the learning of the executive virtues of courage, nerve, follow-through, attention, etc., play an essential role in (a) the creating, (b) the sustaining, of the very possibility of this *phronêsis/sophrosynê*, this motiva-tional focus, or this unifiedness of a system of practical commitments? Surely it is necessary in both of the ways (a), (b). But then is it more than a question of words whether we are prepared to call continence (ditto nerve, the dispositions to persevere, to pay attention, etc.) 'a virtue'?

(I notice McDowell having a cognate worry when he writes in his §5, 'Aristotle's picture leaves plenty of room for cases where continence might figure not exactly as an executive *virtue*, but as an executive disposition that is required if the agent is to act, as, in a way, he realizes he should; this realization being, from the terms of the case, less perfectly meshed with his motivational susceptibilities than in the ideal case.') My question is this: what is to be said about this executive disposition for the ideal as well as the non-ideal case? Echoing what I suggested in reply to Lovibond, I ask: does not the unifiedness of a system of practical commitments in the ideal case depend in part on the owner's possession of certain irreducibly executive dispositions? If I put the question like that, maybe all three of us will answer 'yes'. Or will Lovibond and McDowell say that that suggestion invites us to engage in a sort of double counting?

Reply to Roger Crisp

51.   Roger Crisp notes that, among value cognitivists in general, there are some who maintain that genuine evaluative properties are natural properties or like natural properties. The 'best moral theory' will find them out there in the world – alongside the properties discovered by the best theory of the natural world. Amiably and reassuringly, he points to the differences between this position and the value cognitivism that I have tried to help to formulate and, independently of problems of formulation, have speculated about how to test and confirm or refute. (See Pt 5 below.) Then, equally amiably and reassuringly, Crisp seeks not only to raise various questions about values as I have proposed that one might see them but also to release my account from the burden that it has accumulated of sundry misreadings and of interpretations that credit me with an interest in questions I have not been concerned with.

52.   Casting about for ways to sharpen the debate between naturalist and non-naturalist cognitivism, Crisp seeks to distinguish the positions by a 'causal criterion', a 'discipline criterion' and a 'standpoint criterion'. The chief remark that I want to make about his whole paper is one that I can readily affix to his brief discussion of the first of these, namely the causal criterion. (The remark is a general one, however.)

In a vindicatory explanation, as I envisaged such a thing, a belief is vindicated if identifying the best explanation of the belief's having come into being commits the explainer himself to share in the same belief. When things are like this, what happens is that the resulting commitment to the belief in question commits the explainer to the existence of the property that the belief attributes to that which the belief is about. I find it odd to describe what goes on here by saying that the *explanation* postulates the existence of the property. The explanation first postulates the obtaining of the belief. Then the explanation seeks for that to which the belief responds. If the explanation finds that and finds it compelling, the belief is vindicated, but the explanation brings this about by virtue of the belief itself being seen as an intelligible and correct response. It is this last which commits us to the property. Consider. If we say that the belief that $7 + 5 = 12$ is best explained by the subject's having thought such and such (where such and such is a calculation or a proof), then do we have by that token to say that $7 + 5$'s equalling 12 *causes* the subject's thought that $7 + 5 = 12$? And must we then struggle with questions about the causal properties of the numbers? Isn't this perfectly silly? The causality in question is between the subject's being party to certain considerations and that subject's arriving at a certain view. It is the compellingness of the considerations leading to the belief, the belief which commits the believer to the property, that makes the property objective – not the other way around.

At this point, I am moved to allude to the remark of Kreisel that is often quoted and approved by Michael Dummett:[37] 'the question is not whether there are mathematical objects but whether mathematical statements are objective'. I think that it is this sort of thought, apparently familiar to me for almost as long as I can remember,[38] that has motivated everything I have ever written about value cognitivism. The Platonism to which I subscribe about values is a Platonism that takes off from an optimistic view of the objectivity of valuational thinking. It does not explain that objectivity. It derives from it.

Persisting in that Platonism, let me now insist that there really is a point in calling ethical properties non-natural. Whatever I may have added to G. E. Moore's way of claiming that such properties are non-natural, and whatever I may have subtracted[39], I must insist that non-naturalism about a given class of properties is *not* the claim that the properties in question cannot cause anything or that they lie outside time. The goodness of nature of some Samaritan can have all sorts of effects, for instance. Some people may owe their life to it. Others may owe their life to the example that it set. Nor, I would add, and Crisp agrees with this, are ethical properties well described as *shapeless*! They do however answer to interests that are pretty alien to a scientist's interest in certain special sorts of prediction and control. Their shape is different from the shape of properties that are stood for by predicates that pull their weight in science.[40]

53. I like a good deal of what Crisp has to say about the role that responses play in the constitution of the senses of evaluative predicates. When he says that to think that this reference to responses 'commits one to reference to [responses] in an account of the properties [themselves that are] judged from [a] perspective, would be to be guilty of an error similar to that of confusing the genealogy and the content of morals', I see a distinctive addition to the claim I was making at §44 above in reply to Lovibond. But I cannot agree with Crisp when he goes on to propose to me that the non-naturalist should answer one of the several questions that Warren Quinn once asked by saying that a response – the response that one cannot be a stranger to if one understands a certain kind of value-predicate – may be 'logically divided into the pure cognition of a property and some non-cognitive correlative state'.

Crisp proposes this because he thinks that non-naturalists will then be able to 'make sense of those cases where a person can see from an anthropocentric perspective that certain actions will be described approvingly by some as, say, straightforwardly "macho", "chaste" or "pious" and [he] grasps the point of those descriptions but fails to approve or disapprove of those actions'.

The thought is familiar. It also underlies the standard way of differentiating 'thick' and 'thin' predicates.[41] But I could not be party to the idea which Crisp's use of the word 'pure' suggests here, and I never have been party to it.

54. When we train our moral or aesthetic interest on what lies outside us and we find the value V in object x, this response to x of finding V in it cannot surely consist of a cognitive act that discerns that x qualifies as lying in the extension of V, *followed by* or *simply accompanied by* a separate or separable reaction, a reaction simply on the level of affect, towards x as a member of that extension. For the prior grasp of the extension needs to be sustained by the *interest* with which the extension is demarcated. The point that is visible to this interest that attaches to applying or withholding the predicate is simply invisible in the absence of the interest. What is needed is the *simultaneous* understanding of what the things that belong to the extension are like, how they affect us and how exactly it matters whether x does or does not belong to that extension. It follows that no part of the response can be cognitive-in-abstraction-from-affect. Nor yet can the other part of the response be sheer affect in abstraction from that to which it is a reaction – affect abstracted from its intentional object. (One should not too lightly assume that arbitrarily different attitudes to what a certain word stands for will cohere with the understanding that open-endedly generates a given extension.)

It is certainly harmless to say that our evaluations are 'world-guided' if 'the world' is used here in an all-inclusive sense. (The claim simply condenses a longer account.) But, if the phrase 'the world' is used in a narrower sense suggested by the empiricist *préjugés* that make such a business of any and every attempt to account for ethical and aesthetical properties, then it is absurd to say that evaluation is world-guided.

55. How then, declining Crisp's suggestion, shall we account for evaluations like 'macho', 'chaste' or 'pious', in the cases where we want to remain detached or uncommittal? Well, when we employ such attributions, we have to make as if to enter into the world view of those whose thoughts we seek to understand – or we have to enter into that world view and *then* express our reservations about it. On these terms, we must first recognize, but then we must prepare to abdicate from, the question of vindicatory explanation and the question of explaining others' beliefs as a reaction to that which is actually macho or chaste or pious. The question 'is x (really) macho/chaste/pious?' was there, but then, in remaining uncommittal, we distance ourselves from it. The question that was there was a question of what the extension really was, but then, in abdicating, we have lost that question of what the extension really is. Once we started to engage again with the question of whether *x* was really in the extension of 'chaste', we should face a host of questions for which we are no longer prepared or are actively disprepared, once we decide we are uncommitted in the way Crisp envisages.

An example. We may seek to understand why, in *Tess of the D'Urbervilles*, Angel behaves as he does to Tess after their marriage and his discovery that she had had a child by another man – which is something that she justifiably took him to know already when they were joined in marriage. One cannot understand Angel's behaviour to Tess without making reference to his thought that she had been unchaste. But few readers of the book will be content to see Angel's reaction as a reaction to Tess's actually belonging in the extension of the predicate *unchaste* 'in Angel's sense' or 'as Angel will have been brought up to use the predicates "chaste" and "unchaste" '. For if Angel and his kind of people had used the word 'unchaste' in that way and applied it so to Tess, they would have been wrong. Indeed, if they had used it in that way of Tess knowing her whole history, then they would have been insane! You cannot touch on the question of the word's extension without thought of its actual extension and you cannot do that without engaging with the point of the attribution of unchastity (in which case Tess will not lie within it). You can, however, enter into the thoughts of Angel and, in doing so, you can grasp well enough what mistake he was making, the mistake he began at the end to see for himself.

56. Crisp ends his paper with some questions. Some of them I think he has answered himself. Others he gives the recipe for answering. See his last sentence. Yet others I believe I may have cast a little more light upon in two pieces subsequent to those that he cites.[42]

Reply to Anthony Savile

57. Back now from post-Moorean non-naturalist subjectivism to Hume's own subjectivism and to Anthony Savile's interpretation of the essay 'Of the Standard of Taste'. Savile sets out persuasively the extreme difficulties any construal of Hume's theory would incur if it made the favourable responses of the sound judge *constitutive* of the literary merit of a book or a poem. By implication he suggests comparable difficulties that would arise if one sought to make the responses of sound judges constitutive of the 'moral standard by which [one] judges' questions of manners or virtue. As Savile makes evident, the constitutive interpretation can easily be married to a suggestion that is the semantical counterpart of that which Roger Crisp has provoked me to discuss in §55 above.

> A particular term, 'elegance', say, or 'fustian', comprises two distinct elements, one that is quite neutral with regard to sentiment and the other . . . sentiment- involving . . . . People agree readily enough about the applicability of a term's neutral element, but differ in the sentiment that they attach to it. And just because, in our ordinary meaning, 'elegant' *analytically* implies favourable response, these divergent judges, in so far as they use that word, must be using it in a different sense from the rest of us.

I shall add to Savile's decisive refutation of this interpretation of Hume just two points.

First, the bad interpretation takes 'different meaning' to mean 'different sense'. But Hume's use of the word 'meaning' almost always requires to be explained in terms of reference or of denomination. In the second place, contrary to what the bad interpretation suggests, Hume *cannot* have meant to drive a wedge between seeing what is on display *for what it is* and our reaction to it, as if it were up to me to react as I will 'once my judgement of the facts is made'. That is not Hume's doctrine at all – neither in morals nor in taste nor in the philosophy of mind. When Hume says that it is not contrary to reason to prefer the destruction of the world to the scratching of my finger, this is a remark about the limits of theoretical reason, not an invitation to behave in that way if you feel like it!

In 'A Sensible Subjectivism' ((1991a), Essay V) I sought, a little impatiently perhaps, to exempt any proper development of Humean subjectivism from the dead weight that would impede it if a sound judge's favourable response *were* the aesthetic or ethical merit of that to which he responds. Savile has done something more interesting for Hume. He has distanced Hume from that idea by suggesting more positively that the whole essay 'Of the Standard of Taste' is a contribution to the theory of aesthetic evidence, not to the theory of aesthetic nature.

> . . . The good judge tries to show the disputing parties what to see. He operates not by enouncing what Peter is to believe, but by getting him to respond to the poem with which he is having difficulty in the light of suggestions about what to look for. Belief is concurrent with response here: it does not precede it. The evidence of the good judge is indicative.

Yes! I have reread the essay in this light. I am relieved not to have committed myself to anything that would make such a way of reading it difficult. For reading it so, I find Hume's essay a yet clearer and more amiable work.

5 Truth, Marks of Truth and the Vindication of Belief

58. From values then, and the things we say about them, to the status of that which we say about them and its status with respect to truth in particular.

After nearly seven decades of experiment with the alternatives, the obvious thing still stares us in the face. From the nature of their declarative purport, judgements of obligation and value aspire to be true. To the extent that they really are true, they surely direct our attention to properties that things and situations really can have.[43] But the existence of the aspiration itself shows nothing at all about the success of the aspiration or about the existence of such properties. So is *true* ever a fair verdict on judgements that are as essentially contestable, or as perspectively dependent in respect of their sense, or as special in other ways, as value judgements are?

Ethical cognitivism is the thesis that there is a considerable body of cases where the verdict of truth is the right or correct (or true) verdict on a moral judgement.[44] Cognitivism need not deny that there are classes of judgement that are problematic or under-determinate for truth. But, on pain of vacuity, it had better insist that the truth that is in question is ordinary or plain truth, not some custom-made dilution of the property.

This will bring me to the subject of the essays of Wilfrid Hodges and Adrian Moore. But, before I engage with them, I want to emphasize the distinctness of two distinct tasks. One task is to determine sufficiently neutrally for the purpose what we should expect of truth taken as a property of judgements. Hodges's essay belongs chiefly in this area (or that is where I seek to place it). So in another way does Adrian Moore's. The other task is to find ways to determine whether value judgements do or can attain to it. Here we are involved in one way or another with the construal or reconstrual of the standards that actually prevail in ethical thinking it and describe it as we know it. Here or hereabouts belong the essays of Edward Hussey and Cheryl Misak.

There is one other preliminary on which I would insist, and this is the need for each of these two tasks to be seen on its merits and inde-pendently of emphases suggested by those whose primary concern is the relative merits of realism and anti-realism. Such emphases are no more neutral with respect to the question at hand than are the projects of building up to a metaphysical notion of truth by further and better specification of the normally received idea of correspondence or building down to an anti-metaphysical notion of truth by further and better specification of the idea of coherence.

Reply to Wilfrid Hodges

59. It would be good to transcend all these influences. But, if we are too ambitious, then it may seem that the issue between cognitivism and non-cognitivism cannot be decided without a new definition of truth. And if that were right then the issue would remain forever unresolved. For no plausible properly analytical definition exists. Nor will it ever, I think. Tarski's work shows how the extension of various restrictions (or sub-properties) of truth may be determined. But it does not do this in a way that says what truth is like. (For Tarski, definition is a matter of the reliable determination of an extension. It is not the traditional project.) Correspondence and coherence accounts of truth, even if we forget the other complaints against them, suffer from the defect that every passable version of either has a secret need of the idea of truth in order to achieve a passably correct or plausible definition of 'correspond'/'cohere'.

In this philosophically familiar situation my response has been to urge that we should forget definition and look instead in the direction of the elucidation of the idea of truth. Let us look for statements or truisms that bring truth into interesting or fruitful connection with concepts that are distinct but coeval or collateral with it, and let us see what we can learn about it in that way.[45]

The truism from which I have sought to extract most information about truth is a claim made by Frege and Wittgenstein about sense. My suggestion has been that we should ask what truth must be like if the following is to stand as a correct claim about truth: truth is a property such that to know what the declarative sentence s *means* is to know under what conditions s *is true*. Or leaving out knowledge, the question becomes: What must truth be like if the claim is to stand that s means that p just if whether s is true or not depends upon whether or not p?

Working from this basis, we might discover something interesting. But we can get much more information about what truth is like if we transform the Fregean equivalence at the right hand side, as we have strong independent reasons to do, and change the entering question correspondingly to read as follows: What must truth be like if the following claim is to stand: that s means that p in language L just in case the statement that s is true if and only if p can be derived from that method of determination of the extension of 'true' among the sentences of L which best complements and assists in the task of describing and understanding the conduct and doings, both linguistic and non-linguistic, of speakers of L?

It is from the answer I offer to this question that I once claimed to generate five preliminary or basic marks of truth (then a less basic one in (1990/1)). Then I asked how the standard of correctness that applies in practice to various kinds of moral judgement compares with the standard that is set by the conjunction of these five marks (or is set by any other marks that we may in due course generate). This is the way in which I have tried to engage with the questions of truth, objectivity and the rest in ethics.

Here Wilfrid Hodges's friendly essay – containing things I could never have imagined he would find to say about me – raises all sorts of questions. I shall try to answer his questions in the same I–thou mode that he adopts.

60. The first question arising from Wilfrid's essay is: whence do I derive the equivalence that is the basis of the derivation of that mark of truth? Wilfrid thinks I see it as something to be derived from Tarski's Convention T. I mean that I think he sees me as arriving at the equivalence by some transformation of Convention T. (Nor is it impossible that that is where Donald Davidson thinks that his own version of it is based.) But the source I get it from is Frege, *Grundgesetze* 1.32 (see Frege

(1967)), and Wittgenstein, redeploying Frege, at *Tractatus Logico-Philosophicus* 4.024. I am afraid this misunderstanding affects whole paragraphs of Wilfrid's §§2 and 3.

Unlike some of the other bases on which one might try to generate the marks of truth, the Fregean equivalence that I call in evidence is scarcely a truism or a platitude. But I think it is a truth, and a truth that becomes deeply interesting when, as in the final version, we cease to take 'means' for granted (as this occurs in the Frege-Wittgenstein proposal and its variants). The interpretational framework within which we seek to supersede or reinforce 'means', 'translates', (etc.) is available, I would add, even if one rejects – as I do and always have – the extreme Quinean-cum-Davidsonian claim that Wilfrid records in the words 'the only *semantic* facts we would need to know about [a linguistic] community in order to unravel their language are facts of the form "sentence s is true" '. This is a fair account of something that Davidson has claimed: but there lurks here a reductionism about meaning that I for one could never take seriously. I do not have to take it seriously in order to adopt the interpretational framework. Meaning and truth are correlative notions: that is what makes it possible to elucidate the one in terms of the other. But there is no way by which either might reduce or absorb the other.

The next set of questions relates to the issue of 'marks' (see Wilfrid's §7). But first a word more on the elucidatory approach to truth. I see this, with hindsight, as a variant upon the same old strategy that was used in *Identity and Spatio-Temporal Continuity* (1967). In that book and in *Sameness and Substance* (1980a), I thought I saw quite clearly that identity, like so many of the other things that exercise us in philosophy, was indefinable; but I thought that we could still advance the subject by asking what the individuation of things would have to be like and issue in for the formal properties of identity, its reflexivity and congruence, to be safeguarded in our judgements of identity. When truth became a matter of concern, as it began to do in 'Truth, Invention and the Meaning of Life',[46] the question became what declarative discourse must be like in order to provide for the possibility of truth or what a belief or judgement must be like for its acceptability or correctness to count as nothing less than truth. There was an analogy between the two problems. But there was also a difference. It was almost completely clear in advance (even if one had to remove things that obstructed the view, and then extend the view) what identity was like. It is much more contestable what truth is like. Nor are the marks of truth, either those one begins with or those one ends up with (in the two-way flow of philosophy), stateable in the simple way in which the marks of identity were.

61. Why call the features of truth that I want to derive from the constraints that interpretation places upon truth 'the marks of the concept true'? I simply meant by this the properties that a belief or statement has, *if* it is true. Here I was following Frege, and my understanding of Frege's use was based upon 'On Concept and Object',[47] where he says:

> If the object Γ has the properties Φ, X, and Ψ, I may combine them into Ω; so that it is the same thing if I say that Γ has the property Ω, or, that Γ has the properties Φ, X, and Ψ. I then call Φ, X, and Ψ marks of the concept Ω, and, at the same time, properties of Γ. It is clear that the relations of Φ to Γ and to Ω are quite different, and that consequently different terms are required. Γ falls under the concept Φ; but Ω which is itself a concept, cannot fall under the first-level concept Φ; only to a second-level concept could it stand in a similar relation. Ω is, on the other hand, subordinate to Φ.

So, as in Frege's example, if 2 is a positive whole number less than 10, then *to be a positive number, to be a whole number, to be less than 10* each appears as a property of the object 2 and appears also as a mark of Ω if Ω is the concept *positive whole number less than 10*.

In the light of this explanation, I hope it will also be clear that the five marks I claim to derive are only claimed to be some of the marks of truth: that I do not need to say that a belief's satisfying all five would be sufficient for its being true. The five marks are not necessarily exhaustive of truth and, as Wilfrid says, I never say they are. The ones I chose are certainly distinctive of truth, but in the way in which being fierce or stripy is distinctive (i.e. partially diagnostic) of being a tiger. That the stated marks are in this way distinctive, however, does not follow from their being marks, but from their being worth singling out for notice. I would add that the ones I chose are not only distinctive. They are also challenging. They are challenging because it is far from obvious that moral judgements that pass as correct have these marks. In a preliminary treatment of my problem, it was more than enough to explore whether moral judgements that pass as correct *could* have these marks. If they couldn't, that would settle the matter negatively. The purpose was not to find a way to determine the passable correctness of this or that moral judgement – we have that already – but to cast light on the question of how impressive we could take that received kind of correctness to be. How like was it to plain truth?

I think that what I have said here ought to answer all the questions that Wilfrid raises in his §7. If it doesn't, then someone must complain. For the line I am taking here is that the various suggestions that Wilfrid offers to me obscure the strategy I wanted to adopt.

Two more observations are still called for, however, about the marks that I single out for attention. First, the arguments I gave for them were meant to arise out of the interpretational construal of the right hand side of the Fregean equivalence that figures in my mark-generating question about truth. If they do not arise from that, then they are a failure.

In the second place, I am grateful to Wilfrid for pointing out my dreadful lapse in the formulation of the first mark. I should have given the mark as he does first, before he shifts over to another more Kantian reading of 'mark'. Or I should have given it as follows:

> If x is true, then x passes muster in that dimension of assessment that is correlative with what x is, which is the dimension of assessment in which x demands, simply by virtue of what it is, to be assessed.

If x is a belief then by virtue of its being that sort of thing, truth is the first dimension for its assessment.

62. Wilfrid says that my 'trek from the prime question [whether moral judgements can be plain true] to the marks of truth runs neither by logical deduction nor by free association, but somewhere in the space between these two'. Where in that space?

Given the prime question whether moral judgements can be plain true, we need to know what truth is like. (An ordinary piece of dialectic, this transition.) Given that need, we press into service a Fregean truth about truth and meaning. (More dialectic.) From this we deduce (however informally) what truth must be like in order to be related in the right way to meaning, meaning itself being collaterally characterized. The deduction gives marks. We then mount an initial investigation whether the standard of correctness or acceptability by which we assess moral judgements has any chance of coinciding with the newly elucidated standard of truth. (Dialectic, somewhat discursive.)

Allowing that to summarize my response so far, I turn now to Wilfrid's §§3–6, in order to measure the contribution to all this of Tarski's truth definition and to refine the understanding of that contribution. But let me precede my responses by pointing out that the *only* use to which Tarski's work is put in the exercise just summarized comes at the point where we seek to improve and amplify the Fregean insight about truth and meaning that forms the basis of the derivation of marks of truth. We begin with 'To understand a *Satz* means to know what is the case if it is true' (*Tractatus 4.024*). We force the right construal on to this by using Tarski's idea of a truth definition to rewrite it as 's means that p in L if and only if it is derivable from the Tarskian definition of truth in L that s is true iff p'.[48] Then we renaturalize everything that this transformation imports. (For 'definition of truth' imports the idea of determining the extension of 'true' in a way subject to a constraint that Tarski states by use of the idea of translation, which is as ripe for elucidation as that of meaning.) We rewrite the Fregean insight without 'translation' as 's means that p in L if and only if we may derive that [s is true if and only if p] from the grammatical and referential stipulations (or findings) which most satisfactorily subserve the effort to interpret (i.e. subserve the effort to describe and understand all the doings of) speakers of L'. (Cf. §59 above.) Which last is a project we understand well enough independently of the specifically semantical. Finally, as already explained, we ask what marks truth must have for the true/false contrast to play the role it needs to play here in the interpretation of speakers of L.

63.   So all that we take from Tarski is the idea of a truth-definition for a delimited language – which is the idea of pretty much the same thing that Frege had once furnished for the formal language of his *Begriffsschrift*. To speak of 'definition' in *this* sense does not, within the framework proposed, give us back anything mysteriously semantical. Any orderly, systematic reckoning of the resources of a language such as that which Tarski condenses into his definition of satisfaction, and which enables us to pair each sentence of the language with a T-sentence in the form [s is true if and only if p], will suffice, provided that, by virtue of the pairings it generates, the reckoning *reliably grasps the actual meaning of the notion as it is known intuitively*. Here I adopt the very words that Tarski himself uses in a closely related connection.[49] Or, as I preferred to put it in the words that Wilfrid has questioned, it must be no accident that the extension that the reckoning or definition generates is the extension of (the restriction to L of) the concept *true*.[50] In the early thirties, Tarski called himself an 'intuitive formalist'. I interpret that here as follows: the proposals he makes must ensure that the notion of truth he introduces is manifestly correct, free of paradox and not to be despised by mathematicians. But the notion must also be recognisable as a notion of truth. Formalism must be both mathematically and intuitively correct. The second of these things Tarski ensures in the paper on truth by means of Convention T or 'the Criterion of Material Adequacy'.[51]

Wilfrid suggests that, on my reading of Convention T, 'translation' there must have some philosophical or more than ordinary content, or arise from something I want to think of as Tarski's philosophy of meaning. But I think that Wilfrid only says I need that because he thinks that I think I must get the Fregean equivalence from Convention T. I get it from Frege and Wittgenstein. For me as for everybody else, the ordinary content of 'translation' is more than enough – even if Convention T itself, as it derives from Kotarbinski, was part and parcel with thoughts that played a more philosophical role in Frege and Wittgenstein.

Reply to Adrian Moore

64. My improvidence with the space provided for these replies matches, I fear, my improvidence with the life with which I have been furnished for the study *inter tot alia* of Kant's first and second *Critiques*. Adrian Moore's Kantian adventure deserves a longer, stronger reply than I am going to muster. So do the qualities of the other excellent essays that remain.

Moore studies the meaning and the further philosophical usefulness of a form of words I have sometimes used, namely 'There is nothing else to think but that . . . '. Where there are many to whom I dismally failed to explain what I meant by it, Moore steers confidently past the extant misreadings to which I have laid myself open – except that he suggests at one point that what I meant was something indexical, i.e. that there is nothing else to think at the moment, say, or at any moment that *we* can conceive of, but that . . . . But then he puts matters straight by reconstruing the claim non–indexically or absolutely – as I would wish and have always intended it to be read – rightly insisting that, when there is nothing else to think but that p, this amounts to there being nothing else to think for anyone who understands properly what is said by the sentence that says that p. That is right. When one finds that there is nothing else to think, one may well do this on the preliminary basis of being oneself unable to think anything other than that p. But that is not all one is saying when one says there is nothing else to think. Nor is it anything so easy as this that one needs to be prepared to give reasons for. One needs to be ready to show how the apparent alternatives are generated and then excluded.

65. Moore points out that, in deploying this form of words, I was aiming to show forth a scheme that would cover both the empirical and the non-empirical cases, both the necessary and the contingent cases, etc. What I was concerned with was truth in general. The thought was that, once we contemplate and make room for arguments that gain their force *cumulatively*, we can break the association between the modal status of necessity and the dialectical status of conclusiveness. Conclusiveness can be achieved in any sphere of thought where there can be truth or falsehood.

But why such lust for generality? Here Moore and I would give different answers. The generality I was concerned with arose from the attempt to show that there was no obstacle to empirical beliefs, perceptual beliefs, arithmetical beliefs and moral beliefs, despite their undoubted differences, all possessing the same marks of truth. This mark for instance: if it is true that p then, in so far as it can be known that p, someone can believe that p precisely because p. Any beliefs of any of these various kinds could qualify as having this mark, I claimed, by virtue of admitting of a vindicatory explanation.[52] From this concern on my part there resulted a test that it is hard for moral judgements to pass. It is a test that calls not for a re-run of old bits of metaphysics or philosophy of mind, but for our surveying the richness, variety and strength of the modes of moral persuasion. (It is not clear to me whether there is some test weaker than the vindication test by which to show that moral judgements that normally pass as correct also enjoy this mark of truth.)

The generality that Moore is concerned with is rather different. It arises from his special interest in whether one may treat the formula 'there is nothing else to think but that p' as a necessary and sufficient condition for truth itself. Postulating this equivalence, he asks how, on these terms, one might fill the gap ' . . . ' in 'any thinker who . . . is bound to think that p'. He settles down to the following putative equivalence: 'It is true that p if and only if any thinker who has an unconditioned belief about whether or not p is bound to think that p'. And from there he sets forth upon a Kantian exploration of ideals of rational volition and rational agency – an exploration that would rapidly carry me out of my depth if I were to try to participate in it. Prescinding from those concerns, let me simply enter two comments about Moore's thought that 'There's nothing else to think but that p' should be both sufficient and necessary for it to be true that p.

66.   The first doubt one might have concerns how well such a condition, if it is put forward as sufficient *and* necessary for the truth of the statement that p, coheres or consists with the essential contestability of the statement, in the case where it is essentially contestable. The essential contestability of a claim implies (I suppose) that, from the nature of what it says, there can be no circumscription in advance of that which bears upon its correctness. But as regards this doubt, I think Moore might fend off objections by pointing out that essential contestability does not exclude the possibility that the local, contextually specific accumulation of relevant considerations can prevail. (They can surely prevail at least as well as anything can prevail in any case that explicitly or implicitly imports generality.)

67. The second doubt is more general. Truth is not in itself an epistemological notion, however epistemological we may allow our formulations to be of its marks and attributes.[53] It was for this sort of reason that, in the formulation of the mark of truth given at paragraph two of §65, I entered an explicit restriction to truths that were knowable. But how do matters stand with Moore's proposal? He remarks in his note 18 that there is a problem with false propositions with respect to which no thinker ever satisfies the condition. He does not solve the problem except by deprecating premature formalization of this proposal. My problem is not so much that I feel it must be formalized to be intelligible as that every possible clarification seems to induce some problem. If 'any thinker who has an unconditioned belief about whether p is bound to think that p' carries existential import (in Aristotelian fashion) then Moore is committed to something like idealism. If there is no such import what is the answer to the question in note 18? Is the whole right-hand side modal then? What then happens to the case of a truth that could not be known? Or is the claim that there could not be such a thing?

Reply to Edward Hussey

68. Edward Hussey's Protagoras, who believes that ordinary physical objects and processes have a non-subjective reality that is not unknowable in principle, opposes to this reality a subjective sphere where there is no objective knowledge and no objective truth. This latter is a sphere in which secondary qualities and values subsist (undifferentiated) and in which a certain paradox (familiar from life itself) has to be defused. The paradox is that our opinions, about the temperature of the wind, say, or the moral excellence of a certain line of conduct, strike each of us as simply true-for-us, so that the wind has coldness-for-us and such and such an act has moral-excellence-for-us, yet these opinions *also* strike us as open to improvement or correction by someone wiser or more enlightened than we are. The paradox is defused, first by our declining to refer these raw opinions to the objective sphere or to any other sphere of reality beyond the opinions or semblances themselves; and then by our viewing each of the totality of raw opinions as a potential contribution to the shared task of *constructing* a new and 'better' opinion (Hussey's §7, para. 2) – the negotiative undertaking in which Protagoras sees himself as having an important role to play of leadership or expertise. 'Any human being can contribute to the process of approximation by bringing the evidence of her or his "measurements" to bear in the (joint) construction of "better" opinion'. Any human being can contribute: but many will

want their efforts to be influenced by one who has thought longer and harder than they have about what is being attempted.

To what does this better opinion relate or refer? Hussey does not say but maybe his answer to the question is that better opinions relate to the reality that is to be found by those who are to conceive it and be its measures. What kind of knowledge can they have of it? One answer is that there is no *knowledge* of it. Another answer might invoke something akin to Vico's *maker-knowledge* – i.e. the knowledge of x proprietary to one who creates x –, where the hyphenation may be seen as holding in suspension the whole question whether this state of mind could ever approximate to *knowledge*. What then is the standard by which to evaluate the judgements that arise from the new conception and purport to find this or that 'out there'? Hussey's answer is that the opinions that these judgements express must be 'persuasive', 'worthwhile', 'as good as absolutely true' (Hussey's §7, end) and 'better both in the sense-perceptions of individuals and in the flourishing of the community' (Hussey's §8, beginning) as this last is judged from within 'the going concern' of negotiation and construction.

69. On this interpretation, what we have in addition to the schematic physical world and the raw uncriticized perceptions and findings of individual subjectivity is an emerging, advancing *intersubjectivity* of better opinion. And by this intersubjectivity is raised up an altogether new creation – the conception of a putative reality that a pragmaticist moral philosopher might tentatively or experimentally compare with 'the real' that C. S. Peirce, thinking of the empirical and objective spheres, described as follows:

> The real then is that which, sooner or later, information and reasoning would finally result in, and which is independent of the vagaries of me and you. Thus the very origin of the conception of reality shows that this conception essentially involves the notion of a COMMUNITY, without definite limits and capable of a definite increase of knowledge. (1931–5), vol. V, §311.

Shall we say then that, even as the new reality is found which the moralist who conceives it wants to compare with the empirical reality that Peirce is describing here, there comes into being the language of intersubjectivity – with all the attributes that have already come under consideration in connection with Lovibond's and Crisp's essays?

70. If we are to think clearly about this possibility – as intriguing in Protagoras (happily liberated in Hussey's thoughts from the shackles of

received interpretations) as it is in Hume – then there are precautions we must take.

First, I believe we must uncouple the objective/non-objective distinction from the non-subjective/subjective distinction[54] and reserve the second for a distinction of content between that which does or does not relate (and is or is not answerable for its correctness) to the consciousness of subjects – while deploying the first contrast only in connection with truth, falsehood and their congeners.

Secondly, we must see what is constructed as belonging on the level of sense or content not reference or truth-value.[55]

Thirdly, we must embark on the project described in the last paragraph of Hussey's §9 with a proper sense of the complexity of what is involved. The marks of truth that he enumerates will open out into highly substantial requirements upon the argumentative resources of received methods of dialogue and negotiation. Nor do these marks necessarily exhaust the exigent requirements for whatever passes for correctness to coincide with plain truth.[56] Pending real progress in this area, we should encourage the new Protagoreans to withhold judgement on the question of whether there really is moral truth and moral knowledge.

Reply to Cheryl Misak

71. Cheryl Misak laments the distortions that have resulted from seeing sensory judgements, among which she includes propositions of any kind that rest upon the evidence of the senses, not merely as unproblematic candidates for truth and knowledge but as paradigms of what truth and knowledge require. She proposes that we should take our stand in the fashion of an epistemological holist upon a broader and less specifically empirical conception of experience and then ask ourselves what judgements such experience can sustain or be recalcitrant to. Here, and in treating moral judgements as judgements along with others (empirical, sensory, mathematical and all the rest), Misak would claim to be following through a philosophy of inquiry that other epistemological holists have followed through less consistently, less even-handedly, and less radically. Indeed, in respect of their treatment of moral judgements, she would say that they have been arbitrary or *parti-pris*.

If I understand the proposal correctly, then experience as broadly conceived has among its special cases: that of finding the arithmetical claim that $7 + 5 = 12$ either self-evident or proven by a calculation; that of colliding with a tree blocking our way, this sustaining the finding 'a tree is in the way'; or that of perceiving a loaf on the table and then tasting some of it, this sustaining the claim 'that is bread'. Some experience does and some does not relate to 'ears, eyes, nose and skin'. None is raw or unconceptualized. The *genus* to which the evidence of 'ears, eyes, nose and skin' belongs is that which is 'compelling, surprising, brute, unchosen, impingeing or insistent'. She quotes Peirce to the effect that 'There will be a wider genus of things *partaking* of the character of perception if there be any matter of cognition which exerts a force upon us' (Peirce (1958), vol. VII, §623) – a possibility she finds that Peirce illustrates by reference to thought experiments and operations upon diagrams.

There are impressive differences between the subject matters of morality and arithmetic and there are further differences between the world of morality and the world that we explore by sense. But in all three spheres the same compulsiveness or 'secondness' can attach to the findings of that which the radical semantical holist counts as experience. Experience so conceived is what all inquiry – or all inquiry that is non-authoritarian and non-dogmatist and that lays itself open to what Peirce sometimes calls *Reals* – latches upon, goes forward from, or goes backwards or sideways from.

72. There are good things and bad things about this proposal, I believe. It is good in so far as it encourages us to explore any analogies that there may be between what sense experience does for empirical knowledge, what felt response does for ethics (or for aesthetics), and what the experience of being simply unable to find any other possibility does in the primitive combinatorics that are presupposed to elementary arithmetic and logic.[57] It is good again in so far as it makes us have regard for the frequency with which empirical, ethical and logical claims are fused in the ordinary motivations of life, and have regard for the way in which the marks of truth are common marks, present wherever truth is present. (Hence my own interest in the 'there is nothing else to think' formula, which in my usage is conclusory rather than initiatory or observational.)

I think it is a defect in radical epistemological holism, however, if it discourages us from attending in detail to the need for each sort of discourse and each sort of subject matter to be furnished with an account proprietary to it of its intellectual aims and methods, its sources of evidence and the link between what arises from these sources and the contents of its ordinary judgements. In this essential task, we should be just as interested in any differences as in any similarities that hold between the judgements of empirical exploration and the judgements of arithmetic, of morality or of aesthetics.

73. If someone constantly emphasizes certain features of the empirical and faults other subject matters for lacking them, then either we can try to show that, on a proper understanding, these other subject matters do not lack these features or else we can show that truth-directedness does not in itself require them. ('Why does arithmetic or ethics *need* any starting points?', we can ask. Or 'may it not be that arithmetic needs *no* foundations?')

Misak's response to those who fault the judgements of morality for lacking reference to experience conforms to the first of these patterns. But it would be a pity not to explore the prospects for the second pattern of response too. So with a view to motivating the second pattern (or motivating a mixed strategy that Misak may find more congenial), I shall make one or two general remarks about the ideas of experience and/or observation and try to point to that which is distinctive of them within the empirical sphere that is their ordinary habitat.

Since the ensuing remarks will smack of epistemological foundational-ism, let me begin by distinguishing the foundationalist impulse to which I confess (i) from the philosophical hunger for Cartesian certainty and other forms of immunity from error; (ii) from the search for a preconceptual given; and (iii) from the search for that to which certain basic sentences can correspond (in some philosophical sense of 'corres-pond'). In itself, the foundationalist impulse represents only the innocent idea that, in our linked interrogations of the empirical world and of the beliefs about it that we find ourselves possessed of, there has to be *relatively* direct knowledge of how things are in particular places at particular times; there has to be knowledge which can be supplied at need to other fields of inquiry; there has to be knowledge that presup-poses *relatively* little and which we can avail ourselves of without being required to embark upon a potential infinity of antecedent precautionary routines.[58] Our relatively direct ways of getting hold of information do not need to be invariably or incorrigibly correct. To give us the direct knowledge we need, their findings only need to be (i) *relatively non-com-mittal with respect to collateral information,* (ii) *relatively reliable* (something one does not have to establish about them from within a Cartesian project), (iii) *relatively less at the mercy of interfering or defeating factors, and relatively less controversial than most other kinds of findings are.* The public account of how these findings arise will have to confirm and explain these facts about them along with the directness of the knowledge that they furnish us with.

74. There is much more to say here: but the more of it one says, and the clearer one becomes about the way in which other inquiries lean upon

our empirical knowledge, the lesser will the temptation be to insist that the finding 'that was cruel' is like an experiential claim – especially when it is so unclear as yet that ethical knowledge really needs anything analogous to the experiential judgements that empirical inquiry needs. 'That was cruel' can certainly come to our lips unmediated by argument and that is important. But it is not non-committal with respect to collateral information (concerning intentions etc.). It is open to a significant extent to interfering or defeating factors (concerning intentions, concerning what really happened and why). It is potentially controversial and it is essentially contestable (which is not at all to say that it is *for that reason* problematic for being true or false). *A fortiori*, the account of how such judgements arise does not confirm but rather subverts the title of the judgement to the special privileges of judgements like 'there's a tree in the way' or 'there's a loaf of bread on the table'.

NOTES

1 If only to make sense perhaps of the experience that overwhelmed us all in these two forms at St Paul's, contemporaries who migrated to science have told me that it was an incomparably good training for their training in science. Would it be a good thing if this sort of education were still offered? The school education I have described is a timeless good – most especially in its focus upon faithful, idiomatic, two-way translation of substantial writings of drama, lyric, history and rhetoric. To perfect the form to which I submitted and preserve the space it offered humane letters, it would suffice for each pupil to choose one scientific or mathematical subject to study concurrently.
2 Different modes of conceptualization, one might say. For the reservations about that way of putting it, see *Sameness and Substance*, ch. 5.
3 Why can one not deliberate under democratic and open minded procedures about matters of ends? Because a decision about ends may bear hard upon a minority, perhaps? But a democratic decision about the means to things desired can bear equally hard upon a minority.
4 Invaluable to me at that time as a co-experimenter was my former New College student Wilfrid Hodges, soon to be my colleague at Bedford College, London.
5 I had heard Quine lecture in Oxford as Eastman Professor, when I was an undergraduate.
6 I say I forced it upon them. But they did not object or even murmur. John McDowell, whom I thank here for his kind words in this volume and his close attention to the two pieces he comments upon, was one of these pupils. Many years later, I tried to expound to him my explanation of why it was and how it was that Davidson, when eventually he came to give the John Locke lectures, took Oxford by storm. I gave my theory that Davidson showed one how to like Austin *and* like Quine. McDowell looked blankly at me for a moment, as if

unaware that there was anything to be explained. So I asked him whether he did not agree that this helped one to explain the reception of Davidson's ideas in Oxford. He replied, 'I thought Davidson was important because you told me he was – and I believed you'. Such is the short-lived authority of the young philosophy tutor.

7 I applaud particularly his explanation of the limitations of the would-be purely theoretical model-theoretic determination of modal claims that are metaphysically significant. 'As usual in modal logic, we cannot decide the correctness of contentious principles by appeal to model theory, for [model theory] comes in too many varieties'. Here I espy the point that I needed in order to complete the denunciation that I was attempting in *Sameness and Substance* (1980a) (note 4.02) of the model-theoretic craze of the 1970s, which so greatly overestimated the power of possible world semantics to make informal semantics and discursive metaphysical argument redundant in the assessment of modal claims.

8 That is to say that this is many more times evident than it is that, if everything that obtains in a world w_1 could obtain in world w_2, then everything that obtains in world w_2 could obtain in world w_1. What does 'could' mean here? Does it mean could *regardless* of the quantity and quality of the disruption that would be involved in realizing in w_2 everything that is possible in w_1? If so, then symmetry of accessibility is unproblematical, but it may appear that *on these terms* all worlds are accessible to one another. (Perhaps that is the right view to take of the flat metaphysical 'could'.) If the issue is whether, by some definite standard, the disruption that would be involved in realizing w_1's possibilities in w_2 might be *greater* than that involved in realizing w_2's possibilities in w_1, then symmetry becomes highly questionable. (And now I look back at my argument in the text, 'If A holds, how could it help but be the case that A is possible', and I worry that the most that it shows is a *necessitas consequentiae* not a *necessitas consequentis*.) But the fact that the clearest way of illustrating this difficulty is the case where all the laws of w_2 are laws of w_1 but not all the laws of w_1 are laws of w_2, suggests that here we have travelled a great distance from the question as originally posed about the status of

$$A \rightarrow \square\lozenge A.$$

What does 'it is nomologically necessary that it's nomologically possible' mean? The original question was about metaphysical 'could'.

9 An analogy. It makes no more sense to require that identities should announce themselves from out of the properties and relations within the world of a supposition than it does to suppose that it is constitutive of a picture's being a portrait of x that any pictorially competent observer should be able to tell *from looking into the picture* that the person in the picture is x.

10 Whatever we ask about what a thing could do or be or could have done or been, the answer will be *yes*!

11 See Quine (1960), p. 230. For some comments on this, see *Sameness and Substance* (1980a), pp. 199–201.

12 'Pure' means here not specified by use of the identity predicate or equipollent devices.
13 See (1967), pp. 37–8; (1980a), p. 92.
14 See (1980a), pp. 97–99.
15 He vindicates it whichever way you construe it, as concerned with 'definitely' in the sense of 'it is definite that' (my reconstruction) or 'it is definite whether' (the usual reconstruction).
16 Frege was concerned with the case where the conditions of identity and difference can be given explicitly, as they are in 'direction d_1 = direction d_2 if and only if the corresponding lines are parallel'.
17 For there to be an absolute relation of identity, it suffices that we should think of the range of properties in respect of which congruence holds as extensible beyond any stated limit. Compare the way in which Tarski's theorem, to the effect that there is no universal T-predicate, allows more and more comprehensive truth-predicates and warns us *not* that there is no such property as truth, but only that there exist limits to the definability of truth.
18 Though I do in fact doubt the coherence of the procedures by which the relation of being-the-same-surman as gives rise in due course to 'Chones' as the name of the one and only surman all the Joneses are. Is this not a creative definition of Chones?
19 I let this pass, though I could not concur in the suggestion that it makes any difference to the *logical form* of 'a=b' or '$a=_f b$' whether or not what is at issue turns on persistence through time.
20 I will give an argument for that. Suppose that we can make sense of a and b's being identical *at time* t, or

$$a \underset{f,\,t}{=} b.$$

Suppose then that it is true that

$$a \underset{f,\,t}{=} b$$

and suppose that, in addition to existing at t, *a* also exists at t′. Then we must also have

$$a \underset{f,\,t'}{=} a$$

But then, by Leibniz's Law, however times t and t′ are related, we shall have

$$b \underset{f,\,t'}{=} a$$

and

$$a \underset{f,\,t'}{=} b$$

So generalizing this, we have

$$\exists t\, (a \underset{t}{=} b) \to \forall t'\, (a \underset{f,t}{=} a \to a \underset{f,t}{=} b).$$

21 Or, in the wireless parlance of the military, 'on net' with us. In (1987b), I try to make candidature for reciprocity consequential upon and part and parcel with candidature for interpretation.

22 In a way in which neither 'human being' nor 'horse' is indexical. 'Human being' and 'horse' are extension-involving but precisely not indexical. Cf. my (1993a) and (1993c). In (1987b), I was trying to make the indexicality point by marking off a certain sense in which 'person' is, as I then elected to say, *relative*; see pp. 69–70.

23 Not alone. Cf. Bernard Williams's various writings on personal identity. And among more recent writings, see Gillett (1987).

24 The concept of animal is only, I said, a determinable awaiting further determination.

25 I find that, with rare prescience, I have explicitly refused to deny that a higher animal or organism could be synthesized. See *Sameness and Substance* (1980a), p. 175, note 30.

26 Vol. 7, *Oeuvres de Descartes*, Adam et Tannery, p. 201.

27 The Latin word *persona* means primarily (1) a mask or (2) a character in a drama. What first pushed the word in the direction of its modern meaning was the task of codifying the Roman law.

28 See his note 8.

29 For what it is worth, my view is set out in my (1994a).

30 For reservations about that particular manner of argument, see (1971a), p. 33.

31 These two cases fall within the ambit of the Aristotelian doctrine that G. E. L. Owen calls that of 'focal meaning'. See Owen (1986).

32 Or not straightforwardly so: it would take much local stage setting, *ad hoc*, to make them available. Contrast 'healthy urine'.

33 Ruling at the same time that all parts of the elucidation must pull their weight in the application to each input. For the need for such a ruling, compare again (1971a), p. 31 ff.

34 Cf §13 of my (1990/91), from which I have borrowed here a sentence or two.

35 Cf. *Needs, Values, Truth* (1981a), p. 331.

36 It is on this basis that Michael Woods, in his translation of *Eudemian Ethics* (see his note on 1216b 17–19, Aristotle (1982)) remarks that in our Bk VII passage the word *poietikais* is used in the same undifferentiated sense as it bears elsewhere in the *Eudemian Ethics*.

37 E.g. at Dummett (1981a), p. 508, or p. xxi.

38 But, now that I reflect, I am certain that I first got it from Dummett by hearing him lecture in the early sixties.

39 For the subtraction, see note 4 of (1993b).

40 Better, if we must speak of shape, to speak of the shape of their extensions.

41 For a different distinction that might do some of the work of the thick/thin distinction – but certainly not all of the work to which it has been harnessed – see *Needs, Values, Truth* (1991a), pp. 95–6.

42 (1990/1) and (1995/6).

43 The claim can be misconstrued – see §52 – but this does not lay it open to denial.

44 On these matters, my (1990/1) is clearer than *Needs, Values, Truth* (1991a), p. 141, which it supersedes.

45 Concerning elucidation, compare Wittgenstein, *Tractatus* (1961), 3.263, 4.026, 4.112; *Sameness and Substance* (1980a), pp. 2–4, 49–55; *Needs, Values, Truth* (1991a), p. 142. See below, note 53. See also reply to Williams, §40.

46 The relevant section is (1991a) §8 (= VII of the original publication (1976a)). Cf. also (1980c).

47 See Frege (1952), p. 51.

48 For the difficulties it faces otherwise, see *Needs, Values, Truth* (1991a), pp. 142–3.

49 See lines 1–4 of p. 129 of the text in Tarski (1983) of 'On Definable Sets of Real Numbers'.

50 A Tarskian fixing of the extension of 'true' that relied for its correctness on the fact that it is raining would scarcely 'grasp the notion reliably'. A definition would be perfectly acceptable, however, which depended upon the windfall that Tarski harvested (here I am reacting to the last but one paragraph of Wilfrid's §4), when he found the equivalence of every sentence of the elementary algebra of the real numbers to some quantifier-free sentence. At note 15 of his (1951), Tarski proposes a truth definition precisely so dependent. He proposes it as an alternative, at once safe and illuminating, to a truth-definition made by the standard method. When he does this, he is not departing from the demand for the sort of reliability that is spoken of in the quoted sentence from 'On Definable Sets of Real Numbers'.

51 Which I think that he gets from Tadeusz Kotarbinski's discussion of truth. See pp. 106–7 of Kotarbinski (1966), a translation of Kotarbinski (1929), to which Tarski refers. I quote the passage at *Needs, Values, Truth* (1991a), pp. 333–4, and quote it again with more discussion in 'Meaning and Truth-Conditions: from Frege's Grand Design to Davidson's', (1996). Let me take the opportunity to stress that Kotarbinski's discussion of truth is professedly anti-correspondentist. Unless someone can show that Tarski dissented under this score from his mentor's philosophical views, Tarski must have seen his definition of true-in-L as doing for the correspondentist any legitimate thing that the correspondist wanted done – but no more.

52 Vindicatory explanations at once justify a belief, as the only belief that is open to one who understands what is at issue, and also, by reference to that, explain the belief's coming into being.

53 The generalization of this point: practitioners of the elucidatory method must constantly rebut the suggestion that, because they elucidate the concept Φ through its connections with concept Ψ, they think of Φ as a Ψ sort of concept.

54 Cf. *Needs, Values, Truth* (1991a), p. 201.

55 Cf. §44 above; also §7.

56 (1990/1), which I have been referring to, adds to *Needs, Values, Truth* (1991a), which adds to the requirements given in (1980c) that Hussey cites.
57 What gives us the right to be sure that there will be just eight lines in the truth-table for a formula in three propositional variables? What underlies the certainty we attach to the combinational formula 2^n, or to the subcalculations into which any particular calculation of possibilities could be dismantled?
58 Cf. my (1992d).

Philosophical Works of David Wiggins

1963   'The Individuation of Things and Places', *Proceedings of the Aristotelian Society*, Supplementary Volume 37, 177–202. Reprinted in corrected form in M. Loux (ed.) *Universals and Particulars*. New York: Doubleday 1967.

1965   'Identity-Statements' in R. J. Butler (ed.) *Analytical Philosophy*, 2nd series. Oxford: Blackwell. Reprinted in German as 'Identitatsaussagen', trans. Matthias Schirn, in Kuno Lorenz (ed.) *Identität und Individuation. Band 1: Logische Probleme in historischem Aufriß*. Stuttgart-Bad Cannstatt: Frommann-Holzboog 1982. (The chief thesis of this paper was recanted in 1967, note 7, and 1971a, p. 17 note (b).)

1967   *Identity and Spatio-Temporal Continuity*. Oxford: Blackwell.

1968   'On Being in the Same Place at the Same Time', *Philosophical Review* 77, 90–95.

1969   'Reply to Mr Chandler', *Analysis* 29, 175–176.

1970   'Freedom, Knowledge, Belief and Causality' in G. Vesey (ed.) *Knowledge and Necessity*. London: Macmillan.

1971a   'On Sentence Sense, Word Sense and Difference of Word Sense: Towards a Philosophical Theory of Dictionaries' and 'Reply to Mr Alston' in D. Steinberg and L. Jakobovits (eds) *Semantics: An Interdisciplinary Reader*. Cambridge: Cambridge University Press. Translated into Greek in *Deucalion: A Quarterly Review* 31, 1980. (Amplified here in the Reply to S. G. Williams.)

1971b   'Sentence Meaning, Negation, and Plato's Problem of Non-Being' in Gregory Vlastos (ed.) *Plato I*. New York: Doubleday.

1973   'Towards a Reasonable Libertarianism' in Ted Honderich (ed.) *Essays on Freedom of Action*. London: Routledge & Kegan Paul (amended edn 1979). (Rewritten for 1987a/1991a.)

1974   'Essentialism, Continuity, and Identity', *Synthèse* 28, 321–359.

1975   'Identity, Designation, Essentialism and Physicalism', *Philosophia* 5, 1–30.

1975/6 'Deliberation and Practical Reason', *Proceedings of the Aristotelian Society* 76, 29–51. Reprinted in A. O. Rorty (1980). (Rewritten for 1987a/1991a. An excerpt was rewritten for 1978c.)

1976a   'Truth, Invention and the Meaning of Life', *Proceedings of the British Academy* 62, 331–78. Reprinted in G. Sayre-McCord (ed.) *Essays on Moral Realism*. Ithaca: Cornell University Press 1988. (Rewritten for 1987a/1991a.)

1976b   'The *De Re* "Must": A Note on the Logical Form of Essentialist Claims' in Evans and McDowell (1976).

1976c   'Locke, Butler and the Stream of Consciousness: and Men as a Natural Kind', *Philosophy* 51, 131–158. Reprinted in A. O. Rorty (ed.) *The Identities of Persons*. Berkeley: University of California Press 1976. Also reprinted in H. Noonan (ed.) *Personal Identity*. Aldershot: Dartmouth Publishing 1993. (Rewritten for 1980a, ch. 6. See also Reply here to Snowdon.)

1976d   'Frege's Problem of the Morning Star and the Evening Star' in M. Schirn (ed.) *Studies on Frege II: Logic and Philosophy of Language*. Stuttgart-Bad Cannstatt: Frommann-Holzboog.

1976e   'Identity, Necessity and Physicalism' and 'Reply to Professor Marcus and Mr. Hacking' in Körner (1976).

1978a   'Are the Criteria of Identity that hold for a Work of Art in the Different Arts Aesthetically Relevant? Reply to Richard Wollheim', *Ratio* 20, 52–68.

1978b   'Aurel Thomas Kolnai (1900–1973)'. Introduction (written with Bernard Williams) to A. T. Kolnai, *Ethics, Value and Reality*, ed. B. Klug and F. Dunlop. London: Athlone Press.

1978c   'Deliberation and Practical Reason' in J. Raz (ed.) *Practical Reasoning*. Oxford: Oxford University Press.

1978/9 'Weakness of Will, Commensurability, and the Objects of Deliberation and Desire', *Proceedings of the Aristotelian Society* 79, 251–277. (Reprinted in A. O. Rorty (1980). Rewritten and corrected for 1987a/1991a.)

1979a   'Ayer on Monism, Pluralism and Essence' in G. F. MacDonald (ed.) *Perception and Identity: Essays Presented to A. J. Ayer*, Ithaca: Cornell University Press. (Corrected by 1987d.)

1979b   'The Concern to Survive', *Midwest Studies in Philosophy* IV, 417–22. (Rewritten for 1987a/1991a.)

1979c   'On Knowing, Knowing that One Knows and Consciousness' in E. Saarinen (ed.) *Essays in Honour of Jaako Hintikka*. Dordrecht: Reidel.

1979d   'Mereological Essentialism, Asymmetrical Essential Dependence, and the Nature of Continuants', *Grazer Philosophische Studien* 7/8 (*Festschrift* for Roderick Chisholm), 297–315. (Corrected/recanted by 1980a, p. 93, note 16.)

1980a   *Sameness and Substance*. Oxford: Blackwell. (A second impression appeared in 1981 with *errata* and *addenda*. A second edition will appear in due course with Cambridge University Press.)

1980b   ' "Most" and "All": Some Comments on a Familiar Programme, and on the Logical Form of Quantified Sentences' in M. Platts (ed.) *Reference, Truth and Reality*. London: Routledge & Kegan Paul.

1980c   'What would be a Substantial Theory of Truth?' in Zak van Straaten (ed.) *Philosophical Subjects: Essays Presented to P. F. Strawson*. Oxford: Clarendon Press.

1980d   'Contingency, Identity, and *de re* and *de dicto* Necessity' in Dancy (1980).

1980e   'Truth and Interpretation' in W. Leinfellner, R. Haller, A. Hubner and P. Weingartner (eds) *Proceedings of the 4th International Wittgenstein Symposium, Kirchberg 1979*. Vienna: Hölder-Pichler-Tempsky.

1981   'Public Rationality, Needs, and What Needs are Relative to' in P. Hall and D. Bannister (eds) *Transport and Public Policy*. London: Mansell.

1982   'Heraclitus' Conceptions of Flux, Fire, and Material Persistence' in M. Nussbaum and M. Schofield (eds) *Language and Logos*. Cambridge: Cambridge University Press.

1984   'The Sense and Reference of Predicates: A Running Repair to Frege's Doctrine and a Plea for the Copula', *Philosophical Quarterly* 34, 311–328. (This issue of *Philosophical Quarterly* was also published as Wright (1984).)

1985   'Claims of Need' in Honderich (1985). (Rewritten for 1987a/1991a.)

1985/6   'Verbs and Adverbs and some other Modes of Grammatical Combination', *Proceedings of the Aristotelian Society* 86, 273–306.

1986a   'On Singling Out an Object Determinately' in Philip Pettit and John McDowell (eds) *Subject, Thought and Context*. Oxford: Clarendon Press. (Corrected here by the Reply to Williamson.)

1986b   'Teleology and the Good in Plato's *Phaedo*', *Oxford Studies in Ancient Philosophy* 4, 1–18.

1987a   *Needs, Values, Truth: Essays in the Philosophy of Value*. Oxford: Blackwell.

1987b   'The Person as Object of Science, as Subject of Experience, and as Locus of Value' in A. Peacocke and G. Gillett (eds) *Persons and Personality*. Oxford: Blackwell.

1987c   'Needs, Need, Needing' (with Sira Dermen), *Journal of Medical Ethics* 13, 61–68.

1987d   'The Concept of the Subject contains the Concept of the Predicate: Leibniz on Reason, Truth and Contingency' in J. J. Thompson (ed.) *On Being and Saying: Essays for Richard Cartwright*. Cambridge, Mass.: MIT Press. (Reprinted in Roger Woolhouse (ed.) *Leibniz: Critical Assessments*, vol. II, 141–163. London: Routledge 1994.)

1990/1   'Moral Cognitivism, Moral Relativism and Motivating Moral Beliefs', *Proceedings of the Aristotelian Society* 91, 61–85. Reprinted in *Archivio di Filosofia Analitica*. Roma: Lithos 1993.

1991a   *Needs, Values, Truth* (2nd edn, revised). Oxford: Blackwell.

1991b   'Categorical Requirements: Kant and Hume on the Idea of Duty', *The Monist* 74, 83–106.

1991c   'Ayer's Ethical Theory: Emotivism or Subjectivism?', *Philosophy* 30 (Supplement), 181–196. (This is an abbreviation of 1992a. The same Supplement of *Philosophy* was published as A. Phillips Griffiths (ed.) *A. J. Ayer: Memorial Essays*. Cambridge: Cambridge University Press 1991.)

1991d   'The Principle of Hypothetical Necessity in Jules Vuillemin's Reconstruction of the Master Argument of Diodorus Cronus' in G. C. Brittan Jr (ed.) *Causality, Method and Modality (A Festschrift for Jules Vuillemin)*. Dordrecht: Kluwer.

1991e   'Pourquoi la notion de substance paraît-elle si difficile', *Philosophie 30*, 77–89.

1992a   'Ayer on Morality and Feeling: From Subjectivism to Emotivism and Back?' in L. E. Hahn (ed.) *The Philosophy of A. J. Ayer*. LaSalle, Illinois: Open Court.

1992b	'L'éthique et la raison', *Studia Philosophica* 51, 75–87.
1992c	'Meaning, Truth-Conditions, Proposition: Frege's Doctrine of Sense Retrieved, Resumed and Redeployed in the Light of Certain Recent Criticisms', *Dialectica* 46, 61–90.
1992d	'Remembering Directly' in J. Hopkins and A. Savile (eds) *Psychoanalysis, Mind and Art: Essays for Richard Wollheim.* Oxford: Blackwell.
1993a	*'Sinn, Bedeutung,* et les mots d'espèce', *Revue de Theologie et de Philosophie* 24, 225–237. (Translated and rewritten as 1993d.)
1993b	'Cognitivism, Naturalism, and Normativity' and 'A Neglected Position?' in J. Haldane and C. Wright (eds) *Reality, Representation, and Projection.* Oxford: Oxford University Press.
1993c	'Time, Ability and Real Choice' in P. Horak (ed.) *Responsibility (Actes de l'I. I. P. à Prague 1990).*
1993d	'Putnam's Doctrine of Natural Kind Words and Frege's Doctrines of Sense, Reference and Extension. Can they Cohere?' in A. W. Moore (ed.) *Meaning and Reference.* Oxford: Oxford University Press 1993. Also in P. Clark and B. Hale (eds) *Reading Putnam.* Oxford: Blackwell 1994; and in J. Biro and P. Kotatko (eds) *Sense and Reference One Hundred Years Later.* Dordrecht: Kluwer 1995.
1994a	'The Kant–Frege–Russell View of Existence: A Rehabilitation of the Second Level View' in W. S. Armstrong, D. Raffman and N. Asher (eds) *Modality, Morality and Belief: Essays for Ruth Barcan Marcus.* Cambridge: Cambridge University Press.
1994b	'Vérité et morale', trans. Monique Canto-Sperber from 1990/1, in M. Canto-Sperber (ed.) *La philosophie morale britannique.* Paris: Presses Universitaires de France.
1995a	Preface for *The Utopian Mind,* a posthumous work by Aurel Kolnai, ed. F. Dunlop. London: Athlone Press.
1995b	'Eudaimonism and Realism in Aristotle's Ethics: A Reply to John McDowell' in Robert Heinaman (ed.) *Aristotle and Moral Realism.* London: UCL Press.
1995c	'Categorical Requirements' in R. Hursthouse, G. Lawrence and W. Quinn (eds) *Virtues and Reasons.* Oxford: Oxford University Press. (The longer version of 1991b, corrected.)
1995d	'Substance' in A. Grayling (ed.) *Philosophy: A Guide through the Subject.* Oxford: Oxford University Press.

1995/6a   'Objective and Subjective in Ethics, with two Postscripts about Truth', *Ratio*. To appear in another form in M. Canto-Sperber (ed.) *Dictionnaire de philosophie morale*. Paris: Presses Universitaires de France.

1995/6b   'In a Subjectivist Framework: Categorical Imperatives and Real Practical Reasons' in C. Fehige, G. Meggle and U. Wessels (eds) *Preferences*. Berlin: de Gruyter.

1996   'Meaning and Truth Conditions: From Frege's Grand Design to Davidson's' in B. Hale and C. Wright (eds) *Blackwell Companion to the Philosophy of Language*. Oxford: Blackwell.

Forthcoming (a): 'Incommensurability: Four Proposals' in Ruth Chang (ed.) *Incommensurability*. Cambridge, Mass.: Harvard University Press.

Forthcoming (b): 'Natural Languages as Social Objects' in Menno Lievers (ed.) *Language and Speakers' Knowledge*.

Forthcoming (c): 'Natural and Artificial Virtues: A Vindication of Hume's Theoretical Scheme' in Roger Crisp (ed.) *The Virtues*.

Forthcoming (d): 'Sufficient Reason: A Principle in Diverse Guises, both Ancient and Modern', *Acta Philosophica Fennica*.

Bibliography

Anscombe, G. E. M. (1981), *Collected Philosophical Papers*, 3 vols. Oxford: Blackwell.

Aristotle (1954), *The Nicomachean Ethics of Aristotle*, ed. and trans. David Ross. Oxford: Oxford University Press.

—— (1961), *De Anima*, ed. David Ross. Oxford: Clarendon Press.

—— (1975), *Posterior Analytics*, ed. and trans. Jonathan Barnes. Oxford: Clarendon Press.

—— (1982), *Eudemian Ethics*, Books I, II and VIII, ed. and trans. Michael Woods. Oxford: Clarendon Press.

Austin, J. L. (1970), 'The Meaning of a Word' in *Philosophical Papers* (2nd edn). Oxford: Oxford University Press.

Baldwin, Thomas (1975), 'Quantification, Modality, and Indirect Speech' in S. Blackburn (ed.) *Meaning, Reference and Necessity*. Cambridge: Cambridge University Press.

Barcan, Ruth C. (1947), 'The Identity of Individuals in a Strict Functional Calculus of Second Order', *Journal of Symbolic Logic* 12, 12–15.

Bernays, Paul (1935), 'Sur le platonisme dans les mathématiques', *L'enseignement mathématique*, 1st series 34. English translation by C. D. Parsons in P. Benacerraf and H. Putnam (eds) *Philosophy of Mathematics* (2nd edn). Cambridge: Cambridge University Press 1983.

Blackburn, Simon (1981), 'Reply: Rule-Following and Moral Realism' in Holtzman and Leich (1981).

—— (1985), 'Error and the Phenomenology of Value' in Honderich (1985).

Bostock, David (1988), *Plato's Theaetetus*. Oxford: Clarendon Press.

Boyd, Richard N. (1988), 'How to be a Moral Realist' in G. Sayre-McCord (ed.) *Essays on Moral Realism*. Ithaca: Cornell University Press.

Bradley, F. H. (1914), *Essays on Truth and Reality*. Oxford: Oxford University Press.

Brink, David O. (1989), *Moral Realism and the Foundations of Ethics*. Cambridge: Cambridge University Press.

Burgess, J. A. (1989), 'Vague Identity: Evans Misrepresented', *Analysis* 49, 112–19.

Burnyeat, M. F. (1976), 'Protagoras and Self-Refutation in Plato's "Theaetetus"', *Philosophical Review* 85, 172–195; also in Everson (1990).

—— (1980), 'Aristotle on Learning to be Good' in A. O. Rorty (1980).

—— (1990), *The Theaetetus of Plato*. Indianapolis: Hackett.

Candlish, Stewart (1991), 'Das Wollen ist auch nur eine Erfahrung' in Robert L. Arrington and Hans-Johann Glock (eds) *Wittgenstein's Philosophical Investigations: Text and Context*. London: Routledge.

Carnap, Rudolf (1947), *Meaning and Necessity*. Chicago: University of Chicago Press.

Cartwright, Richard (1979), 'Indiscernibility Principles', *Midwest Studies in Philosophy* IV, 293–306; also in R. Cartwright *Philosophical Essays* (MIT Press, 1987).

Chandler, Hugh S. (1967), 'Plantinga and the Contingently Possible', *Analysis* 36, 106–9.

Charles, David and Lennon, Kathleen (eds) (1992), *Reduction, Explanation and Realism*. Oxford: Clarendon Press.

Chellas, B. F. and Segerberg, K. (1994), 'Modal Logics with the MacIntosh Rule', *Journal of Philosophical Logic* 23, 67–86.

Classen, C. J. (1989), 'Protagoras' *Alêtheia*' in P. Huby and G. Neal (eds) *The Criterion of Truth*. Liverpool: Liverpool University Press.

Cornford, F. M. (1935), *Plato's Theory of Knowledge*. London: Kegan Paul, Trench, Trubner.

Crossley, John N. and Humberstone, I. Lloyd (1977), 'The Logic of "Actually"', *Reports on Mathematical Logic* 8, 11–29.

Dancy, Jonathan (ed.) (1980), *Papers on Language and Logic: Proceedings of the 1979 Keele Conference*. Keele: Keele University Library.

—— (1986), 'Two Conceptions of Moral Realism', *Proceedings of the Aristotelian Society*, Supplementary Volume 60, 167–87.

Davidson, Donald (1967), 'Truth and Meaning', *Synthèse* 17, 304–23; also in Davidson (1984).

—— (1970), 'Mental Events' in L. Foster and J. W. Swanson (eds) *Experience and Theory*, London: Duckworth.

—— (1973), 'Radical Interpretation', *Dialectica* 27, 314–28; also in Davidson (1984).

—— (1979), 'Moods and Performances' in A. Margalit (ed.) *Meaning and Use*. Dordrecht: Reidel. Also in Davidson (1984).

—— (1983), 'A Coherence Theory of Truth and Knowledge' in D. Henrich (ed.) *Kant oder Hegel?* Stuttgart: Klett-Cotta.

—— (1984), *Inquiries into Truth and Interpretation*. Oxford: Clarendon Press.

Davidson, Donald and Harman, Gilbert (eds) (1972), *Semantics of Natural Language*. Dordrecht: Reidel.

Davies, Martin (1978), 'Weak Necessity and Truth Theories', *Journal of Philosophical Logic* 7, 415–39.

—— (1981a), *Meaning, Quantification, Necessity*. London: Routledge & Kegan Paul.

—— (1981b), 'Meaning, Structure and Understanding', *Synthèse* 48, 135–61.

—— (1987), 'Tacit Knowledge and Semantic Theory: Can a Five Per Cent Difference Matter?', *Mind* 96, 441–62.

DePaul, Michael R. (1990), 'Critical Notice of *Needs, Values, Truth*', *Mind* 99, 619–33.

Derrida, Jacques (1982), *Margins of Philosophy*, trans. Alan Bass. Brighton: Harvester Press.

Descartes, René (1964–76), *Oeuvres de Descartes*, ed. C. Adam and P. Tannery. Paris: Vrin/CNRS.

—— (1970), *Philosophical Writings*, trans. and ed. G. E. M. Anscombe and P. T. Geach. London: Nelson.

Diels, H. and Kranz, W. (eds) (1960), *Die Fragmente der Vorsokratiker* (10th edn). Berlin.

Dummett, Michael (1978), *Truth and Other Enigmas*. London: Duckworth.

—— (1981a), *Frege: Philosophy of Language* (2nd edn). London: Duckworth.

—— (1981b), *The Interpretation of Frege's Philosophy*. Cambridge, Mass.: Harvard University Press.

—— (1991a), *The Logical Basis of Metaphysics*. London: Duckworth.

—— (1991b), 'Does Quantification Involve Identity?' in H. A. Lewis (ed.) *Peter Geach: Philosophical Encounters*. Dordrecht: Kluwer.

—— (1993), *Origins of Analytical Philosophy*, London: Duckworth.

Evans, Gareth (1976), 'Semantic Structure and Logical Form' in Evans and McDowell (1976); also in Evans (1985).

—— (1977), 'Pronouns, Quantifiers, and Relative Clauses (I)', *Canadian Journal of Philosophy* 7, 467–536; also in Evans (1985).

—— (1978), 'Can there be Vague Objects?', *Analysis* 38, 208; also in Evans (1985).

—— (1981), 'Semantic Theory and Tacit Knowledge' in Holtzman and Leich (1981); also in Evans (1985).

—— (1982), *The Varieties of Reference*, ed. John McDowell. Oxford: Clarendon Press.

—— (1985), *Collected Papers*. Oxford: Clarendon Press.

Evans, Gareth and McDowell, John (eds) (1976), *Truth and Meaning: Essays in Semantics*. Oxford: Clarendon Press.

Everson, Stephen (ed.) (1990), *Epistemology* (Companions to Ancient Thought 1). Cambridge: Cambridge University Press.

Farrar, Cynthia (1988), *The Origins of Democratic Thinking*. Cambridge: Cambridge University Press.

Fine, Kit (1975), 'Vagueness, Truth and Logic', *Synthèse* 30, 265–300.

Foot, Philippa (1972), 'Morality as a System of Hypothetical Imperatives', *Philosophical Review* 81, 305–16.

Frege, Gottlob (1950), *The Foundations of Arithmetic*, trans. J. L. Austin. Oxford: Blackwell.

Frege, Gottlob (1952), *Translations from the Philosophical Writings of Gottlob Frege*, ed. P. T. Geach and M. Black. Oxford: Blackwell.
—— (1967), *The Basic Laws of Arithmetic*, trans. M. Furth. Berkeley: California University Press.
Geach, Peter (1973), 'Ontological Relativity and Relative Identity' in M. K. Munitz (ed.) *Logic and Ontology*. New York: New York University Press.
—— (1980), *Reference and Generality* (3rd edn). Ithaca: Cornell University Press.
Gillespie N. (ed.) (1986), *Spindel Conference: Moral Realism* (Southern Journal of Philosophy Supplement).
Gillett, G. (1987), 'Reasoning about Persons', in A. Peacocke and G. Gillett (eds) *Persons and Personality*. Oxford: Blackwell.
Goldfarb, Warren D. (1984), 'The Unsolvability of the Gödel Class with Identity', *Journal of Symbolic Logic* 49, 1237–52.
Grandy, Richard (1973), 'Reference, Meaning and Belief', *Journal of Philosophy* 70, 439–52.
Grice, H. P. (1991), 'Logic and Conversation', in Frank Jackson (ed.) *Conditionals*. Oxford: Oxford University Press.
Griffin, J. (1992), 'Values: Reduction, Supervenience and Explanation by Ascent' in Charles and Lennon (1992).
Habermas, Jürgen (1987), *The Philosophical Discourse of Modernity*, trans. Frederick Lawrence. Cambridge, Mass.: MIT Press.
Hare, R. M. (1952), *The Language of Morals*. Oxford: Clarendon Press.
—— (1963), *Freedom and Reason*. Oxford: Oxford University Press.
Harman, Gilbert (1977), *The Nature of Morality: An Introduction to Ethics*. New York: Oxford University Press.
—— (1982), 'Conceptual Role Semantics', *Notre Dame Journal of Formal Logic* 23, 242–55.
—— (1986), 'The Meaning of the Logical Constants' in E. LePore (ed.) *Truth and Interpretation: Essays on the Philosophy of Donald Davidson*. Oxford: Blackwell.
Hegel, G. W. F. (1975), *The Encyclopedia of the Philosophical Sciences Part One ('Logic')*, trans. William Wallace. Oxford: Oxford University Press.
—— (1977), *Phenomenology of Spirit*, trans. A. V. Miller. Oxford: Clarendon Press.
Heitsch, E. (1969), 'Ein Buchtitel des Protagoras', *Hermes* 97, 292–296; also in C. J. Classen (ed.), *Sophistik* (*Wege der Forschung*, vol. 187, Darmstadt 1976).
Hodes, H. T. (1984), 'Axioms for Actuality', *Journal of Philosophical Logic* 13, 27–34.
Hodges, Wilfrid (1977), *Logic*. Harmondsworth: Penguin.
Holtzman, Steven and Leich, Christopher (eds) (1981), *Wittgenstein: To Follow a Rule*. London: Routledge & Kegan Paul.
Honderich, Ted (ed.) (1985), *Morality and Objectivity: A Tribute to J. L. Mackie*. London: Routledge & Kegan Paul.
Hookway, Christopher (1990), *Scepticism*. London: Routledge.
Hughes, G. E. and Cresswell, M. J. (1968), *An Introduction to Modal Logic*. London: Methuen.

Humberstone, I. L. (1983), 'Karmo on Contingent Non-Identity', *Australasian Journal of Philosophy* 61, 188–91.

Hume, David (1888), *A Treatise of Human Nature*, ed. L. A. Selby-Bigge. Oxford: Clarendon Press.

—— (1975), *Enquiries Concerning Human Understanding and Concerning the Principles of Morals* (3rd edn), ed. L. A. Selby-Bigge. Oxford: Clarendon Press.

—— (1987), *Essays: Moral, Political, and Literary* (revised edn), ed. Eugene F. Miller. Indianapolis: LibertyClassics.

Hussey, E. (1972), *The Presocratics*. London: Duckworth.

—— (1990), 'The Beginnings of Epistemology' in Everson (1990).

Irwin, Terence (1977), *Plato's Moral Theory*. Oxford: Clarendon Press.

Johnston, Mark (1989), 'Dispositional Theories of Value', *Proceedings of the Aristotelian Society*, Supplementary Volume 63, 139–74.

Kant, Immanuel (1933), *Critique of Pure Reason*, trans. Norman Kemp Smith. London: Macmillan.

—— (1948), *Groundwork of the Metaphysic of Morals*, trans. H. J. Paton as *The Moral Law*. London: Hutchinson.

—— (1952), *Critique of Judgement*, trans. J. C. Meredith. Oxford: Clarendon Press.

—— (1956), *Critique of Practical Reason*, trans. Lewis White Beck. Indianapolis: Bobbs-Merrill.

—— (1960), *Religion Within the Limits of Reason Alone*, trans. Theodore M. Greene and Hoyt H. Hudson. New York: Harper and Row.

—— (1992), *Lectures on Logic*, ed. J. Michael Young. Cambridge: Cambridge University Press.

Kaplan, David (1990), 'Thoughts on Demonstratives' in P. Yourgrau (ed.) *Demonstratives*. Oxford: Oxford University Press.

Karmo, T. (1983), 'Contingent Non-Identity', *Australasian Journal of Philosophy* 61, 185–7.

Kenny, Anthony (1966), 'The Practical Syllogism and Incontinence', *Phronesis* XI, 163–84.

—— (1979), *Aristotle's Theory of the Will*. London: Duckworth.

Kerferd, G. B. (1981), *The Sophistic Movement*. Cambridge: Cambridge University Press.

Körner, Stephan (ed.) (1976), *Philosophy of Logic*. Oxford: Blackwell.

Kotarbinski, Tadeusz (1929), *Elementy Teorji Poznania*. Lwow = (1966), *Gnosiology: The Scientific Approach to the Theory of Knowledge*, trans. Olgierd Wojtasiewics. Oxford: Pergamon Press.

Kripke, Saul A. (1972), 'Naming and Necessity' in Donald Davidson and Gilbert Harman (eds), *Semantics of Natural Language*. Dordrecht: Reidel.

—— (1980), *Naming and Necessity*. Oxford: Blackwell.

Lemmon, E. J. (1966), 'Sentences, Statements, and Propositions' in B. Williams and A. Montefiore (eds) *British Analytical Philosophy*. London: Routledge & Kegan Paul.

Lewis, David (1973), *Counterfactuals*. Oxford: Blackwell.

Lewis, David (1983), 'General Semantics' in *Philosophical Papers*, vol. 1. Oxford: Oxford University Press.
—— (1988), 'Vague Identity: Evans Misunderstood', *Analysis* 48, 128–30.
—— (1989), 'Dispositional Theories of Value', *Proceedings of the Aristotelian Society*, Supplementary Volume 63, 113–37.
Locke, John (1975), *An Essay Concerning Human Understanding*, ed. P. H. Nidditch. Oxford: Clarendon Press.
Lovibond, Sabina (1989/90), 'True and False Pleasures', *Proceedings of the Aristotelian Society* 90, 213–30.
—— (1992), 'Feminism and Pragmatism: A Reply to Richard Rorty', *New Left Review* 193, 56–74.
Lycan, W. (1986), 'Moral Facts and Moral Knowledge' in Gillespie (1986).
MacIntyre, Alasdair (1981), *After Virtue*. London: Duckworth.
Mackie, J. L. (1977), *Ethics: Inventing Right and Wrong*. Harmondsworth: Penguin.
Matthen, Mohan (1985), 'Perception, Relativism and Truth: Reflections on Plato's Theaetetus 152–160', *Dialogue* 24, 33–58.
McDowell, John (1977), 'On the Sense and Reference of a Proper Name', *Mind* 86, 159–85.
—— (1978), 'Are Moral Requirements Hypothetical Imperatives?', *Proceedings of the Aristotelian Society*, Supplementary Volume 52, 13–29.
—— (1979), 'Virtue and Reason', *The Monist* 62, 331–50.
—— (1981), 'Non-Cognitivism and Rule-Following' in Holtzman and Leich (1981).
—— (1983), 'Aesthetic Value, Objectivity and the Fabric of the World' in E. Schaper (ed.) *Pleasure, Preference and Value*. Cambridge: Cambridge University Press.
—— (1985), 'Values and Secondary Qualities' in Honderich (1985).
—— (1994), *Mind and World*. Cambridge, Mass.: Harvard University Press.
McGinn, Colin (1977), 'Semantics for Nonindicative Sentences', *Philosophical Studies* 32, 301–11.
—— (1983), *The Subjective View*. Oxford: Clarendon Press.
McNaughton, David (1988), *Moral Vision: An Introduction to Ethics*. Oxford: Blackwell.
Mellor, D. H. (1988/9), 'I and Now', *Proceedings of the Aristotelian Society* 89, 79–94.
Millikan, Ruth Garrett (1984), *Language, Thought, and Other Biological Categories*. Cambridge, Mass.: MIT Press.
Minow, M. (1990), *Making All the Difference: Inclusion, Exclusion, and American Law*. Ithaca: Cornell University Press.
Misak, Cheryl J. (1991), *Truth and the End of Inquiry: A Peircean Account of Truth*. Oxford: Clarendon Press.
Moore, A. W. (1987), 'On Saying and Showing', *Philosophy* 62, 473–97.
—— (1990a), *The Infinite*. London: Routledge.
—— (1990b), 'A Kantian View of Moral Luck', *Philosophy* 65, 297–321.

—— (1991), 'Can Reflection Destroy Knowledge?', *Ratio* (New Series) 4, 97–107.

—— (1992), 'Human Finitude, Ineffability, Idealism, Contingency', *Noûs* 26, 427–46.

Moore, G. E. (1903), *Principia Ethica*. Cambridge: Cambridge University Press.

—— (1959), *Philosophical Papers*. London: George Allen & Unwin.

Moretti, Franco (1987), *The Way of the World: The Bildungsroman in European Culture*, trans. Albert Sbragia. London: Verso.

Noonan, Harold (1989), *Personal Identity*. London: Routledge.

Nussbaum, Martha C. (1986), *The Fragility of Goodness*. Cambridge: Cambridge University Press.

Owen, G. E. L. (1986), *Logic, Science and Dialectic: Collected Papers in Greek Philosophy*, ed. M. Nussbaum. London: Duckworth.

Papineau, David (1987), *Reality and Representation*. Oxford: Blackwell.

Peacocke, Christopher (1976), 'What is a Logical Constant?', *Journal of Philosophy* 73, 221–40.

—— (1987), 'Understanding Logical Constants: A Realist's Account', *Proceedings of the British Academy* 73, 153–99.

Pears, David (1978), 'Aristotle's Analysis of Courage', *Midwest Studies in Philosophy* III, 272–85.

—— (1980), 'Courage as a Mean' in A. O. Rorty (1980).

Peirce, C. S. (1931–5), *Collected Papers of Charles Sanders Peirce, Vols. I–VI*, ed. C. Hartshorne and P. Weiss. Cambridge, Mass.: Belknap Press.

—— (1958), *Collected Papers of Charles Sanders Peirce, Vols. VII and VIII*, ed. A. Burks. Cambridge, Mass.: Belknap Press.

—— (1982), *Writings of Charles S. Peirce: A Chronological Edition*, ed. M. Fisch. Bloomington, Ind.: Indiana University Press.

Pettit, Philip (1987), 'Humeans, Anti-Humeans, and Motivation', *Mind* 96, 530–33.

Plato (1973), *Theaetetus*, trans. J. McDowell. Oxford: Clarendon Press.

—— (1974), *The Republic*, trans. Desmond Lee. Harmondsworth: Penguin.

—— (1976), *Protagoras*, trans. C. C. W. Taylor. Oxford: Clarendon Press.

Platts, Mark (1979), *Ways of Meaning*. London: Routledge & Kegan Paul.

Popper, Karl (1959), *The Logic of Scientific Discovery*. London: Hutchinson.

Prior, A. N. (1955), *Formal Logic*. Oxford: Clarendon Press.

Putnam, Hilary (1962), 'The Analytic and the Synthetic' in *Minnesota Studies in the Philosophy of Science*, vol. 3, ed. H. Feigl and G. Maxwell. Minneapolis: Minnesota University Press.

Quine, W. V. (1953), *From a Logical Point of View*. Cambridge, Mass: Harvard University Press.

—— (1960), *Word and Object*. Cambridge, Mass.: MIT Press.

—— (1970), *Philosophy of Logic*. Englewood Cliffs: Prentice Hall.

—— (1974), *The Roots of Reference*. La Salle, Illinois: Open Court.

—— (1975), 'The Nature of Natural Knowledge' in S. Guttenplan (ed.) *Mind and Language*. Oxford: Clarendon Press.

Quine, W. V. (1981), 'On the Nature of Moral Values' in *Theories and Things*. Cambridge, Mass.: Belknap Press.

—— (1986), 'Reply to Roger Gibson Jr' in L. E. Hahn and P. A. Schilpp (eds) *The Philosophy of W. V. Quine*. La Salle, Illinois: Open Court.

—— (1987), *Quiddities: An Intermittently Philosophical Dictionary*. Cambridge, Mass.: Harvard University Press.

—— (1990), 'Three Indeterminacies' in R. Barrett and R. Gibson (eds) *Perspectives on Quine*. Oxford: Basil Blackwell.

Quinn, W. (1978), 'Moral and Other Realisms: Some Initial Difficulties' in A. Goldman and J. Kim (eds) *Values and Morals*. Dordrecht: D. Reidel.

Railton, P. (1986), 'Moral Realism', *Philosophical Review* 95, 163–207.

Rorty, Amélie Oksenberg (ed.) (1980), *Essays on Aristotle's Ethics*. Berkeley: University of California Press.

Rorty, Richard (1982), *Consequences of Pragmatism*. Brighton: Harvester Press.

Russell, Bertrand (1905), 'On Denoting', *Mind* 14, reprinted in *Logic and Knowledge*, ed. R. C. Marsh. London: George Allen & Unwin 1956.

—— (1967), *Introduction to Mathematical Philosophy*. London: George Allen & Unwin.

Ryle, Gilbert (1949): *The Concept of Mind*. London: Hutchinson.

Salmon, Nathan (1982), *Reference and Essence*. Oxford: Blackwell.

—— (1989), 'The Logic of What Might Have Been', *Philosophical Review* 98, 3–34.

Sayre-McCord, G. (1986), 'The Many Moral Realisms' in Gillespie (1986).

Schiller, F. C. S. (1908), *Plato or Protagoras?* Oxford: Oxford University Press.

—— (1912), *Studies in Humanism* (2nd edn). London: Macmillan.

Searle, John (1984), *Minds, Brains and Science*. London: BBC.

Searle, John (1992), *The Rediscovery of the Mind*. London: MIT Press.

Segal, Gabriel (1991), 'In the Mood for a Semantic Theory', *Proceedings of the Aristotelian Society* 91, 103–118.

Smith, Michael (1986), 'Should we Believe in Emotivism? in G. F. MacDonald and C. Wright (eds) *Fact, Science and Morality: Essays on A. J. Ayer's Language, Truth and Logic*. Oxford: Blackwell.

—— (1987), 'The Humean Theory of Motivation', *Mind* 96, 36–61.

—— (1988), 'On Humeans, Anti-Humeans and Motivation: A Reply to Pettit', *Mind* 97, 589–95.

—— (1989), 'Dispositional Theories of Value', *Proceedings of the Aristotelian Society*, Supplementary Volume 63, 89–111.

—— (1991), 'Realism' in Peter Singer (ed.) *A Companion to Ethics*. Oxford: Blackwell.

Snowdon, Paul (1989), 'On Formulating Materialism and Dualism' in J. Heil (ed.) *Cause, Mind and Reality*. Dordrecht: Kluwer.

—— (1991), 'Personal Identity and Brain Transplants' in D. Cockburn (ed.) *Human Beings*. Cambridge: Cambridge University Press.

—— (1995), 'Persons, Animals and Bodies' in J. Bermudez, N. Eilan and A. Marcel (eds) *The Self and the Body*. Cambridge, Mass.: MIT Press.

Spinoza, Benedictus de (1959), *Ethics*, trans. Andrew Boyle. London: Dent.

Stevenson, C. L. (1963), *Facts and Values*. New Haven: Yale University Press.

Strawson, P. F. (1959), *Individuals*. London: Methuen.

—— (1971), 'Identifying Reference and Truth-Values', in *Logico-Linguistic Papers*. London: Methuen.

Stroud, Barry (1986/7), 'The Physical World', *Proceedings of the Aristotelian Society* 87, 263–77.

Sturgeon, N. (1984), 'Moral Explanations' in D. Copp and D. Zimmerman (eds) *Morality, Reason and Truth*. Totowa: Rowman and Allanheld.

—— (1986), 'What Difference Does it Make whether Moral Realism is True?' in Gillespie (1986).

Tarski, Alfred (1951), *A Decision Method for Elementary Algebra and Geometry* (2nd edn). Berkeley: University of California Press.

—— (1983), *Logic, Semantics, Metamathematics*, trans. J. H. Woodger and ed. J. Corcoran. Indianapolis: Hackett.

Taylor, C. C. W. (1980), 'Plato, Hare and Davidson on Akrasia', *Mind* 89, 499–518.

Thomson, Garrett (1987), *Needs*. London: Routledge & Kegan Paul.

Unger, Peter (1990), *Identity, Consciousness and Value*. Oxford: Oxford University Press.

Urquhart, A. (1986), 'Many-Valued Logic' in D. Gabbay and F. Guenthner (eds), *Handbook of Philosophical Logic III: Alternatives to Classical Logic*. Dordrecht: Reidel.

Vlastos, Gregory (1956), *Plato's Protagoras*. Indianapolis: Bobbs-Merrill.

von Wright, G. H. (1963), *The Varieties of Goodness*. London: Routledge & Kegan Paul.

Williams, Bernard (1973), 'Imperative Inference' in *Problems of the Self*. Cambridge: Cambridge University Press.

—— (1978), *Descartes: The Project of Pure Enquiry*. Harmondsworth: Penguin.

—— (1981), *Moral Luck*. Cambridge: Cambridge University Press.

—— (1985), *Ethics and the Limits of Philosophy*. London: Fontana.

Williamson, Timothy (1987/8), 'Equivocation and Existence', *Proceedings of the Aristotelian Society* 88, 109–27.

—— (1988), 'First-Order Logics for Comparative Similarity', *Notre Dame Journal of Formal Logic* 29, 457–81.

—— (1990a), *Identity and Discrimination*. Oxford: Blackwell.

—— (1990b), 'Necessary Identity and Necessary Existence' in R. Haller and J. Brandl (eds), *Wittgenstein – Towards a Re-Evaluation: Proceedings of the 14th International Wittgenstein Symposium*, Kirchberg, 1989, vol. I. Vienna: Hölder-Pichler-Tempski.

—— (1994), *Vagueness*. London: Routledge.

Wittgenstein, Ludwig (1961), *Tractatus Logico-Philosophicus*, trans. D. F. Pears and B. F. McGuinness. London: Routledge & Kegan Paul.

—— (1965), 'A Lecture on Ethics', *Philosophical Review* 74, 3–11.

—— (1967), *Philosophical Investigations*, trans. G. E. M. Anscombe (3rd edn). Oxford: Blackwell.

Wittgenstein, Ludwig (1978), *Remarks on the Foundations of Mathematics* (revised edn), ed. G. H. von Wright, R. Rhees and G. E. M. Anscombe, trans. G. E. M. Anscombe. Oxford: Blackwell.

—— (1979), *Notebooks 1914–1916* (2nd edn), ed. G. H. von Wright and G. E. M. Anscombe, trans. G. E. M. Anscombe. Oxford: Blackwell.

Wollheim, R. (1989), *The Thread of Life*. Cambridge: Cambridge University Press.

Wright, Crispin (ed.) (1984), *Frege: Tradition and Influence*. Oxford: Blackwell.

—— (1988), 'Moral Values, Projection and Secondary Qualities', *Proceedings of the Aristotelian Society*, Supplementary Volume 62, 1–26.

—— (1992), *Truth and Objectivity*. Cambridge, Mass.: Harvard University Press.

Index

Wittgenstein, Ludwig 74, 84, 90n,
  92n, 93n, 113, 125, 128n, 166,
  176, 179n, 180n, 183n, 184n, 267,
  268, 271, 272, 283n
Wollheim, R. 47n

Wolf, Naomi 91n
Woods, Michael 282n
Wright, Crispin 93n, 121, 124, 128n,
  180n, 183n